he future

since their inception in
le in the history of the

care for children suffering
blems in the community.
important aspect of child
intervention are being
essional teams working in
effective in-patient care,

ment of a number of key
re in therapeutic schools
d on the importance of
ment and care of difficult
ion.

children

ient care for children and

Jonathan Green is Clinical Director of the Child In-patient Unit at Booth Hall Hospital, Manchester and Senior Lecturer in Child and Adolescent Psychiatry at the University of Manchester. **Brian Jacobs** is Consultant Child and Adolescent Psychiatrist to Bethlem and Maudsley NHS Trust and Honorary Senior Lecturer in Child and Adolescent Psychiatry at St George's Hospital Medical School.

Contributors: Jennifer Beecham; Madge Booth; Maureen Burke; Gerry Byrne; Wendy French; Jonathan Green; Ian Higgins; David Imrie; Brian Jacobs; David Jones; Judith Lask; Jeanne Magagna; Sean Maskey; Cynthia Maynerd; Kathleen Morris; Caroline Newbold; Kenneth Nunn; William Parry-Jones; Richard Rollinson; Michael Shaw; Anna Tate; Chris Wever.

In-patient Child Psychiatry
Modern practice, research and the future

Edited by Jonathan Green
and Brian Jacobs

London and New York

First published 1998
by Routledge
11 New Fetter Lane, London EC4P 4EE

Simultaneously published in the USA and Canada
by Routledge
29 West 35th Street, New York, NY 10001

Typeset in Goudy by Keystroke, Jacaranda Lodge, Wolverhampton
Printed and bound in Great Britain by T.J. International Ltd, Padstow, Cornwall

British Library Cataloguing in Publication Data
A catalogue record for this book is available from the British Library

Library of Congress Cataloguing in Publication Data
In-patient child psychiatry / edited by Jonathan Green and Brian
 Jacobs
     Includes bibliographical references and index.
     1. Child psychotherapy–Residential treatment. 2. Children–
Institutional care–Psychological aspects. 3. Psychiatric hospital
care. 4. Alternatives to psychiatric hospitalization. 5. Child
psychiatry–Differential therapeutics. I. Green, Jonathan.
II. Jacobs, Brian
     [DNLM: 1. Mental Disorders–in infancy & childhood. 2. Mental
Disorders–therapy. 3. Psychotherapy–in infancy & childhood.
4. Hospitalization. 5. Parenting.]
RJ504.5.I56   1998
618.92'89—dc21
DNLM/DLC
for Library of Congress   98–2991

ISBN 0–415–19439–3 (hbk)
ISBN 0–415–14525–2 (pbk)

We would like to dedicate this book to our families; to the staff who work on in-patient child psychiatry units; and to the children and families who have helped us to learn.

Contents

Figures

Tables

Contributors

Jennifer Beecham is a senior lecturer and assistant director at the Centre for the Economics of Mental Health and a research fellow at the personal social services research unit in health economics at the Institute of Psychiatry and at the PSSRU at The University of Kent in Canterbury.

Madge Booth is the director of care for Windows for Children. She has worked for many years with damaged youngsters. She trains in settings across the UK in direct work skills for these children. She has devised a programme of therapeutic play for disturbed children.

Maureen Burke was ward manager of the child psychiatry in-patient unit at Booth Hall Children's Hospital from 1991 to 1993. She is currently nurse consultant at Ashworth Special Hospital, Liverpool.

Gerry Byrne is a nurse specialist at the Park Hospital for Children, Oxford.

Wendy French is the headteacher at Bethlem Royal School. She has a long career in special education. She has trained as a counsellor and published as a poet.

Jonathan Green is senior lecturer in child and adolescent psychiatry at the University of Manchester and honorary consultant at Booth Hall Children's Hospital where he is clinical director of the in-patient child psychiatry unit.

Ian Higgins is a nurse manager at Stepping Stones child psychiatry unit, Sutton, Surrey.

David Imrie is a graduate in experimental psychology, currently working to gain experience of applied mental health with a view to gaining a place on a D. Clin. Psych. Course. He formerly acted as research assistant to the in-patient outcomes project at Booth Hall Hospital.

Brian Jacobs is consultant child and adolescent psychiatrist to Bethlem and Maudsley NHS Trust and honorary senior lecturer in child and adolescent psychiatry at St George's Hospital Medical School.

David Jones is consultant child psychiatrist and honorary senior lecturer,

University of Oxford and director of the family unit at the Park Hospital for Children.

Judith Lask is a senior family therapist and psychiatric social worker. She is a course co-ordinator at The Institute of Family Therapy and trainer on the MSc course at The Institute of Psychiatry. She formerly worked as a family therapist at Acorn Lodge, Bethlem Royal Hospital.

Jeanne Magagna is child and family psychotherapist and head of psychotherapy services at Great Ormond Street Hospital for Children, NHS Trust. She is joint co-ordinator of Tavistock Clinic model child psychotherapy training in Florence and Venice.

Sean Maskey is consultant child psychiatrist at the child in-patient unit, Collingham Gardens, London.

Cynthia Maynerd is a family therapist at Stepping Stones in-patient unit, Sutton Hospital. She has previous experience as a psychiatric social worker and is a family therapy trainer.

Kathleen Morris is a clinical psychologist at Acorn Lodge, Bethlem Royal Hospital. With a background in nursing, she has trained in a variety of parenting approaches. She teaches at The Institute of Psychiatry. She also works with children with learning difficulties in Bromley.

Caroline Newbold is senior social work practitioner with the family unit, Park Hospital for Children, Oxford.

Kenneth Nunn is a consultant child and adolescent psychiatrist at The New Children's Hospital at Parramatta in New South Wales, Australia. He trained in Australia and the UK, holding a senior lecturer post at St Thomas' Hospital, London before returning to Australia.

William Parry-Jones was professor of child and adolescent psychiatry at Yorkhill Hospital in Glasgow until his death in July 1997. He was formerly consultant to the Highfield Adolescent Unit, Oxford.

Richard Rollinson is the director of the Mulberry Bush School in Oxfordshire. He has a background in social work. He was a lecturer at Reading University teaching on social work in the department of community studies.

Michael Shaw is consultant child and adolescent psychiatrist at the St Helier Trust and Stepping Stones children's in-patient unit, Sutton Hospital. He is an honorary senior lecturer at St George's Hospital Medical School, London.

Anna Tate is teacher in charge of the Mildred Creak unit, The Hospital for Sick Children, Great Ormond Street.

Chris Wever is staff specialist at the Delphis Anxiety Disorders Clinic, Sydney, New South Wales, Australia and was previously staff specialist at the Rivendale adolescent unity in Sydney.

Acknowledgements

The generation of ideas contained in this book owes a great deal to a wide group of professionals involved in in-patient treatment. Firstly we would like to thank the clinical teams with whom we work and with whom we have developed many aspects of our practice. Secondly the informal UK network of clinicians involved in in-patient care known as CIPSIG (Child In-patient Special Interest Group) has provided a valuable forum, and many members of the group have contributed to this book – our thanks to them and to other clinicians involved in this group.

Specific and grateful thanks are offered to the following for advice and comments on drafts of various chapters: Ruth Anson, Dr Rutger van der Gaag, Professor Richard Harrington, Professor Lionel Hersov, Dr Leo Kroll, Dr Zarrina Kurtz, Dr Rod Pipe, Dr Charlie Stanley, Kirsteen Tait, Professor Eric Taylor and Julie Wilkinson.

Personal and heartfelt thanks come from JG to Joanne Turner and Julie Murphy for their exemplary secretarial work on many aspects of the text. From BJ such gratitude is felt to Toby and Guy who have allowed him access to the computer.

Our families have had to put up with our preoccupation and occasional absence while we have been working on this text. We have seen acknowledgement to families in the front of many books – only undertaking a task like this has made us realise the extent of the debt. We are very grateful for their love and patience.

Preface

Professor Lionel Hersov

The notion of removing children and adolescents with severe behavioural disorders and emotional disorders from their homes into an in-patient unit has its attractions. It may appeal to mental health professionals in the community because it permits the separation of the child from the negative influences in the family and community while exposing the child to an organised treatment programme. However, the attractions have to be weighed against the potential negative effects of this experience before the decision to admit is taken. Modern in-patient units take this issue very seriously in their preparation for admission and visiting policies, and by involving the family and the community agencies very fully in the individual treatment programmes for each child.

The earliest in-patient units in the USA had a mainly custodial and management function but later there were moves toward the use of the in-patient setting as a therapeutic agent in itself. Treatment procedures reflected the outpatient procedures of the time. Modern in-patient units usually include the disciplines of child psychiatry, nursing, psychology, social work, education paediatrics, occupational therapy, child psychotherapy and sometimes the experiential therapies. More specialised units may also employ child-care workers and speech and language therapists, depending on the age of the children and the range of disorders treated.

Each of the contributors has brought to this book different experiences and vantage points on the disturbed children admitted to their units. The reader is given a comprehensive picture of the complex nature of the needs to be met, the questions to be asked and how some of the provisions are organised and provided. Although no particular philosophy of treatment is given precedence, it is the variation in outlook of the different disciplines blended together in the interests of the child and family which holds the reader. In-patient child psychiatric units have indeed come a long way since their inception in 1947. Circumstances and purposes differ in different units, as is clear from the contents, but this comprehensive account will stand as a milestone in the history of the service.

Part I

The current context

Introduction

With a long history and tradition behind them, residential psychiatry units for children find themselves now in a period of rapid transition. Health service delivery in the UK is going through rapid change and there is a profound worldwide re-examination of methods of delivery of health care. In adapting to these changing circumstances, there will need to be a continual re-evaluation of our ideas of what residential mental health treatment for children should be like and its place in the overall pattern of mental health services. A number of intellectual and practical challenges have to be faced. Doing so will help clarify the core contribution of this kind of treatment to the mental health of children in the community. The central purpose of this book is to conduct that re-examination of the aims and approaches of child psychiatry in-patient treatment in the light of this changing context. We have aimed to produce a book that reflects the move towards evidence based medicine by emphasising the links between research and practice and, wherever possible, the evidence base for that practice. Where treatments do not have specific evidential support, we have aimed to elucidate the clinical experience behind their advocacy.

In this first section of the book we set the context. First there is a discussion of the current challenges that we believe in-patient child psychiatry faces – the challenges that led us to wish to write this book. Second, we include a review of current provision – based on a questionnaire study of in-patient units that we conducted in 1995. Third, William Parry-Jones gives an account of some aspects of the history of residential psychiatric care for children. Many readers will know that Professor Parry-Jones died tragically and suddenly, soon after delivering the final draft of his chapter to us. The great sense of loss at his death (especially for one of us, once his trainee) is linked to our appreciation that this chapter must represent one of his last pieces of academic work. William was powerfully committed to the view that the study of the history of psychiatry – especially of the waxing and waning of treatment enthusiasms – should provide sobering lessons for our current practices and enthusiasms. This could lead him at times to a pessimistic view of progress in psychiatry and certainly his chapter here has an almost elegiac tone in relation to residential treatment of children. His warnings and reminders at the end of this section act as a foil for the committed work and attitudes described elsewhere in the book.

1 Current challenges

Jonathan Green and Brian Jacobs

This book is written in the context of a number of challenges to the appropriateness and effectiveness of residential psychiatry treatment of children. The challenges come from many directions: from economic and political developments in many countries; from shifts in the social attitudes towards children and family life; from within the profession and from other professional groups. Let us begin by identifying some of the most salient.

SECULAR SHIFT IN USE OF HOSPITALS

There has been a general shift towards reduced use of in-patient treatment throughout medicine including paediatrics and adult mental health. In-patient child psychiatry has been no different and the total number of in-patient child psychiatry beds has certainly decreased over a number of years. It is not now felt to be essential for each health district to have its own in-patient facility, although all districts should have access to in-patient child psychiatry beds on a supra-district basis (Royal College of Psychiatrists 1992). A recent UK review (NHS Health Advisory Service 1995) identifies the core need for in-patient services as a 'Tier 4' specialist resource available in the context of tertiary referral. Thus in-patient child psychiatry has become a low volume, high cost, supra-district service with similarities to other highly specialist or intensive care facilities throughout medicine. This position within the NHS purchaser provider structure creates particular challenges for the negotiation of contracts and financing. Creative solutions involving consortium contracting and joint funding will have to be sought and these issues are discussed in detail in Part VII of this book. There is a risk that poor management of such co-ordinated contracting might result in the closure of units through default.

DEVELOPMENT OF INTENSIVE OUTREACH

In parallel with the relative decline in the use of in-patient facilities has come the growth in sophistication and application of various new forms of outpatient treatment. Intellectually, there have been arguments in favour of an increasing amount of treatment taking place within the child's natural context, and for the professional service to reach out to the child rather than have the child come into a specialised environment away from the natural setting of school and home. Such a move away from institutional care towards family care has occurred on many fronts, for instance in the social services field. Additionally, the growth of family based approaches to treatment such as family therapy has led many professionals within child mental health to question the wisdom and efficacy of separating young children from their family for the treatment process. In this context, child in-patient units can be seen as anachronistic hangovers from an 'institutional' past and likely to do more harm than good. There have, of course, been parallel movements within adult psychiatry, focused on the development of community care and the closure of mental hospitals.

These are persuasive arguments. Most clinicians would agree that the increase in community outreach and family based care when coherently and effectively organised with skilled personnel offers an effective and probably optimal treatment for *most* child mental health problems in the current community. However, it is likely that the shortcomings of a purely outreach based approach will become increasingly apparent for a core group of serious problems in the community. There may be a danger in idealising community outreach such that its overall effectiveness will be over-emphasised and insufficient attention paid to children who are unable to benefit from such work. There are also dangers, to be discussed at several places in this book, that a number of areas of serious psychopathology in children may currently be under-recognised or under-treated. This can apply to biological disorders such as undiagnosed epilepsy or developmental disorder, to psychological disorders such as unrecognised mood disorder or attention problems, and to psychosocial traumas such as undisclosed abuse or privation. The intensive residential assessment of such children can reveal problems that are not apparent in the outpatient setting, and intensive residential treatment may be able to promote change and developmental progress when outpatient treatment cannot. Naturally, it is going to be critical to provide evidence for such assertions. Much will be found throughout this book, especially in Parts V and VI. Further it is essential that future research strategies within the in-patient field concentrate on these issues and the 'added value' that in-patient assessment and treatment may or may not bring in certain situations (see Chapter 27).

QUESTIONING THE MILIEU

Another important challenge to traditional modes of in-patient child psychiatry treatment relates to the concept and efficacy of the so-called therapeutic 'milieu': that environment of care within which much of the therapeutic effect deemed distinctive to in-patient therapy is felt to take place. Some have developed attitudes hostile to any form of non-family care. These combine with pressures towards financial economy and the 'efficiency' of high throughput. They have led to the development of the notion, particularly in the USA, that in-patient units should provide the bare 'minimum necessary' intervention in order to return the child to the home environment. Children are admitted for a few days or at most a few weeks and intensive programmes are supposed to produce a proscription for services that will then be provided in the community. This model is described in detail in chapter 8. This does represent a significant challenge from within and without the profession to traditional notions of in-patient milieu therapy. From within the profession it partly stems from changes in treatment philosophy from ones based on psychodynamic principles with broad goals and an expectation of slow change, to more focused goal directed therapies such as cognitive behavioural therapy and behavioural management techniques.

We welcome many of these changes. However, shortening treatment times beyond a critical point will lead to a collapse of any proper notion of in-patient psychological treatment, and replace it by the most short term triage or superficial symptom control. Much of the re-definition of in-patient therapy that we are arguing for in this book does involve the incorporation within in-patient care of new styles of treatment delivery often initiated within the outpatient context, such as systemic, group and cognitive behavioural treatments. The challenge is to integrate these within a residential environment along with the best of what the traditional milieu has to offer, transforming them both in the context of overall shorter treatment admissions. Much of the thinking within Parts III and VI of this book is concerned with just this evolving practice. In the end, what it is that is efficacious about the complex intervention within in-patient care needs to be a matter of continuing intellectual debate and research initiatives. Such questions have proved difficult to research systematically in the past, but in Part VI we present such findings as there have been and suggest research initiatives for the future.

FAMILY CENTRED APPROACHES

The theory behind family centred treatment approaches strongly suggests that it is illogical to treat children outside the immediate context of the family. This has been another powerful challenge that has needed consideration. Most in-patient units have made great strides towards adapting their practice towards a family centred approach. Methods have been devised to keep a family focus of while admitting the child and keeping a focus from the beginning on 'family restoration'. Parts II and III of the book consider these matters as they affect the family engaging with the unit, during admission and post discharge. The admission of whole families is a radical solution to this problem and procedures to do this have been developed in the UK particularly at the Cassel Hospital and the Park Hospital, Oxford. A flexible use of family admission during the course of a child's treatment is being increasingly contemplated by many units but there are, of course, resource implications and the effectiveness of this manoeuvre needs to be tested. The effect of a family on the unit and the effect on an admitted family of being there need careful consideration in those units where there is limited or no separate specialist provision.

A second response to the challenge of an exclusively family centred approach lies in the realm of individual child rights. In some sense the admission of a child for its own assessment and treatment away from the family is an assertion of a child's right to be considered as an individual in some contexts, separate from the family and environment. Attention to the individual child in this way may be essential to uncovering individual developmental or biological difficulties with strong impact on the child's development. Alternatively the temporary removal of a child from the family home may prove to be the only way in which key origins of disturbance such as covert abuse may be identified. A child can have just as much right to this kind of individual assessment and care as it has a right to grow within a family context.

A DEVELOPMENTAL PERSPECTIVE

A further source of challenge to in-patient treatment is temporal. In-patient treatment is relatively short term and even if, as often happens within a protected and modified environment, the child is relieved of symptoms and makes developmental growth, the risk is that return to the same environment following discharge may result in a reversion to the original state with nothing much gained. This serious consideration has meant that in-patient practitioners have increasingly turned their gaze from a primary focus on the in-patient environment itself out to the child's developmental context both before admission and after discharge. Modern preadmission work aims to gain a good insight into the current context of a child's development and is described in Chapters 4 and 5. Emphasis is placed on preadmission engagement and contracting with families and others in the environment. Equally there is good evidence that post-discharge care plays a critical part in long-term outcome after in-patient treatment (Chapter 7). Increasing attention is paid to discharge planning and the offering of bridging 'care' following discharge before the further involvement of local services. In-patient treatment will only be most effective if it exists in a context of secondary care and follow-up. For many disorders it is increasingly useful to see the period of admission within the context of the whole developmental span of childhood. With a greater understanding of the developmental trajectory of different disorders it becomes possible to identify critical inputs that may alter a subsequent developmental pathway, and often the long-term aim of admission is to set in motion just such a significant change for the child. In-patient care here is seen as one component of a linked series of initiatives and interventions over time: collaboration with other services becomes vital. Research into the efficacy of in-patient treatments would ideally show such an impact into developmental trajectories; however such studies are difficult and have yet to be done.

For a minority of children in in-patient care it becomes apparent that the time period typical for modern in-patient child psychiatry treatment in the UK (three to nine months – see Chapter 28) is going to be inadequate. Here the in-patient service needs to be able to articulate with a range of longer term resources such as therapeutic schools, therapeutic children's homes, and therapeutic communities. Part VIII of this book is devoted to an examination of such contexts. It is an urgent matter to know whether such a large investment pays developmental dividends and whether the costs in terms of community dislocation for the child are more than matched by the benefits accruing to psychological development. Equally, within in-patient psychiatry care, the true costs of these units needs to be seen within the context of potential social gains in other spheres during later development. Are the economic costs warranted? An approach to these issues is discussed in Chapter 30.

REFERRING CONSTITUENCIES AND THE FUTURE

The in-patient psychiatry unit serves a number of different constituencies. The **courts** will often see them as useful places for structured and intensive assessments for medical legal purposes, particularly in the context of planning a future care placement. **Social services** may see the in-patient unit as a resource for some of their most complex and multi-problem children in whom care issues and psychological morbidity usually covary. On occasion the in-patient unit has to resist becoming a substitute care environment for highly disturbed but socially deprived children. **Paediatricians** of all kinds will often look to the child in-patient unit for help with difficult psychosomatic and conversion disorders or children with significant psychological comorbidity to their physical problems. The role of child psychiatry in-patient units within specialist paediatric hospitals has been particularly fruitful and this relationship is likely to continue. For **child psychiatrists** in-patient units are a resource for some of the most difficult and complex children in psychiatry practice though there is often ambivalence about the share of the limited financial resources that in-patient units can consume.

To thrive into the next millennium, child in-patient psychiatry units will have to redefine themselves and articulate their values in respect of all these different constituencies. They will need to prove their worth within the context of evidence based medicine and a strict managerial pressure on costs. Despite the relative complexity and arduousness of developing and maintaining a good in-patient treatment environment, practitioners within in-patient child psychiatry will continue to promote this work. Why? Because of their belief that well functioning in-patient environments provide the most powerful and complete response to some of the most complex and challenging difficulties presenting in child mental health. We hope in this book to contribute to a necessary re-evaluation and re-definition of in-patient care in the face of these current challenges. We are sustained in the belief that in-patient treatment is, and will remain, a challenging, fascinating and valuable resource within Child Mental Health.

REFERENCES

Association of Directors of Social Services and the Royal College of Psychiatrists (1995) *Joint Statement on an Integrated Mental Health Service for Children and Adolescents.* North Allerton: Royal College of Psychiatrists.

Department of Health (1995) *A Handbook on Child and Adolescent Mental Health.* London, HMSO.

NHS Health Advisory Service (1995) *Thematic Review. Together We Stand: The Commissioning Role and Management of Child and Adolescent Mental Health Services.* London, HMSO.

Royal College of Psychiatrists (1992) *Mental Health of the Nation: The Contribution of Psychiatry*, Report to Council No. 16. London: Royal College of Psychiatrists.

Royal College of Psychiatrists and the Faculty of Public Health Medicine (1993) *Psychiatric Services: The Report of the Joint Working Group on the Purchasing of Psychiatric Care*, Report to Council No. 25. London: Royal College of Psychiatrists.

2 Current practice: a questionnaire survey of in-patient child psychiatry in the United Kingdom

Jonathan Green and Brian Jacobs

INTRODUCTION

Child psychiatry in-patient units in the UK are widely distributed geographically. In the past there has been little co-ordination of their efforts. Some have been concerned about idiosyncratic diversity in their practice (Wrate and Wolkind 1991). The aim of this study was to investigate current practice. We wished to test whether previous impressions of idiosyncratic practice and standards were justified, and to examine the current state of this treatment in the context of recent reports (The Children Act 1989; NHS Executive 1994; Kurtz, Thornes and Wolkind 1994; NHS Health Advisory Service 1995).

We identified twenty-nine in-patient units in the UK admitting children up to 13 years. There is no centrally held record of such units. Partial lists were obtained from the Department of Health and the Association of Child Psychology and Psychiatry database. Each health region was approached for local lists. Data collection was undertaken in late 1994 and 1995 by postal questionnaire. Responses were received from the consultants responsible for all units. Telephone contact was used to clarify details. Data was analysed using SPSS. Distribution of responses was summarised using median and mid-quartile range and associations were tested using Pearson correlation coefficients.

RESULTS

Distribution of units

Broadly, the distribution of units follows patterns of major conurbation through the UK (Table 2.1). The distance people have to travel to an in-patient unit are uneven but the populations served show less variability. Seventeen units considered themselves to be regional or supra-regional services and another eleven supra-district. Only one offered a purely district service. Fifteen units served one to two million population. Four units provided for five million or greater: two in London, one in Manchester and one in Birmingham.

Table 2.1 Distribution of units

Area	No. of Units
South East	8
South West	2
Midlands	4
North West	6
North	3
Wales	1
Scotland	4
Ireland	1

Size and activity

The maximum age accepted for admission was 13 years (mid-quartile range 12–14). Twelve units opened seven days a week, seventeen units opened five days a week and all but one unit also offered day-patient admission. Units were similar in size irrespective of geographical area served.

Admission rates varied but length of stay and throughput per bed were less diverse. Median length of assessment admission was six weeks with only four units reporting assessment admissions lasting longer than two months. Length of treatment admissions was also similar (median sixteen weeks) with only four units reporting usual treatment stays above twenty weeks (Table 2.2). It was very rare for treatment admissions to last over one year.

Table 2.2 Size and activity of units

	Median	Mid-quartile range
In-patient places (maximum capacity)	10	8–12
Day patient places (maximum capacity)	5	3–6
No. of in-patient admissions per year	25	22–38
Bed occupancy (%)	80	70–85
Usual length of assessment admission (weeks)	6	5–8
Usual length of treatment admission (weeks)	16	12–20
Minimum length of treatment admission (weeks)	7	2–13
Maximum length of treatment admission (weeks)	39	23–52
In-patient throughput (patients per bed per year)	3	1.8–3.4
Cases followed up as outpatients (%)	72	16–88

Caseload

Overall frequency of diagnostic groups admitted is shown in Table 2.3. There were striking differences between units. Ten units did not admit conduct disorders and five did not admit emotional disorders. Seven units did not see neuropsychiatry cases but for one unit these represented 60 per cent of the

Table 2.3 Caseload: percentage split of admissions by diagnosis

Diagnostic group	Median (%)	Mid-quartile range (%)
Conduct disorder	25	0–35
Emotional disorder	20	5–25
Mixed disorder of conduct and emotion	25	8–35
Neuropsychiatry	5	0–12
Somatising disorder	5	2–9
Elimination disorder	9	3–9.5
Eating disorders	4	0–7
Psychosis	2.5	0–4.5
Developmental disorders	4	0–5

caseload; similarly two units reported 30 per cent of their work as somatising disorders. Five units did not see psychotic disorder and ten did not admit developmental disorder. A high proportion of admissions of developmental disorders such as Pervasive Developmental Disorder was correlated with a higher patient throughput per year (Pearson r = 0.6942, p<0.01, 1-tailed), suggesting that these may often be shorter assessment admissions.

Staffing

Nursing

The overall nurse–patient ratio was similar in most units. Only six units had a ratio greater than 1 nurse to 1.2 children. No unit had a ratio less than 1 : 1.1 (Table 2.4). Most units had specific night staff and in addition twenty units operated an internal rotation for night cover. There was a Senior Nurse (Grade

Table 2.4 Staffing

	Median	Mid-quartile range
Consultant	4 sessions	2–5.8 sessions
Senior Registrar	3 sessions	0–7 sessions
Registrar	4 sessions	0–8 sessions
Total nursing complement	13	10.5–18
Nurse–patient ratio	1 : 1.2	1 : 1.1–1 : 1.5
Night Nurses	2	0–2.8
Junior Nurses (Grades A–C)	5	3–6.2
Staff Nurses (Grades D and E)	5	4–7
Charge Nurses (Grade F)	1	
Senior Nurses (Grades G, H, and I)	18 units have 1 / 6 units have 2 / 4 units have 3 or more	
Psychology sessions [N = 20]	1	0–4.8
OT sessions [N = 16]	1	0–6.5

G and above) on all units and four units had a nurse at Grade I. The number of junior nurses varied considerably. Six units reported that they had non-qualified staff such as postgraduate students working on the ward.

Medical

See Table 2.4. All units were consultant led. Eight units had no senior registrar and eight no registrar; two ran with no junior doctors at all. Five units had sessions of other associate medical staff.

Other staff

Units varied greatly here. Nine units had no psychologist, thirteen had no occupational therapist, only five had a child psychotherapist and (remarkably) only three had social work sessions. Few units had sessions in experiential therapies: only seven had any art therapy; only two drama or music therapy. Just four units had any dedicated family therapist time; but in two this was a full-time post.

Staff roles

Typically in the in-patient teams there are discipline-specific roles and therapeutic roles that bridge disciplines. To investigate this we asked about the tasks that individual disciplines undertook and found a wide variation. As an example Table 2.5 illustrates the various work roles undertaken in different units by three disciplines.

School

Provision of specialised schooling is essential for in-patient functioning. Eight units had dedicated schools on site whereas the other units in this survey shared school facilities with other patient groups. Eighteen units had a headteacher and two a teacher in charge; eleven had no teaching ancillary staff. Excluding the Head, there was a median of two trained teachers per school (mid-quartile range 2–3.5). In all but two units the local education authority funded the school.

Treatment philosophy

The data did not support the view that in-patient units show a variety of idiosyncratic styles. One unit described itself as psychodynamic and another was organised around family systems theory. The rest (27 units) reported an eclectic or mixed therapeutic orientation. Many units reported special expertise in particular areas, most commonly in parenting assessment and treatment, psychosomatic disorders, eating disorders and neuropsychiatry.

Table 2.5 Profession and work role (the number of units employing each of three professions in various roles)

	Psychology	OT	Psychotherapy
Individual child psychotherapy/play therapy	12	15	2
Psychometric testing	5	1	0
CBT, behaviour treatment	7	0	0
Group work	1	11	0
Consultation staff supervision/support	2	0	3
Family work	7	2	
Parent training	2	1	
Motor assessment	0	1	
Speech and language assessment	1		

Twenty units had exclusion criteria relating to admission; most common of these were for learning disability (6 units), aggression or dangerousness (5 units), poor family motivation or lack of a clear carer (6 units).

Three-quarters of the units reported using goal-orientated treatment planning but less than half assessed goal outcomes.

Behavioural management

Units were asked to describe their approach to behavioural management, the circumstances in which these strategies would be used, the method of application, any consent procedures used and whether their policy was consistent with the 1989 Children Act.

Time out

Seventeen units used formal time out procedures. In ten units it was used for disruptive behaviour and acts that were abusive to adults or peers; in five it would be used when the child could not cope with a situation or where there was social breakdown. One unit would use time out for a child who was behaving dangerously towards adults or who was out of the control of the staff. No unit used the procedure for absconding children.

Units used a variety of methods of time out, ranging from the child sitting on a special chair or bench in a communal area (11 units) to using the child's own bedroom or dormitory (10 units). Five units had a dedicated time out room. For only one unit was a room with a lockable door used for time out.

Thirteen units considered that parental consent for time out was covered by pre-admission agreements and unit information policy. Five units sought general pre-admission consent from the child whilst only one unit obtained specific consent at the time the treatment was prescribed. Most units that used time out did not think they needed to make changes in their procedures.

Physical restraint

Twenty-five units used this; twenty-three for abusive behaviour and aggression towards peers as well as for disruption. About half of the units used restraint for self-harming behaviour whilst only four used it for challenging behaviour or when the child was threatening adults. Two units used formal restraint procedures when children threatened to abscond.

Thirteen respondents used a specific room for restraining a child. No unit would use a child's bedroom. Eight units used a specific holding technique. Specific consent at the time was obtained in only two units but fourteen units considered that they had gained general consent for such procedures pre-admission. Four units sought consent from the child at the time. Sixteen units considered their restraint procedures met the requirements of the 1989 Children Act, whilst ten thought that they might need to make changes.

Segregation

Twenty-one units used segregation (that is separating the child from the rest of the group, usually into a quiet place – sometimes described as 'destimulation'). Eighteen units used this for children who were disruptive, abusive or aggressive to their peers. In two units it would be used for challenging behaviour or behaving dangerously to adults. Three units stated they did not use segregation. Consent would be obtained by general pre-admission agreement in five units but it seems to have been rarely discussed with the child before admission. Usually, a quiet room with soft furnishings was preferred. Sometimes the child's bedroom would be used. Time out rooms were not used for segregation.

Most units were happy with their current policy on segregation and did not think it needed amendment.

Seclusion

Six units used seclusion (placing a child in a room from which they cannot leave). It was mainly used for abusive and aggressive behaviour towards peers or because of self-harming behaviour. One unit stated it would use seclusion when other methods had failed. Respondents did not give challenging behaviour or aggression towards adults as a reason for its use. The site of seclusion varied with one unit using the child's bedroom, one unit using a specific room and three units mentioning isolation but not specifying how this was achieved. General parental consent was sought in only two of the units but most discussed the procedure before admission. Two units made no mention of gaining consent.

Attitudes to children's rights

We asked at what age a child might refuse management or treatment requiring degrees of coercion or force and whether the child's intellectual abilities would affect the clinician's judgement on such matters. There was a range of views. For non-coercive treatments most clinicians used age thresholds in determining whether child consent was needed: these were 10 years or under (7 clinicians), 11 years (3 clinicians), 13 years (3 clinicians). Only two clinicians would use Gillick criteria and for four parental consent was always paramount. For coercive treatments and treatment requiring force, the pattern was similar except that the age thresholds were higher. For forceful treatments, four clinicians had an age threshold of 11 years and three of 13 years. Only one clinician would use Gillick criteria for these situations and for three the parental consent was primary.

Involvement of parents

All units said they work actively to engage the whole family in treatment. One unit involved a parent in management of the unit school whilst five units had other approaches to involve parents in managerial aspects of the unit. Seven units ran groups for the parents and four units provided specific clinical activities for parents on the wards. Four respondents cited parents' contributions towards case reviews as an aid to parental involvement.

Use of medication

Medication is not a common form of first line treatment in child psychiatry, but given the nature of the cases treated in in-patient units, one would expect the use of medication to be relatively higher than in other child psychiatry practice, and this proves to be the case (Table 2.6). The indications cited for antidepressant usage are most commonly depression but also OCD, enuresis and school non-attendance. Stimulants are used solely for disorders of overactivity and inattention. Twelve units used anxiolytics rarely, usually in the context of desensitisation in anxiety disorders or school non-attendance. Anti-psychotic medication is used for psychotic disorders or Tourette Syndrome. Only three units reported ever using anti-psychotic medication specifically for sedation or behavioural control and only two for mood disorders. Other drugs reported as occasionally used were laxatives, clonidine, lithium and anticonvulsants. We examined the data to see if there was an increased use of medication in units where morale was low but did not find this.

Table 2.6 Use of medication (frequency of usage by percentage of respondents)

	Often (%)	Quite often (%)	Rarely (%)	Never (%)
Antidepressants	3.4	20.7	65.5	10.3
Antipsychotics	3.4	10.3	69	17.2
Anxiolytics	0	0	45	55
Stimulants	3.4	20.7	55.2	20.7

Contracting and financial viability

There was a very high level of block contracts in all units (median 90 per cent of all contracts). Eight units were completely dependent on block contracting. The use of ECR contracts varied widely: in nineteen units they accounted for less than 25 per cent of contracts and in a minority of three units they accounted for between 25 and 50 per cent of contracts. Only two units had rolling contracts applying to more than one year. Ten units reported problems with funding related to contracting.

Confidence and morale

Fifteen units in the survey described themselves as 'thriving' but nine felt that they were 'just surviving' and five were under 'imminent threat'. Staff morale was reasonable with twenty-one units describing morale as good or very good and eight units describing morale as fair. No units described poor morale.

A number of factors correlated with units' sense of thriving and staff morale. A unit's 'thriving' was significantly related to serving a larger catchment area ($r = 0.6028$, $p < 0.01$; Pearson correlation coefficients, 1-tailed significance levels) and admitting fewer children with antisocial behaviour – conduct disorder plus mixed disorder of conduct and emotions – ($r = 0.7346$, $p < 0.001$). Unit 'morale' was correlated with a higher nurse : patient ratio ($r = 0.6230$, $p < 0.01$) and admitting less antisocial disorder ($r = 0.7141$, $p < 0.01$).

General comments

Clinicians were asked for their comments on particular pleasures and problems in working in in-patient units now and any other comments that they wished to make. A number of themes emerged.

Firstly, the NHS reorganisation was largely seen as a problem rather than an opportunity. A number of units found themselves surprised to be on a good financial footing; a number of consultants referred to the success of their units within the new management environment and the pleasing increase in referrals that they were witnessing. However, a greater number experienced the reorganisation as a destabilisation and a threat. Management work, the struggle for resources and recognition within the larger service environment were seen as the least attractive parts of the work.

There was much comment on the increasing numbers of highly disturbed and disruptive conduct disordered boys referred to in-patient units: these children are generally seen as problematic and have relatively poor outcomes. Better outcomes were associated with less overt behavioural disturbance. Nursing shortage was felt to be highly stressful, damaging to morale and limiting to creativity.

Overall, the main pleasures of the work remained in the clinical contact with parents and children and successful working within the multi-professional team. The sense of success in witnessing change in children and families; team work;

watching staff grow and develop and express their creativity; and the building of efficient practices: these were core pleasures communicated.

DISCUSSION

Are the extent and distribution of in-patient units adequate?

The NHS Health Advisory Service thematic review (Health Advisory Service 1995) describes in-patient treatment as a 'Tier 4' specialised service to be provided on a subregional or a regional basis. Current recommendations from the Royal College of Psychiatrists (Royal College of Psychiatrists 1992) are for two to four child in-patient places at any time per district of 250,000 population. The median of ten beds per unit found in this study would therefore indicate a need for one in-patient unit per 0.6–1.2 million population. Our findings show that in-patient provision is indeed now largely regional or subregional, but that the median population served (between 1 and 2 million) is greater than that recommended in the Royal College guidelines. However, no systematic needs assessment for child in-patient treatment has been done. This would require evaluation of the population prevalence of complex and severe problems in children, and the methodologies to do this are only just being developed (Kurtz 1994)

The data does suggest that child in-patient units are fairly rationally spread across the country, concentrated in areas of major conurbation. This means that there are likely to be significant problems with transport and maintenance of family involvement in rural units – clinicians do report these anecdotally.

How diverse are practices between units?

Contrary to some expectations, there is convergence in a number of aspects of units' function: size, activity, lengths of admission are rather similar throughout the country; there is no evidence of great diversity in treatment philosophy. All but two units describe themselves as eclectic. All units say they involve the whole family in the treatment process. In nearly a fifth, parents were involved in some way in the management of the unit. There is a low use of medication compared to adult psychiatry and no evidence of medication used in any widespread way for sedation or behavioural control. A high proportion of cases is followed up as outpatients after discharge, despite the large geographical area served by each unit. We do not have data on how long such patients are followed up. Clinicians may be reflecting in their practice here the association between good aftercare and long term outcome following admission (Pfeiffer and Strzelecki 1990). Alternatively, the finding might reflect difficulties in handing back care to local services.

There are a number of variations in practice identified in the data, not least in the profile of disorders treated. Given their high prevalence in the population, it is not surprising that disorders of conduct, emotion, and mixed disorders are highly represented in many units – although a minority do not admit them at all. A number of other disorders are more highly represented than one would expect from population prevalence rates. These include somatisation, psychosis and neuropsychiatric disorders. This is unsurprising as these disorders are often disabling and complex in their presentation and treatment. A number of units make these admissions their main work. This variability of admission pattern has implications for health service strategic planning. In-patient units are a scarce resource. Most districts will not have access to more than one unit within reasonable distance. Arguably, most units must maintain the potential to admit children across the broad range of diagnoses besides developing specialisms. Specialising is of course simpler and can be more efficient since the milieu environment, staffing and training can be fine-tuned to a particular need (see Chapter 9). There is research evidence to back clinical impression that different milieu styles can selectively benefit different problems (Friis 1986). Maintaining flexibility may be more difficult – it requires more staff to manage a more complex environment (see Chapter 9).

A high level of admissions of antisocial disorder is associated with poor staff morale and lack of unit confidence. Clinicians commented on the greater pressure to admit conduct disorders in recent years. The treatment of conduct disorder in itself raises important questions. There is evidence against in-patient psychiatry as an effective treatment for pure conduct disorder (Pfeiffer and Strzelecki 1990). Maintaining a therapeutic milieu intact in the face of a high proportion of conduct disordered patients is stressful and perhaps impossible. On the other hand, there is preliminary evidence to suggest that the in-patient assessment of some cases of severe conduct disorder can be very fruitful in defining covert comorbidity which may be treatable (Hill-Smith et al. 1994). The development of more sophisticated criteria for the admission of conduct disorder and research on assessment and outcome will be a significant task for the future.

In the management of antisocial or dangerous behaviour, most teams use some form of physical restraint with their children although only in a minority are there standardised holding techniques; a third of units are concerned that their measures (1995) may not be compatible with the Children Act. These results suggest the need for systematic national protocols based on legal advice and training in restraint techniques. The majority of units use time out techniques, and this use appears to be associated with better morale in the unit. The dilemmas are discussed in Chapter 29.

Learning disability is frequently an exclusion criterion for admission. There can be problems in integrating children with significant mental handicap into an in-patient milieu. Unfortunately this reflects inadequacies in mental health provision for this group generally (Kurtz, Thornes and Wolkind 1994).

How are the units staffed?

The bulk of in-patient treatment is delivered through direct staff–child contact and the staff resource represents by far the greatest cost in treatment. The staff profile of units is of critical importance. Staffing is very variable and grossly inadequate in some areas, particularly among professions allied to medicine and nursing. The data shows considerable variability in nursing skill mix but with reasonable, high grade, nursing leadership. Nonetheless, we were concerned at the number of units without senior nurse leadership. Evidence points to the critical importance of good nursing staff–patient ratios: low ratios are correlated with poor morale. There is no guidance in the UK from Royal College of Nursing on this area, but the median overall nurse–patient ratio of 1 : 1.2 found in this study implies a likely difficulty of getting a shift ratio much above 1 : 5. Recommendations in the USA are for shift ratios considerably higher than this (American Academy of Child and Adolescent Psychiatry 1990). Levels of non-nursing staff are also critical. In our study, the provision of psychology and occupational therapy is patchy, and other specialisms are very poorly represented. The lack of child psychotherapy and experiential therapies in the great majority of units is a concern when children with such complex psychopathologies are being treated. The stark absence of social workers reflects a nationwide with-drawal of social workers from hospital practice and many respondents particularly commented on how regrettable this was. Chapter 9 contains a detailed discussion of the implications of these staffing issues.

We found as predicted that work roles often bridge disciplines. While this may often represent an appropriate flexibility in a work group it can also often raise issues of training, status and supervision (see Chapters 16–18). Moreover one does need to ask how often this form of working is actually a counsel of desperation in the context of staff shortage and difficulties in recruitment.

Consent to treatment

There was a patchy response to questions of consent to treatment. All but one clinician answered questions on non-coercive treatments, but only a third responded in relation to coercive or forceful treatments. The majority of units practice coercive methods at some time; thus clinicians have either not thought through issues of consent or are reluctant to address them in surveys. These are difficult issues. It is unlikely that an angry, distressed child who perceives, often wrongly, that the world has ganged up on them will give consent for treatments that restrict their liberty. They may withdraw consent previously given. Should this mean that their liberty cannot be restricted at that moment? The Children Act gives guidelines on the use of restriction of liberty (see Chapter 29). It does not envisage that a child's view should necessarily prevail. The survey suggests that there is not yet a general agreement about when informed consent can be given on the basis of age.

Shaw (1993 and Chapter 29) suggests a distinction between coercive treat-ments such as time out, and positive reinforcement and restriction of liberty as defined in the 1989 Children Act. In practice, there is overlap. The use of time out frequently requires the restriction of liberty as defined by the Act. This is an area of practice that needs further discussion and the generation of an agreed set of guidelines which safeguards the child's civil rights but does not deprive them of treatment that can help them. There is the reciprocal danger of labelling restriction of liberty as a treatment. If such restriction (for instance in time out) were to be regarded as somehow separate from the business of the Children Act, there would be a danger of abuse of the regulations.

How should the services be contracted?

Recent reports have dealt with the issue of contracting specialised services in general and in-patient child psychiatry in particular (NHS Executive 1994, NHS Health Advisory Service 1995). In the light of their recommendations, the data from this survey is concerning. Both reports address the issue of the purchasing of specialist services. Both conclude that block contracts are quite inappropriate and that purchasers should commit themselves to specifying care using advanced contracts even of low volumes rather than using ECR referrals. Various forms of multi-purchaser agreements are suggested, for instance insurance-based consortia and subscription services. There is also a suggestion (NHS Executive 1994) that specific contracts for specialised service should be underwritten at regional or national level. Above all, the contracting of low volume, relatively high cost services 'requires protection (from the market) and proactive management' (NHS Executive 1994).

At the time of this study, progress towards specialised contracting arrangements had hardly begun. While many units may be protected for the time being within larger blocks, developing a more sophisticated practice in the future over contracting is going to be crucial. Contracting issues are discussed in further detail later in Chapter 31 of this volume.

Conclusion

This survey suggests a convergence in treatment philosophy and practice in child in-patient units that could presage the development of common clinical standards of care in some areas. The results also point to a number of issues requiring further attention:

- The variation in admission profiles nationally.
- The admission of children with severe antisocial or aggressive behaviours. How are they to be selected, and how may the presence of comorbidity affect treatment outcome?
- The need for national guidelines for adequate staffing. Is the effectiveness of units impaired by the often limited range of professions we find working in them?
- The need for a general policy of training on the use of specific methods of restraint.
- More discussion of the issues of children's consent to treatment.
- The need for more attention to be paid to methods of contracting.

REFERENCES

American Academy of Child and Adolescent Psychiatry (1990) *Task Force on Adolescent Hospitalisation. Model for Minimum Staffing Patterns for Hospitals Providing Acute In-patient Treatment for Children and Adolescents with Psychiatric Illnesses.* Washington DC.

The Children Act (1989). London: HMSO.

Cotton, N.S. (1993) *Lessons from the Lion's Den: Therapeutic Management of Children in Psychiatric Hospitals and Treatment Centres.* San Francisco: Jossey-Bass.

Friis, S. (1986) 'Characteristics of a good ward atmosphere', *Acta Psychiatrica Scandinavica.* 74: 469–473.

Hill-Smith, A., Spender, Q., Glaser, D. and Jacobs, B.W. (1994) *Comorbidity Found in Recruits to the Pilot Phase of a Treatment Trial for Conduct Disorder.* Presentation at Royal College of Psychiatrists, Child and Adolescent Annual Conference, September.

Kurtz, Z., Thornes, R. and Wolkind, S. (1994) *Services for the Mental Health of Children and Young People in England: A National Review.* London: South Thames Regional Health Authority.

Kurtz, Z. (1994) *Treating Children Well.* London: Mental Health Foundation.

Marsden, G., McDermott, J.F. and Miner, D. (1970) 'Residential treatment of children: a survey of institutional characteristics', *Journal of the American Academy of Child Psychiatry.* 9: 332–346.

NHS Executive (1994) *Contracting of Specialised Services: A Practical Guide.* London: HMSO.

NHS Health Advisory Service (1995) *Thematic Review. Together We Stand: The Commissioning Role and Management of Child and Adolescent Mental Health Services.* London: HMSO.

Pfeiffer, S.I. and Strzelecki, S.C. (1990) 'In-patient psychiatric treatment of children and adolescents: a review of outcome studies', *Journal of the American Academy of Child and Adolescent Psychiatry.* 29, No. 6, 847–853.

Royal College of Psychiatrists (1992) *Mental Health of the Nation: The Contribution of Psychiatry.* Report to Council No. 16. London: Royal College of Psychiatrists.

Shaw, M. (1993) *On the Road to Clarification: Good Practice for Child and Adolescent In-patient Units in the Light of the Children Act 1989.* Presentation at the Royal College of Psychiatrists, Child and Adolescent Psychiatry Section, September.

Wrate, R.M. and Wolkind, S. (1991) 'Child and adolescent psychiatry in-patient units', *Psychiatric Bulletin,* 15, 36.

3   Historical themes

William Parry-Jones

The justification for historical analysis is the contribution it can make to the clarification and resolution of current issues, such as the vagaries of service evolution in the field of residential treatment and ideological dilemmas intrinsic to institutional care of children and adolescents (Parry-Jones 1989). From identifiable origins in the eighteenth century, there is a long-standing history of residential care, confinement and treatment as part of society's response to psychotic, mentally handicapped, or just homeless children, and to those presenting with a wide range of emotional and behavioural disorders and deviance. Current challenges and recommendations for future developments in Child Psychiatry need to be set into this broad historical context.

There have been few systematic studies of the history of the residential care and treatment of children in hospital, e.g. Beskind (1962) in the USA and Barker (1974) in the UK. Published accounts tend to go back only as far as the 1920s and 1930s and modern writers have made little exploration of pre-twentieth century developments. Additionally, there are a few reviews of the history of residential child care in Europe (Buckle et al. 1972; Cotton and Hellinckx 1993; Madge, 1994). In this chapter, emphasis will be on the history of provision for mentally ill young people in hospital settings in the UK, referring to influential developments in the USA.

EIGHTEENTH AND NINETEENTH CENTURY ORIGINS

Workhouses and houses of correction

From antiquity onwards, protective services for children lacking parents or parental care have always been based on institutional management or fostering initiated by concerned individuals, philanthropic societies or the state. The effectiveness of the Elizabethan Poor Law Act, 1601, in protecting helpless children was variable and abandonment of unwanted offspring, including the mentally and physically defective, continued (Boswell 1988). Before the widespread establishment of lunatic asylums, workhouses provided both short- and long-term care. They were expected to contain disturbed young people, especially the mentally handicapped, and only dangerous, acute or curable cases were transferred, often belatedly, to asylums. Separate lunatic and infant wards were established in some workhouses, but overcrowding and inadequate care predominated. Very little is known about the welfare of the young mentally ill or mentally handicapped, either in British workhouses or in American poor houses. Such residential institutions retained a central role in child welfare right up until the reforming Children Act (1948) established Children's Departments as free-standing local authority units.

Institutions for destitute children

The first specialised institution for destitute children, the London Foundling Hospital, opened in 1747 (McClure 1981) and became widely imitated. Despite its admirable objectives, opposition emerged on the grounds of encouraging abandonment, deprivation of parenting and high levels of institutional infant mortality. By the early nineteenth century, there were numerous orphans and foundlings in overcrowded, insalubrious workhouses. Gradually, educational provisions were made in workhouses, and the use of district schools and boarding-out in families developed. Philanthropic concern for needy children was pioneered by nineteenth-century rescue societies, notably the Destitute Children's Dinner Society, 1864, the National Children's Home and Orphanage, 1869, and Dr Barnardo's Homes, 1870.

Industrial and reformatory schools

The conspicuous social problems of vagrant children in the late eighteenth and early nineteenth centuries precipitated the Ragged School Movement. The Marine Society, 1756, established a school for convicts' children, although the Philanthropic Society, 1788, is generally recognised as the first institution for delinquents. However, these organisations made little impact on the incidence of early nineteenth-century juvenile crime, when any child aged over seven could be considered capable of committing felony. Convicted juveniles were still sent to prisons and houses of correction, despite growing dissatisfaction about numbers and recidivism. Later, encouraged by Carpenter's pioneering work in Bristol (Carpenter 1851) and concern about harsh conditions at Parkhurst Prison for Boys, industrial and reformatory schools were set up for training, detention and social rehabilitation (Carlebach 1970; Bridgeland 1971). Borstal institutions were established from 1908 to train young offenders who needed higher levels of security than in the reformatory schools (Barman 1934). Chisholm (1996a) has drawn attention to the special contribution of early Scottish initiatives.

'Reform' schools were replaced in 1933 by approved schools and remand homes, both of which were succeeded by 'community homes' following the Children and Young Persons Act, 1969. Thereafter, short-term secure accommodation was provided in observation and assessment centres, while community homes with education on the premises supplied longer-term needs. In the 1980s, the approved school population declined sharply, reacting against the philosophy of the 1969 Act, especially the use of care as a 'sentence,' and with doubts about the effectiveness of residential care in changing delinquent behaviour.

Infirmaries, early general and specialist children's hospitals

It was not until the mid-nineteenth century that paediatrics emerged as a medical speciality. Although a few dispensaries had catered for sick children from the late eighteenth century, not all early infirmaries and general hospitals accepted children, except for emergency surgery. The Liverpool Infirmary for Children opened in 1851 and the Hospital for Sick Children, Great Ormond Street, London, in 1852. The public appeal preceding the latter emphasised the inadequacy and inappropriateness of general hospital facilities for children and the urgent need to treat larger numbers of children successfully, while recognising the potentially adverse effects of removal from home.

Subsequently, similar foundations in other large cities created the institutional framework for the new discipline (Franklin 1964), but no systematic provision was made for mentally ill children (Parry-Jones 1994). However, 'disorders of the mind' and mental handicap did feature in the writings of prominent paediatric physicians (e.g. West 1854) and the records of general hospitals in the late nineteenth and early twentieth centuries indicate that children with a range of 'functional nervous diseases' were admitted. Even after the development of specialist in-patient psychiatric units for children, some psychiatrists continued to advocate the diagnostic and therapeutic benefits, for emotionally disturbed children, of short-term hospitalisation in a children's hospital. This view was based, partly, on the perceived therapeutic benefits of parental separation (Solnit 1960, Laybourne and Miller 1962). As specialist psychiatric units expanded, some were located as wards in children's hospitals (Copus and Walker 1972).

Lunatic asylums

At Bethlem from 1772 to 1787, 4.7 per cent of the 2829 admissions were aged under 20 years, with only one under 10 and most between 15 and 20 (see Parry-Jones 1994). Throughout the nineteenth century, there is conclusive evidence that children were admitted alongside adult patients to madhouses, county, borough, and public subscription asylums, but information is variable and often physically difficult to access, particularly for younger children and especially for the early period. Statistics for many European and American asylums indicate that up to about 8 per cent of admissions were aged under 20 years (Parry-Jones 1994). Modern studies of the records of Bethlem (Wilkins 1987) and of private and public asylums in Oxfordshire (Parry-Jones 1972, 1990) corroborate these nineteenth-century statistics.

Reasons for confinement

Nineteenth-century physicians and alienists generally favoured removal from home to establish control, unhindered by parental and family interference. One madhouse proprietor, Bakewell (1836), maintained 'No patient has a fair chance of recovery unless he be separated from family . . . influence . . . and under non-irritating control'. In contrast, West (1854) favoured residential family care by 'some person competent to enter into their pursuits and to share their pleasures', although post-pubertal deterioration might necessitate asylum admission. Allbutt (1889) insisted that insane children, unless seriously disturbed, could be managed at home, thereby avoiding 'the systematic watchfulness' of asylum doctors. Sometimes, the notion of asylum care for children was disputed. Nevertheless, despite public sensitivity concerning asylum confinement, no scandalous accounts of juvenile maltreatment have emerged nor did children receive any special, or separate, consideration in Reports of Commissioners in Lunacy.

Diagnostic categories

Precise diagnostic statements in asylum records were rare, permitting only speculative retrospective diagnosis. A study of young people admitted to Oxfordshire asylums (Parry-Jones 1990) provides an illustration of presenting disorders. In a series of forty-six patients aged up to 16, admitted to Oxfordshire County Asylum from 1846 to 1866, the sexes were about equal and the youngest were aged five. Twenty-five epileptics presented major management problems and many early fatalities. Nineteen patients were diagnosed as 'idiotic'. Acutely disturbed, noisy and destructive behaviour was characteristic in this study and in many contemporaneous case reports and, of four children with delusional ideas, two were paranoid. In this series, no patients were termed melancholic, but depressive features were recognisable and one boy aged 15 showed manic-depressive phenomena. Several were suicidal and some excited states suggested mania.

Treatment philosophy and outcome

In the first three decades of the nineteenth century, the concept of moral management emerged, incorporating the replacement of external coercion and physical restraint by the encouragement of self-restraint in a humane and salubrious environment (Scull 1993). As was the case with adults during the nineteenth century, education was used extensively, together with bathing and prescribed dietaries. Children benefited from the advantages implicit in this approach, particularly minimal restraint, the practice of grouping according to clinical state, the provision of amusements, exercise, employment, educational activities and religious services. Selective use of seclusion, strait waistcoats or cotton restraining dresses continued in phases of acute disturbance.

Length-of-stay figures showed considerable variation. In the Oxfordshire study (Parry-Jones 1990), length of stay of county asylum pauper patients was consistently longer than for paying patients at a neighbouring public-subscription asylum, where there was more active treatment, a different range of disorders and the economic constraint of fees. In a modern study of Bethlem admissions, from 1830 to 1899, juvenile cure rates were 63 per cent (males) and 68 per cent (females), these high percentages probably reflecting the selective admission criteria (Wilkins 1987). At the Royal Edinburgh Asylum, from 1874 to 1879, where 10 per cent of admissions were 14–21 years, 93 juveniles were discharged recovered, 40 relieved, 26 became incurable and three died, supporting the conclusion that adolescent insanity was 'very curable' (Clouston 1898). However, the degree of recovery in children and adolescents remains difficult to evaluate retrospectively, owing to variable statistics and ambiguous terminology. Generally, restoration was gauged by the degree of symptom removal or the return to socially acceptable behaviour.

Specific adaptation for young people

The only published reference to special provisions for accommodating children on adult wards comes from the Oxfordshire County Asylum. There, very young or delicate children lived on the female side with boys being transferred to male wards when about seven years old (Parry-Jones 1990). Routine treatment of small numbers of juveniles in nineteenth-century asylums was facilitated by the prevailing tendency to interpret the behaviour of lunatics as childlike and responding to them as if they were dependent children.

Management of the mentally handicapped

Mental handicap and its residential management are integral to the history of psychiatry and especially relevant in child and adolescent psychiatry (Rosen, Clark and Kivitz 1971; Parry-Jones 1994). Although from medieval times, 'idiots' were distinguished from 'lunatics', systematic improvement of the condition of mentally handicapped children started only in the nineteenth century, when behaviourally disturbed, handicapped youngsters not kept at home were confined in madhouses, asylums and workhouses. The Idiots Act, 1886, was the first to provide separately for mental handicap.

Schools for 'fatuous patients' opened in France in the early nineteenth century. In Britain, child provisions commenced with a small private institution in Bath, and the Earlswood Idiot Asylum, Surrey, both in 1847, followed by the Idiot Asylum, Parkhouse, London, in 1849. Others were established shortly after (Parry-Jones 1994). In Scotland, Baldovan Asylum for Imbecile Children, Dundee, opened in 1853, and the Scottish National Institution for the Education of Imbecile Children, Larbert, in 1862. Similar institutions developed throughout Europe and the USA, the earliest being privately run as schools (Barr 1904).

Some county asylums built annexes for retarded children. Superintendents of idiot asylums advocated institutional training in a 'family home' setting and separate management according to the degree of handicap. Pessimism about curability of inherited disease and fears, fostered by eugenic ideology, concerning the proliferation of retardation, encouraged institutionalisation. Segregation in colonies, particularly of delinquents and females of child-bearing age, persisted into the 1950s. However, a degree of optimism prevailed in educational, industrial and moral training, involving both physicians and teachers. For feeble-minded children who were neither 'certifiable imbeciles' nor in need of confinement, belated special educational provisions were made in the UK, under the Elementary Education (Defective and Epileptic Children) Act, 1899. The Education Act, 1944, initiated the integration of some mentally handicapped children into ordinary schools.

Although the study and management of mental handicap in children and young people during the twentieth century deviated from child psychiatry, these fields remained closely allied. Valuable common ground was shared in managing disordered behaviour and idiot asylums and colonies 'served as a model for organ-isation of large groups of in-patient children with educational and behavioural problems' (Von Gontard 1988).

PROGRESS IN THE EARLY TWENTIETH CENTURY

The emergence of child psychiatry

There was a particular interrelationship between the evolving medical speciality of child and adolescent psychiatry and the use of residential care and treatment (Parry-Jones 1994). The roots of child psychiatry extend back to asylum practice in the nineteenth century, although the boundaries of the modern speciality were not formed until the 1920s, with the emergence of the child guidance movement. This new, multi-disciplinary speciality was the product of an exciting convergence of interest and expertise from adult psychiatry, mental deficiency, psychoanalysis, medical psychology, social work, remedial teaching, criminology and paediatrics. Child psychiatrists rejected the physically orientated approach and the residen-tial ethos of the asylum era. The trend was directed away from organ pathology, syndromal description and classification, and towards individual psychotherapy. Divergent models of service delivery were established, with child guidance clinics and health service-based child psychiatry services having responsibility for catering for the whole range of disturbed children in the population.

Early therapeutic communities and progressive schools

In the early twentieth century, pioneering innovations in the USA and the UK involved the establishment of residential communities for delinquent children, based on ideals of self-government. These represented the first stages of an enduring series of approaches based around the concept of planned environment therapy (Righton 1975). Early experimental developments included Rendel's work in the Caldecott Community, founded in 1911, and Homer Lane at the Little Commonwealth, Dorset, from 1913 to 1918 (Bazeley 1928).

During the 1920s, such models encouraged a new progressive education movement, which led to the founding of a number of schools which became notable for their Freudian psychoanalytic approach, combined with revolutionary emphasis on permissiveness and self-government rather than the rigours of traditional education. The leaders included Neill (1968) at Summerhill School, founded in 1921, Shaw at Red Hill and Docker-Drysdale at the Mulberry Bush School. One of the dilemmas concerned the extent to which the roles of principal and therapist could be combined (Chisholm 1996a). The notion of shared responsibility was further developed by Wills (1971), in the setting of an approved school.

In the USA, from the 1930s onwards, non-medically based residential units for treating severely disturbed children of all types were established. The most influential protagonists were Aichorn (1935), Bettelheim (1950; Bettelheim and Sanders 1979) and Redl and Wineman (1957). The overall approach, initially psychoanalytically based, attempted to utilise the residential milieu itself to facilitate behaviour control, personality growth and resolution of intrapsychic problems (Whittaker 1979). Later, behaviourally oriented approaches were to become more fashionable, laying practical emphasis on overt behaviour disturbance. The milieu therapy application of the planned environment therapy concept has to be seen in the same context as therapeutic communities developed in the 1960s, principally for adults, but utilised actively in early psychiatric adolescent units. Kennard (1983) stated that these principles were applied also in the Camphill Schools, established principally for mentally handicapped and maladjusted children, inspired by the work of Rudolf Steiner.

Schools for maladjusted and emotionally behaviourally disturbed (EBD) children

Several of the first residential schools for maladjusted children were run by psychiatrists, e.g. Dodd, 1920 and Fitch, 1935, who utilised their schools to minimise adverse effects of parental problems. Later, schools such as the Mulberry Bush and the Cotswold Community, run by Balbernie, conducted on rigorous milieu therapy lines, were influential in shaping developments and apparently successful. From the 1980s, such schools began to fall from favour, despite increasing numbers of children needing help, largely because of the changed approach by education authorities towards utilisation of local and less costly provisions.

Children's homes

Children's homes constituted one of the categories of community homes under the Children and Young Persons Act, 1969. They could be provided by local authorities or voluntary child care bodies, such as Dr Barnardo's, the National Children's Home and the Children's Society. Their use declined similarly from the 1960s, especially for younger children (Berridge 1985), with a corresponding increase in children staying with their own families or with foster or adoptive parents.

In-patient medically based units: 1920s to World War II

Specialised psychiatric in-patient units for children developed first in the USA during the 1920s to care for children with behaviour disorders following an encephalitis epidemic. The first was established at Bellevue Hospital, New York (American Psychiatric Association 1957; Beskind 1962; Barker 1974). Subsequently, these were used more generally in the residential treatment of emotionally disturbed children, many of whom, otherwise, would have been managed in adult wards. Although the emphasis initially was on containment, by the 1930s detailed diagnostic and treatment programmes were being designed around the application of individual and group psychotherapy, in the context of the therapeutic living experience (e.g. Bender 1937; Klopp 1932; Potter 1934). In the UK, the in-patient department for children at the Maudsley Hospital opened in 1947 (Cameron 1949) and others soon followed (Barker 1974). The first Scottish unit opened at Crichton Royal Hospital, Dumfries in 1951 (Chisholm 1996b) and the description of its organisation provides valuable insight into its therapeutic regime, which Rogers believed was enhanced by association with a mental hospital (Rogers 1954, 1965). Cameron's pioneering account of the organisation, staffing and treatment regime at the Maudsley Hospital department (Cameron 1949) emphasised the importance of broad investigation and assessment, 'total treatment' and continuity with intervention following discharge. Thus, in this early psychiatric setting for children, full consideration was given to the 'socio-psychobiological unity of the child'. These new units focused mainly on children, while adolescents, especially those suffering from major morbidity, were accommodated with difficulty.

RECENT DEVELOPMENTS

Trends in residential child care

Throughout the first half of the twentieth century, residential methods continued to be the mainstay of child care. From the 1950s onwards, especially in the early 1970s, far-reaching changes took place in policy regarding the role of residential care and treatment in child welfare programmes. These included the dramatic reduction in admission rates and in the number of children of all ages living in homes; major changes in the use of homes and hospitals for children with disabilities; the virtual disappearance of approved schools by the 1980s and the decline of voluntary children's homes (Parker 1993). Similar changes occurred in Europe (Cotton and Hellinckx 1993; Madge 1994).

These major changes were related to a number of factors. From the 1960s onwards, research into residential child care increased (Bullock, Little and Millham 1993) and its findings had widespread impact on the decline in services, by questioning the benefits of long-term residential care. The process was affected by the anti-institutional movement influenced by the writings of Goffman, Vaizey, Barton and Tutt and by numerous reports of the potentially adverse effects of institutionalisation on children's development (Wolkind 1974). Vigorous reappraisal of traditional practices occurred, recognising the needs and rights of children and the importance of family care, and responding to reported scandals and tragedies, e.g. the Staffordshire Pindown Inquiry (Levy and Kahan 1991). Alternative, community-based approaches and support, often perceived as cheaper, began to be utilised, including substitute family placement, especially for younger children, and intermediate care; above all, there was new investment in improved preventive work by social services departments.

Central to this trend was loss of confidence and conviction in the benefits of the residential experience. The 'broadly unifying beliefs' that had characterised early forms of residential child care, 'about the pliability of children, about the value of communal living or about the importance of demarcated space to the control of behaviour and relationships', had disappeared (Parker 1993). The existence and role of residential child care had been brought into question, and management, staff recruitment and training suffered accordingly. One English county went as far as closing all its residential facilities for children (Cliffe and Berridge 1992). Utting (1991) comprehensively reviewed the status of residential care in the early 1990s, in the context of the Children Act, 1989. He concluded positively that 'residential child care is, and under the Children Act will remain, an indispensable part of the range of provision for children in public care'. Nevertheless, placement of children supervised by local authorities continued to be controversial because 'child care is driven by strongly held beliefs and political attitudes rather than considered judgement' (Wolkind 1991). Although decisions concerning life-saving operations were made by a trained professional, 'a decision on care . . . may be made by poorly trained, or even untrained, professionals acting according to the changing policies of council committees'.

Expanding in-patient psychiatry services: the 1960s to the 1980s

By contrast, in the late 1950s and early 1960s, there was growing professional and governmental endorsement of the need to expand in-patient psychiatry services. The intention was to relieve pressure on beds, with emphasis on the interim, experimental nature of recommendations, and to cater for severely disturbed children placed inappropriately in other residential settings. Wardle (1991) suggested that the latter process accounted for the paradoxical expansion of in-patient services despite growing recognition of the dangers of institutional-isation. Elsewhere in Europe, similar developments were occurring (Buckle, Lebovici and Tizard 1972). A memorandum issued by the Royal Medico-

Psychological Association (1956) noted that there were 11 units (311 beds) for children. A few years later, far-reaching recommendations for the expansion of services were made (Ministry of Health 1964). By this time, there were 18 in-patient units (370 beds) for mentally ill or maladjusted children, generally aged up to 12 years, and seven units (157 beds) for adolescents. It was recommended that provision for children should be increased to 20–25 beds per million for assessment and short-term treatment, with a further 25 beds per region for long-term treatment. Provision for adolescents was to be raised to 20–25 beds per million, with units having links to a hostel and an approved school. In planning children's units, it was recommended that special consideration be given to prolonged treatment facilities, possibly in 30–50 bedded annexes. The need for integration with other children's services was emphasised, especially residential schools for maladjusted children, approved schools and children's homes.

Most early units catered principally for children, but from the late 1960s there was rapid growth of regional adolescent units in response to the Ministry of Health Memorandum, 1964. Initially, these had highly innovative, but often idiosyncratic, admission and operational policies, reflecting the beliefs and personalities of senior staff. These policies did not necessarily provide a broad-based service for their catchment populations, generating in turn controversy about their optimal role and function (Parry-Jones 1984). By the mid-1980s, however, there was broad acceptance of the necessity for 'general purpose' units, capable of combining emergency, short- and long-term functions (NHS Health Advisory Service 1985).

Despite the distinctive individuality of the early units and the considerable diversity in size, location and character, general consensus emerged about the main objectives of residential treatment. These comprised admission for obser-vation and diagnostic assessment in a controlled setting, which could last up to three months; short-term treatment to resolve a crisis in the home environment; participation in the therapeutic milieu; and, finally, individual psychotherapy in a supportive environment (Noshpitz 1962). Initially, the influence of the child guidance outpatient model on in-patient treatment philosophy was considerable, emphasising the central role of the treatment team and the application of psychoanalytic principles. This gave way gradually to a more eclectic and wider multi-disciplinary model, leaning towards behaviourally orientated programmes. It was recognised that high nurse–child ratios were required to cope with the most seriously disturbed children, and school became a standard component, supported by a variety of other professional staff. Considerable variation occurred in operational policies, as revealed in many published descriptions of units (Barker and Jamieson 1967; Copus and Walker 1972; Barker 1974), but there remains a need for more precise information about the therapeutic ethos of early units, based on the systematic study of hospital records. There appears to have been continuing emphasis on individual psychotherapy, limited use of medication and the widespread application of the principles of the therapeutic milieu, designed to help children with their group relationships (Bettelheim 1950; Rioch and Stanton 1953; Redl and Wineman 1957).

In the UK, the last decade has witnessed growing uncertainty about the status and future of in-patient units for children and adolescents consequent upon a number of interrelated factors. The overriding impetus towards a policy of care in the community has been encouraged in child and adolescent psychiatry by the widespread adoption of various forms of family intervention. The anti-institutional trend, relevant to all forms of residential care and treatment, has provided an enduring background. There has been a growing lack of conviction about the value and appropriate goals of hospitalisation. This negative view has been encouraged by the paucity of health service research into the effectiveness of all aspects of the functioning of in-patient units (Hersov 1994), with the exception of a small number of high calibre studies and reviews (Pffeifer and Strzelecki 1990, Blotcky, Dimperio and Gossett 1984), and the lack of any convincing guidelines for successful treatment programmes. Concern has been voiced about unnecessary admissions and potential unwanted effects (Green 1992). Such fears were especially prominent in the USA in the mid-1970s and 1980s, when rapid changes occurred in the pattern of juvenile institutions, and admissions to private, for-profit hospitals were rising rapidly. The steady improvement of staffing and facilities for outpatient and day-patient care have also had an impact on the perceived need for in-patient services. Financial constraints and emphasis, within the reformed NHS, on demonstrable treatment effectiveness and 'value for money' have had far-reaching effects on the attitude of health-commissioning authorities. Recent developments have highlighted the especial vulnerability of small, cost-intensive in-patient units, for both children and adolescents, to cost–benefit appraisal and cost-cutting exercises. Their predicament has been exacerbated by delay in organising funding from consortia of NHS trusts for the maintenance of units providing services with wide regional or supra-regional coverage. In this context, a recent report has endorsed the essential requirement for in-patient units within the resource centre concept (NHS Health Advisory Service 1995).

CONCLUSIONS

This chapter has described an ever-changing spectrum of residential provisions for emotionally and behaviourally disturbed, and disturbing, children and adolescents in children's homes, schools, health facilities and secure institutions. There has been a fluctuating relationship between voluntary and state provision. This plurality of provision raises the notion of 'trans-institutionalisation' (Woolston 1991, Weithorn 1988), whereby, over time, the same categories of children, regarded as requiring some form of residential protection or care, are shifted for non-therapeutic reasons from one setting to another, as different institutional facilities come and go. Quantification of the number of juveniles implicated in such movement over a historically significant timespan has yet to be accomplished. However, there is little doubt that sequential consignment to contemporaneously fashionable institutional outlets was influenced as much by political and economic factors as by clinical judgement. Like other forms of residential care, mental hospital wards and specialist hospital units have fulfilled varying functions, adopting different treatment philosophies to meet changing perceptions of need. A correlation may be discerned between the rise and fall of in-patient units and prevailing causative models, fashions in treatment and ways of construing disturbance and disorder within medicine and society. One of the most fundamental changes has concerned the replacement of long-term treatment, involving some degree of personality restructuring, by shorter-term focal treatment approaches. However, despite the changing conditions and operational policies there is an enduring core of disordered children and young people who have required containment and treatment in psychiatric settings, largely comprising those suffering from major psychiatric morbidity.

A number of powerful non-clinical factors, particularly economic and political forces, have had a important influence on the confidence and conviction in the status and role of psychiatric in-patient units for children. The reform of the NHS in the UK was triggered essentially by the need to contain costs and to establish an equitable basis for the rationing of services. Coupled with the stated policy of care in the community, a short-term 'value for money' ethos and scrutiny by child advocates and parents, hospital units are now facing a powerful challenge, analogous to those that other, non-medical residential care institutions have confronted in the second half of this century. Current units are addressing a number of core dilemmas (Harper and Cotton 1991). These include a tension between the case for locality-based facilities, as opposed to planned regional or national resources, practical questions about the extent to which a unit should be 'home or hospital' and whether the ward environment should be a neutral background or a major therapeutic agent (Green 1992).

For the greater part of the twentieth century, child and adolescent psychiatry has been influenced strongly by multi-disciplinary principles. As its compass and service boundaries broadened rapidly, child and adolescent psychiatrists followed a variety of trends, regardless of whether they called for conventional medical or psychiatric expertise. During the current phase, characterised by a trend for the re-medicalisation of the speciality, the role and functions of in-patient services are likely to be defined in narrower, more positive terms, concerned chiefly with the highly specialised investigation and treatment of severe disorders. Historical precedent strongly suggests that failure to adapt and establish a clear sense of direction will challenge their continuing survival.

REFERENCES

Aichorn, A. (1935) *Wayward Youth*. New York: Viking.

Allbutt, T.C. (1889) 'Insanity of children'. *Journal of Medical Science*, 35, 130–133.

American Psychiatric Association (1957) *Psychiatric In-patient Treatment of Children*. Baltimore, MD: Lord Baltimore Press.

Bakewell, S.G. (1836) *An Essay on Insanity*. London: E. Cox.

Barker, P. (1974) 'History'. In P. Barker (ed.), *The Residential Psychiatric Treatment of Children*, pp. 1–26. London: Crosby Lockwood Staples.

Barker, P. and Jamieson, R. (1967) 'Two years' admissions to a regional child psychiatric unit'. *British Medical Journal*, 2, 103–106.

Barman, S. (1934) *The English Borstal System. A Study of the Treatment of Young Offenders*. London: P.S. King.

Barr, M.W. (1904) *Mental Defectives. Their History, Treatment and Training*. Philadelphia, PA: P. Blackiston's Son and Co.

Bazeley, E.T. (1928) *Homer Lane and the Little Commonwealth*. London: George Allen and Unwin.

Bender, L. (1937) 'Group activities on a children's ward as methods of psychotherapy'. *American Journal of Orthopsychiatry*, 7, 1151–1173.

Berridge, D. (1985) *Children's Homes*. Oxford: Basil Blackwell.

Beskind, H. (1962) 'Psychiatric in-patient treatment of adolescents: a review of clinical experience'. *Comprehensive Psychiatry*, 3, 354–369.

Bettelheim, B. (1950) *Love is Not Enough*. New York: Free Press.

Bettelheim, B. and Sanders, J. (1979) 'Milieu therapy: the orthogenic school model'. In J.D. Noshpitz (ed.), *Basic Handbook of Child Psychiatry* Vol. 3, *Therapeutic Interaction* (ed. S.I. Harrison), pp. 216–230. New York: Basic Books.

Blotcky, M.J., Dimperio, T.L. and Gossett, S.J. (1984) 'Follow-up of children treated in psychiatric hospitals: a review of studies'. *American Journal of Psychiatry*, 141, 1499–1507.

Boswell, J. (1988) *The Kindness of Strangers. The Abandonment of Children in Western Europe from Late Antiquity to the Renaissance*. New York: Vintage Books.

Bridgeland, M. (1971) *Pioneer Work with Maladjusted Children*. London: Staples.

Buckle, D.F., Lebovici, S. and Tizard, J. (1972) 'The in-patient psychiatric treatment of children in Europe'. In H.P. David (ed.), *Child Mental Health – International Perspective*, pp. 35–50. New York: Harper and Row.

Bullock, R., Little, M. and Millham, S. (1993) *Residential Care for Children. A Review of Research*. London: HMSO.

Cameron, K.A. (1949) 'A psychiatric in-patient department for children'. *Journal of Mental Science*, 95, 560–566.

Carlebach, J. (1970) *Caring for Children in Trouble*. London: Routledge and Kegan Paul.

Carpenter, M. (1851) *Reformatory Schools for the Children of the Perishing and Dangerous Classes and for Juvenile Offenders*. London: Gilpin.

Chisholm, D. (1996a) 'Historical precursors'. In R. Chesson and D. Chisholm (eds), *Child Psychiatric Units. At the Crossroads*, pp. 8–27. Bristol: Jessica Kingsley.

Chisholm, D. (1996b) 'The development of child psychiatric in-patient practice. Past, present and future'. In R. Chesson and D. Chisholm (eds), *Child Psychiatric Units. At the Crossroads*, pp. 28–44. Bristol: Jessica Kingsley.

Cliffe, D. with Berridge, D. (1992) *Closing Children's Homes. An End to Residential Child Care?* London: National Children's Bureau.

Clouston, T.S. (1898) *Clinical Lectures on Mental Disorders*. 5th edn, London: J. and A. Churchill.

Copus, P.E. and Walker, L.W. (1972) 'The psychiatric ward in a children's hospital: a review of the first two years'. *British Journal of Psychiatry*, 121, 323–326.

Cotton, M.J. and Hellinckx, W. (1993) *Child Care in the EC. A Country-specific Guide to Foster and Residential care*. Aldershot: Arena.

Franklin, A.W. (1964) 'Children's hospitals'. In F.N.L. Poynter (ed.), *The Evolution of Hospitals in Britain*, pp. 103–121. London: Pitman Medical.

Green, J. (1992) 'In-patient psychiatry units'. *Archives of Disease in Childhood*, 67: 1120–1123.

Harper, G.P. and Cotton, N.S. (1991) 'Child and adolescent treatment'. In L.I. Sederer (ed.), *In-patient Psychiatry Diagnosis and Treatment*, pp. 321–337. Baltimore, MD: Williams and Wilkins.

Hersov, L. (1994) 'In-patient and day-hospital units'. In M. Rutter, E. Taylor and L. Hersov (eds), *Child and Adolescent Psychiatry. Modern Approaches*. 3rd edn, pp. 983–995. Oxford: Blackwell.

Kennard, D. (1983) *An Introduction to Therapeutic Communities*. London: Routledge and Kegan Paul.

Klopp, H.I. (1932) 'The children's institute of the Allentown state hospital'. *American Journal of Psychiatry*, 88, 1108–1118.

Laybourne, P.C. and Miller, H.C. (1962) 'Pediatric hospitalization of psychiatric patients: diagnostic and therapeutic implications'. *American Journal of Orthopsychiatry*, 32, 596–603.

Levy, A. and Kahan, B. (1991) *The Pindown Experience and the Protection of Children. Report of the Staffordshire Child Care Inquiry*. Staffordshire County Council.

McClure, R. (1981) *Coram's Children. The London Foundling Hospital in the Eighteenth Century*. New Haven, CT: Yale University Press.

Madge, N. (1994) *Children and Residential Care in Europe*. London: National Children's Bureau.

Ministry of Health (1964) *In-patient Accommodation for Mentally Ill and Severely Maladjusted Children and Adolescents*. H.M. (64)(4). London: Ministry of Health.

Neill, A.S. (1968) *Summerhill*. Harmondsworth: Pelican.

NHS Health Advisory Service (1985) *Bridges over Troubled Waters*. London: HMSO.

NHS Health Advisory Service (1995) *Together We Stand. The Commissioning, Role and Management of Child and Adolescent Mental Health Services*. London: HMSO.

Noshpitz, J.D. (1962) 'Notes on the theory of residential treatment'. *Journal of the American Academy of Child Psychiatry*, 1, 284–296.

Parker, R. (1993) 'Trends in residential child care'. In: B. Cahan (ed.), *Residential Care for Children. The Report of a Department Invited Seminar 30 October–1 November, 1991 at Dartington Hall, Devon*, pp.77–87. London: Department of Health.

Parry-Jones, W.Ll. (1972) *The Trade in Lunacy. A Study of Private Madhouses in England in the Eighteenth and Nineteenth Centuries*. London: Routledge and Kegan Paul.

Parry-Jones, W.Ll. (1984) 'Adolescent psychiatry in Britain: a personal view of its development and present position'. *Bulletin of the Royal College of Psychiatrists*, 8, 230–233.

Parry-Jones, W.Ll. (1989) 'The history of child and adolescent psychiatry: its present day relevance'. *Journal of Child Psychology and Psychiatry*, 30, 3–11.

Parry-Jones, W.Ll. (1990) 'Juveniles in 19th century Oxfordshire asylums'. *British Journal of Clinical and Social Psychiatry*, 7, 51–58.

Parry-Jones, W.Ll. (1994) 'History of child and adolescent psychiatry'. In M. Rutter, E. Taylor and L. Hersov (eds), *Child and Adolescent Psychiatry: Modern Approaches*, 3rd edn, pp.794–812. Oxford: Blackwell.

Pfeiffer, S.I. and Strzelecki, S.C. (1990) 'In-patient psychiatric treatment of children and adolescents: a review of outcome studies'. *Journal of the American Academy of Child and Adolescent Psychiatry*, 29, 847–853.

Potter, H.W. (1934) 'The treatment of problem children in a psychiatric hospital'. *American Journal of Psychiatry*, 91, 869–880.

Redl, F. and Wineman, D. (1957) *The Aggressive Child*. New York: Free Press.

Righton, P. (1975) 'Planned environmental therapy: a reappraisal'. *Journal of the Association for Workers with Maladjusted Children*, 3, 3–12.

Rioch, D.M. and Stanton, A.H. (1953) 'Milieu therapy'. *Psychiatry*, 16, 65–72.

Rogers, J.B. (1954) 'Child psychiatry. The work of a hospital unit'. *British Medical Journal*, 2, 1544–1546.

Rogers, J.B. (1965) 'Children's in-patient psychiatric units'. In J.G. Howells (ed.), *Modern Perspectives in Child Psychiatry*, pp. 534–561. Edinburgh: Oliver and Boyd.

Rosen, M., Clark, G.R. and Kivitz, M.S. (1971) *The History of Mental Retardation. Collected Papers*, 2 vols. Baltimore, MD: University Press.

Royal Medico-Psychological Association (1956) *In-patient Accommodation for Child and Adolescent Psychiatric Patients*. London: RMPA.

Scull, A. (1993) *The Most Solitary of Afflictions. Madness and Society in Britain 1700–1900*, pp. 96–103. New Haven, CT: Yale University Press.

Solnit, A.J. (1960) 'Hospitalization: an aid to physical and psychological health in childhood'. *American Journal of Diseases of Children*, 99, 155–163.

Utting, W. (1991) *Children in the Public Care. A Review of Residential Child Care*. London: HMSO.

Von Gontard, A. (1988) 'The development of child psychiatry in 19th century Britain'. *Journal of Child Psychology and Psychiatry*, 29, 569–588.

Wardle, C.J. (1991) 'Twentieth-century influences on the development in Britain of services for child and adolescent psychiatry'. *British Journal of Psychiatry*, 159, 53–68.

Weithorn, L.A. (1988) 'Mental hospitalization of troublesome youth: an analysis of skyrocketing admission rates'. *Stanford Law Review*, 40, 773–838.

West, C. (1854) *Lectures on the Diseases of Infancy and Childhood*, 3rd edn. London: Longman, Brown, Green and Longmans.

Whittaker, J.K. (1979) *Caring for Troubled Children*. San Francisco, CA: Jossey-Bass.

Wilkins, R. (1987) 'Hallucinations in children and teenagers admitted to Bethlem Royal Hospital in the 19th century and the possible relevance to the incidence of schizophrenia'. *Journal of Child Psychology and Psychiatry*, 28, 569–580.

Wills, W.D. (1971) *Spare the Child. The Story of an Experimental Approved School*. Harmondsworth: Penguin.

Wolkind, S.N. (1974) 'The components of affectionless psychopathy in institutionalised children'. *Journal of Child Psychology and Psychiatry*, 15, 215–220.

Wolkind, S.N. (1991) 'Child placement. Driven by belief rather than research'. *British Medical Journal*, 303, 483.

Woolston, J.L. (1991) 'Psychiatric in-patient services for children'. In M. Lewis (ed.), *Child and Adolescent Psychiatry. A Comprehensive Textbook*, pp. 890–894. Baltimore, MD: Williams and Wilkins.

Part II

Treatment process

4 The process of admission

Sean Maskey

INTRODUCTION

Admission to an in-patient unit should not be thought about in isolation from other child mental health care, or indeed the full range of a child's social environment, including parental, educational and other inputs. The Health Advisory Service Review *Child and Adolescent Mental Health Services: Together We Stand* (Williams and Richardson 1995) describes four tiers of formal service, over the base of informal care and treatment. Numerically the services together form a pyramid. Parents, teachers and other informal helpers work with the 20 to 40 per cent of children with minor psychological problems. Services at Tier One, self-referral or informal referral, and Tier Two, formal referral from a child centred professional (e.g. teacher, social worker) or General Practitioner to a single member of a clinical team, will see some 1 to 2 per cent of all children. Tier Three, Multidisciplinary Outpatient teams working with complex cases, see 0.1 per cent and Tier Four, Specialist Outpatient, Day and In-patient Services, treat some 0.01 to 0.03 per cent of children per year. (See Table 4.1.) Cost per case is an inverse of this pyramid, mirroring case complexity and severity.

The not unreasonable expectation of the HAS model is of progression of a case through the tiers of service, with treatment resources being provided at the level appropriate to the needs of the child, which will vary over time. Figure 4.1, taken from *Together We Stand*, illustrates the progression of a child through the various systems.

Most children who are referred to in-patient services should have had the benefit of full multidisciplinary outpatient work-up, including liaison with education, as it is highly unlikely that a child whose problems are so severe as to

Table 4.1 Health advisory service tier model

Tiers	% of child population
1 *Self-referral (no filter)*	1–2
2 *Lone CMH practitioner*	1–2
3 *Multidisciplinary team*	0.1
4 *Very specialised assessment and treatment in or outpatient*	0.01–0.03

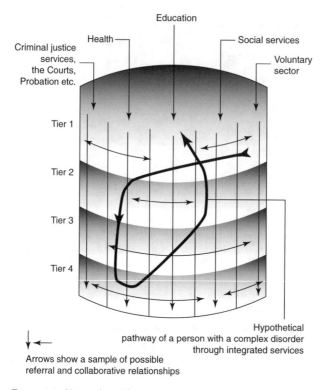

Education

Health

Criminal justice
services,
the Courts,
Probation etc.

Social services

Voluntary
sector

Tier 1

Tier 2

Tier 3

Tier 4

Hypothetical
pathway of a person with a complex disorder
through integrated services

Arrows show a sample of possible
referral and collaborative relationships

Figure 4.1 (Reproduced by permission of HMSO) The integration of the sectors of care

require in-patient treatment does not have problems in the school setting. Where appropriate, Educational Psychology, Paediatrics and Social Services will have been involved.

The 1993 Education Act implemented a Code of Practice (COP) requiring schools to demonstrate that they had completed certain tasks at each defined stage in identifying and providing for children experiencing problems at school. Some 20 per cent of children are identified by schools as having some form of special needs, which are met within school resources, COP Stages One and Two. If the school has to involve outside services, the Education Psychologist or Child Mental Health clinic, the child moves to Stage Three of the COP. If additional resources are likely to be required, the Local Education Authority formally considers this, Stage Four, and if warranted, provides additional help in a mainstream or specialist school, by the production of a statutory Statement of Special Education Needs. Some 2 per cent of children will reach this stage. The Statementing process is bureaucratic, protracted and has fixed time limits. It is essential therefore, if a child is to have a smooth transition back to permanent education provision, that the Local Authority, in parallel with any therapeutic work, is actively addressing the educational needs.

At Collingham Gardens, as in many in-patient services, we start from the premise that children should not be in hospital if this can possibly be avoided, and if they must be admitted, the length of stay should be as short as possible. There are two principles underlying this. Firstly for the individual, any treatment should be the least restrictive possible, in accordance with the United Nations Convention on the Rights of the Child. Secondly, that access to a limited resource should be available to as many as possible. If the unit is full, children who need help have to be turned away at least temporarily, and in a high cost-per-case service, unnecessary or protracted admissions deny funds to other patients.

SOURCES OF REFERRAL AND ADMISSION THRESHOLD

Before the introduction of purchasing in the NHS, referral routes to in-patient treatment were often multiple, coming from social services and educational psychologists who knew about the service, as well as non-medical members of community child mental health teams (Barker 1974). Purchasers have been concerned to limit these uncontrolled costs on their budgets, as well as to develop a full picture of the needs of their health district. As a result of this and in line with *Together We Stand*, in-patient units are now less likely to take referrals from sources other than consultant child and adolescent psychiatrists. A major exception to this will be selected referrals from social services, when there is a request to recommend a care plan in complex cases, often where there is dispute. The Local Authority will usually have to fund this separately.

Use of in-patient units should be reserved for the most severe and/or complex cases that cannot be managed effectively by community resources. Referrals are drawn from a large area, covering many health districts and local services. The admission threshold cannot be an absolute, based on factors restricted to the specific case, but has to allow for the expertise and resources in the referrer's service, and other local resources. In a study of decision making about admission for adolescent suicide attempts, Morrissey et al. (1995: 902–11) showed that the choice of hospitalisation was inversely related to clinical experience. Other factors that the clinicians considered included adequacy of social support, openness to outpatient treatment and prior response to treatment. Costello, Dulcan and Kalas (1991: 823–8) provide an excellent critique of the complexity of the decision to refer for in-patient treatment. Their study, carried out in 1981, looked at 389 children aged 2–12 years referred for in-patient evaluation (22 per cent were admitted within three weeks). They derived six factors that, when suitably weighted, discriminated well between cases offered residential and outpatient treatment. Costello's checklist factors are broadly in line with two UK studies (Garralda 1986, Wolkind and Gent 1987). In the British literature, there is more emphasis on complex needs and (co-morbid) psychiatric disorder and less on aggression as an indicator for admission (Table 4.2). It is clear from this work, and other American and (the more limited) British literature, that

Table 4.2 Indications for admission in three studies

Costello 1991	Garralda 1986	Wolkind and Gent 1987
• Is the patient's condition deteriorating rapidly or failing to improve despite adequate outpatient treatment?	• Acute disabling psychiatric states	• Severe emotional disorders
• Have aggressive outbursts occurred towards animals or objects?		• Severe conduct disorders – bizarre and borderline behaviours
• Have aggressive outbursts occurred towards other people?		• ditto
• Are there physical or neurological conditions or a psychotic disorganised state that requires hospitalisation to initiate treatment or to establish a diagnosis?	• Diagnosis • Treatment: medication or behavioural • High risk/severe disorders	• Psychosis • Neuropsychiatric disorder
• Does a pathological or noxious situation exist among patient's family or associates that makes treatment without hospitalisation impossible? Or, does the patient's disordered state create such difficulties for family that he or she has to be hospitalised? (Include danger of child abuse.)	• Separation from home as a management strategy – psychosomatic or school refusal	• Psychosomatic disorders
• Does evaluation of patient's condition require 24-hour observation and evaluation that only a hospital can provide? (Include stabilisation or re-evaluation of medication.) Or, is patient referred for treatment of drug or alcohol dependence?	• Neuropsychiatric assessment and evaluation	• Complex co-morbidity

there are no absolute indications for in-patient treatment. Rather a combination of factors determines referral, which may or may not match the admission decision criteria.

Psychosis and neuropsychiatric disorders are relatively uncommon in the community. Most if not all will be referred for the multi-faceted simultaneous assessment and treatment that it is not usually possible to deliver in a community service, including total nursing care, medical investigation, developmental and neuropsychological assessment, and expert supervision of psychotropic medication.

Emotional and conduct disorders, in contrast, are extremely common. When mixed with specific developmental delays or communication disorders, they can present a very odd picture that is quite intractable in the outpatient clinic if the various problems are not managed conjointly. Severe emotional, or internalising, disorders may by themselves merit admission, e.g. for the management of persistent suicidal behaviour.

Conduct disorder in isolation is best managed away from medical settings as there is no reasonable evidence of effectiveness, and 'medicalising' the behaviour may give it a spurious legitimacy. In-patient units are very often asked to aid the 'understanding' and advise in care planning for highly disturbed aggressive youngsters that Social Services cannot foster and do not wish to place in children's homes. This presentation, assuming reasonable outpatient assessment to exclude other unusual causes, is almost invariably a manifestation of severe attachment problems which result in intense psychic turmoil when the child experiences the 'ordinary' emotional demands of family life in foster care. The picture is often compounded by a failure to provide any useful 'permanency' structures in the Care Plan. There is a limited role here for in-patient assessment in stabilising and structuring the management of the child, allowing a transition to a longer term 'Therapeutic Community' setting (see chapters 25 and 32 for further discussion of this).

Psychosomatic disorders range from the somatising problems such as chronic fatigue syndrome through encopresis, to diabetes and anorexia nervosa. The capacity to address the physical and psychological at the same time and provide the expert nursing required to manage these, often very long term, and sometimes life-threatening problems, is a prerequisite for success. Moreover the child and family are usually involved in such a way that pressure from the parents produces increasing physical disturbance in the child, much to their distress and sometimes anger. The decision about admission (i.e. separation) can be a major step on the path to re-establishing parental authority and control.

Garralda lists indications for in-patient treatment, which have a more paediatric-psychiatric perspective, with more emphasis on the assessment, diagnosis and treatment facilities unique to the in-patient setting (Garralda 1986). She recognises that differences in ethos and location will modify the admission criteria for different units, as to some extent will the expertise and resources available in the local clinics.

MODELS OF ASSESSMENT AND ADMISSION

Many units operate alongside outpatient services with part-time consultants (see chapter 28). The Royal College of Psychiatrists guidelines for consultant job descriptions implicitly support this in expecting consultants to have some outpatient work in addition to in-patient responsibilities. In this context, cold admissions are often brought in through the outpatient service, which facilitates the development of a therapeutic relationship with members of the in-patient service prior to referral. This model has been consistently described since the first in-patient unit opened in England at the Maudsley in 1947 and in the United States (Hoffman 1982). A small number of units do not offer outpatient treatment prior to or as an alternative treatment to residential work. It is perhaps easier in this setting to be clear about the task of admission, as the formal negotiation between the referring network, family and in-patient team prevents any possible drift into residential status that may occur if outpatient work is 'stuck', and the referrer is also the in-patient consultant.

Gutterman et al. (1993) examined one system through which children and adolescents with acute psychiatric illness were admitted to an in-patient child mental health facility. They found that children and adolescents assessed at the regional centre associated with the in-patient service had an odds ratio for in-patient referral of 6.6 compared with those screened at a local centre distant from the regional service. Cases screened at the regional centre were more likely to be in current treatment ($p < 0.001$) and the authors argue that admission is associated with breakdown in outpatient treatment. However, the odds ratio for hospitalisation based on current treatment was only 2.2, and the study does not show figures for admission by site of assessment controlling for the effect of treatment status. Another interpretation of the data is that direct access to in-patient treatment makes in-patient referral an easier choice for the assessing clinician. It would be instructive to plot admission rates (in the UK) by ease of access to in-patient units.

REFERRAL AND RESPONSE

Referrals fall into one of three groups. In the 'enquiry', the referrer is uncertain about the suitability of the case for in-patient treatment, or of the unit for the case, and wants to discuss matters. The 'referral' occurs when where the referrer is reasonably clear about the needs of the case, and knows or expects that the unit can meet them. The 'emergency' is more often a crisis – the request is for the in-patient team to take over responsibility and management at once.

The true emergency is rare, occurring for example in acute onset psychosis, suicidal depression, and incapacitating obsessional states. The crisis is more common, and usually means the carers, and sometimes the referrers, have reached the limit of their resources to cope with prolonged difficult behaviour. There are very few emergency admissions in the UK, which contrasts greatly with the picture in the USA, where both the admission and emergency admission rates are much higher. US National Institute of Mental Health data for 1986 indicated 5 per cent of children receiving psychiatric services were hospitalised (Pottick et al. 1995); some 130,000 children under 13 each year (Costello, Dulcan and Kalas 1991). Over a six-month period in a mixed geographical area of 672,000 people 31 per cent of 226 children and adolescents presenting as emergencies to mental health assessment centres were recommended in-patient treatment (Gutterman et al. 1993). The majority of UK children's units do not admit emergencies, or take just a few each year.

At Collingham Gardens, which serves a minimum population of 3.5 million, or 420,000 5 to 14 year-old children in NW Thames Region, with more in other regions, the current referral rate is 80–100 cases per annum, with 35–45 being admitted, from a clinic pool of (very roughly) 5000 cases. This represents a rate of admission from outpatients which is one fifth that of the American NIMH figure, or one tenth of the Gutterman study rate. Why should this be so? One possible explanation might be real differences in prevalence, but it would be surprising if this were able to account for the order of magnitude of the differences seen. More likely is the very low supply of all child mental health provision in the UK compared with the USA, with this absence of provision resulting in an apparent absence of need. The drive in the USA has been for short duration (up to four weeks) of in-patient assessment and treatment coupled with an extensive range of non-residential options. In the UK, there is no expectation of an equivalent variety of treatment provision. Seventy-eight per cent of the provider units that responded to the recent HAS survey (1995) had less than the 'irreducible minimum' (2 per 200,000) of consultant child and adolescent psychiatrists recommended by the Royal College of Psychiatrists. Given that most children and families only have access to the limited outpatient services operating at HAS Tier One or Two, with occasional Tier Three, multidisciplinary work, some children will be in in-patient treatment who could be managed in a more intensive local service. Many more however will be in outpatient clinics who should be in more intensive treatment. Up to half the children and adolescents looked after by the Social Services in one region had diagnosable mental health problems and had not received any treatment (McCann 1996)

In the UK, admission is almost invariably a prolonged process, involving two or more meetings with the referring network and family as well as the child. This serves several purposes. It allows case planning to occur in conjunction with the other agencies involved. There is little benefit gained, for example, in removing a child from school at the point when the educational psychologist is about to visit to assess the child in order to commence the 'Statementing' process. It permits exploration of alternative management strategies, avoiding admission, and gives the child and family time to prepare, psychologically and practically, for the admission. In the interval, the unit can also prepare for the child. Finally, a 'crisis' that was forcing the child into a medical role and out of the family may well pass, allowing outpatient work to continue.

THE COLLINGHAM MODEL

At Collingham Gardens, a small team of senior staff forms a rota to respond to, and follow through, referrals, to aid continuity for each case and ensure a prompt response. Each case is discussed with the wider staff group at the weekly referral meeting to draw on the multidisciplinary perspectives available in formulating an initial hypothesis and highlighting issues to explore in the first meeting. It is also the venue for management of cases moving along the admission process, so that bed occupancy and case mix can, to some extent, be controlled. A second person with skills relevant to the problem, e.g. a teacher for a child who appears to have special educational needs, is attached to the case at this stage. Admission of the occasional emergency is discussed with the consultant and senior nursing staff to ensure the unit (children and staff) can cope with the unexpected demands.

The referrer, who is a consultant child and adolescent psychiatrist, or member of their team, is telephoned to discuss the case. The aim is to ascertain the nature of the problem; the referrer's expectation (assessment or assessment and treatment); the legal status of the child and location of parental responsibility; the support network, formal and informal, around the child; who, if anyone, is missing from this network, and why. The degree of urgency of response is established with the referrer and a date agreed for a first meeting.

Responsibility for the case remains firmly with the referrer at this stage, and they are asked to convene the meeting. Parents or those with parental responsibility are essential. We prefer the index child to attend, if the referrer thinks the child can cope. A school representative – ideally the special needs co-ordinator or a senior teacher who can commit resources, is necessary. Since the advent of contracts for services, the source of funding for the referral is now ascertained at this point.

The first meeting, at the referrer's base, begins with introductions and clarification of the purpose of the meeting. These are

- To hear about the concerns of those present, particularly the family members
- To review what has and has not been possible therapeutically prior to the referral
- To clarify plans from all parties
- To offer preliminary information about Collingham Gardens
- To determine whether or not an in-patient stay seems appropriate and practical.

All present are asked to state their concerns and worries, and describe the changes they think need to take place in order for the problems to be manageable by outpatient and local resources once again. If the network has worked well with the family, admission is a probable outcome. Dovetailing of plans begins here (e.g. for 'Statementing', social work input, outpatient investigations, etc.), and will continue throughout the in-patient process. The teachers from the hospital school will contact the child's current school or education authority if they are out of school, to gather specific information about the strengths and weaknesses in the class setting. As the case progresses through the unit, the flow of information reverses, with review and discharge meetings giving information and ideas about management to the referring network. Assuming we and the family agree that there is a task for hospital assessment plus or minus treatment, the family are invited to Collingham for a further meeting, with the social worker if the child is 'looked after' or on the Child Protection Register.

In-patient referral is sometimes used as a means of settling disputes within a network, or avoiding difficult decisions. The most common clue is the very large number of people wanting to attend the referral meeting, asking for yet another 'assessment'. In these circumstances we ask, 'What is it that you want to know that you do not already know, and how will that make a difference to your management plan?' This often serves to focus the network back on their existing information, which may not have been sufficiently processed or organised, allowing progress in the case without recourse to an in-patient unit. Alternatively, it clarifies the task of admission.

On occasion it is not appropriate to admit a particular child, the prime reason being that they will not benefit from the treatment on offer. Published outcome research is not conclusive on this point, and while Pfeiffer and Strzelecki's review (1990) does not offer conduct disorder as an indicator of poor outcome, others have demonstrated little benefit from residential as opposed to other forms of treatment for this disorder (Grizenko and Papineau 1992). Most pre-adolescent units now avoid primary conduct disorder, in contrast to the early 1970s (Barker 1974; see also chapters 19 and 2). The level of aggression and violence presented by children with reactive attachment disorder, pervasive developmental disorders and post-traumatic stress disorder is often high in the early stages of an admission before staff engage well with the child. This creates more than enough challenging behaviour for staff to manage, without adding conduct disorder per se.

At the second meeting, we make it absolutely clear that a decision to admit a child for in-patient care rests with the parents or social worker if the child is in care. This much less formal meeting has two tasks. The nursing staff show parents and children around the building, and answer any questions that may arise. The person who led the first meeting then meets the family, and this is observed and recorded through a video link, with the parents' and child's consent. The screening team is multidisciplinary, and the video allows other nursing staff who are not available to gain a picture of the child before admission. Further questions about care and treatment are answered, to give the parents as much information as possible in order to reach their decision about admission. If they agree, the parents are asked to respond formally to the proposal to admit their child. If they do not wish to proceed, this will have become clear in the discussion, and alternative strategies are discussed. These are fed back to the referrer and network as appropriate, as the unit does not offer outpatient work.

The second part of the meeting involves the clarification of the goals for the admission. These will be refined or adapted during the course of treatment; however the aim is to define concrete changes that each member of the family wants to see. Our brief intervention in their lives is emphasised, with the expectation not of complete resolution of problems, but of loosening up and creating the possibility of much greater, long-term improvements post discharge. The goal setting might develop as follows.

A 12-year-old boy has been out of school for the last four years, because he collapses 'unconscious' at home and at school. Despite extensive investigations, no medical cause has been found. Parents want him to be at school but do not want him to come to any harm. The major effect of this on the family is that they have stopped going out together, because Gordon cannot go out, nor can he be left, for fear of an attack. The parents wanted a cause and a cure.

We agreed with them that they would know things were improving considerably if the whole family were able to go out together to watch a film at the local cinema, something they had previously enjoyed. This focus allowed us, with the family, to begin to develop the things they could do, concentrating on the processes that were maintaining the problem, rather than remain locked into a fruitless search for the 'cause' which had probably stopped operating several years ago. At the same time, knowing that a diagnosis of hysterical conversion is associated with a surprisingly high morbidity and mortality, we reviewed very carefully the previous assessments and investigations.

If the admission is specifically for assessment, then goals will be more staff-focused in terms of the components of the assessment and the question that the assessment is intended to resolve. The unit may be asked to describe the education setting best suited to the child or advise on future therapeutic strategy or assess response to medication. When social services are involved, separate goals may be set with the allocated social worker. These will usually be around the area of assessment of parenting or capacity for change within the family. Again it is essential to have clear and explicit tasks that the family is aware of and understand the consequences of the outcome. Borrowing an acronym from management, goals should be SMART: that is Simple, Measurable, Achievable, Relevant and Time limited. Once on the unit children set a weekly goal with their key nurse, which should link to the overall admission goals.

Sometimes, usually in the context of an acrimonious and dependent relationship with their child, a parent may be anxious that the child will be angry and reject them if they are 'sent away'. Parents then try to obtain permission from the child for the admission. We point out that this is asking the child to take responsibility for the treatment decision, which is unreasonable, given the difficulty the adults are having in making it. Children often look relieved when we intervene to locate the authority and responsibility with the parents in this way. Some however decline to relinquish their power in the family so easily and protest vehemently at the prospect. Reassuring and supporting the parents to enable them to take control once again is often the major therapeutic task, such as when, for example, an 11-year-old girl avoids school and, because she feels unwell, the parents do not feel able to insist on regular attendance.

When parents have separated but hold joint responsibility, both parents are invited to the unit. This can be a difficult encounter, and preliminary work may need to be done in order to prepare antagonistic adults to focus on the needs of their child rather than on their own battles. Hospital admission is not a trivial matter, and the gravity of the situation can be used to encourage embattled parents to separate in their minds the marital role (which has ended) and parental role which continues.

When the admission and the goals have been agreed, we finalise the approximate length of stay, six to eight weeks for assessments and sixteen to eighteen for assessment and treatment. The family is offered an admission date, normally within one or two weeks, and the referrer is advised of the position.

Clinical services such as in-patient units have traditionally been reactive in the sense that they wait for referrals to arrive, and then assess the suitability of the case against more or less well defined criteria. This derives partly from a medical culture where the ill come to the doctor rather than vice versa, and especially so in the more acute end of treatment. Preventative and community services are where most case finding work occurs. Moreover the belief that a service will be overwhelmed by demand if active recruitment takes place also discourages this process. Some change has occurred in this way of thinking with the setting of target occupancy levels, contracts for activity with purchasers, and funding dependent on level of bed occupancy. This has resulted in clinicians marketing their service, primarily by talking and listening to referrers. In contrast, the academic sector actively recruits cases for specific research projects, and may engage in extensive screening as a case finding exercise. The work by Zarina Kurtz for the Department of Health highlights the small, finite pool of cases in the catchment of any in-patient unit with severe and complex psychiatric disorder (Kurtz 1996). These difficult and demanding cases are almost always known to one of the children's agencies, but not necessarily to child mental health, whence referral to in-patient services can most readily occur. Perhaps we should be out looking for cases far more actively, if we are to make the best use of our scarce and expensive resources?

REFERENCES

Barker, P. (1974) The Aims and Nature of the In-patient Psychiatric Treatment of Children. In P. Barker (ed.), *The Residential Psychiatric Treatment of Children*. London: Crosby Lockwood Staples.

Costello, A.J., Dulcan, M.K. and Kalas, R. (1991) A Checklist of Hospitalisation Criteria for Use With Children. *Hospital and Community Psychiatry*, 42, 8, 823–8.

Education Act Part 3 (1993) London: HMSO.

Garralda, E. (1986) In-patient Treatment of Children: A Psychiatric Perspective. In G. Edwards (ed.), *Current Issues in Clinical Psychology*, Vol. 4. New York: Plenum Press.

Grizenko, N. and Papineau, D. (1992) A Comparison of the Cost Effectiveness of Day Treatment and Residential Treatment for Children with Severe Behaviour Problems. *Canadian Journal of Psychiatry*, 37, 6, 393–400.

Gutterman, E.M., Markowitz, J.S., LeConte, J.S. and Beier, J. (1993) Determinants for Hospitalisation from an Emergency Mental Health Service. *Journal of the American Academy of Child and Adolescent Psychiatry*, 32, 1, 114–22.

Hoffman, L. (1982) *The Evaluation and Care of Severely Disturbed Children and their Families*. Jamaica, N.Y.: Spectrum Publications, Inc.

Kurtz, Z. (1996) *The Incidence of Severe Mental Illness in Children and Adolescents*. Paper given to the Child and Adolescent Section of the Royal College of Psychiatrists Spring Meeting.

Mabe, P.A., Riley, W.T. and Sunde, E.R. (1989) Survey of Admission Policies for Child and Adolescent In-patient Services: A National Sample. *Child Psychiatry and Human Development*, 20, 2, 99–111.

McCann, J.B., James, A., Wilson, S. and Dunn, G. (1996) Prevalence of Psychiatric Disorders in Young People in the Care System. *British Medical Journal*, 313 (7071), 1529–1530.

Morrissey, R.F., Dicker, R., Abikoff, H., Alvir, J.M., DeMarco, A. and Koplewicz, H.S. (1995) Hospitalising the Suicidal Adolescent: An Empirical Investigation of Decision Making Criteria. *Journal of the American Academy of Child and Adolescent Psychiatry*, 34, 7, 902–11.

Pfeiffer, S.I. and Strzelecki, S.C. (1990) Inpatient Psychiatric Treatment of Children and Adolescents: A Review of Outcome Studies. *Journal of the American Academy of Child and Adolescent Psychiatry*, 29, 6, 847–853.

Pottick, K., Hansell, S., Gutterman, E. and White, H.R. (1995) Factors Associated with In-patient and Outpatient Treatment for Children and Adolescents with Serious Mental Illness. *Journal of the American Academy of Child and Adolescent Psychiatry*, 34, 4, 425–33.

Psychiatry Star Team (1996) Fact sheet No. 42, http://www.psych.med.umichedu/web/aacap/factsFam/continum.htp

Williams, R. and Richardson, G. (eds) (1995) *Child and Adolescent Mental Health Services: Together We Stand*. London: HMSO.

Wolkind, S. and Gent, M. (1987) Children's Psychiatric In-patient Units: Present Functions and Future Directions. Special issue: Residential Provision. *Maladjustment and Therapeutic Education*, 5, 2, 54–6.

5 Goal setting

Michael Shaw

Goal setting features in the guidelines for the Children Act 1989, the NHS reorganisation (HAS 1995), and is increasingly becoming part of in-patient clinical practice (see Chapters 1 and 2). It is a way of making our work more effective and accountable (see Table 5.1).

Table 5.1 Principles of goal setting

- Part of engaging the family in treatment.

- Establishes priorities for what the family wants.

- A starting point for all subsequent discussion of the case.

- Basis for planning treatment.

- Basis for judging outcome.

Described here is the approach established by my own unit Stepping Stones. Variants are used by a number of children's in-patient units in the UK. We draw up goals on every child admitted at a meeting specially set aside for this purpose. The best time for goal setting is when the family has committed itself to an admission. This could be after two or three meetings but occasionally it takes much longer. For example:

> An 11-year-old boy with a severe mixed disorder of conduct and emotions is violently opposed to admission at referral. His mother is desperate for help but being undermined by her own parents (with whom she always lived until a year ago). They are extremely critical of her parenting, claim that there is nothing wrong with the boy and no need for treatment. We did not rush things, and spent six months discussing admission with the family. During this period the mother grew in confidence and authority and the grandparents were increasingly sidelined. The boy relaxed and was able to come in willingly. (These changes were maintained throughout the admission and since.)

Children referred for psychiatric admission have no shortage of difficulties. Setting goals identifies the top priorities from what might otherwise be an overwhelming list. In introducing goal setting to the family we ask them to think about what they hope will come out of the admission. We want to know what problems they think are having the greatest impact on the child's (and family's) quality of life. It is crucial for the family to feel that their concerns are being listened to and taken seriously. Admission makes huge demands on the family but they will work hard to achieve goals they see as their own (see chapter 12).

The child is likely to be the main focus of the goals, but it is important that the parents also commit themselves to change. Parents often find this difficult. A non-judgmental approach and an emphasis on how things can be improved in the future may help. But sometimes fear of criticism and guilt prevent parents from looking at their own behaviour. This needs to be tackled.

> The parents of a 12-year-old boy with a severe mixed disorder of conduct and emotions are extremely angry. They feel their concerns have not been listened to at the previous clinic and that a diagnosis of hyperactivity has been missed. They are also highly critical of the past involvement of social services. Suddenly, in the midst of their anger the mother is offended by a neutral comment from the interviewer. The interviewer manages to gently point out what has just happened, while at the same time acknowledging how painfully criticised the mother feels. Whereupon the mother bursts into tears and both parents begin to talk about guilt and feeling they have failed. (This dynamic was reworked many times over the course of treatment.)

There are various different types of goal. In an assessment orientated admission the goals are usually about gaining a better understanding of a problem, for example whether a diagnosis of hyperactivity is appropriate or adds anything to treatment of the child's behavioural problems. Goals in a more treatment orientated admission tend to be about changing a pattern of behaviour or interaction, for example reducing sexualised behaviour. Alternatively the emphasis may be on building confidence or learning new skills (such as expressing anger without hurting people). Nearly all children need further help after discharge and a common goal will be to identify and make recommendations about their future needs (treatment, educational, placement etc.)

Around five goals is manageable; more, and the sense of priority gets lost. Wherever possible the goals should be expressed in the family's own words, and better still, in the words of the child. Sometimes naming a problem is a crucial step in treatment. For example:

> A 9-year-old boy was adopted at the age of 5 after horrendous abuse and neglect at the hands of substance-abusing parents. He flies into a terrible rage whenever he feels left out or forgotten. His adoptive mother vividly describes a look of appalling hatred and terror in his face. He is quite inconsolable and will brutally attack her if she comes near. After an episode

he is unable to acknowledge what has happened or talk about his feelings. A crucial point in helping this (very dissociated) boy came when he named the episodes 'megas'.

Regardless of whose words are used the goals must be easily understood. The goals need to be realistic and achievable in the time allowed. There may be a clear target, such as to stop spitting. More often it is a direction in which progress is hoped for, such as improving self-confidence. When setting goals it is useful to think about how the outcome might be judged. At the end of an admission we review progress with each goal. Progress can be quantified if goals have identified something measurable. The most robust method is to measure change in frequency of a specific behaviour. For example a goal might be '*To help James not hurt his sister so much*'. A weekly count can be kept of the number of incidents based on a specially constructed definition of '*hurt his sister*'. Sometimes more abstract qualities (such as self-esteem) can be measured using rating scales. However, rating scales may not be particularly sensitive to change.

Sometimes the referrer or other professionals have a specific question they want clarified (such as whether the child has a developmental disorder). We would include this in the goals after discussion with the family. Very occasionally children are admitted at the request of the court in the context of care proceedings. Under these circumstances it is the guardian ad litem, social workers or even the judge who defines the goals of admission. The parents may be hostile and contribute very little to the process.

There are always senior members of our team involved in goal setting. We also include the staff who will work directly with the family during admission. Being involved in the goal setting seems to be a vital step in staff feeling orientated and engaged with the case. The goals of admission are typed up and distributed to parents and (with the parent's consent) the referrer, GP and other relevant professionals (see Table 5.2.). The goals are filed at the front of the child's notes and an overhead transparency copy is made for use at meetings.

Table 5.2 Goals of admission

Andrew Smith	Admission 3.4.97
dob 13.9.89	Miniteam C

GOALS OF ADMISSION

1. To try to understand why Andrew has such difficulty making friends.

2. To help Andrew not hit his sister so often.

3. To help Andrew express his anger without hurting people.

4. To help Andrew's family work more as a team.

5. To advise on Andrew's treatment, education and placement after he leaves.

We complete the goals of admission prior to a pre-admission case conference; this meeting takes place a week or so before admission and has two parts. In the first half the team meet without the parents, referrer or other outside professionals. We discuss the pre-admission assessment and develop hypotheses about the case. The parents and outside professionals join the second half of the meeting when the treatment plan is drawn up. The hypotheses highlight what we see as the key problems and the critical steps in achieving change. For example:

- The girl's difficulties are closely related to her mother's depression and probable personality disorder.
- She will make better progress if her mother seeks treatment.

The goals are the priorities agreed between the family and therapeutic team. The hypotheses are additional priorities for the team based on theory and experience. The treatment plan is the team's prescription for addressing the goals and hypotheses. The goals, treatment plan and hypotheses become the starting point for all subsequent discussion of the case. The treatment plan and hypotheses will be revised but the goals remain the same. As mentioned above, at the end of the admission the progress with each goal is reviewed.

Table 5.3 Checklist for goal setting

- Responsibility of the senior staff doing pre-admission assessment.

- In combination with the staff who will be working with the family during admission.

- Completed before pre-admission case conference.

- Drawn up and agreed with the family.

- Professional network contributes where there are statutory proceedings.

- Establishes priorities.

- Part of engaging the family.

- Main focus likely to be child.

- Important parents also commit themselves to change.

- Common types of goal:
    Understanding a problem.
    Changing dysfunctional patterns of interaction.
    Learning new skills.
    Identifying future needs.

Goals should:

- Be achievable.
- Have clear targets, e.g. *stop spitting.*
- Set a direction in which progress is hoped for, e.g. *improve self-confidence.*
- Use the family's own words whenever possible.
- Be clearly worded.
- Number around five.
- Target something that can be measured.
- Follow standard document format.
- Be distributed to parents and professionals (consent).
- Be photocopied on to overhead transparency.
- Be stored in the KEY INFORMATION section of casenotes.
- Be used (along with the hypotheses) to generate the treatment plan.
- Be the starting point for all discussion of the case.
- Be reviewed as *Progress with Goals* at final Case Conference.

REFERENCES

Department of Health (1991) *The Children Act 1989, Guidance and Regulations, Volume 4, Residential Care.* London: HMSO.
NHS Health Advisory Service (1995) *Child and Adolescent Mental Health Services: Together We Stand.* London: HMSO.

6 Initial assessment

Brian Jacobs

The process of engaging the family, the child and the wider system has been described in the previous two chapters in discussing the process of admission and goal planning. This frames the admission like an arch but it is not sufficient. A thorough child psychiatric and mental health work-up is necessary.

This process begins with taking a full psychiatric history from the parents. It should be carried out after the initial meeting but before a final decision about admission is taken. It must cover the presenting difficulties in detail with examples, and previous interventions, with the effect of these. Specific examples of current and past behaviour should be sought. If not already discussed in the initial family interviews, then past interventions and the parents' own attempted solutions, what has worked and what failed, need detailed discussion. The interview will move to asking about current daily life, the child's likes and dislikes, concurrent physical illness and any past illnesses that may be relevant. Details of the mother's pregnancy, her and her partner's attitude to the forthcoming child and what else was going on in their lives at the time help to provide a picture of early attitudes to the pregnancy. It may also provide a clue to domestic violence which is common (Mooney, 1993) and occurs particularly in the first year of life (Gielen, O'Campo, Faden, Kass and Xue, 1994; Mezey and Bewley, 1997). Illnesses during the pregnancy, the use of any drugs, prescribed or otherwise, exposure to any adverse environments or toxins and any difficulties with the birth are relevant. It is often helpful to ask for permission to obtain the child's and mother's birth records at this point. For example:

> A 5-year-old boy was admitted with his mother. Among other difficulties, she had a history of alcohol abuse extending through most of her pregnancy. She had sought help and was said to have stopped drinking subsequently. The boy was said to be hyperactive, to have a poor sense of danger and to have a difficult relationship with his mother. We were asked by social services to assess the degree to which his behaviour was a reaction to his mother's management, the degree to which these patterns could be altered and the viability of his remaining with his mother. The diagnosis of foetal alcohol syndrome helped achieve an understanding of his difficult behaviours. Simply removing him from his mother's care would not settle his behaviour. Work with the mother and son on her parent management and on

their relationship led to improvements which enabled him to stay at home with continuing social services support.

The child's early development and temperament as well as the way they are described are again helpful indicators of developing attitudes as well as providing a template against which to assess the child's subsequent development. If specific memories of the child at different stages can be retrieved by parents through linking them to particular salient events, this will improve the quality of the history. Any neurological illness or insult should be carefully documented (see Chapter 22 by Kenneth Nunn).

A history of each parent's background and of their relationship is important even if the couple have subsequently separated. For a step-family, their description of the effect of arrival and presence of the step-parent in the family is often illuminating. A psychiatric history for each parent is important both because of biological continuity and because it may have given rise to separations, emotional unavailability of one or both parents, other caretaking arrangements or a change in attitudes subsequently because of the trauma.

Following a car accident, the mother of 8-year-old James became over-protective towards him. She had suffered chronic physical illness as a child. When he subsequently developed a limb weakness she was convinced that this was as a direct result of the accident and took him to many doctors. An in-patient psychiatric admission became necessary when he developed a paralysis and behavioural difficulties. It was uncertain whether this was a physical or hysterical illness.

A history of any medical condition in the child or parent should be sought. Particular attention should be given to possible epileptic phenomena in the child. In our experience this is a poorly questioned area during a general child psychiatric history. It can be very relevant to a child's behaviour whether aggressive, apparently disoriented and confused or, more rarely, associated with specific sensations or distortions of memory (see Chapter 22).

Sometimes it is important to obtain additional historical interviews from other informants, either because the child has spent part of their life with other caretakers or because there is some doubt over the history obtained.

The interview with the child is important. It has been well described by Angold (1994). It will include a mental state examination of the child. However it is also very important to begin to establish a rapport with the child and to understand the world from their perspective. It is also important to ascertain their view of the possible admission. Do they regard it as welcome? Do they see themselves as being punished? Has possible admission been used as a threat by a parent or others? Each of these will colour the attitude of the child and needs discussing openly with them and later with their parents if the child is willing. It is helpful at this stage to elicit the child's self-view. Do they see themselves as having a problem? If so, what? Does this agree with their parents' views?

PHYSICAL EXAMINATION

The child must have a physical examination (Bailey, 1994). Abnormal facial appearance and other dysmorphic features should be noted. Limb or midline body asymmetries may be important. Tics, tremors and other movement abnormalities should be noted (Robertson and Eapen, 1995). Height, weight and head circumference should be measured and plotted onto growth charts (Tanner and Whitehouse, 1976). A general physical examination and a more detailed neurological examination, including examination for neurological soft signs (Rutter, Graham and Yule, 1970) is appropriate. Neurological soft signs are insufficient by themselves to be interpreted as evidence of neurological disorder. This examination will give some idea of developmental delays or particular motor or perceptual difficulties. Child psychiatrists responsible for in-patient units should be familiar with the various physical illnesses which can mimic psychiatric illness or present with behavioural disorder (see Chapter 22) (Bailey, 1994; Gillberg, 1995; Harris, 1995; Aicardi, 1992). Many of these are rare and a child psychiatrist will only see them very sporadically. It is important that we are alert to the possibility of organic causes and that expert paediatric neurological opinion is sought as necessary. A history that suggests a falling off of intellectual development or loss of skills should particularly alert one to the need for further investigation. Similarly, organic causes for psychotic presentations should not be forgotten.

MEDICAL INVESTIGATION

Investigations are usually tailored to the history and examination. Children will sometimes require a blood screen for moderate learning difficulties. Chromosome analysis may be appropriate as well as specific tests for fragile X syndrome. Specific blood tests will be required if disorders such as thyrotoxicosis, drug abuse, acute intermittent porphyria, etc., are suspected.

EEG examination is quite commonly requested. Partly this arises from a careful history but also it may arise from observations of the child on the ward. We have seen several children where previously unexplained behaviour has, in part, been found to be caused by epileptic phenomena; it has improved with appropriate anticonvulsant medication. This does not contradict the finding of common EEG abnormalities without clinical features that is seen in between 2 and 9 per cent of the child population (Aicardi, 1994). Similarly, if there is a history suggestive of a developmental disorder or other brain dysfunction then it is legitimate to request an MRI examination.

A refugee child from a third world conflict was admitted with hallucinations and a paranoid illness with aggressive behaviour. He had witnessed terrible violence. Close observations by the nursing team suggested that he was having brief episodes when he appeared to scratch at his arm followed by a short time (30 seconds to 1 minute) when he was inaccessible to those around him. He was found to have EEG abnormalities suggestive of complex partial seizures and an MRI showing limited temporal lobe damage suggesting old infarction. Treatment of his epilepsy with carbamazepine led to substantial resolution of his hallucinations and epileptic phenomena but some persistence of his difficult behaviour.

PSYCHOLOGICAL TESTING

It is important to have the support of a clinical psychologist on a children's in-patient unit, though this is not universally available. Psychometry forms an important part of the work-up of these children. Many of the children have general or specific learning difficulties that have not been noticed previously or whose salience for the child's behavioural disorder has not been recognised. Thus many children with behavioural problems have specific reading difficulties. Equally, children with uneven cognitive profiles may be difficult or quite withdrawn. Adults easily misunderstand behaviour as deliberate when the child may not understand. For other children intellectual deterioration is occurring and important to note. Is it an early sign of dementia or a sign that concomitant epilepsy has deteriorated?

Usually a WISC (Weschler Intelligence Scales for Children) III (Weschler, 1992) is performed for school age children and on occasions the WPPSI (Weschler Preschool Primary Scale of Intelligence) (Weschler, 1990a) is carried out on younger children. The WORD (Weschler Objective Reading Dimensions) (Weschler, 1990b) is currently used as an assessment of reading ability and comprehension as it can be correlated with the measures of general intelligence. Other tests are appropriate on occasion for children who will not speak, as in selective mutism, including the Leiter, and the WOND (Weschler Objective Numerical Dimensions) can be very helpful. If language difficulties are found Reynell Developmental Language Scales are useful in further specifying their nature. Access to specialist neuropsychological testing is necessary from time to time (Spreen, Risser and Edgell, 1995; Harris, 1995).

Many children will need to be statemented under the Education Act. Psychometry during the admission and other observations will contribute to this and facilitate correct decisions being made.

USE OF SEMI-STRUCTURED INTERVIEWS AND RATING SCALES

Administration of other psychological measures of functioning can be very helpful. They are not currently used routinely in the UK but can form a helpful basis for diagnostic confirmation of findings and for follow-up studies. We use most of the instruments below on some occasions, often as confirmation of

Table 6.1 Commonly used instruments for assessment

What	By whom	With what purpose	Reference
Semi-structured interviews (s/s i/v)			
Child and Adolescent Psychiatric Assessment – CAPA	Parent and child versions	A detailed psychiatric s/s i/v leading to DSM IV and ICD 10 diagnoses. [*Mainly a research instrument but can be useful clinically to examine one area of psychopathology in detail; disadvantage that it takes a long time.*]	(Angold, 1989)
Kiddie – SADS	Parent and child versions	As above but DSM and RDC criteria only. [*It has a restricted range of diagnoses.*]	(Puig-Antich and Chambers, 1978)
Autism Diagnostic Interview – ADI	Parent	s/s i/v of parent to provide evidence for autism spectrum diagnosis. [*A very useful instrument with algorithms to help assist in diagnosis of pervasive developmental disorders; best used in combination with the ADOS.*]	(Lord, Rutter and Le Couteur, 1994)
Harter Self-Esteem Scale	Child	Child's self-esteem. [*Can be useful clinically as well as part of a research battery.*]	(Harter, 1982)
Adult Attachment Interview	Mother	i/v to delineate mother's representation of childhood attachment. [*This is a research instrument currently because it takes so long to rate the transcripts of interviews. The principles of the interview can be applied clinically.*]	(Main and Goldwyn)

continued

Table 6.1 continued

What	By whom	With what purpose	Reference
Checklists			
CBCL	Parents and home schoolteacher	General child symptom checklist. [*A widely used checklist which may not be very sensitive at high levels of psychopathology. Its sensitivity to change is uncertain.*]	(Achenbach and Edelbrock, 1981)
Birleson Depression Rating Scale	Child	Rating scale of depression in the child. [*A clinically useful instrument in middle childhood and older.*]	(Birleson, 1981)
Revised Child Manifest Anxiety Scale	Child	Rating scale of anxiety in the child. [*Useful for clinical work and research.*]	(Reynolds and Richmond, 1978)
Mood and Feelings Questionnaire	Child	Emotional symptoms. [*Good patient acceptability, useful for age 6 and over.*]	(Costello and Angold, 1988)
Strengths and Difficulties Questionnaire	Parent, teacher, ward staff	Screening instrument and possible measure of change. [*This appears a promising instrument and may provide a more sensitive measure of change. It is also quite brief.*]	(Goodman, 1997)
Observation schedules			
Attachment Play Scenarios	Child	Child's attachment representations. [*This is one of several instruments that are appearing for the assessment of childhood attachment representations. It is not yet clear which most usefully measures this important element to a child's difficulties.*]	(Cassidy, 1988)
Parent/Child Game Observation Schedule	Parent and child	[*This schedule can be used as a measure of change resulting from the specific treatment intervention.*]	(Jenner, 1997)

continued

Table 6.1 continued

What	By whom	With what purpose	Reference
Conners Rating Scales	Nurses, teacher, parent	Child's overactivity and attention deficits. [*We use only the hyper-activity scales from this instrument on the ward and in our school. It is sensitive to change.*]	(Conners, 1982)
Autism Diagnostic Observation Schedule [ADOS]	Trained interviewer	Autism spectrum disorders. [*A very useful confirmatory observation interview for diagnosing pervasive developmental disorders.*]	(Lord et al., 1989)

clinical diagnostic conclusions but sometimes to measure change. The latter seems to be the most difficult to measure reliably and with validity.

Observations in the ward setting form a vital part of the assessment phase of admission. Nurses and others use structured tools. The team will plan their observations and safety measures to protect the child. These will take account of the known risks posed by the child from the history. Strategies for absconding, suicidality or aggression will have been set up and will be modified with the child's actual behaviour. These care plans may require a nurse to remain in close proximity to the child in the early stages of the admission.

Structured observation instruments such as the Conners rating scale (Conners, 1982) require consistent thresholds for ratings. The reliability of the instrument depends upon this. Ideally, the staff should be formally trained. An alternative is for the key nurse to consult others on the shift before rating the instrument. This produces a shifting pattern of consensus ratings so damping the variance that would occur with multiple raters. The potential for variability needs to be taken into account when interpreting neat graphs of results.

The child's ability to regulate himself in the face of frustration, difficult demands, changing activities, his peer interactions and style are carefully noted. Self-care skills and age-appropriate worries are recorded. Independence, risk-taking behaviours and positive personality attributes are also observed as are any likes and dislikes that the child has.

Structured observations of parent–child interactions may be undertaken as in the parent–child game (Jenner, 1997). Other settings will also be used to gain access to parent–child interactions and relationships. These can include unstructured time together as well as specific assessments. Cooking and craft work provide two useful informal settings both for assessment and inter-vention.

The child's attachment to their parents can be assessed through guided dolls play that requires the child to imagine separation from their parents (Cassidy, 1988). This can illuminate some of the processes contributing to the child's behaviour towards others. It can also complement observations and interviews with the parents and principal caretaker, usually the mother (see Chapters 25 and 26).

Assessment of the child in the hospital school setting provides helpful information in terms of the child's self-esteem as a pupil, his areas of skill and of deficit. Some attainment measures, for example using the Aston (Aston Index, 1989) scales, are obtained. Again, his peer interactions and attitudes to adults are noted in that setting. Any perceptual difficulties often become apparent in the school and in assessment by the occupational therapist.

Simultaneously a picture will be built up of the family relationships and of the child's view of his family. Which are the points of support and which those of stress? These observations in structured and unstructured settings, in work and play allow the development of a focused intervention programme for the child and for the family.

The synthesis of observations from different sources on the in-patient unit requires a careful balancing of the information, the context in which it was obtained, the timing of the observations and the degree to which one assesses the reliability of the observer for this particular type of child. Sometimes information is altered by the preconceptions of the beholder, so that it is very important to get detailed observations of behaviours and what the child actually says, as well as the understanding that the staff members have developed. There are different styles for synthesising this information. In one unit the observations may be those of the key nurse, whilst in another the key nurse will summarise the observations of several people working on a shift together. These differences can produce subtle changes in how the observations are understood. Achieving consistency and accuracy is a matter for careful supervision. Similarly, observations between different disciplines need to be understood in terms of their professional background, their differing tasks as well as the ethos of the unit.

All observations are also subject to the effects that the child has upon the staff members. These aspects of the counter-transference are difficult to acknowledge and to describe. For example, some badly behaved children are still likeable whilst others are not. This can be an important quality in terms of how they are described and also for their prognosis. If we are able to develop an early understanding of this during our assessment then we are sometimes able to prevent ourselves idealising a child or failing to see their strengths. This can be very important for their treatment with us and for their future elsewhere.

In summary, the assessment of a child in an in-patient setting is an unrivalled opportunity for detailed observation. Careful weighing of the history and examination of the child is necessary and appropriate investigations must be undertaken. For many of these children it is an unique opportunity for a detailed medical assessment to be integrated with complex psychosocial factors.

REFERENCES

Achenbach, T. M., and Edelbrock, C. S. (1981). Behavioural problems and competencies reported by parents of normal and disturbed children aged four to sixteen. *Monographs of the Society for Research in Child Development, 46, 1*, iv–82.

Aicardi, J. (1992). *Diseases of the Nervous System in Childhood.* Oxford: MacKeith Press / Blackwell Scientific.

Aicardi, J. (1994). Diagnosis and differential diagnosis. *Epilepsy in Children.* New York: Raven Press (pp. 354–380).

Angold, A. (1989). Structured assessments of psychopathology in children and adolescents. In C. Thompson (ed.). *The Instruments of Psychiatric Research.* Chichester: Wiley.

Angold, A. (1994). Clinical interviewing with children and adolescents. In M. Rutter, E. Taylor and L. Hersov (eds). *Child and Adolescent Psychiatry: Modern Approaches.* Oxford: Blackwell Scientific (pp. 51–63).

Aston Index (1989). *The Aston Index: A Classroom Test for Screening and Diagnosis of Language Difficulties (Age 5–14).* Wisbech: Learning Development Aids.

Bailey, A. (1994). Physical examination and medical investigations. In M. Rutter, E. Taylor and L. Hersov (eds). *Child and Adolescent Psychiatry: Modern Approaches.* Oxford: Blackwell Scientific (pp. 79–93).

Birleson (1981). The validity of depressive disorder in childhood and the development of a self-rating scale: a research report. *Journal of Child Psychology and Psychiatry, 22*, 73–88.

Cassidy, J. (1988). The self as related to child–mother attachment at six. *Child Development, 59*, 121–134.

Conners, C. K. (1982). Parent and teacher rating forms for the assessment of hyperkinesis in children. In P. A. Keller and L. G. Ritt (eds). *Innovations in Clinical Practice: A Source Book* (vol. 1) Sarasota FL: Professional Resource Exchange.

Costello, E. J., and Angold, A. (1988). Scales to assess child and adolescent depression: checklists, screens, and nets. *Journal of the American Academy of Child and Adolescent Psychiatry, 27*, 726–737.

Gielen, A. C., O'Campo, P. J., Faden, R. R., Kass, N. E. and Xue, X. (1994). Interpersonal conflict and physical violence during the childbearing year. *Social Sciences Medicine, 39*, 781–787.

Gillberg, C. (1995). *Clinical Child Neuropsychiatry.* Cambridge: Cambridge University Press.

Goodman, R. (1997). The strengths and difficulties questionnaire: a research note. *Journal of Child Psychology and Psychiatry and Allied Disciplines, 38*, 581–586.

Harris, J. C. (1995). *Developmental Neuropsychiatry: Assessment, Diagnosis and Treatment of Developmental Disorders.* Oxford: Oxford University Press.

Harter, S. (1982). The perceived competence scale for children. *Child Development, 53*, 87–97.

Jenner, S. (1997). Assessment of parenting in the context of child protection using the parent/child game. *Child Psychology and Psychiatry Review, 2*, 58–62.

Lord, C., Rutter, M. and Le Couteur, A. (1994). Autism diagnostic interview – revised: a revised version of a diagnostic interview for caregivers of individuals with possible pervasive developmental disorders. *Journal of Autism and Developmental Disorders, 24*, 659–685.

Lord, C., Rutter, M., Goode, S., Heemsbergen, J., Jordan, H., Mawhood, L. and Schopler,

E. (1989). Autism diagnostic observation schedule: a standardised observation of communicative and social behaviour. *Journal of Autism and Developmental Disorders*, *19*, 185–211.

Main, M. and Goldwyn, R. (1985–94). Adult attachment scoring and classification system. (Unpublished manual, Department of Psychology, University of California, Berkeley.)

Mezey, G. C., and Bewley, S. (1997). Domestic violence and pregnancy. *British Medical Journal*, *314*, 1295.

Mooney, J. (1993). *The Hidden Figure: Domestic Violence in the North London Borough of Islington*. London Centre for Criminology, Middlesex University.

Puig-Antich, J. and Chambers, W. (1978). The schedule for affective disorders and schizophrenia for school-aged children. (Unpublished manuscript obtainable through the New York State Psychiatric Institute, 722 West 168 Street, New York, New York 10032, USA.)

Reynolds, C. R. and Richmond, B. O. (1978). What I think and feel: a revised measure of children's manifest anxiety. *Journal of Abnormal Child Psychology*, 6, 271–280.

Robertson, M. R., and Eapen, V. (1995). *Movement and Allied Disorders in Childhood* (1st edn). Chichester: John Wiley.

Rutter, M., Graham, P. and Yule, W. (1970). *A Neuropsychiatric Study in Childhood*. London: S.I.M.P. / Heinemann.

Spreen, O., Risser, A. T. and Edgell, D. (1995). *Developmental Neuropsychology*. Oxford: Oxford University Press.

Tanner, J. M. and Whitehouse, R. H. (1976). Clinical longitudinal standards for height, weight, height velocity, weight velocity and the stages of puberty. *Archives of Diseases of Childhood*, *51*, 170–179.

Weschler, D. (1990a) *Weschler Preschool Primary Scale of Intelligence*. Sidcup: The Psychology Corporation/Harcourt Brace Jovanovich.

Weschler, D. (1990b) *Weschler Objective Reading Dimensions*. Sidcup: The Psychology Corporation/Harcourt Brace Jovanovich.

Weschler D. (1992) *Weschler Intelligence Scale for Children*, 3rd edition. Sidcup: The Psychology Corporation/Harcourt Brace Jovanovich.

7 The treatment and discharge phases of admission

Brian Jacobs

TREATMENT

Treatments need to be tailored to the individual needs of the child and their family. Nevertheless there are generic elements for all children. The specific components of treatment will be described in greater detail in other sections of this book.

It can be difficult to completely separate assessment from treatment in the in-patient service. Often it is necessary to try treatment interventions as a probe to test their likely efficacy either as a continuing intervention in the unit or as a treatment after discharge.

The cornerstone of all treatments in the in-patient service is both therapeutic of itself and provides the setting for all other treatment interventions; it is the milieu (see Chapter 9). The interchanges that the child has with his peers and the adult staff provide much material for social skills interventions and developing and practising new ways of behaving with others. They provide an opportunity to learn mutually supportive ways of relating as well as coping with the inevitable rivalries over friendship and leadership that occur in the changing group, as children are admitted and others leave. They can be a fertile arena for obtaining feedback about the effects of one's behaviour on others. Opportunities must be sought throughout for praising the child appropriately whenever possible.

Some units have a system of mini-team organisation in addition to the child having a key nurse. In such a system a small group of professionals, including the key nurse, meet each week to review progress and adjust the treatment programme. Major changes are discussed with the larger team. This system allows better co-ordination of several treatment interventions; however, there are sometimes difficulties in timetabling mini-team meetings.

Similarly, the child has opportunities in the hospital school to extend these skills in another controlled setting. Outings and special activities such as swimming and horse riding, which may be available from the unit, are not just fun; they provide essential arenas for extending and developing social skills and self-esteem. Some units organise adventure or other holiday trips for the children each year. These can be wonderful opportunities for observing the children in different settings and for them to practise feeling good about themselves through participative success.

Little plays can be put on with, or for, unit staff and parents; sports events that are run in a collaborative style, modulating the competitive element so that they do not overwhelm the children, can also be milieu contributions to developing self-esteem and a co-operative attitude.

Most units run a community group. This provides an opportunity for the children to review their activities for the day or the week. It allows tensions between them to be aired and difficult behaviour to be addressed. It is helpful if several disciplines from the staff are represented at this meeting. However, care must be taken not to outnumber the children. Some hospital schools run a separate review group towards the end of each week for the children from these units. Their achievements, academic, social and personal, are reviewed and the children are asked to rate themselves. Their peers then give them a rating with support from the staff. This can be a revelation for the child and often leads to them realising greater success than they would allow themselves.

Embedded in the milieu of most eclectic units will be general rules of behaviour towards one another and the fabric of the unit. In addition children will have targetted behavioural programmes to help them learn new behaviours and ways of managing themselves. These are reviewed regularly and adjusted so as to maintain the momentum of treatment. Access to dedicated clinical psychology time is invaluable in this task (see Chapter 10).

Individual experiential work with the child may be based on a talking therapy (see Chapter 11), an approach using structured or unstructured play for younger children or the developmentally immature child. For other children, a non-verbal therapeutic approach is more appropriate. These can include art therapy (Mills, 1991), a movement-based therapy (Jennings, 1987), or music therapy (Goodman, 1989; Friedlander, 1994). Unfortunately, only some units have access to any of these approaches. In our experience many children can benefit from an arena that allows them to explore something of their inner world in the presence of a safe adult.

Another style of working with the children might be described as task-centred. Such approaches will include cognitive approaches to depression and behavioural difficulties (Kendall, 1991), anger management training (Lochman, Lampron, Gemmer and Harris, 1987; Lochman, White and Wayland, 1991), relaxation training etc. These can be delivered to a single child or sometimes to small groups of children. The material and approaches do not differ greatly from those used in an outpatient setting. The difference lies rather in the observed opportunities for skills practice and debriefing that are inherent to an in-patient service.

Children can use psychotherapy groups on in-patient units but they are not good at using free-floating psychodynamic groups at this age. Groups function better if they are task centred (Dwivedi, 1993). Thus a cookery group or other activity can be run, in which comments on the co-operation, sharing and positive help that children give to each other and how they perhaps make each other feel by nice and nasty comments and actions, can be incorporated. I once helped at a cookery group shortly before I left a unit in which the children's anger with the occupational therapist and me resulted in our being tied up by them with sellotape! Fortunately, interpretation of their anger led to our being cut free again before they went for lunch. Earlier interpretation might have prevented it.

Success for the children breeds a new attitude to being successful, often for the first time in their memories. The children gradually stop sabotaging their own achievements and can tolerate achievement. This provides a platform for the difficult task of transferring their skills to the outside world.

Occupational therapists will work with other team members including the nurses and school staff in activity based treatments with the children. These will include learning to cook and learning to use their hands in model making, pottery and other craft skills. The children will also work with an occupational therapist around specific manual and other skill deficits that have an organic origin. Carefully chosen sports activities are again very useful in helping a child with balance or co-ordination difficulties.

For youngsters with eating disorders, the advice of a dietician in the hospital can be invaluable (Lask and Bryant-Waugh, 1993). It is important that the dietician advises the staff rather than the youngster directly. Otherwise splitting of the staff group with differing opinions set off against each other and orchestrated by the anorectic patient can occur.

Most of the children will be spending the weekends at home. Some children will only be admitted for part of each week. This time at home is an important element of the treatment. It provides a laboratory for testing out what has been achieved so far and for allowing tuning of the child's and family's treatment programme.

Simultaneously, much work will be taking place with the parents. For all parents or other carers there is the need to exchange information about the time the child has spent on the ward during the week and to obtain detailed feedback about the weekend for most of the children who spend the weekends at home. Occasionally, children will spend their weekends in local authority care or with other relatives. In all these cases, feedback is important for the in-patient unit. This is not always realised by outside agencies and requires careful and sometimes delicate liaison from unit staff.

There are many other needs for communication between the parents and unit staff. There should be both informal and more formal opportunities for this. This also places an onus on staff to monitor the interchanges and to ensure that a consistent but not a rigid position is taken.

Formal family therapy is also a vital element of work. This will sometimes involve the whole family and sometimes subsystems of it (see Chapter 8). Working with parents on their parenting and their attitudes to their partner's parenting is delicate but vital. Similarly, disentangling this from their own relationship is important. They may want to work on the latter but it is not a necessary focus. Behavioural shifts and attitudinal changes can be powerfully affected by this intervention, particularly when it is carefully dovetailed with other therapeutic approaches.

At times, a parent or sometimes both parents need a series of individual sessions to begin to come to terms with events in their own past lives. This can be essential for them to be able to start treating their child differently. For some insight is necessary, but it is often insufficient for behavioural change, and practice using parenting techniques learnt through the parent–child game (Chapter 26) or Webster-Stratton parent management training can be very helpful. For others insight is unbearable and can be counterproductive, alienating the parent from other approaches.

During the admission, continuing liaison with local services from the referring area is important. It is very helpful if the child's school and mental health service are each able to send a consistent representative to clinical reviews. It aids better planning for the child's discharge and a smoother handover to those services that will be carrying the long-term responsibilities. It can also help to avoid setting up those services for failure, by working out ways with them that certain elements of the in-patient treatment programme may be continued post-discharge. When it is not possible for a member of the referring CAMHS to attend it is very important for a consistent member of the unit staff to provide feedback. This can be organised by the leader of the mini-team, where such a system operates. Sometimes closer liaison with the referring team is possible through joint work, often in the family therapy through the admission. Usually this is not possible because of time and distance constraints but it can work well and can ease discharge.

One major issue that repeatedly confronts us is the handling of therapeutic work with the family. If the in-patient unit does it all then the family often develops trust in our staff and is reluctant to return to local services. However, it is inappropriate for in-patient units to provide the continuing care for most of the children they have seen. The liaison relationships between child mental health services and other services will be closer in the child's home community – they have more dealings with one another over many children. Sometimes it is possible to include a professional from the home community in the treatment delivered at the in-patient unit. On other occasions a pattern of shared care can alleviate these difficulties. Often however, the most important contribution to be made is the careful attention to detail in the process of handing back the case to the local team.

Planning for discharge needs to begin early in the admission, particularly where special resources will be needed for the child post-discharge. Thus it is very important to involve the child's education authority from an early stage if residential schooling or an unexpected special school placement will be sought. Close liaison from the hospital school headteacher greatly eases this process. Similarly if there is a question of the child not returning to live with their family, this needs to be addressed early. Having a social worker with dedicated sessional time for the unit greatly helps this liaison task. Surprisingly often, local social services departments have not had a very disturbed family brought to their attention. They are not always overjoyed to hear from our services.

Few children's in-patient units now have a social worker attached to their service (see Chapter 2). This is a great loss. A social worker who knows the workings of the unit but who is actually employed by the local authority provides an independent but sensitive view of child welfare issues. These include restriction of a child's liberty, consent to treatment and the balance of when it is legitimate and necessary to involve social services departments and when not.

DISCHARGE

A case where there has been no need for further work has not occurred in my experience. Thus, liaison with local services and ensuring good post-discharge arrangements are extremely important. Children's services are not required to follow the Care Planning Approach that has been introduced to adult psychiatry in the UK, but it is good practice to follow a parallel, adapted process. Careful handover to the local CAMHS of all aspects of the treatment and information about which approaches have best suited the case is essential. When appropriate, medication regimes must be communicated. A detailed multi-disciplinary report is prepared, summarising the admission, discussed with the parents and circulated to those professionals who will have to continue aspects of the work. The child's general practitioner must be sent a letter summarising the salient points of the admission in brief. Detailed psychiatric summaries are probably not appropriate for this purpose.

As the child's discharge approaches there will be a need to review progress, gains made and those not achieved so far. The child is often reluctant to leave and anxious about the future. Similarly, parents are wary and have often made strong emotional investments in the unit and particular staff members. There are often associated setbacks at this stage of the treatment. They have to be forecast as 'what we expect to happen at this stage' and as obstacles to be overcome with a sense of achievement, not as mountains that block further progress.

Rituals of leaving are important for all family members. The focus is the child but covertly they are just as important for the parents. A celebration of the child's time on the unit, their achievements and the thoughts of those they are leaving are important to them. Often one finds that families have found common ground whilst their children have been in-patients and they remain in contact for some years thereafter.

Helping the child and family to disengage from the in-patient service and to move towards the much less intense tempo of outpatient work can feel like a yawning chasm to them. Similarly it is easy for the child's local mental health services to be seen as failures since they cannot possibly provide the breadth or intensity of service that the family has experienced in the unit.

There are differing ways of trying to overcome these difficulties and make this transition (see also Chapters 11 and 12). That it is a vital phase of the admission there is no doubt. Research shows that follow-up by in-patient services is a strong predictor of final outcome for the children (Pfeiffer and Strzelecki, 1990). At the

Bethlem, we cannot provide a long-term outpatient service. What we can do is arrange a few meetings with the family post-discharge and arrange one or two handover meetings as part of this process to the child's local service. These may occur symbolically on our territory first and then at the local clinic. We also encourage children to feel that they can contact or visit our unit some time later. We periodically have visits from young people who were patients some years before. Similarly parents will sometimes contact us and we will try to help them by guiding them gently back into their local service if appropriate. Sometimes they have completed treatment locally and no longer need a mental health service but want some informal advice. This may be frowned upon by some but it is perhaps inevitable when people have been through a powerful and sometimes pivotal experience.

REFERENCES

Dwivedi, K. N. (1993). *Group Work with Children and Adolescents: a handbook*. London: Jessica Kingsley.

Friedlander, L. H. (1994). Group music psychotherapy in an in-patient psychiatric setting for children: a developmental approach. (Special Issue: Psychiatric music therapy.) *Music Therapy Perspectives, 12*, 92–97.

Goodman, K. D. (1989). Music therapy assessment of emotionally disturbed children. *Arts in Psychotherapy, 16*, 179–192.

Jennings, S. (1987). *Drama Therapy: therapy and practice for teachers and clinicians*. London: Croom Helm.

Kendall, P. C. (1991). *Child and Adolescent Therapy: cognitive–behavioural procedures*. New York: Guilford.

Lask, B. and Bryant-Waugh, R. (1993). *Childhood Onset Anorexia Nervosa and Related Eating Disorders*. Hove: Lawrence Erlbaum Associates.

Lochman, J. E., Lampron, L. B., Gemmer, T. V. and Harris, R. (1987). Anger coping intervention with aggressive children: a guide to implementation in school settings. In P. A. Keller and S. R. Heyman (eds), *Innovations in Clinical Practice: a source book*. (vol. 6, pp. 339–356). Sarasota, FL: Professional Resource Exchange.

Lochman, J. E., White, K. J. and Wayland, K. K. (1991). Cognitive–behavioural assessment and treatment with aggressive children. In P.C. Kendall (ed.), *Child and Adolescent Therapy: cognitive–behavioural procedures*. (pp. 25–65). New York: Guilford.

Mills (1991). Art therapy on a residential treatment team for troubled children. *Journal of Child and Youth Care, 6*, 49–59.

Pfeiffer, S. I. and Strzelecki, S. C. (1990). In-patient psychiatric treatment of children and adolescents: a review of outcome studies. *Journal of the American Academy of Child and Adolescent Psychiatry, 29*, 847–853.

Part III

Therapeutic elements in in-patient treatment

8 Engaging and working with the family

Judith Lask and Cynthia Maynerd

Family relationships play a significant role in the aetiology and course of psychiatric problems in childhood (Quinton and Rutter, 1984; Garmezy and Masten, 1994). Increasingly, family and carers take part in treatment programmes (Howlin and Rutter, 1987; Russell et al., 1987; Kazdin et al., 1987; Webster-Stratton C., 1991). Ensuring this involvement presents a particular challenge for the staff of in-patient units who will have the care of the child throughout the week but have limited opportunities to meet with family members. The distance of the unit from the family home can be an added complication. This situation may intensify the focus on the child and lead to a marginalisation of other important factors in the child's family relationships and wider environment. It can place the main burden of change on the child whose best efforts may be counteracted by what is happening in 'life outside the unit'. The admission might also be seen itself as a solution, leading to a decrease in motivation to address family relationship issues (Harbin, 1982). Over time, in-patient units have developed a variety of ways of working with parents and families and many of these will be described in other chapters (see chapters 24–26 and also chapter 32 for strategies in another setting). Work with families will usually include many approaches and a range of professionals but in recent years a number of units have created specific family therapist posts to assist the development of work in this area. Family therapists usually come from a health or social services related profession and have undertaken a specialist four-year training in systemic family therapy. Although their main concern is with assessing families and working with them therapeutically to create change, they are also interested in understanding complex professional systems and the way in which they impact on families. To this end they may meet with whole families, part families, couples, individuals and professional systems as well as thinking about the ways in which work with families is undertaken, in relation both to individual children and the ethos of the whole unit. Some units are able to admit whole or part families during a child's admission and involve them more intensely (Brown, 1991; Didyk et al., 1989). This chapter aims to put forward some guidelines for good practice as well as examining issues that arise when working with families in the context of child in-patient settings. Many of the ideas will have direct relevance to other forms of residential setting.

SOME THEORETICAL CONSIDERATIONS

One of the strengths as well as one of the potential hazards of in-patient units is that they contain professionals who may have differing views about children and their families. Units will devise structures and systems for formulating and co-ordinating work but unless professionals discuss their different theoretical positions they may have problems in understanding one another or working together in a collaborative way. For this reason it seemed important to outline some of the key theoretical ideas that underpin systemic family therapy, and these are found in Table 8.1. Readers who want a fuller account are directed to other texts (Burnham, 1986; Goldenberg and Goldenberg, 1996).

Table 8.1 Key family therapy concepts

Family system	Family members interconnect to form a system in which the behaviour of each member affects and is affected by the behaviour of the others.
Context	Behaviour can only be understood in the context in which it occurs. Just as individuals operate within contexts such as family or peer group, the family operates within the context of wider systems such as community, culture and society.
Circularity	No relationship is one way or linear. Any attempt to formulate a clear cause and effect is a 'punctuation' of a circular process.
Behaviour, beliefs and relationships	All of these are part of human interaction and are interdependent.
Pattern and process	As well as the content of what people say and do it is possible to observe persistent patterns which may be helpful or unhelpful. The structure and organisation of families is one such pattern. Process refers to the way things are done or said, by whom and in what way. Family therapy focuses on relationships and patterns and these are likely to be the focus for interventions.
Change and homeostasis	Families, like all systems, work hard to achieve a balance between necessary change and stability. Under stress they often become stuck in old unhelpful patterns. The focus of therapy is often to help families become 'unstuck' and find ways of moving forward.
Narrative	Through social interactions we develop 'narratives' to make sense of complex lived experience. These narratives have dominant themes and they influence the way we live our lives. By examining these narratives and the way they are formed, other, more positive themes may be revealed which may help individuals and families to make changes in their lives.

THE ROLE OF THE FAMILY THERAPIST IN INITIAL MEETINGS

It is important that child, family and professional system are all considered at this early stage. Whatever the developmental history of the problem it will have begun to have a life of its own. The family, professionals and others will have formed a system, sometimes called the 'problem determined system', around it (Selvini Palazzoli et al., 1980). Within this system there may be multiple understandings of the problem, different views about what has been helpful, and whether or not a referral to an in-patient unit is appropriate. To address these issues and to maximise collaboration, many units convene an initial meeting which includes both professionals and family. This may be the first time that everyone involved has had the opportunity to sit down and talk together (see chapters 4 and 5).

The systemic perspective brought by the family therapist can be very helpful in understanding the complexities of a referral (Reder and Kraemer, 1980; Dare et al., 1990). It also gives an opportunity for the family therapist to become acquainted with those most closely involved with the child and to identify positive resources that can be used by the family. Family therapy can help the family to mobilise their own resources in a more effective way. One unwanted side effect of an admission can be that other professionals cease to be involved (see chapter 18). Meeting the family affords an opportunity to explain the importance of family involvement and what expectations there will be, and to begin the process of engagement with them. Particular questioning techniques developed within family therapy can be used with good effect in initial meetings as well as in direct work with individuals, couples and families. Circular or reflexive questions are used both as a way of eliciting systemic information and as an intervention strategy (see below, pp. 87–88). There are many elaborate descriptions of categories of circular questions (Fleuridas et al., 1986; Tomm, 1987) but some brief examples are listed below.

Questions which elicit and explore difference

- Out of the professionals involved with John who is the most worried?
- Who will be the most important person you need to persuade that an in-patient assessment would be useful?
- How do you understand the fact that you have different ideas about what is best for John?

Questions which explore beliefs, behaviour and relationships

- I wonder if you can explain the views that lead you to feel so strongly that in-patent help is not appropriate?
- How is your own experience of being in care influencing your idea about what is best for your daughter?

- What does the social worker do to make you think that she is on your side?
- When you and the teachers are not getting on what is the effect on your relationship with your son?

Questions which help to clarify aims and objectives

- What would be the first sign to you that John had benefited from our help?
- How would you know that things had improved?
- What would your social worker want to be different for your daughter to come home?
- What would have to happen to convince you that this child should not return home?
- In three years time what would you all like to be doing?
- What could you (your son, social worker, partner etc.) do to make a difference?

Questions are designed to elicit new information and are based on the notion that people are more open to ideas which they formulate for themselves than those which are given by others. The family therapist will usually formulate some 'hypotheses' or possible explanations about the referral and the questions will link to these. The aim of this enquiry is not so much to seek out 'the truth' but to come to a mutual understanding and agreement that will help everyone move forward together.

THE ROLE OF THE FAMILY THERAPIST IN FAMILY ASSESSMENT

The assessment of an individual child and the family is a complex process involving many of the multidisciplinary team and is described in detail in chapters 4, 5 and 6. It is very important that all of those involved in the assessment have thought clearly about their roles and what is to be achieved. It is of no service to the family if tensions and differences between staff are apparent in the session.

There have been attempts in the past to categorise particular patterns of family organisation and communication and link them with presenting problems. An example of this would be Minuchin's idea of the 'psychosomatic family' (Minuchin et al., 1978). Further research has challenged the validity of these categorisations (Wood, 1993) and it seems more important to look at the 'fit' between what goes on in the family, its current tasks and the problems presented. Research shows that well functioning families are categorised by a moderate degree of flexibility, clear rules and relationships that are neither too distant nor too close (Olsen, 1986).

ENGAGING WITH FAMILIES

A two-way process

Engaging families is a two-way process. It is very important that the family develops trust in the unit and that enough shared aims are identified to ensure collaboration and teamwork between family and staff. Similarly, the unit staff need to become interested in the family, understand their aims and particular circumstances and develop respect for both family strengths and constraints. Unit staff have to work very hard to avoid unhelpful polarisation in their views and the involvement of a range of staff in this initial process can be helpful. Some of this can be achieved through discussions in meetings and the use of one-way screens and videos.

Curiosity and questioning are an important part of this process. Unit staff have to think about the way in which a particular family might experience the referral and contact with the unit, questioning their own assumptions; for example, apparently honest explanations of restraint procedures may be experienced by families as punishing and abusive. All communications with the unit affect engagement. The messages families take from small things such as a smile of welcome, pleasant surroundings and clear information can go a long way in encouraging a positive working relationship between family and unit.

Culture and power

Another important element is the sensitive consideration of culture and power issues such as those associated with race, gender and class (Goldner, 1985; Messent, 1992; Kingston, 1987; Boyd-Franklin, 1989). Families make rapid assumptions about the capacity of a unit to understand their positions and listen to their voices. Units which have a staff reflecting the cultural diversity of potential referrals will have an advantage. This is especially relevant when there are issues of power to be considered. In a climate of societal racism a black family may easily feel misunderstood by white staff; similarly, middle-class decor and mealtime rituals may make some working-class families feel alienated when they visit. It is dangerous to make stereotypical assumptions but a willingness to continually question, review work and learn from the experience of families will help safeguard good practice.

Beginnings

A major element of the engagement and assessment process is to understand the views and concerns of family members. It can be hard work (Minuchin, 1974). The task is not only to show respect for the whole family structure but also to make individual connections with each family member. Most family therapists will begin by introducing themselves, asking to be introduced to each family member, and pausing for a brief conversation with each on a positive or neutral topic. This contact will need to take account (among other things) of age, developmental level, gender and culture. It is also helpful to elicit everyone's understanding of the meeting and referral, making sure that even the youngest child present is able to make some sense of it. The family therapist tends to avoid a checklist approach to gaining information and will initially track information given by the family. Later in the interview there will be more structure to the questions. The value of this approach is to help families feel relaxed and avoid closing down important areas.

KEY AREAS FOR FAMILY THERAPY ASSESSMENT

Family composition

This involves obtaining information about family members not present as well as those present. It is useful to begin to place the information on a genogram or family tree. This is an easy way of conveying many facts such as ages, and dates of important events, as well as showing family patterns over time. The usefulness of inviting other family members may become apparent. Family members not present can be included by asking what their views would be if they were there.

Family process

As well as taking full account of the content of the discussion, it is important to note who gives which information, what the effect of this is on others, non-verbal elements to communications and repetitive processes such as a child's interruption when a parent looks sad. The process gives important information about how a family operates and may sometimes contrast with the family's account.

Family life-cycle stage

Families have to change their ways of relating to suit their particular life-cycle stage and the development of individuals is to some extent dependent on these changes. This need for change is particularly strong at critical times such as the birth of a first baby or a child starting school. The development of problems can often be related to these points, especially if a family faces multiple life-cycle stages together with other stresses such as illness or unemployment (Carter and McGoldrick, 1989).

Family structure

Families develop structures in the same way as organisations. Sometimes these do not work well and one way of intervening is to help families make changes in these organisational arrangements (Minuchin, 1974). An assessment of current structure will be based to a large part on observations within the session and will take account of boundaries, rules, hierarchy, alliances and coalitions. It will look at triangular relationships within families and especially at the ways in which children can get caught up in parental conflicts through diversions or unhelpful alliances. The lack of effective mechanisms to deal with conflict can be a key element in family interaction. There is a danger that professionals will impose their own idea of what an ideal family should look like and it is important to remember that many different family forms operate successfully.

History of the problem

The family therapist will be more interested in family views about this rather than in obtaining a 'true' picture. There are often differing and strongly held beliefs about the problems and their development. This story or 'narrative' of how the problem developed can itself constrain family solutions. An important intervention can be to help family members to discover alternative ways of thinking about the problem; for example, headaches which the family saw as evidence of physical illness may come to be seen as symptoms of anxiety and fear.

Solutions

It is useful to know what families have already done to address their child's difficulties and what has been helpful or unhelpful. This gives insight into family modes of problem solving, information about approaches that are unlikely to be successful and ideas of what might be needed to make previous approaches more successful. It also serves to remind both family members and professionals of the family's resourcefulness and past successes.

Important beliefs

Beliefs concerning religion and culture are particularly important. For example, attempts to help a psychotic girl from a Muslim family to be more outgoing were countered by the adult family members – they feared that she would become too 'Western'. Sometimes parents may discover the conflict between a firmly held belief and behaviour, such as the father who recognised the clash between his belief that children should be treated kindly, and his aggressive style with his son. This became a focus for further work. Beliefs may be handed down through generations and can lead to the formation of both reparative and replicative scripts (Byng-Hall, 1988). Beliefs about parenting are especially important. Parents may find themselves unable to offer appropriate limits to behaviour as a reaction against their own punitive parenting or be filled with guilt because they see themselves as not measuring up to family ideals of parenthood. Unless these ideas are explored staff may find themselves blocked in by tightly held beliefs and unable to develop collaborative relationships.

Family strengths

Family strengths are crucial for change so their careful assessment is vital. It is easy for all to lose sight of what goes well and what the family has been doing to prevent even worse problems developing. Spending time on this area can help make strengths more visible and more available for the work of the unit.

Hopes for the future

Family members will have most energy for change if they feel that the work is going in a direction relevant to them. Precise descriptions of the most important changes sought by the family will help. Questions such as the ones outlined in the section on the initial meeting can be very helpful. Another question asks, 'If a miracle happened overnight and the problem with John disappeared how would you know?' (Berg, 1991). This gives an opportunity to explore all the effects of the problem on family life and an opening to the process of designing a better future. Asking each family about their three wishes is another way of gaining information. It can be surprising to parents when their children express clear ideas about what they want to happen and important for them all to know that everyone wants change.

Attitude to admission

Family members will have many complex feelings associated with an in-patient admission. It may be the first time that a child has stayed away from home. Nursing staff usually visit the home to learn about particular routines such as bedtimes and mealtimes. This is very important for the child and the parents to know that the unit is not taking over and undermining what they think. It is also helpful to know something about the past relationships with other professionals. If these have been fraught, unit staff may need to put in extra effort to build a collaborative relationship

Other stressors

These may include financial concerns, health worries and housing conditions as well as employment and relationship problems. They affect families and children (Kingston, 1987). It is important to take them into account and to avoid making unrealistic demands on families.

Formulation

The formulation will pull together important information and give ideas about ways of working with the family. These will be discussed with the multi-disciplinary team when a package of help is being designed.

FAMILY WORK, ADMISSION AND THE MULTIDISCIPLINARY TEAM

The more one thinks about multidisciplinary teams the more it seems like a miracle that they work so well. Work with families presents particular challenges including the fact that most staff on the unit will have contact with families and will make interventions. These interventions will range from family therapy to information about a child's week in school. Family members may choose different members of staff in whom to confide and policies relating to confidentiality have to be clear and ensure that important information is shared with those making decisions. Staff will also experience different aspects of family life and will form a variety of views about the family. Staff who are focused mainly on the children may not appreciate the needs of other family members. Similarly, there is a risk that family therapists may not take full account of individual child issues. It is unrealistic to expect that all the work will be co-ordinated perfectly but there needs to be sufficient time for those involved to get together, discuss what is happening and identify differences and problem areas. Occasionally units can find themselves in more serious trouble with some staff always speaking for the parents and others always being critical. This kind of 'stuck' position needs to be addressed as a unit issue (see chapter 14).

It is important not to overload families with different therapies so that they cannot use the time in between to work on issues for themselves. Parents also need sufficient time on the unit to engage in ordinary activities with their child.

Parents on the unit

Views vary on how much time parents should spend on the unit. There is value in families being involved as much as possible in the unit programme so that they can carry on interventions following discharge. In addition there are negative effects on young children of being separated from their parents and an effect on the family balance of having a member away for a time. Arguments for limiting family contact include the impact on the unit routine and the effect on the children who have few visits. A balance has to be achieved but it is very important that when families are on the unit they feel welcomed. They must have sufficient room and privacy to spend time together, access to suitable refreshments, and arrangements must be made to accommodate to the needs of the other children in the family. A welcoming and caring atmosphere is very important when families are asked to work on difficult areas both inside and outside family therapy sessions.

Family/parent meetings

The admission itself generates much work in communicating with parents and families. Decisions have to be made, problems and misunderstandings resolved (Chesson et al., 1997). Some units create special family meetings, separate from family therapy sessions, to tackle these issues. This model increases the number of meetings but decreases the tasks that have to be dealt with in family therapy sessions. More time is available for discussion of underlying issues. There are arguments for these communication meetings being 'adult' only, with information conveyed separately to younger members of the family. Systemic skills and techniques can still be as useful but the emphasis is on information exchange and decision making.

FAMILY THERAPY

Parents feel a great deal of guilt that their child has needed an admission to an in-patient unit. This may be the case even if the underlying problems are mainly biological. The suggestion that they take part in family therapy can reinforce feelings of being criticised. Some units avoid the term 'family therapy' and may use the term 'family meeting' or 'family consultation'. However some parents and families value a space that is called 'therapy' and the opportunity to reflect on themselves and their relationships. Family therapy should be seen as part of the package of help and not a sign of particular pathology.

Family therapy and the busy in-patient unit

There are particular challenges in setting up family therapy sessions on an in-patient unit, some of which resemble the challenges of doing family therapy in a client's own home (Cottrell, 1994). The timetable for the unit may run over or an unexpected event lead to carefully timed sessions being cancelled, postponed or shortened. Shortage of staff may mean that co-workers are unavailable. Family members may come into the room preoccupied with events on the ward. The child who is on the in-patient unit may want to go back to play in their own room. When it is necessary to meet with parents on their own it may not be possible for other staff to watch over the children. It is very important that other unit staff understand the purpose of the sessions, that the work is done as economically as possible and that the unit respects the basic need for time and private space in order for therapeutic work to be achieved. The family therapist must liaise closely with ward staff so they understand why a child is upset or difficult afterwards.

Another issue that sometimes arises is how far therapy sessions should be exempt from unit rules and on-going behavioural programmes. This needs agreement between staff. It is not helpful for sessions to be constrained by having to comply with detailed programmes, but it is important that therapist rules for the session broadly accord with unit rules.

Family members included in therapy sessions

Gone are the days when some family therapists would only consider meeting with 'whole' families. It is important to meet with as many family members as possible on some occasions; this may include grandparents or other relatives. Sometimes, family friends are also crucial participants in family life and parents may want them to be involved. At times it is more appropriate to work with parents alone or other combinations of family members. These decisions must be made with the family and in the best interests of the work. Cultural issues may influence which family members it is most appropriate to see.

Therapist issues

It is not only trained family therapists who will do 'family therapy' but it is likely that someone with training will be more effective and work at a faster pace. Working with families is difficult and it is important that everyone involved in the work has good support and supervision. The use of one-way screens and/or video can greatly enhance this support. Some units set aside a particular time of the week when families are seen so that more staff can learn. Other units have group family therapy supervision sessions. These opportunities lead to greater effectiveness but are always difficult to arrange when some staff work on changing shifts and the children have to be cared for.

Matching therapists to families requires thought. The admission is relatively short and there is not always time to overcome strong feelings about aspects of a therapist. Often women who have been the victims of male violence find it much easier to relate to a woman therapist. It is usually unhelpful for therapists to work with families or problems closely mirroring their own, or with families for whom they play another significant role on the unit.

Aims of therapy

These will vary from family to family but are always connected to the overall aims of the admission. Decisions about the focus of family work are made at the unit planning meeting but work depends on the agreement made with the family. It is influenced by the time scale available and whether or not the therapy can continue following discharge. Family therapy can be very unpredictable and what

Table 8.2 Some common aims for family therapy on an in-patient unit

- To provide an opportunity for all family members to be involved in and support the admission and to provide a forum for them to discuss their feelings and the impact on family life.
- To help improve communication within the family so that they can more easily work on issues for themselves.
- To help families adjust to chronic problems or disabilities.
- To help parents work together more effectively to help their child(ren).
- To help families and family members to discover their strengths and resources and to devise more effective solutions to their problems.
- To help families change their ways of relating to one another.

seems to be a fairly straightforward piece of work can open up new areas of concern and the need for review. The problems presented by children requiring in-patient admission are complex and often have a strong biological substrate. In consequence the focus of therapy may sometimes be on helping the family accommodate to long term difficulties such as psychosis whilst meeting the needs of the whole family. Table 8.2 outlines some of the kinds of work that may be done in family therapy sessions. In view of the short length of admissions and the amount that has to be achieved it is important that realistic aims are set. If families experience some success and positive change they can often go on to continue the work themselves or with the help of other professionals.

Approaches to therapy

There are many different approaches to family therapy and therapists will have their own particular style. However all will pay careful attention to engagement and to reframing the child's problem as one which involves the whole family. This does not imply that the family has 'caused' the problem but rather that the problem always influences the family and the family always influences the problem: the family can contribute to its management and hopefully its resolution. In some situations it might be clear that the problem the child presents has arisen out of family dysfunction and may even be serving a particular function for the family.

Thinking about family structure at different stages in therapy

Although family therapists are used to a certain amount of activity and confusion in therapy sessions there are pieces of work that cannot be achieved without a degree of order in the room.

> Catherine, a 7 year old, was admitted with a variety of phobias and frequent aggressive episodes which it was suspected had some kind of organic basis. The family presented a number of difficulties including much sadness associated with the death of a very involved grandmother. It seemed useful to provide an opportunity for the family members to talk about the effect on them of this loss. Neither parent found it easy to be firm with the four children; they were chaotic and rude to their parents, interrupting when any serious topic was discussed. The initial work was to help the parents to take more charge and create clearer rules about the way that they wanted the children to behave. This was difficult but eventually the sessions were calmer and more containing and it was possible to talk about difficult topics. The family gained from their experience of different relationships and said that this made things easier in other settings.

A hallmark of the structural approach is to work with 'enactments' in the session so that, with the support of the therapist, family members can experiment with different ways of relating. With other families it may be necessary to explore underlying themes before it is possible for them to begin to relate differently together.

Brief solution approaches to therapy

In this approach the therapist helps the family move from a 'problem saturated' description to a more solution focused conversation (Mittlemeier and Freidman, 1993). In the above case example the therapist might begin asking about the times when Catherine was less fearful than usual or when she managed to avoid losing her temper. The family would be encouraged to think about what was different at those times that may have contributed to the 'success'. They might then be asked to explain what would have to happen for them to think that the problem had improved a little more and encourage the family to think of ways of moving things to that point. This approach can increase energy and optimism. With its focus on small achievements, it can give a sense of empowerment and success. It is less useful when emotionally laden issues need to be explored or the families require the therapist to really understand how dreadful things have been. In this situation there may need to be more 'problem talk' before moving towards solutions. If other work on the unit has a similar focus the effectiveness is likely to be intensified.

Strategic approaches

The term 'strategic' encompasses a wide range of approaches which are concerned with repetitive processes between people rather than with overall family organisation (Cade, 1987). They focus on the problems that clients bring, seeing the 'problem as the problem'. Some focus on changing repetitive behavioural sequences and others on changing the way that problems are viewed. Some therapists pay more attention to the way that problems can be part of the system and to the gains and losses that might occur when a problem is diminished. Specially designed tasks are a feature of this approach and help families to make changes in their own context. The non-blaming focus, emphasis on the problem and creative use of story, metaphor and tasks can make them helpful in a children's in-patient setting. The approach attracts criticism for being potentially manipulative. It is important that other unit staff understand the rationale for any task set. In the above example the parents might be asked to set a time every day when the children are encouraged to interrupt as much as they like. The rationale for this would be to diffuse the emotion attached to 'interrupting', reduce the challenge to the parents' wish for the children to express themselves, remove it from the usual battles and hopefully lead the children and parents to view it from another perspective.

Milan/post Milan

What does Milan mean to therapists? These approaches derive their name from the Italian city in which the four originating therapists lived. They emphasise the way in which our beliefs drive our behaviour and relationships. Circular questioning is used to bring forth new information. The therapist (and frequently the team) generate ideas about the way in which the presenting problem may be connected to beliefs, relationships and behaviour. Questions are used to explore these ideas and new ideas formulated in the light of feedback from the questioning process. The hope is that this new information will lead family members into new ways of thinking about and approaching the difficulties (Jones, 1993)

> In the above example, it was revealed that the mother was rather shy and fearful and in the early days of their marriage her husband protected her and gave her confidence. More recently he was working very long hours and she found some comfort in her daughter staying at home. The other children talked about how difficult the current situation was for them and this led the parents to see the cost to the family of the current situation and to think about ways of going forward which also addressed the mother's lack of confidence.

Narrative approaches

This approach might have been taken to explore themes of self-doubt and inferiority that were potent for the parents. Their experience of being poor immigrants and the effects of poverty and failure in education helped shape these themes which their children took up. One of the effects of this was for all the family to rely heavily on each other and be distrustful of people outside the family. By exploration of past successes and the times when people had not let them down it might have been possible to think with the family about what could happen if 'inferiority' was less a part of their life (White, 1989). The technique of 'externalising the problem' is one that can be very useful and carried through to other work on the unit. Its rationale is based on the idea that the problem is often thought of as being the referred child, rather than the problem itself. The effect can be that whole families focus their anger on the child, who becomes increasingly defeated and low in esteem. The therapist begins to talk about the problem as if it is 'outside' the child and to encourage the whole family to join together to defeat it. A child might be asked who in the family is on the side of defeating the problem and promote discussion about the extent to which the child and family have control over the problem and how this control can be increased. For example there are usually times when 'temper' does not get its way or only manages to be boss for a short time. Unit staff can be brought in as allies in the fight and activities such as the drawing of 'anti-temper' posters undertaken. The use of certificates and celebrations of success can intensify the work.

Working with young children in family therapy

There is some work that is better done without small children present, especially when discussions focus on adult relationships. It is, however, important that when young children are present in family therapy sessions they are involved as much as possible. To enable children to feel comfortable the room should be designed with them in mind and contain suitable, age appropriate toys (which do not make too much noise). There should be opportunities through drawing and play for non-verbal communication and therapists should be attentive to this during the session (Dare and Lindsay, 1979). Verbal communications should take account of age and developmental level, and young children will need special care when any aspect of the session is explained. They may need to check that they have their parents' permission if asked about a potentially difficult area and the therapist should facilitate this. Aids such as mobiles can be used to explain ideas about family members being affected by each other, and the use of puppets, imaginary creatures and stories can capture a child's imagination. There is no doubt that if the energy of adults and children can be utilised to overcome difficulties more progress can be made than if left to adults. The work of Michael White and David Epston (White, 1984; Epston, 1986) gives useful ideas for engaging young children in working towards change. Young children cannot manage long sessions and it is better to end them before they, the therapists or parents disintegrate.

Ethical issues

As in all work which involves children the needs of the children are paramount and accepted child protection procedures must be followed if the family therapist becomes sufficiently concerned about anything that is said or done in sessions. Issues of confidentiality need to be well worked out and explained. For example, what will happen if one parent reveals information that they wish kept secret from the other parent? There are often concerns about how much of the detail of information given in sessions will be shared with other in-patient staff or other outside professionals involved with the family. Videos, screens and teams should be carefully explained and permission to video should be sought in writing as well as through a verbal agreement. Families should be given every opportunity to say no to the use of video without this jeopardising the help offered. They should also be clear about how the video will be used and stored and have opportunities to ask for video taping to cease.

Working within a statutory framework

Sometimes families will have children on the child protection register or be admitted whilst assessments are being made about the viability of their care. The family therapist will need to be clear about the nature of the work being done. Is it assessment or therapy, and whose aims are driving the work? Whilst families may not see the need for therapy themselves they may be motivated by the desire to convince social workers that they can manage. The content of reports should wherever possible be shared with the family and be written in a clear, jargon free fashion which clearly addresses the questions being asked.

THINKING ABOUT DISCHARGE

How long family therapy continues will depend on the work being done and the accessibility of the family to the unit. It is clearly not practical for in-patient units to carry on therapy for a considerable period following discharge but the family therapist can have an important role to play in the transition from unit to community care (see chapter 7). Space can be made available within sessions to discuss the effects of the transition on individuals and family relationships and to explore the availability and use of community resources. It is not uncommon for difficulties to become worse during this period and families may need help in holding on to their optimism and all that has been learned and achieved during the admission. The family therapist may consult the family about what they have learned, perhaps asking, 'If I were to meet another family with similar problems, what have you learned from your experience that would be helpful to them and me?' Families also need a space to acknowledge disappointment about what has not been achieved, to set goals for the future and predict setbacks and how they will deal with them. It can be useful for families to have tangible evidence of the work they have done and a video of this review could be given to them. Children (and adults) appreciate certificates and 'awards' for what has been achieved and some units routinely put together a book of information about the child's stay with them. Letters can also be used over this transition (White and Epston, 1990). They can be written to the whole family and work best when they reflect on what has come up in therapy and highlight strengths and achievements. It is easy for depression and hopelessness to creep in when something small goes wrong.

SUMMARY OF THE ROLE OF FAMILY THERAPY IN IN-PATIENT SETTINGS

Family therapy can have an important role to play alongside a range of treatment interventions. Although systems theory provides the main theoretical framework, interventions are often multilayered and involve ideas and skills from other frameworks such as child development. The length of admission and complexity of problems may well limit what can realistically be achieved but in any case a systemic approach and family therapy skills can be used to facilitate engagement with families, maximise their involvement on the ward, and help them to move forward. The family therapist will need to have access to a range of approaches and to respect and work alongside other professionals. Their work will not be limited to families but will include couples, groups, individuals and professional and network meetings. Their approach enables them to take a broad focus which can be especially valuable in complex situations. However family therapy has limitations and the most useful family therapist will be the one who acknowledges these and continues to work with colleagues to develop new and better ways of helping these very troubled families.

REFERENCES

Berg, I.K. (1991) *Family preservation: a brief therapy workbook*. London: BT Press.

Boyd-Frankin, N. (1989) *Black families in therapy: a multi-systems approach*. New York: Guilford Press.

Brown, J. (1991) Family involvement in the residential treatment of children: a systemic perspective. *Australian and New Zealand Journal of Family Therapy 12*, 17–22.

Burnham, J. (1986) *Family therapy*. London: Tavistock.

Byng-Hall, J. (1988) Scripts and legends in families and family therapy. *Family Process 27*, 167–179.

Cade, B. (1987) Brief and strategic approaches to therapy: a commentary. *Australian and New Zealand Journal of Family Therapy 8*, 37–44.

Carter, B. and McGoldrick, M. (eds) (1989) *The changing family life cycle: a framework for family therapy* 2nd edn. New York: Allyn and Baker.

Chesson, R., Harding, L., Hart, C. and O'Loughlin, V. (1997) Do parents and children have common perceptions of admission, treatment and outcome in a child psychiatric unit? *Clinical Child Psychology and Psychiatry 2*, 257–270.

Cottrell, D. (1994) Family therapy in the home. *Journal of Family Therapy 16*, 189–198.

Crowther, C., Dare, C. and Wilson, J. (1990) Why should we talk to you? You'll only tell the court: on being an informer and family therapist. *Journal of Family Therapy 13*, 105–123.

Dare, J., Goldberg, D., and Walinets, R. (1990) What is the question you need to answer? How consultation can prevent professional systems immobilising families. *Journal of Family Therapy 12*, 355–366.

Didyk, B., French, G., Gerbman, C., Manson, N. and O'Neill, I. (1989) Admitting whole families: an alternative to residential care. *Canadian Journal of Psychiatry 34*, 694–699.

Epston, D. (1986) Night watching: an approach to night fears. *Dulwich Centre Review* 28–39.

Fleuridas, C., Nelson, T. and Rosenthal, D. (1986) The evolution of circular questioning: training family therapists. *Journal of Marital and Family Therapy 12*, 113–128.

Garmezy, N. and Masten, A.. (1994) Chronic adversities. In Rutter, M., Hersov, L. and Taylor E. (eds) *Child and adolescent psychiatry: modern approaches*, Oxford: Blackwell, pp. 191–208.

Goldenberg, D. and Goldenberg, H. (1996) *Family therapy: an overview* 4th edn. Pacific Grove: Brookes/Cole.

Goldner, V. (1985) Feminism and family therapy. *Family Process 24*, 31–48.

Harbin, H. (1982) Family treatment of the psychiatric in-patient. In Harbin, H. (ed.) *The psychiatric hospital and the family*. Lancaster: Mand P Press, pp. 3–25.

Howlin, P. and Rutter, M. (1987) *Treatment of autistic children*. Chichester: John Wiley.

Jones, E. (1993) *Family systems therapy: development in Milan Systemic therapy*. Chichester: John Wiley.

Kazdin, A.E., Esveldt-Dawson, K. and Unis, A.S. (1987) Effects of parent management training and problem solving skills training combined in the treatment of antisocial child behaviour. *Journal of the American Academy of Child and Adolescent Psychiatry, 26*, 416–424.

Kingston, P. (1987) Family therapy, power and responsibility for change. In Walrond-Skinner, S. (ed) *Ethical issues in family therapy*. London: Routledge, pp. 84–96.

Messent, P. (1992) Working with Bangladeshi families in the east end of London. *Journal of Family Therapy 14*, 287–304.

Minuchin, S. (1974) *Families and family therapy*. London: Tavistock.

Minuchin, S., Rosman, B. and Baker, L.(1978) *Psychosomatic families: anorexia nervosa in context*. Cambridge, MA: Harvard University Press.

Mittlelmeier, C. and Freidman, S. (1993) Towards a mutual understanding: constructing solutions with families. In Freidman, S. (ed.) *The new language of change*. New York: Guilford Press, pp. 158–184.

Olsen, D. (1986) Circumplex model vii validation model and FACES iii. *Family Process* 25: 337–351.

Quinton, D. and Rutter, M. (1984) Parents with children in care: 1. Current circumstances and parents; 2. Intergenerational continuities. *Journal of Child Psychology and Psychiatry 25*, 211–231.

Reder, P. and Kraemer, S. (1980) Dynamic aspects of professional collaboration in child guidance referral. *Journal of Adolescence 3*, 165–173.

Russell, G., Szmuckler, G., Dare, C, and Eisler, I. (1987) An evaluation of family therapy in anorexia nervosa and bulimia nervosa. *Archives of General Psychiatry 44*, 1047–1056.

Selvini Palazzoli, M., Boscolo, L., Cecchin, G. and Prata, G. (1980) The problem of the referring person. *Journal of Marital and Family Therapy 6*, 3–12.

Tomm, K. (1987) Interventive interviewing part 2: reflexive questioning as a means to enable self healing. *Family Process 26*, 167–183.

Webster-Stratton, C. (1991) Annotation: strategies for helping families with conduct disordered children. *Journal of Child Psychology and Psychiatry 32*, 1047–1062.

White, M. (1984) Pseudo-encopresis: from avalanche to victory. *Family Systems Medicine 2*, 115–124.

White, M. (1989) *Selected papers*. Adelaide: Dulwich Centre publications.

White, M. and Epston, D. (1990) *Narrative means to therapeutic ends*. New York: Norton.

Wood, B. (1993) Beyond the 'psychosomatic family': a biobehavioural model of pediatric illness. *Family Process 32*, 261–278.

9 The ward as a therapeutic agent

Jonathan Green and Maureen Burke

Creating a milieu treatment adapted to the often extreme and varied needs of children within residential psychiatric care is an exciting and major challenge. Any unit's response to this challenge will be influenced by a philosophy of treatment and prevailing social and economic conditions, but it should now also be a matter of empirical testing rather than ideology as to what forms of milieu provide the best and most economical treatment for different kinds of problems. This chapter reviews a variety of solutions to the task of milieu care and important themes that have emerged in practice. It treats the in-patient environment as a treatment modality in its own right; looking at the elements that make up the treatment and the mode through which they may act. Other chapters address the efficacy of this treatment (chapter 27) and its potential unwanted effects (chapter 18). As a treatment modality it has been subjected to little empirical research (see chapter 27): milieu programmes in the future will need to address these empirical issues explicitly and research is greatly needed into the dimensions of care best suited for different disorders.

RESEARCH MODELS

There has been virtually no systematic research into the child psychiatry milieu. In adult psychiatry, by contrast, Moos and colleagues (Moos 1974) have developed sociometric instruments to measure the social climate of the psychiatric ward. The 'Ward Atmosphere Scale' (WAS) addresses three aspects of ward functioning. A *'relationship'* dimension contains scales relating to characteristics of staff involvement, support and spontaneity. A *'treatment programme'* dimension evaluates a ward's treatment style in relation to issues such as emotional expressiveness, orientation towards patients' practical or personal problems and patient autonomy. An *'administrative or system structure'* dimension evaluates characteristic approaches to order and organisation, clarity of programming, and staff control. Using such dimensions in a study of 144 treatment programmes in the USA (Price and Moos 1977), Moos developed a taxonomy of in-patient treatment environments (Table 9.1). Milieu style has been associated with outcome (Moos, Shelton and Petty, 1973), and different WAS atmospheres have been shown to benefit psychotic and non-psychotic patients (Friis 1986), in work that echoes the three UK hospitals studies of Wing and Brown (1970). The WAS has been adapted for use in an adolescent setting (Steiner et al. 1991) and a newer instrument, based on the same sub-scales, has been specifically developed for children's units and is in the process of validation (Green and Imrie, unpublished).

Colton (1988) studied the extent of child or institutional orientation in children's residential (but not psychiatric) environments. His 'index of child management' builds on King et al. (1971), in identifying rigidity of routine, homogeneity of treatment, depersonalisation and social distance between staff and children as characteristics of institutionalised care (Goffman 1961). He also measured the quality of community involvement, physical environment and staff control. On all these dimensions residential children's homes scored extremely poorly compared to a comparison group of foster homes. While some of these differences are confounded by choice of items (such as the presence of 'exit' signs being inevitable accompaniments to institutional environments), this work was important and does provide concepts and instruments with which to evaluate the health of a ward environment.

Work such as Colton's has certainly fuelled a recent bias against residential treatments (chapter 3, this volume). However as Bettelheim points out (1995, chapter 1.1), it is not necessarily institutional environments per se that are at fault but the *kind* of institution. The heterogeneity of treatment environments found by Price and Moos supports the view that no over-generalisations about therapeutic milieus should be made.

Table 9.1 A taxonomy of ward treatment environments

- The *therapeutic community orientation* emphasises patient involvement in relationships, open expression of feeling and concern with patients' personal problems, but low emphasis on 'rules', programme planning and goals.

- *Relationship orientated programmes* emphasise interpersonal relationships and programme clarity, but less on specific therapy programming.

- *Action orientated programmes* emphasise early patient autonomy, staff control and early discharge; attempting to minimise 'secondary gain' from hospitalisation.

- *Insight orientated programmes* have less emphasis on milieu relationships and more on individual insight orientated therapeutic work.

- *Control orientated programmes* show little emphasis on relationships or programming and high emphasis on ward order, organisation and staff control. This cluster, representing a third of programmes in the sample, resembles the 'total institution' described by Goffman (1961) and later investigated in a child context by King et al. (1971) and Colton (1988).

- *Disturbed behaviour programmes* emphasise programme clarity and patient expressivity. This cluster is composed primarily of programmes designed to handle acutely disturbed patients on admission wards.

Source: Moos et al. 1973

Table 9.2 Key dimensions on which to investigate the milieu

- Characteristics of interpersonal relationships fostered.

- Characteristics of therapeutic programme.

- Child centeredness versus institutional centeredness.

- Staff control versus permissiveness.

- Quality of physical environment.

Source: adapted from Moos et al. (1900) and Cotton (1993).

CLINICAL MODELS

Psychodynamic

Although not strictly a child psychiatry setting, the example of Bruno Bettelheim's Orthogenic School in Chicago remains deeply attractive to many workers within children's units. This is hardly surprising. Bettelheim elevated the role of the therapeutic milieu to an almost heroic agent of profound contact with children's distress and radical therapeutic change. His moving clinical accounts make compelling reading, and the involvement of the unit's staff was intense. His model has remained a powerful influence up till the present, despite the fact that many of the details of his milieu are best appreciated in their historical context and despite the serious challenges to both the methods and the original claims of their effectiveness that have emerged since Bettelheim's death (Sutton 1996). Bettelheim described a 'total institution' of care, whose effect is quite purposefully to remove the child from other influences. Although often empathic towards parental perspectives and difficulties, the implicit message of his practice was to remove the child from the harmful influence of parents – who were not allowed to enter the residential part of the Orthogenic School (Bettelheim 1955). Visits home early in admission were not allowed and parental contact was limited to meetings in a reception area. Parental care was completely taken over by the staff and stays were relatively long (mean of three years in one report). The child's psychopathology was seen in psychoanalytic terms and expected to show gradual change. On the one hand the therapeutic programme could be seen as highly child orientated: unit rules and staff reactions were individualised to the child and staff were often very permissive with behaviour. On the other hand, the principles by which the milieu operated were implicit rather than explicitly made available to the children, and the staff's parental role could foster considerable dependency. There was relatively little emphasis on the potential therapeutic effects of the peer culture. In the UK a similar philosophy has underpinned the 'planned environment therapies' within therapeutic schools and communities (McCleod et al. 1996; Dockar Drysdale 1968).

Eclectic

More recent therapeutic formulations of the milieu within a hospital environment incorporate much of the passionate structure of Bettelheim's milieu but with less emphasis on psychoanalytic stage development and much more emphasis on empathy, communication and behavioural control. Cotton's account of a child psychiatry unit at New England Memorial Hospital is a classic of this kind (Cotton 1993). She describes an active treatment programme based around current interactions and explicit ward rules and structure. The concurrent focus on warm rapport, active communication and staff control embodies many current concepts of good parenting and can provide a persuasive model for many therapeutically orientated units. There is also emphasis placed on the peer context and culture, reminiscent of adult therapeutic communities and planned environment therapies in child care (Kennard 1983). The relentless level of zest energy and high expectations might prove a little overwhelming for fragile children (and perhaps staff). This milieu has the many of the characteristics that Friis (1986) identifies from WAS studies as optimal for non-psychotic disorders.

Systemic

Much recent theory takes a more open systems approach to unit organisation. Not only do staff need to devote themselves to maintaining the internal milieu of the ward, they also need to be aware of their position in interaction with wider systems, including family and other agencies. Increasingly the milieu is seen as a more transitory period within a wider developmental context. This 'Janus-faced' position (Green 1992, 1993) greatly increases the complexity and difficulty of the task for staff. It has led to sophisticated developments in referral and admission practice and relationship with parents (chapters 3 and 8). Woolston (1989) uses a systems view to re-conceptualise the role of the in-patient milieu; locating it in a bridging role mediating child, family and other institutional interactions. The child's psychopathology is seen transactionally as lying in the lack of 'fit' between a child's capacity and the expectations and realities of the environment: the ward's role is to work to improve that goodness of fit. Parents participate in all aspects of the child's hospitalisation, from practical care to implementing treatments, attending for at least two days a week. Other authors have described a family systems orientation to in-patient care (Blotcky et al. 1983, 1987; Hildebrand et al. 1981; Jenkins and Loader 1984).

These systemic orientations can seem to reduce the prominence given to the nurturing or parental substitute role of the ward staff. However, unless there is a full family residential treatment, a systemic approach that emphasises the wider context of in-patient care cannot change the reality that when a child is admitted a structural change occurs which inevitably means that the staff to some degree take on a quasi parenting role (Green 1992). Issues relating to ward milieu thus still remain.

Brief hospitalisation

A powerful recent development, seen especially in the USA, is the move towards brief hospitalisation (Harper 1989; Nurcombe 1989). In these developments, explicitly the result of financial necessity as much as professional conviction (Nurcombe 1989), the focus is on stabilisation and the 'minimum necessary change' needed before discharge. Explicit goals for behavioural change (Nurcombe 1989) or the 'focal problem' (Harper 1989) are identified and time constraints for treatment laid out. With their emphasis on symptom stabilisation and early discharge, these units have the characteristics of the 'action orientated' milieu described in Price and Moos (1977). Here there is likely to be less emphasis on the interpersonal relationships of staff and children, but a high emphasis on the clarity of programming, independence and the reduction of symptoms. There are many, particularly in the United States, who see in-patient child psychiatry as becoming increasingly focused on such a model of diagnostic assessment and containment (Jemerin and Philips 1988; Perry 1989). This really dispenses with the notion of the ward environment as a therapeutic agent and suggests a return of hospital treatment to the role of containment and crisis intervention that characterised early developments (chapter 3, this volume; Chisholm 1996).

Current data in the UK (chapter 2) suggests that this stabilisation and containment model has not yet made a significant appearance in this country. Most units see themselves as eclectic, with an assessment and a medium term treatment role. Only one unit in the country described itself as having an exclusively psychoanalytic orientation.

THE ELEMENTS OF MILIEU TREATMENT

The physical environment

Much information on the effect of the physical environment on psychological state and behaviour is relatively inaccessible to health professionals; however the nature of the physical environment is a critical aspect of milieu care. Whitehead et al. (1984) found that re-design of an adult psychiatric ward encouraging social interaction around ward activities correlated with reduced psychopathology. Corey et al. (1986) used the Ward Atmosphere Scale to show improvements in the therapeutic culture after refurbishment of an in-patient unit. When budgets for 'ward decoration', refurbishment or 'fixtures and fittings' are traditionally non-clinical costs, it can be tough to persuade managers that the physical environment of a psychiatry ward is a treatment cost *equivalent* to that of drugs or medical equipment.

Fortunate is the unit that has purpose built space. Most will have a compromise conversion of wards originally designed for different purposes. Cotton and Geraty (1984) described the process of converting a conventional paediatric ward into a child psychiatry milieu and give useful theoretical and practical guidance – as they say, 'Design details articulate treatment goals'.

Therapeutic space design

'Therapeutic space design' personalises space – in contrast to the homogenous and impersonal 'institution' (Colton 1988). It can promote engagement and a sense of safety as children first enter the environment with heightened awareness. Bettelheim (1955) describes how his patients 'actually hug the walls; they like to sit or lie on the floor. It is as if they press against the wall or the floor in order to gain support in withstanding the stresses of life. Only later does the counsellor's lap become their refuge.' When they feel more at home, there are many ways in which design can help them make use of the space according to their needs. Wards should be split into age-related spaces with appropriate furniture. Cotton (1993) suggests personalised bulletin boards while Cotton and Geraty (1984) and Bettelheim (1955) advise that children should contribute to design planning. Rotating decorations can represent the single or communal efforts of the particular group of patients at any one time.

Many disturbed children have problems with psychological boundaries; the distinction between private and public, intrapsychic and overt behaviour, what belongs to them psychologically and what to the environment. A poorly planned milieu can reinforce these confusions while a well-planned space can model psychological boundaries and a sense of self. Well-constructed environments will contain an understandable gradation between public spaces, such as dining areas, kitchen and play areas, and private spaces, such as bedrooms, bathroom and quiet room. Provision of privacy is crucial, and within the limits of safety there can be rules governing certain thresholds, for instance knocking and asking permission to enter bedrooms. Gradations can be reinforced by furnishings and colour. The use of carpets, non-institutional colour schemes and wallpaper is crucial. Door jambs can be painted to emphasise important transitions in the space; painted signs label rooms in a non-institutional way (Arts for Health 1989).

Long corridors with fire doors and exits can encourage a 'racetrack' environment for physically active children; they make control by staff difficult. Simple physical adjustments can make a big difference to the children's behaviour. We had a problem where children were getting up onto our (flat) roof, with all the dangerousness and perverse excitement that it can bring for some children. Observation of the typical route that the children used and a strategically placed piece of wood completely prevented this behaviour. Our play area and play apparatus is designed around the principle that many children need frequent physical release and exciting muscular activity. At other times they need to have provision for co-operative and socialising play and competitive games. We have therefore swings, a place for 'assault course' type activities, a basketball net and space for team games.

Toys and other play materials can be subject to a kind of 'ward entropy' which results in an undifferentiated mass of damaged articles. Active storage and tidying of materials is therefore crucial. Cotton describes generic toy boxes containing basic toys that are always available to children, lockable toy cabinets containing activities that need more supervision, a 'visiting time' box with family materials, a 'personal time' box with toys for intimate play and a 'fantasy trunk' for dramatic play containing dressing up clothes etc. She also advocates posters, quotations, children's productions and other material in the public spaces, to emphasise the unit's values and to convey hope and pride in progress.

Boundaries and safety

Children will be acutely aware of the external as well as internal boundaries of the unit space. Depending on their life experience they may feel either imprisoned and unable to get out or vulnerable that intruders could get in. Staff concern will be for safe containment of children as well as the danger of intruders (particularly at night). Bettelheim used doors that would open from the inside but were locked from the outside. He felt that children will often need to experiment with 'physical closeness and emancipated distance' and if the internal boundaries of the unit allow distancing and privacy then it is less likely that the child would need to breach the external boundaries of the unit by absconding. Locked environments cause unease in relation to the Children Act but it will be important to generate sensible case law so that the in-patient environment is safe and containable (see chapter 29). Cotton advocates the need to be able to 'lock down' the unit at certain times with certain groups of children. Each unit will need to make its own physical solution that reflects a balance of safety and openness.

Care for the fabric

The physical fabric is a feature that will remain permanent through changes in staff and patient group. A milieu that is well organised, physically resilient, aesthetically pleasing and protected will allow trust and relaxation for both staff and children. The fabric needs care and attention and repair at all levels. All materials should be resilient and of the highest quality. For many children, making imaginative use of their environment will involve attacking and trying to damage it and the physical environment needs to be able to show resilience in the face of attacks if child's anxiety and lack of trust is not to be further increased.

For the children, routine care of their private and communal spaces can help counteract a sense of institutionalisation and physical entropy. Care of the environment after a child has assaulted it, when timed correctly, can be reparative. Specific staff time needs to be set aside for care, renewal and planning of the environment and a recurrent budget *must* be negotiated with managers to fund the inevitable structural repairs and renewal that will be necessary. Like staff, the environment takes a battering.

The staff

Milieu treatment is primarily delivered through relationships between children and staff. The whole weight of organisation, planning, training and support is channelled to foster the quality of these staff/child relationships and the specific treatment programmes that are mediated through them. The bridge from the treatment plan to its enactment in practice has to be constantly maintained. Moreover the modern ward milieu is a complex arena, where basic milieu care intersects with many other tasks (Table 9.3). Milieu staff experience intensity, teamwork, and exposure in equal measure; their work is carried out in the glare of exposure to children and other staff. This can make for wild oscillations between the exhilaration of success and confidence, and potential embarrassment, humiliation and public disarray. Add to this the many instantaneous decisions that they have to make concerning their reactions to the children – to know when firmness is necessary and when empathy is required; which situations are likely to escalate and which can be left; to integrate the needs of the group with those of the individual; to handle the powerful feelings that children can evoke in them – these are personal and professional demands of the highest order. The staff need to feel that their efforts and mistakes are understood, that fears for their own safety are often justified and that there is an atmosphere of support around them from the other staff.

The staffing ingredients necessary to deliver such milieu care are succinctly summarised by Cotton (1993), 'a sufficient *quantity* of people selected for certain *qualities*, *trained* to deliver therapeutic management, and arranged in an *organisational* structure'.

Staff numbers

Milieu treatment is a labour intensive activity and attempts to operate with too few staff are a recipe for stress, burn out and institutional decay. For ward staff, the

Table 9.3 Typical range of tasks that milieu staff undertake

- Basic care to the children: insuring basic safety, nutrition, comfort and cleanliness.
- Maintenance of the space and time organisation of the unit: activity schedules, programmes etc.
- Structured nursing and psychiatric assessments for individual children, such as autism rating scales, behaviour rating scales and observations of socialisation.
- Individual counselling relationships with specific children.
- Maintaining a healthy group dynamics amongst the patients through active early interventions and group work.
- Delivering specific psychological treatments such as CBT or anxiety management.
- Delivering and monitoring medications.
- Taking part in team meetings or case conferences and presenting assessments.
- Managing interactions with families at visiting times, including informal but intense communications from distraught or angry parents.
- Maintaining the physical organisation and tidiness of the environment.

Table 9.4 Patient factors needing higher shift ratios

- Greater number of patients

- Broader range of ages

- Larger spans of levels of developmental functioning and diagnosis (e.g. combining cognitively impaired or psychotic children with brighter, behaviourally disordered children)

- Greater severity and pervasiveness of impairments

- More severe lethality of symptoms, such as suicidality, aggressiveness, sexualisation

- Lack of family or support systems outside the hospital

- Poor therapeutic alliance (e.g. families with statutory orders or referred from Courts)

- Frequent staff turnover

- Shorter lengths of stay (more acute admissions and an inability to develop routines and relationships)

Source: Cotton 1993

important variable is the actual staff present during a shift (and with sickness and other absence this may differ substantially from the theoretical complement). There has been no standard or guidance within the UK on staff numbers within psychiatric units, but explicit guidance has been formulated in the USA. The American Academy of Child and Adolescent Psychiatry (1990) recommends shift ratios of 1:3 for times of basic observation and maintenance of safety, 1:2 or 4:6 for active milieu therapy and 1:6 as a minimum for night-time. Other American authors recommend staff/patient ratios of at least a 1:2 for active milieu therapy (Dalton and Foreman 1992), 2:5 during mealtimes (Pines et al. 1985), 4:6 during active therapeutic programming times (Marsden et al. 1970), and 1:4 during less intense occupational activities (Rinsley 1980). Cotton describes a ratio of five or six staff to twelve patients during the daytime shift, four or five staff for the evening shifts and three or four staff at weekends with fewer patients (Cotton 1993). She suggests critical variables creating higher dependency and staffing need (Table 9.4).

Staff numbers in the wider team also need to be considered. The American Academy of Child and Adolescent Psychiatry (1990) recommends five hours per week child psychiatrist time for each patient, to include medical management, staff contact, conferences etc. At least one social worker for every ten patients is suggested, with responsibilities for family assessments, social assessment, agency contact and team activities, including family therapy. The presence of at least one psychologist in the team is taken for granted. Steiner et al. (1991) suggest a formula for the time commitment of a medical director of 0.06 WTE (whole time equivalent) per bed, including eight to ten hours per week meeting time, two hours a week for medical staff supervision and a further two hours a week administration. In the UK, staffing levels reported in our survey (chapter 2) are far below this level. Only two units in the UK currently report having social workers at all and only two-thirds have any psychologist sessions. The lack of central guidance in the UK on staffing norms needs urgent attention.

Skill mix and professional qualities

Milieu staffing in the UK has been primarily a nursing task, drawing from both general children's nursing and Registered Mental Nurse (RMN) training, to some extent depending on where the unit is based (Paice 1996). The strong move recently is for RMN qualification to be the primary requirement (Hinks et al. 1988) but Registered Children's Nurse (RCN) or double qualified nurses are likely to remain valuable, particularly in paediatrically orientated settings. This contrasts with the tradition in the United States where there is a much greater emphasis on non-nursing graduate employees, often psychology students on interim placements of one or two years (Ney and Mulhivill 1989, Cotton 1993). Perhaps too little interest is taken in the UK in this possibility. Senior staff and culture carriers within the milieu should be nursing staff, but a number of other young graduate staff from other disciplines could be employed in primary care roles.

Qualities looked for in psychiatric nurses working in the milieu have often reflected a view of their role as intuitive; included are warm-hearted, caring, personal stability, capacity to tolerate anxiety, and a sense of humour (Brown et al. 1974). The modern milieu demands sophisticated skills in addition to these, at least in the senior staff. More recently Cotton (1993) emphasised staff qualities of respect and empathy, self-reflection and self-awareness, energy, resilience, co-operation, intellectual curiosity, and playfulness.

THE THERAPEUTIC PROCESS

Ward culture

A coherent culture – 'like a well-conducted orchestra' – is strongly related to therapeutic outcome (Pfeiffer and Strelecki 1991) but hard to analyse. Successful milieux are said to show: 'responsiveness and flexibility in an environment of clear organisation and structure' (Swartz et al. 1988), 'involvement and validation along with containment and structure' (Gunderson 1978), 'corrective relationships along with internalisation of external controls and the capacity to resolve conflict' (Fineberg et al. 1980). Other factors are likely to be staff morale, consistency, good communication and self-confidence. A milieu has above all to remain functionally intact in the face of staff and patient turnover, disruption and conflict, and assaults from the patients, individually and as a group. Self-confidence will communicate itself to the children and increase their ability to trust. The instilling of hope is one of the first consequences of successful therapy and the milieu is no exception.

At a wider level the therapeutic milieu will embody cultural and moral, as well as professional beliefs about how disturbance in children should be approached. This can be graphically seen in their historical development (chapter 3). As Kennard notes, it is no accident that there were powerful religious impulses behind the early ideas of therapeutic residential child care and planned environment therapy, as well as various forms of therapeutic community development (Kennard 1982). However, history is replete with examples of cultures that have grown too strong and rigid and have lost a responsiveness to patients: at this point the environment of the milieu can rapidly become dangerous (Kennard 1982). Perhaps the best safeguard is to establish a culture that is committed and coherent but open to new ideas, and in particular to scientific enquiry.

Relationships

A constant theme since the early days of moral treatment has been that the child needs a milieu which promotes relationships and is responsive and empathic. This kind of empathy and responsiveness can only come from individuals, who must be able to act within that relationship as authentic individuals. The milieu with an over-emphasis on programmes and organisation will lose this capacity for individual relating. Much of the administrative structure of the milieu should be directed towards allowing the individual staff to relate authentically within a consistent treatment programme and milieu philosophy. All the evidence points to the fact that such relationships are made easier when there are good levels of staff/patient ratio, small groups (Bailine *et al.* 1977), and when a key worker or primary care taker system is used (Kutchinski 1977).

The provision of an adapted care which is responsive and empathic and which can remain so, more or less, in the face of difficulties, is likely to have the same beneficial effect as it would do in individual therapy. The child will then be able to take the risk of dropping defences and communicating distress. The subjective state of very many disturbed children is desperate loneliness. Their escalating behaviour is often a way of triggering responses that will relieve tension and populate the subjective space of the child, diffuse loneliness and perhaps find containment. The child knows, with a sense of relief and hope, when he is somehow being *recognised*, responded to and held by another person or the environment. 'Children experience support when they sense staff's genuine interest in their ideas, attitudes and perceptions. But the child's sensitivities are often hidden beneath anger, sadness and confusion' (Redl and Wineman 1951). When responses from staff deepen in this way the child will feel supported and less defensive. This level of communication can only be achieved when staff are emotionally available.

In a responsive environment many children, particularly those whose main problem has been difficulties in interpersonal care, will develop powerful attachments to the ward and to individuals within it. Severely disturbed children may 'regress' behaviourally or show exaggerated dependency. Should the in-patient milieu be encouraging such developments? Historically, there has been a tradition within residential care to allow and encourage such regression at the service of psychological growth and this became a common feature of a number of therapeutic communities, as well as the Orthogenic School. The practice has also been seriously abused on occasion as a means of gaining perverted control over children. As they begin to trust the ward, children with complex, disturbed behaviour will often signal unresolved and contradictory patterns around primary attachments and dependency and these will reflect powerful and early unmet needs. In the milieu and in the child's psychological therapy, staff do have the opportunity of meeting these needs and giving the child a precious psychological experience. This also promotes a relationship that allows work on the development of more adaptive behaviours. But the idea that children can 'regress to the beginning and start again' is theoretically naive. We advocate a milieu culture that is sensitive but basically reality orientated. The message from staff should be of respect for the universal need for dependency; being with the child and meeting the needs of this kind when they arise. Important therapeutic work can be done at these times on basic attachments and then in joining with the child in working towards the return back to age appropriate skills when possible. High dependency regressive behaviour can be encouraged to emerge in the more intimate and 'private' spaces on the ward (for instance the child's bedroom), and in the company of key workers or other identified staff, so that the 'public' space of the ward is preserved for the adaptive efforts of the rest of the group. It can be a fine judgement as to when to understand and respond to a child's behaviours as communications of this kind and when to see them as maladaptive behaviours to be reduced. Much team discussion and supervision will inevitably focus on issues of this sort, which also need to be addressed in therapeutic planning.

This general environment of adapted care provided by the milieu must be capable of modification in order to meet the special needs of particular children and disorders. Many of these modifications are described in Part V of this volume. Strategies of modified care are informed by specific assessments. The milieu is well placed both clinically and in research to investigate and understand how specific disorders can impact on the capacity of children to form relationships and attachments. Children with neuropsychiatric disorder, attachment disorder or Pervasive Developmental Disorder (see chapters 22, 23, 25) may have particular needs for understanding. The ward is a place where techniques of specialised care in extreme situations can be usefully developed and researched.

Structuring space and time

Recent in-patient programmes have tended towards increased levels of structure. In part this is a need to structure time over a short admission for maximum benefit. It also tends to reduce the potential for group chaos, emotional expressiveness and regression. In other words it encourages a culture of reality orientation and relative control ('action orientated' and 'disturbed behaviour' programmes, in Moos's taxonomy). The structures of ordinary child care are here seen as necessary to reduce arousal and anxiety, as well as improving group morale and motivation. However, an over-intrusive structure can reduce child orientation. Rigid timetables are usually seen as characteristics of institutions and a negative effect of residential care (Moos's 'institutional' programmes; see Colton 1988). There is a balance to be struck here. It is a critical part of child care to structure space and time and this can be particularly important for children who are disorganised and disturbed. We advocate predictable structures regarding getting up, going to bed, chores, mealtimes, school times etc., as a structure to the day. 'Staff provide an environment where choices are clear and the day follows a predictable pattern. A sense of order and stability is critical for children, especially if their home life has been chaotic' (Delaney 1992). However, a prime goal should be to respond to the individual child's needs and this may on occasion mean he is treated differently from others. Most children can understand this as long as there is staff consistency. This is an area where clarity of staff leadership and communication is very important. A scheduled day, focused around individual as well as group needs, will avoid overstimulation on one hand and isolation on the other. Structure enhances the sense of community for the children. The unit should develop systems of supervision that can balance keeping watch on the children and being unobtrusive. In a relaxed atmosphere staff can engage in activities whilst remaining vigilant to the children's whereabouts.

In meeting the more personal basic needs of children staff can develop close relationships and encourage the development of trust. Mealtimes often elicit powerful issues related to nurturing (Delaney 1992). Younger children respond particularly well to some kind of reward system around the issue of eating together, i.e. finishing your meal, good behaviour, star charts.

Containment and behavioural change

The great majority of UK in-patient units practise some form of systematic behavioural management, such as time out, seclusion, withdrawal or restraint (see chapter 2). Detailed discussion of cognitive behavioural methods in the milieu is given in chapter 10, and of the management of oppositional and aggressive behaviour in chapter 16. Cotton has an excellent discussion of issues of behavioural management in an eclectic unit (Cotton 1993, chapters 4, 5 and 6). Pychotherapeutically orientated units may consider behaviour modification and containment without insight and empathy as of little value (McCleod 1996; Cotton 1993) but there is no incompatibility between a broadly psychotherapeutic milieu approach and the short term control and modification of behaviours informed by ideas from learning theory. As Bettelheim himself discusses in his case history of 'Harry' (Bettelheim 1955), over-permissiveness towards extreme behaviours can create great anxiety in the child as well as others. Nevertheless, one of the legacies of the approach of Bettelheim and others has been to make some milieu care staff unclear and ambivalent about the place of behavioural control. Staff are also rightly influenced by the current legal climate in terms of any physical contact that could be interpreted as intrusive or intimidating. Sensitive but confident handling of behaviour is a core staff skill and the individual team member needs the support and understanding of the group and the wider professional network. It is important for there to be well worked out procedures that are supported by the authority of the institution, although the individual must have the opportunity of questioning procedures if necessary (see chapter 17).

Peer relationships

In environments where there are low scores on the control and organisation dimension of the WAS (as in therapeutic communities) it is the peer culture that is given responsibility for coherence and control on the unit. In our view this is a quite inappropriate burden to place on young children and is likely to lead to problematic dynamics. In adolescence it may be more possible and a number of experiments over the years, beginning with the Little Commonwealth institutions, have attempted to generate this culture. In children's units the peer culture can be mobilised helpfully but in a structured and planned way (Cotton 1993).

Play provides a rich opportunity for the child to have fun and for staff to observe the child at play, with particular reference to the development of socialisation and peer relationships (Kahan 1994). The unit needs to remain flexible and not to institutionalise the concept of play. Choices of group activity and singular occupations need to be on offer. Providing play can become a complex and sometimes disheartening experience for staff, especially if children act out or withdraw in spite of enormous efforts to engage them (Petrillo and Sanger 1972). A powerful shift can be achieved if the children, as a group, plan the activities for the week with staff. This encourages ownership, imagination, group cohesion and peer pressure to participate. There soon develop favoured groups of activities that have a greater success rate in terms of the children attending, participating and enjoying.

The peer group can be a source of difficulty and amplification of children's problems. But it can also be the source of peer support and modelling, an opportunity for reparative activity and the development of social sensitivity and enjoyment. Well designed group activities maximise the positive aspects.

REFERENCES

American Academy of Child and Adolescent Psychiatry (1990). *Task force on adolescent hospitalisation. Model for minimum staffing patterns for hospitals providing acute in-patient treatment for children and adolescents with psychiatric illnesses.* Washington DC.

Arts for Health (1989) National Conference: *A Vision of Caring Environments.* Manchester, November.

Bailine, S.H., Katch, M. and Golden, H.K. (1977) Mini groups: maximising the therapeutic milieu on an acute psychiatric unit. *Hospital and Community Psychiatry* 28 (6), 445–447.

Bettelheim, B. (1955) *Truants from life.* New York: Free Press.

Bettelheim, B. (1974) *A home for the heart.* New York: Knopf.

Bettelheim, B. and Sylvester, E. (1948) A therapeutic milieu. *American Journal of Ortho-Psychiatry 18*, 191–206.

Blotcky, M.J., Dimperio, T.L., Blotcky, A.D. and Looney, J.G. (1983) A systems model for residential treatment of children. *Milieu Therapy 3 (2)*, 3–13.

Blotcky, M.J., Dimperio, T.L., Blotcky, A.D. and Looney, J.G., (1987) A systems model for residential treatment of children. *Residential Treatment for Children and Youth 5 (1)*, 55–66.

Bowlby, J. (1981) *Attachment and loss*, Vol 3. Harmondsworth: Penguin (Reprinted 1991).

Brown, S., Kolvin, I., Scott, D. and Tweddle, E.G. (1974) The child psychiatric nurse: training for residential care. In P. Barker (ed.), *The residential psychiatric treatment of children.* London: Granada Publishing.

Chisholm, D. (1996) The development of child psychiatric in-patient practice, past, present and future. In R. Chesson and D. Chisholm (eds), *Child psychiatric units at the crossroads.* London: Jessica Kinsgley.

Colton, M. (1988) Dimensions of foster and residential care practice. *Journal of Child Psychology and Psychiatry 29 (5)*, 589–600.

Corey, L.J., Wallace, M.A., Harris, S.H. and Casey, B. (1986) Psychiatric ward atmosphere. Fifth institute for psychiatric nurse clinicians. *Journal of Psycho-social Nursing and Mental Health Services 24 (10)*, 10–16.

Cotton, N.S. (1993) *Lessons from the lion's den: therapeutic management of children in psychiatric hospitals and treatment centres.* San Francisco, CA: Jossey-Bass.

Cotton, N.S. and Geraty, R. (1984) Therapeutic space design: planning an in-patient children's unit. *American Journal of Ortho-Psychiatry 54*, 624–636.

Dalton, R. and Foreman, M.A. (1992) *Psychiatric hospitalisation of school-aged children.* Washington DC: American Psychiatric Press Inc.

Dartington Social Research Unit (1995) *A life without problems.* (Response to research at the Caldecott Community) Dartington: DSRU.

Delaney, K.R. (1992) Nursing in child psychiatric milieus. *Journal of Child Psychiatric Nursing 5(1)* 10–15.

Dockar Drysdale, B. (1968) *Papers on residential work: therapy in child care.* London: Longman.

Faber, A. and Maxzlish, E. (1980) *How to talk so kids will listen and listen so kids will talk.* New York: Avon Books.

Fineberg, B.L., Sowards, S.K. and Kettlewell, P.W. (1980) Adolescent in-patient treatments: a literature review. *Adolescence 15 (60)*, 913–925.

Friis, S. (1986) Characteristics of a good ward atmosphere. *Acta Psychiatrica Scandinavia 74*, 469–473.

Friis, S., (1986) Measurements of the perceived ward milieu: a re-evaluation of the ward atmosphere scale. *Acta Psychiatrica Scandinavia 73*, 589–599.

Goffman, E. (1961) *Asylums: essay on the social situation of mental patients and other inmates.* Garden City, NY: Doubleday.

Green, J.M. (1992) Personal practice: inpatient psychiatry units. *Archives of Diseases in Childhood 67*, 1120–1123.

Green, J.M. (1993) Inpatient treatment. In M.E. Garralda (ed.) *Managing children with psychiatric problems.* London: BMJ Publications.

Gunderson, J.G. (1978) Defining the therapeutic process in psychiatric milieu. *Psychiatry 41 (4)*, 327–335.

Harper, G. (1989) Focal inpatient treatment planning. *Journal of American Academy of Child and Adolescent Psychiatry 28 (1)*, 38–37.

Hildebrand, J., Jenkins, J., Carter, D. and Lask, B. (1981) The introduction of a full family orientation in a child psychiatry in-patient unit. *Journal of Family Therapy 3 (2)*, 139–152.

Hinks, M., Crosby, C., Adams, M., Skinner, A., Cooper, G. and King, M. (1988) Not child's play. *Nursing Times 84 (38)*, 42–44.

Jemerin, J.M. and Philips, I. (1988) Changes in in-patient child psychiatry: consequences and recommendations. *Journal of the American Academy of Child and Adolescent Psychiatry 27*, 397–403.

Jenkins, J. and Loader, P. (1984) Family therapy in an in-patient unit – whose problem is it anyway? In E.J. Anthony (ed.), *Yearbook of child psychiatry*. Chichester: Wiley.

Kahan,B. (1994) *Growing up in groups*. National Institute for Social Work Research Unit. London. HMSO.

Kellmer Pringle, M. (1974) *The needs of children*. London: Hutchinson.

Kennard, D. (1983) *An introduction to therapeutic communities*. London: Routledge and Kegan Paul.

King, R.D., Raynes, N.V. and Tizard, J. (1971) *Patterns of residential care: sociological studies in institutions for handicapped children*. London: Routledge and Kegan Paul.

Kutchinski, W.R. (1977) Milieu therapy under the primary care taker system at the University of Michigan's Children's Psychiatric Hospital. *Child Psychiatry and Human Development 8 (1)*, 31–42.

Little, M. (1995) *A life without problems: the achievements of a therapeutic community*. London: Arena.

Marsden, G., McDermott, J.F. and Miner, D. (1970) Residential treatment of children: a survey of institutional characteristics. *Journal of the American Academy of Child Psychiatry 9*, 332–346.

McCleod, D. Chesson, R., and Chisholm, D. (eds) (1996), *Child psychiatric units at the crossroads*. London: Jessica Kingsley.

Menzies Lyth, I. (1985) The development of the self in children in institutions. *Journal of Child Psychotherapy 11 (2)* 49–64.

Menzies Lyth, I.(1988) *Containing anxiety in institutions: selected essays*. London: Free Association Books.

Moos, R. (1974) Evaluating treatment environments: a social ecological approach. Transaction Publishers.

Moos, R., Shelton, R. and Petty, C. (1973) Perceived ward climate and treatment outcome. *Journal of Abnormal Psychology 82*, 291–298.

Ney, P. and Mulhivill, D. (1989) *Child psychiatry treatment*. London: Croom Helme.

Nurcombe, B. (1989) Goal directed treatment planning and the principles of brief hospitalisation. *Journal of the American Academy of Child and Adolescent Psychiatry 28 (1)*, 26–30.

Paice, R. (1996) Nursing in a child psychiatric unit. In R. Chesson and D. Chisholm (eds), *Child psychiatric units at the crossroads*. London: Jessica Kingsley.

Perry, R. (1989) The medical in-patient model. In R.D. Lyman, S. Prentice-Dunn and S. Gabel (eds), *Residential and in-patient treatment of children and adolescents*. New York: Plenum Press.

Petrillo, M. and Sanger, S. (1972) *Emotional care of hospitalised children: an environmental approach*. Philadelphia, PA: J.B. Lippincott.

Pfeiffer, S.I. and Strzelecki, S.C. (1990) Inpatient psychiatric treatment of children and adolescents: a review of outcome studies. *Journal of the American Academy of Child and Adolescent Psychiatry 29(6)*, 847–853.

Pines, R., Kupst, M. and Natta, M. (1985) Staff/patient ratio and type of interaction on a child psychiatry in-patient unit. *Child Psychiatry and Human Development 16*, 4–29.

Price, R.H. and Moos, R.H. (1977) Toward a taxonomy of in-patient treatment environments. *Journal of Abnormal Psychology 84 (3)*, 181–188.

Rapoport, R.N. (1960) *Community as doctor*. London: Tavistock.

Redl, F. and Wineman, D. (1951) *Children who hate*. Glencoe, IL: Free Press.

Redl, F. (1959) The concept of a therapeutic milieu. *American Journal of Ortho-Psychiatry 29*, 721–736.

Redl, F. (1966) The life-space interview – strategy and techniques. In F. Redl (ed.), *When we deal with children: selected writings*. New York: Free Press.

Rinsley, D. (1980) Principles of therapeutic milieu with children. In G. Sholevar, R. Benson and B. Belinder (eds), *Treatment of emotional disorders in children and adolescents*. New York: SP Medical and Scientific Books (pp. 191–208).

Scharer, K. (1982) In service training. In J.L. Schulman and M. Irwin (eds), *Psychiatric hospitalisation of children*. Springfield, IL: Charles Thomas.

Scoles, J. (1996) Staff role transitions and emotional labour in NDUs. *Nursing Times*, 31 July 92 *(31)*,

Steiner, H., Marx, L. and Walton, C. (1991) The ward atmosphere of a child's psychosomatic unit: a ten year follow-up. *General Hospital Psychiatry 13*, 246–252.

Sutton, N. (1996) *Bruno Bettelheim, a life and a legacy*. New York: Westview Press.

Swartz, M.S., Hargett, A.B., Fraker, W.W. and Noll, B.K. (1988) The in-patient milieu: organisation and functional principles. *Psychiatric Annals 18 (2)*, 80–84.

Walker, M. (1994) Principles of a therapeutic milieu: an overview. *Perspectives in Psychiatric Care 30 (3)*, 5–8.

Whitehead, C.C., Polsky, R.H., Cruickshank, C. and Fik, E. (1984) Objective and subjective evaluation of psychiatric ward re-design. *American Journal of Psychiatry 141 (5)*, 639–644.

Wing, J.K. and Brown, G.W. (1970) *Institutionalism and schizophrenia*. Cambridge: Cambridge University Press.

Woolston, J.L. (1989) Transactional risk model for short and intermediate term psychiatric in-patient treatment of children. *Journal of the American Academy of Child and Adolescent Psychiatry 28 (1)*, 38–41.

10 Behavioural and cognitive therapies

Brian Jacobs

INTRODUCTION

Behaviour therapy as a generic term is based on a variety of models which place learning theories in a central role as explanations of human behaviours. On children's in-patient units, behaviour therapy techniques are widely used often in combination with other therapeutic frameworks that may provide a framework for diagnosis and hypotheses about maintaining factors. Behaviour therapy is essentially a problem-solving approach to treatment (Yule, 1985). It takes as its starting point the idea that any observed behaviour occurs in an immediate context and leads to certain reactions from those around the child; this then forms the basis for subsequent behaviours. This is a common observation of parents. It leads to a view of disturbances in behaviour as not being due to hidden and inaccessible motives that are inexplicable except by experts, but rather as due to readily observable chains of events that are amenable to change by encouraging or discouraging the production of particular behaviours.

Four theoretical frameworks underpin behavioural treatments used in the in-patient setting.

1) Treatments which are based on stimulus–response theories.
2) Operant conditioning theories use schemes of positive and negative reinforcement to modify behaviour.
3) Cognitive theories suggest techniques which seek to alter repetitive trains of thought that lead to unwanted behaviours.
4) Social learning theory leads to a group of interventions using modelling, role-play and social skills training.

Extensive accounts of behavioural approaches can be found in Gelfand and Hartmann (1984) and in Herbert (1981). This chapter can only summarise methods; they need application with care and skill.

Application of behavioural techniques in an in-patient setting provides an approach to the analysis of complex problems. The provisional results of the behavioural analysis can be applied to help the child working firstly with the unit staff. They can then be taught to parents and other important adults, such as teachers, for application at home and elsewhere.

ASSESSMENT

Functional analysis

The first stage in developing behavioural interventions requires a functional analysis. For each difficulty, an 'ABC' (antecedents, behaviour and consequences) description is developed. Understanding what type of event regularly precedes the behaviour, the characteristics of the behaviour itself and what are the regular consequences for the child of the particular behaviour forms the focus of a functional analysis. It is obtained through a careful history from the child's parents and school teacher. Observations are made in the child's classroom setting before admission and then on the ward and at the hospital school. A clear ranking of the priorities for changes in behaviour is necessary. This may require working with parents to revise unrealistic expectations of the child arising from the latter's developmental immaturity.

Setting

Some variables are given and will not alter in the time span of the treatment. They include the child variables such as age, temperament, etc. and family variables such as parental ill-health and recent major life events.

> One child was very difficult with her parents at mealtimes, throwing food around and eating very messily. Observation on the in-patient unit and a detailed neurological examination revealed her motor clumsiness. She had developed a very oppositional style with her parents, at least in part, as a way of avoiding the use of cutlery which she could not manage.

Baseline observations

Baseline structured observations are essential to the development of a treatment programme. The in-patient unit is a very good setting for these observations. Some difficulties may only occur at home but getting the parents to spend time with the child on the ward will often reveal such interactions.

The hospital school setting and a variety of activities available to the children as well as the behaviour towards the staff and the other children, all provide fertile ground for observations. Staff need to be trained to carry out structured observations and to pay attention to detail.

Observations may well be supplemented by asking the parents to keep a diary at home when the child is with them for the weekend. They might be asked to keep a diary of particular target behaviours, such as temper tantrums, noting each occasion on which they occur, what behaviours of the child and others including themselves preceded the tantrum, what they did about it and the outcome. They would be asked to try to note how long each tantrum actually lasted – people's sense of time becomes distorted under such circumstances. One advantage of getting the person who is complaining of the child's behaviour to make the observations is that they can come to a more objective view of the difficulties, their magnitude or otherwise. It also helps them begin to observe for themselves the triggers, the antecedents and their own responses. It allows the ward staff to assess how this person will be able to help in any intervention and the difficulties that may have to be overcome for this to happen in a positive way for the child.

Structured observations on the in-patient unit may be obtained using methods described in Gelfand and Hartmann (1984):

1) Event recording – the number of occurrences of the event are noted in a particular time frame. For behaviours that are frequent, it is best to use quite short time samples e.g. 5 minutes. In the in-patient setting several observation periods may be made during a shift by different observers and the results compiled to produce a more robust measure. It is less dependent on a particular observer being on shift to measure change in due course.

2) Duration recording – how long is the behaviour performed for during the particular observational period?

3) Momentary time sampling – is the behaviour actually occurring at specified time marks? Is the child performing the behaviour at the end of each five minute cycle?

4) Interval recording – the observation period is broken into short time intervals and the presence or absence of the target behaviour is noted for each interval. Did the child carry out the target behaviour at any time during the last five minutes?

Behavioural codes and coding sheets are used that can be completed as simply as possible during the observation period. Whatever methods are used they should be specific, for example behaviour that meets a described, simple criterion, repeatable across time and observer.

As implied above, particular care needs to be taken to ensure that reliable observations are made, ones not coloured by sympathy or irritation in staff members. A consensus across a shift can be very illuminating both for the functional analysis and in understanding some of the differing effects the same behaviour can have on different people.

Assets

The child's and parents' behavioural and personality assets are an important component of developing a successful programme. They can help the child's self-esteem. Often the parents come with a guilt-filled self-view though this may be hidden behind a blaming attitude towards the child or others. Such views need to be addressed, often privately and sometimes in individual therapy for the parent.

Identification of reinforcers

Anything that increases the likelihood of a particular behaviour being repeated is called a reinforcer. Reinforcers form one of the mainstays of behavioural interventions. During the functional analysis one must consider what can be used during the treatment programme to encourage the behaviours that are wanted. The crucial question that needs to be addressed here is, what will act as reinforcers for this particular child? Are there natural reinforcers, i.e. ones that form part of the existing system? Can they be harnessed? Broadly, reinforcers fall into four categories: things that the child is given; activities that he is allowed to carry out; privileges; and social praise. Often the last has been lacking or become extinct. Adults often expect children to do what they are told without any recognition that they have done well or that it might have been difficult for this particular child to manage. Reinforcers are frequently seen as bribes rather than a legitimate means to help the young person change their behaviour. The adults often fear that it is a slippery road and that other siblings or class members will be jealous. Failure to be praised by their parents is particularly common for children that are seen on in-patient units. In its extreme it forms a pattern of scapegoating that overlaps with emotional abuse of the child.

Reinforcers can therefore be material or social. They can be administered by another person or can be awarded by the child themselves for achieving their goal. In behavioural programmes with children it is usually necessary to have material reinforcers initially. These should be coupled with social praise. Often this is more effective if it takes place in front of other people. However, some children cannot tolerate social praise in the early stages of a programme. Even here it should be commenced as soon as allowed. Gradually social reinforcement will replace any material reinforcers.

Useful reinforcers (Gelfand and Hartmann, 1984):

- Are resistant to satiation. Using a variety of reinforcers helps this. Generalised reinforcers, such as tokens or stars, together with verbal praise can be very useful immediate rewards working towards later ones. Designing the reward chart so that it appeals to the individual child and feels personal to them is important.
- Should be administered in small amounts.
- Should be administered *immediately* after the occurrence of the required behaviour in the early stages of the programme.
- Should be exclusively under the therapist's control. It is no use giving a child crisps if he is swamped with them outside the programme.
- Should be compatible with the overall treatment programme.
- Must be practical.

For young children, reinforcers may include specific items or activities or they may gain a reward from a bag of hidden items or activities. Sometimes a variant of this, a 'magic tree', can be used; the child chooses a reward to the value of the points he has earned from the tree. For older children, a system of points is often more appropriate but surprisingly often they will want a star chart or reward system similar to that used with their younger peers.

TREATMENT INTERVENTIONS

Co-operation and good communication between different staff group members and professions is essential for the successful application of behavioural programmes. Everybody must understand the programme and stick to it. Difficulties must be discussed with key multidisciplinary team members quickly and alterations to the programme must be shared effectively.

Generally, interventions can 1) be designed to increase behaviours that are absent or infrequent – **deficit behaviours** – or 2) be constructed to decrease unwanted behaviours that are too frequent or occur in inappropriate settings – **excess behaviours**. Other classes of interventions such as relaxation techniques and social skills training will be discussed later.

Procedures to increase deficit behaviour

Positive reinforcement

This is the preferred approach to intervention wherever possible. A key element in any reinforcement schedule is that the child should be working to goals that are going to be achievable for them from the outset and that they are getting rewards they want. *The child must succeed early.* Otherwise, he can become rapidly discouraged.

Functional analysis clarifies the nature of the behaviour which one wishes to alter. A child who constantly argues with adults will be rewarded for speaking nicely and co-operating. Initially the staff may have to watch vigilantly for examples of co-operation, rewarding them immediately as previously agreed with the child. Another regime might allow a certain number of slips by the child in a given time without loss of reward if the task is felt to be very difficult for that child. In general, achievement of the desired behaviour with an 80 per cent success rate is necessary before moving on to the next stage.

Shaping behaviour

This refers to the steady approximation of the child's behaviour towards the target. In the above example the child is first rewarded for managing to speak nicely once or twice more than he would previously have managed in a known time during the baseline observations. The staff would then gradually increase the demands made of him, first with them and then with his parents.

Modelling

These techniques can be helpful in overcoming fears and phobias. It has been found that several models are better than using one alone (Bandura, 1977). The models must be credible for the child and not be perceived by the child as being much more successful than he is in other areas. Equally, adverse modelling can prove a difficulty on in-patient units. A child with behavioural difficulties is likely to join in if he has modelling from peers he respects or fears. This promotes oppositional behaviour and antisocial behaviour. Similarly, there is a careful balance to be sought for having too high a loading of any particular pattern of poor social skills among the children attending the in-patient unit.

Cueing

Often a child will have the desired behaviour within his repertoire but does not produce the behaviour when it is required. This happens for complex reasons but among these is the ambiguous and incorrect cueing that the child has received from his parents or teachers. The unit staff can help greatly by appropriate encouragement of targeted behaviours and modelling.

Social skills training

This provides alternatives to antisocial or withdrawn behaviours and is increasingly addressed in the context of cognitive behavioural approaches.

Procedures to decrease excess behaviours

There is a range of methods that can be applied to decrease or remove unwanted behaviours. Informed parental consent is required before any of these methods are used. It is also important to have explained the programme to the child. Issues of consent are addressed in chapter 29.

Punishment

Parents often use unpleasant consequences (negative reinforcers) and teachers to try to prevent unwanted behaviour. They can be very effective in the short term but effectiveness quickly tends to fade because the child becomes habituated, inviting an unhelpful escalation. It is easy to get into a cycle whereby the child is receiving much attention through punishment without apparent effect. If a child can only get negative attention from adults he will tend to seek it.

Satiation

Where the behaviour is not dangerous or going to cause serious difficulties if allowed to take place then one approach is to allow it to occur or even encourage the child to perform the behaviour until they are thoroughly bored with it. **Massed practice** is a variant of this – an approach that is sometimes used to try to rid children of tics or mannerisms. The child is asked to repeat the behaviour in a rehearsed form for some minutes and to carry out this procedure each hour initially.

Extinction

If the response that the child usually obtains from their behaviour is not forthcoming then it may be expected to decrease and disappear. Often this means ignoring the behaviour so that the social reinforcement of any adult response is removed. This happens but frequently there is an initial increase in frequency or intensity of the target behaviour. This may not be tolerable or safe to ignore.

Unfortunately, the best way to reinforce a behaviour is to reward it inter-mittently. If the adult responds to the unwanted behaviour then they have set themselves a harder task still. Working as a team in the ward milieu can help to avoid this difficulty; there are others to take over if the child threatens to temporarily overwhelm any one adult. This is often not the case at home or in the classroom.

Stimulus change

A child might be separated from another child with whom there is an adverse interchange until they have calmed down and alternative ways of being together can be explored.

It can be very important to notice if a child has great difficulty changing activity suddenly. Giving the child notice and time to prepare himself for such changes can transform previous aggressive responses. Other children may need to work with the same person over into the new activity and setting for a few minutes to feel safe.

Differential reinforcement

Encouraging alternative behaviours that distract the child from the unwanted behaviours or rewarding behaviours that are incompatible with the unacceptable actions is actively pursued are known as differential reinforcement.

One group of techniques that are used in conjunction with the above require 'a price to be paid' for exhibiting the unwanted behaviour.

Response cost

This method gives the child tokens or points for desired behaviours and fines the child if he shows the unwanted behaviour. The tokens can be exchanged for reinforcers at set intervals. It is important to get the right balance between the likelihood of earning points and the size of the fine for undesired behaviours. If this is wrong the child can easily become disheartened or not care about the cost of misbehaviour.

Overcorrection

Essentially, this requires the child to correct and then make additional restitution for the results of his bad behaviour. If possible, the corrective task should relate very directly to the damage done. This can be a useful approach to property damage on the unit.

Time out (from positive reinforcement)

The child is removed from the situation where they are getting reinforced for adverse behaviour to a setting which is unrewarding. It can be a very effective technique if carefully applied but, like other 'negative' techniques, it should only be used in conjunction with positive programmes to encourage wanted behaviours.

The child should have the programme explained to him clearly beforehand. He should be told that he will be given one clear warning but that if his behaviour continues then he will be removed to the designated place. Staff and parents must understand that the purpose is not to punish the child but rather to remove him from reinforcement that is not under the control of the adult. To the child this can be framed as 'a chance to calm down', though the child tends to experience it as punishment. The removal of the child should be done efficiently and with the minimum of fuss; tussles can be very reinforcing to some youngsters. The child should be required to remain in time out for a short specified period. If he is disruptive there, he should know that the time that he stays there begins once he calms himself to an acceptable level. When the child comes out he should be expected to behave calmly. Repetition of the misbehaviour or tantrum results in his immediately returning to the time-out room. If the disruption has stopped the child completing a task then it is desirable that he be made to complete it once the misbehaviour has been dealt with.

Obviously, there are difficulties which need attention in such a programme. The child may be physically too large to be removed to time out. There can be a tendency for the removal of the child to be an over-excited struggle, and there may be no suitable space available.

Any non-stimulating space can be used for time out. Originally the concept suggested a plain, safe area with non-breakable windows, a minimum of furnishings and removal of any surfaces on which the child could harm themselves. More recently we have moved to having a 'quiet room' with soft furnishings such as bean bags, to which the child can take themselves or be escorted if they are unable to go because they are overwhelmed with anger. The child is not shut inside the room without adults unless this has been carefully considered. To do so amounts to seclusion and is a restriction of liberty (chapter 29).

Parents have often sent children to their rooms and then complain that this does not work. Detailed enquiry often reveals that the child has been sent for an indeterminate time in a framework of contingencies that is muddled and inconsistent. The child may have played or been destructive and the parents give up. Clarity and consistency are vital. This can mean repeatedly having to place the child in the time-out situation on the first time that it is tried because the child does not believe that the adults mean what they say and so has to test the situation. Sometimes one finds that this programme turns into a self-regulating one where the child takes himself to time out when he breaks the rules. This should be seen as an advance rather than the child making a mockery of the programme. It represents an internalising of social constraints and self-regulation.

Desensitisation

The simplest example of this technique is the treatment of simple phobias. The child is gradually given increasing exposure to the phobic stimulus, e.g. spiders. It is accompanied by muscle relaxation training to help the child in their anxiety management. More complex programmes of exposure to an increasing hierarchy of feared situations can be used. There are indications that working in actual exposure are better than working using a hierarchy in imagination with children. Successful programmes are careful not to allow the child to proceed faster than they are able in their enthusiasm. The risk is that a panic ensues which will sensitise the child further. This method has been used very successfully in the treatment of school refusal. Children who have intractable school refusal may be helped if the resources of the unit can be mobilised to accompany them to school. This can depend on how locally the child's home school is situated, but with creative use of staff they can support parents in the initial stages.

> For example, Ian, aged 10, had not attended school for nearly a year. Outpatient treatment using parents and teachers to try to insist on his attendance had failed. The apparent original precipitant of his failure to attend school, the death of his grandmother, seemed to have become less relevant than the anxiety associated with anything to do with school. We gradually introduced Ian to our hospital school, initially for half an hour each day. A relaxation programme using imagery and muscle tension exercises accompanied this. He also worked with the nursing staff under supervision of the clinical psychologist to identify a hierarchy of feared situations in his own school. As his time each day in our school increased, his confidence grew and he realised that he was not as behind in his work as he had feared. He was slowly introduced to a programme of exposure to feared situations in his own school, first using photographs of the school and later with school visits. The ascent up his feared hierarchy was controlled so that his impulse to accelerate the programme was resisted. We did not want to precipitate an anxiety attack with the strong negative reinforcement that that would incur. After several weeks, Ian was able to attend his school from

home, first with the support of nursing staff and his parents and then with his parents alone.

Flooding

Here the child is held in the most feared situation of his phobic hierarchy and not allowed to leave it until their anxiety levels have fallen and remained down. It extinguishes the fear. There are particular ethical considerations and issues of consent to be addressed in using flooding with children.

Response prevention

This technique has been successfully applied in obsessional–compulsive disorder (Bolton, Collins and Steinberg, 1983). The rituals are regarded as attempts by the child to manage his anxiety. By preventing the usual ritualistic response the child has to cope with the feelings of anxiety until desensitisation occurs. It works less well if the obsessional symptoms are accompanied by conduct disorder.

CONTRACTS

Staff often like to work in the framework of a verbal or written contract. This specifies for the child:

- What the expected behaviour will be. This is spelt out clearly so that the child understands exactly what is expected of him, where and when and how often.
- What the child can expect if they achieve the set targets.
- What the consequences will be if they fail to achieve the target.
- What the consequences will be if certain unacceptable behaviours occur.

The expectations of the parents are also spelt out clearly so that it is clear if they have not kept to their part of the bargain. Contracts should also specify what the staff will do as their contribution.

Cognitive therapy with children

The application of cognitive–behavioural techniques to child psychiatric problems is relatively new and is still evolving rapidly (Kendall, 1991). They arise from social learning theories (Rotter, Chance and Phares, 1972; Bandura, 1977): the likelihood of a particular behaviour shaping and being shaped by expectations. Central to the models is the idea that much child and adult psychiatric disorder arises from the patient's difficulties in two areas. Firstly they show **cognitive deficits**, an absence of careful information processing that would help the child in the situation; secondly they have **cognitive distortions** – a tendency to misconstrue and distort the situation that faces them, usually in various negative ways.

The techniques have been applied with enthusiasm to a wide variety of child psychiatric disorder, and with some success, though it seems rather too early to say where these methods will finally best be applied in child and adolescent psychiatry. Thus they have been applied to the treatment of conduct disordered youngsters with modest success, to those with anxiety related difficulties and to depressed children (Vostanis and Harrington, 1994; Wood, Harrington and Moore, 1996). They have also been applied to help children with serious physical illness improve their sense of limited mastery of the situation.

Kendall (1991) gives detailed reviews of the approach. For example, Lochman et al. (1991) quote research on three areas of altered or defective cognition in aggressive children.

1) *Social cognitive products* Aggressive children have a bias to being overly sensitive to others' hostile intentions and underestimate their own aggressiveness. They have deficiencies in their social problem solving skills with more solutions involving actions than words. They are poor at correctly labelling their own emotions tending to mislabel other forms of arousal as anger. In addition they are poor at empathising with others' emotions.

2) *Cognitive operations* Attention span is poor and they make mistakes in their short-term memory. The automatic scripts that they tend to retrieve for instant reactions from long-term memory are aggressive.

3) *Beliefs and expectations* These children wish to dominate others and revenge is important to them. They are not very bothered by the possible reactions of the victim or other consequences of their actions. They expect aggression to produce tangible rewards. They have poor self-esteem but they often feel they are 'good at being bad'.

These research findings have led to therapeutic programmes applied in outpatient settings and in schools. They are applicable, with adaptation, in work with children with aggressive behaviour and those with a hyperactive component in the in-patient setting. The therapeutic approach requires careful assessment in each area before a treatment package is designed. Often the young people are treated in small groups to allow for brainstorming of situations and role-play methods. However, this may prove impossible in an in-patient setting because of the severity of the children's difficulties. Programmes have been developed by Webster-Stratton (Webster-Stratton and Hammond, 1997), working with children in groups up to age 8, and by Kazdin (Kazdin, Siegel and Bass, 1992; Kazdin, 1993), who works with individual children to specifically target their social problem-solving skills.

Children are taught to recognise internal emotional states, their precipitants, the accompanying thoughts and the autonomic physiological cues. They are taught to use these bodily cues and non-verbal cues as signals for problem solving. Cognitive self-control strategies are taught through '**self talk**'- what the child can say to himself that will increase or decrease his state of anger.

Social perspective taking is taught through role-play, modelling, group discussion and structured exercises. Everyday situations of potential conflict are used to generate scripts and discussion. There is encouragement to develop alternative understandings about others' thoughts and their intentions. This leads to exercises intended to increase **social problem-solving skills**. Essentially these include problem identification; generation of several possible solutions and their evaluation, predicting the consequences of whatever action they choose. Helping the child spot potential problems early seems crucial so that they have time to think and to implement their new strategies. Backup solutions are important, as is the development of other social skills where these are deficient. Practice in the treatment sessions with peer comment and homework projects is an essential part of this treatment.

Research shows that adults in these families also exhibit some of the cognitive deficits and distortions that are seen in their children and these limit the strategies that they apply in the home in their child management.

Cognitive behavioural approaches for depression have to contend with the poor motivation of depressed youngsters and the boredom induced by their anhedonic state.

The milieu

Many aspects of the milieu are considered elsewhere (chapter 8). For behavioural programmes in an in-patient setting, the ward milieu can offer support in the regular routine and consistent consequences for some common behaviours. However, there are also complications. Two different children may be treated quite differently for what appears to be a similar action. This can lead to dissatisfaction between them and a sense of unfairness. This needs to be watched carefully and may need adjustment of each child's programme. Similarly, the children react with one another so that a negative spiral of behaviours can occur. The use of group contingencies with each child contributing, or otherwise, by earning points towards a shared special event can counteract the effects of negative leadership or negative modelling.

Conversely, positive modelling can be used on the ward to advantage. There are many small instances of positive behaviour that can be encouraged by comment directly or to someone else. Provided that care is taken to spread this social praise around the group an atmosphere of positive behaviour in the group can be created. The 'can do' atmosphere that can be nurtured on the ward also encourages children to try positive behaviours that they would previously have shunned. The feedback they get tends to reinforce further efforts on their part.

Staff must be vigilant both within professional groups and between different settings, e.g. the ward and at the hospital school, that they are consistent in their application of a child's programme. Otherwise it is counterproductive, confusing the child. Interventions can quickly become ineffective.

Transferring behavioural programmes to the child's home needs special attention. Programmes require careful design so that they can be carried out in the family context with parents who cannot leave at the end of their shift and who have competing siblings to contend with. Sometimes the solution to this is to introduce a programme for the siblings which may have direct benefits as well as avoiding jealousies.

SUMMARY

Behavioural techniques are widely used in children's in-patient units. They are applied on the ward and in school as rehearsals for application back at home and in the home school setting. They are used alongside other approaches to increase their effectiveness with the individual child and to increase their utility for the child's parents. Attention to detail is very important in the application of these approaches. A major trap is to produce a programme that cannot be applied at home by parents. It is crucial to remember the limits of numbers and personal resources at home when devising behavioural programmes that will work. On occasion a more sophisticated programme will be applied on the in-patient unit. This must be adapted or faded out by the time the child is due to spend significant time at home or the parents and child will be set up for failure.

The techniques are very helpful but they are not the answer to all the child's difficulties. It is the combined approach of different therapies in detail that allows full use of the in-patient setting.

REFERENCES

Bandura, A. (1977). *Social Learning Theory*. New Jersey: Prentice-Hall.

Bolton, D., Collins, S. and Steinberg, D. (1983). The treatment of obsessive–compulsive disorder in adolescence: a report of fifteen cases. *British Journal of Psychiatry, 142*, 456–464.

Gelfand, D. M. and Hartmann, D. P. (1984). *Child Behaviour Analysis and Therapy* (2nd edn). Oxford: Pergamon.

Herbert, M. (1981). *Behavioural Treatment of Problem Children: A Practice Manual*. London: Academic Press.

Kazdin, A. E. (1993). Treatment of conduct disorder: progress and directions in psychotherapy research. *Development and Psychopathology, 5*, 277–310.

Kazdin, A. E., Siegel, T. C. and Bass, D. (1992). Cognitive problem-solving skills training and parent management training in the treatment of antisocial behaviour in children. *Journal of Clinical and Consulting Psychology, 60*, 733–747.

Kendall, P. C. (1991). *Child and Adolescent Therapy: Cognitive–Behavioural Procedures*. New York: Guilford.

Lochman, J. E., White, K. J. and Wayland, K. K. (1991). Cognitive–behavioural assessment and treatment with aggressive children. In P.C. Kendall (ed.), *Child and Adolescent Therapy: Cognitive–Behavioural Procedures*. New York: Guilford (pp. 25–65).

Rotter, J. B., Chance, J. E. and Phares, E. J. (1972). *Application of a Social Learning Theory of Personality*. New York: Holt, Reinhardt and Winston.

Vostanis, P. and Harrington, R. (1994). Cognitive–behavioural treatment of depressive disorder in child psychiatric patients: rationale and description of a treatment package. *European Child and Adolescent Psychiatry*, 3, 111–123.

Webster-Stratton, C. and Hammond, M. (1997). Treating children with early onset conduct problems: a comparison of child and parent training interventions. *Journal on Consulting and Clinical Psychology*, 65, 93–109.

Wood, A., Harrington, R., and Moore, A. (1996). Controlled trial of a brief cognitive–behavioural intervention in adolescent patients with depressive disorders. *Journal of Child Psychology and Psychiatry and Allied Disciplines*, 37, 737–746.

Yule, W. (1985). Behavioural approaches. In M. Rutter and L. Hersov (eds), *Child and Adolescent Psychiatry: Modern Approaches*. Oxford: Blackwell Scientific.

11 Psychodynamic psychotherapy in the in-patient setting

Jeanne Magagna

INTRODUCTION

Figure 11.1 Trapped

I would love to be a model,
But I know, I do confess,
I really need some help because
My life is in a mess.

But I don't want to put on weight,
I'm scared of growing big
I fear that I will lose control
And end up like a pig.

So, as I said, I feel trapped.
Like I've been left behind,
For me, skinny is attractive
Nothing can change my mind.

'I feel trapped'; with these words 14-year-old Anna spoke of her first night in a psychiatric in-patient unit. She didn't want to be there, and her parents had consented to her admission against her will, yet she was aware of her need for psychological help. This is a common experience of a child entering the in-patient unit. She feels dominated by a set of self-beliefs and yet anxious about the alternative threat of being controlled or changed by the culture of the institution. Individual psychodynamic psychotherapy provides a space for the child to speak or be silent, to choose to examine or ignore the workings of his or her mind (Magagna, 1996b). (The pronoun 'she' will be used for convenience and because the clinical material represented refers to a girl. In fact, 25 per cent of the anorectics I see are boys and 50 per cent of the patients in the unit where I work are generally boys.)

I work as a child psychotherapist in an in-patient unit for ten children between the ages of 7 and 15. In this chapter I shall explore how I approach work as a psychodynamic psychotherapist during various stages of a child's admission. Through vignettes, drawn primarily from Anna's psychotherapy, I hope to show some of the struggles endured in developing a capacity to resolve conflicts, to have concern for the self and others and the courage to return to an ordinary life without the specialness of a severe psychiatric symptom.

In our unit psychodynamic psychotherapy has become an integral part of a therapeutic process involving cognitive and behaviour therapy, individual work, group work, family therapy and an exciting new venture of a weekly parental support group for parents. Medication is also used, in for example psychotic behaviour, epilepsy and depression. I do not see medication as interfering with the process of therapy, for if given in moderation, drugs enable the child to think more fully about the conflicts needing to be resolved. A psychotic adolescent who was being helped by psychodynamic psychotherapy said of her medication, 'What a relief! Now I can dream instead of having hallucinations and having to run away!' (Magagna, 1996a).

It is essential for an individual therapist to be intimately involved in the multidisciplinary staff group, rather than to be isolated as a 'special therapist', having private meetings with patients. It is important to be at team meetings discussing various types of individual work with children and to understand the issues raised in parent support group.

CHARACTERISTICS OF IN-PATIENT PSYCHODYNAMIC PSYCHOTHERAPY

'Total' transference to the institution

In-patient psychodynamic psychotherapy is in my view characterised by a focus upon the transference of the child to the total institution rather than just to the individual therapist (Janssen, 1994). The whole of the child's emotional response to the in-patient environment (the setting, institutional procedures and the range of staff), is understood as gathered into the transference relationship to the therapist. When she speaks of being 'caged in' and 'locked up' I assume that she is talking about being trapped not only by anorectic ideas, her parents' decision to admit her, and the nurses caring for her, but also by me providing the individual therapy.

> *Thoughts of a Captured Bear*
>
> Huddled in a corner
> Chained to the ground,
> Desperately trying
> To escape the sound,
> Of noisy tourists
> Banging my cage,
> Clicking their cameras,
> All in a rage.
> At night I am lonely
> When on my own
> I miss my dear family
> I miss my home.
> I shouldn't be locked up,
> I should be free,
> But, sadly, my keepers
> Do not agree.

I suggest that she wants me to understand how she is feeling trapped right now in the therapy room, rather than suggesting that it is merely the doctors and her parents who have trapped her. Gathering of the total transference to the institution and interpreting it in the context of the child's immediate relationship to the therapist in the consulting room is essential. It avoids a split in which the therapist becomes the good understanding figure, in contrast to parents, doctors and others who become 'bad objects'.

Figure 11.2 Thoughts of a captured bear

Focus on anxieties in the immediate present

My task is to focus on the emotions that are most immediate and pressing in the experience of the therapy session. Underlying this is the idea that internal change can best be facilitated through interpretations which meet anxiety at the moment at which it is being experienced. The material that the child brings is considered for clues it offers to what is actually happening in the session. The aim is to provide a situation in which the child can talk about whatever is on her mind, however insignificant it may seem to her or however controversial she fears it will be (Strachey, 1934). In facilitating the unfolding of the transference, I am concerned with matters of place, time and receptivity (Box et al., 1981).

Place

Conflictual issues described as occurring in another place such as at school, in the family, on the unit are scrutinised in terms of how they relate to the experience in the therapy room. When Anna says her parents have forced her to eat at home during the weekend away from the unit, I listen empathetically to what she says. I then also look with her at how force-fed she feels by my interpretations in the session.

Time

Severe anxieties are often described as having existed in the past or worries are expressed about the future. Anna says she hated the end of term exams and is afraid of failing her GCSEs. She is afraid that the girls at school won't like her when she gets back. All these anxieties about the past and the future are expressing an aspect of her current anxiety in the room. What do I feel about her?

Am I thinking of her as being inadequate because of her admission into an in-patient unit? She is afraid of being judged and disliked at this moment by me in the room as well as by teachers and peers in her past and future.

Emotional receptivity

My capacity to accept and bear the current presenting anxieties, however uncomfortable or painful, is of prime concern to the child. She *feels betrayed* by placating gestures, a too intellectual stance or note-taking on my part. It is not so much the content of the child's communication but more its meaning and significance which is of interest. It is important for the therapist to listen with a third ear to how the story is being told, the mood of the child in speaking and how the child makes her feel. Subsequently, it is essential to listen to the particular way in which the child reacts to the therapist's words and receptivity to the child. It is for this reason that detailed process recordings of the session are essential for self-supervision.

Understanding the countertransference

Once it has become evident that the child is experiencing a particular anxiety, its true nature may only become fully apparent by careful observation of not only what is going on between the therapist and patient, but also of what is going on inside the therapist; what it is that is being transferred by the patient to the therapist, and what exactly this feels like. This is the counter-transference. Through a therapist's ability to discriminate between the different emotions evoked in herself, a clearer picture of the internal world of the child emerges. The figures (or objects) in the child's internal world and their relationships together are projected onto the therapist who receives them and provides an opportunity for them to be re-experienced and re-tested in a new relationship.

Anna at one point had a very 'idealised object', reflected in her intense excitement and pleasure as she talked non-stop to the therapist. When she left the session, she attacked every nurse on the ward who put some restriction on her starving or exercising. By gathering in the 'total transference' of this (Anna's sense of 'the good mother' present in the therapy room and 'the bad father' who put limits on the time in sessions), both loving and destructive feelings could be brought into the relation with the therapist in the therapy session. Subsequently Anna was able to question her notion that a therapist who put limits on time with her was 'simply cruel' and develop a notion that concern for the therapist would involve letting the therapist have the freedom to be with her and also to go away.

The child's eventual capacity to face and bear her own emotions, respond to her own needs and depend on the parents depends on an internalisation of the experience of being helped to bear her emotions with the therapist. Once the therapist is accepted as a reliable, dependent and empathic person, the child can internalise a dependable person and search once again for dependent, intimate links with people in her external world (Rey, 1994).

> In the first session Anna very quickly describes her life; at 6:24 she awakens, at 6:26 she gets out of bed, at 6:28 she puts on her clothes. Every two minutes are programmed while she is getting up. When she eats, every minute is programmed for the ten bites of food which she can eat; at 7:15 she has the first bite of toast, at 7:16 the second bite of toast, etc. Anna continues non-stop until I feel virtually paralysed by the obsessional, clockwork control which has been utilised not only during her day but also during the session.

Anna's words are being used to control and drain me by not allowing any space to feel her emotional experience underneath this obsessional control nor any temporal space to think about the meaning of this 'clock work life'. This bombardment completely drains me. I tell Anna I now have a picture of how necessary it is for her to have every minute controlled. 'Clockwork control' enables her to feel safe.

Anna's predominant anxiety about not having any way of containing her anxieties and impulses pervades her life and is being re-enacted in the present session. In the transference I am perceived as a threat. Rather than remaining separate and experiencing my threatening presence Anna speaks non-stop, invading me, controlling my body and my mind. She omnipotently forces herself into me and becomes fused and confused with me, preventing any experience being separate. At the same time she is tortured by anxieties relating to the loss of Self and the fear of being trapped by me and the hospital staff.

My countertransference is that I am invaded by a torrent of words, emptied of life. I feel a 'damaged mother', invaded by Anna.

In subsequent sessions as Anna finds that I accept her, the presence of my other patients on the unit provokes her jealousy and a phantasy[1] which Anna recounts. As she does so I am uncertain as to whether or not the phantasy will remain a thought or turn into an instruction for action, for it is clear that her obsessional clockwork control is used in lieu of having an inner way of thinking and moderating her impulses to act.

> Anna says she loves being an in-patient in the hospital. She adds though that she is still thinking of suicide. When I explore this thought, she says she thinks she might just jump onto the railway tracks near the hospital, die and join God in heaven. What is in heaven? I ask. She responds that only she and God would be there. She adds that she has also had a dream of having a room to herself where she can eat non-stop without anyone looking.

In her phantasy there should be just two people, her and God. It seemed that there should be just the two of us in the cocoon of my room with me being highly idealised as someone providing wonderful conversations. The other children on the unit should be kicked out of 'the heaven' of the session. Excitement seems to be the primary emotion which Anna experiences in being with me. In her dream she is given permission for a non-stop invasion of the feeding object and no one is to be present to notice her greed. This greed and the need to invade the therapist, through taking all the space for talking available, is probably prompted by Anna's sense of having an empty internal space, a space with a damaged internal mother that cannot allow her to feel able to think safely about her emotions and contain her impulses to act dangerously. In my countertransference I become aware of being invaded by a deep anxiety about whether or not Anna will be safe when she is alone; I feel afraid of her going out of the unit.

One inherent problem with providing psychotherapy as part of treatment on the in-patient unit is that the patient can entertain a regressive phantasy of residing non-stop 'inside the therapist's space' (Magagna and Segal, 1990). This occurred with Anna when her positive transference changed into an idealised transference in which being in the hospital – first experienced as 'being in a cage' – turned into being a 'kind of heaven' as it came to be felt as the 'therapist's residence'. When this 'idealised transference' to the therapist occurs it is essential for the therapist to examine her countertransference. She must avoid the temptation of becoming too intellectual or aloof from the severe anxieties of the patient or becoming cocooned in an idealised transference in which she and the patient feel that the only therapeutic work is being done in the individual therapy – negating the efficacy of the therapeutic milieu and contributions of many others (Rosenfeld, 1987).

In listening to Anna's phantasy I became aware of the problems which occur when the patient begins to depend on the therapist yet has unresolved separation anxieties (Magagna and Segal, 1990). Up to the age of fourteen Anna had managed to remain in her parents' bedroom at night because she was afraid to sleep alone. Her dependence on the therapist was frustrating because not only did Anna feel in a 'bad space' when separate from her, she also felt the jealousy of the 'other patients'. To deal with these mental conflicts Anna resorted to the regressive phantasy of invasion of the therapist represented by 'talking to God in heaven'.

THEMES IN THE TREATMENT PHASE

A deepening of the therapeutic relationship with the patient occurs both in the individual psychotherapy and on the in-patient unit during the middle phase of therapy. There may be the emergence of more severe anxieties and defences as well as a clearer picture of external events which were experienced as traumatising. Issues such as competition between staff members, over-identification with the child and a conflictual relationship with the parents may emerge.

Deepening of trust in the therapeutic relationship

Anna begins to be aware of me as a separate person and she experiences anger with me for going away. This is a development from obsessive control involved in being anorectic and starving herself. However, the problem is that, rather than stay with the feeling of being abandoned between sessions, she projectively identifies with 'the rejecting therapist' and rudely tells the other patients and workers on the unit to 'go away and leave me alone'. Then she feels sad and doesn't know why.

At this stage it was important for me to encourage staff to view Anna's expression of emotion, even negative emotions such as hostile rejection, as progress. In the staff support group we described the different *negative countertransference reactions* evoked in us by Anna's behaviour. We tried to explore how these feelings projected into us by Anna might actually be aspects of her painful sense of rejection which she could not yet bear to own and might have nothing to do with Anna's own likes or dislikes of staff and other patients (Steinberg, 1986).

Acknowledging the presence of psychotic or more severe anxieties and defences against them

As Anna can begin to trust the therapist, the symptom of obsessional control of time, thoughts, emotions and food lessens in severity. Simultaneously an enormous pressure of hitherto hidden and repressed angry and hostile emotional experiences floods to the surface. Anna is no longer the 'perfect adolescent'. Figure 11.2 gives a picture of Anna's state of mind.

I discovered through this drawing that since she was five Anna had heard 'voices' which dictated what she should do (Magagna, 1996b). When I asked her why she hadn't told me about them before she said, 'You never asked me. Anyway, I thought if I told you, you would think that I was crazy.' I learned from my experience with Anna that in the assessment phase I needed to ask questions about suicidal impulses and hallucinatory experiences to enable the child to know that I wasn't afraid to encounter them.

Anna said there were three women's voices which haunted her; cruel witch figures telling her what to do and threatening her if she did not obey them. They criticised her for talking to me in therapy or if she didn't follow her daily routine. She felt herself to be a helpless victim of their cruelty and at times felt suicidal because of their shouting.

I tried to understand the nature of Anna's relationship to 'the voices' as if she were describing a gang to which she was addictively attached. She gradually felt a bit antagonistic towards them, saying that she didn't really like them much, although she didn't want to let them go. As Anna became more in touch with her own possessiveness, jealousy, hate and aggression, the voices seemed to be robbed of some of their virulence. They disappeared much of the time. Anna was aware of their destructive nature, but she was panicked about being alone without their company! She had to face the burden of being alone without the comfort of clinging onto a worrying psychiatric symptom.

Figure 11.3 Anna's state of mind: emotions untrapped

Anna was angry because I did not behave exactly as she wished. I was not under her control as her food was. As I survived her rage without recrimination and as I contained her panic about not being in control of the therapist upon whom she depended, Anna was gradually able to internalise a sturdier maternal figure who could bear her emotions. Thus, the need for splitting off dangerous parts of herself in order to protect and preserve her relationship with her mother was no longer there.

Anna's obsessional control had originally hidden the unspoken internal trauma which her drawing illustrated. The hand can often move, drawing pictures, before the child's mind can find words for her experience. Anna's internal trauma, vividly depicted in her drawing, consisted of a confusion of noises in her head, voices, internal emotional pressure, feelings and conflicting thoughts about her weight.

Exploring the presence of external traumatic events

Around the time that she did the drawing, Anna elucidated her fears through the following dream:

> There is a restaurant with a lot of food; someone is inside drinking coffee there. Anna is sleeping next door with her mother. The bedroom is filled with snakes in cages. There are all sorts of snakes. They are everywhere. There is a huge monstrous boa constrictor as well as other terrible snakes. Someone had let them out of their cages and a cobra had slipped down on her mother. Anna became absolutely terrified and ran off. As she described this dream, Anna said that she felt so bad when she was having this dream that she wet the bed.

I was aware that Anna's drawing with the stars and dots around the face and the big, shocked eyes highlighted the possibility of some external trauma. The dream in which Anna becomes absolutely terrified of the cobra 'down on her mother' could have been considered to be simply a representation of her hatred of the father's sexual life with mother, spoiling her nurturing relationship with her mother. However I was puzzled by the degree of shock and terror present in the dream and drawing. Although I always ask in the initial interview if anyone has touched the child in a way that the child didn't want, Anna had given a negative response to this question and had said that she would tell her mother if anything ever did happen which she didn't like. Of course when the child doesn't trust the interviewer she might conceal the truth (Lask et al., 1991). This necessitates beginning each session with a mind open to facts which contradict those of previous sessions.

I looked with Anna at how the dream suggested that she had possessive wish to have the 'mother–therapist' completely to herself, day and night. I described how she was terrifically hungry to have everything all at once from me. I delineated how in her talking so rapidly, I was to listen and serve her twenty-four hours of sessions in one fifty-minute session. I then wondered about the snake on top of mother. Anna said that she was pleased when her father was travelling outside the country. She said that she didn't want her mother to know that because his absence probably makes her mother lonely.

I then took the liberty of saying I wondered if that was all there was only the feeling that the therapist, mother, should be for her and have no life with a father. I wondered if there wasn't something more about a frightening, bad sexuality being represented in both the dream and the drawing.

Since Anna had developed a more trusting relationship with me, she was safe enough to say, 'Yes, there was more meaning to the dream and the snake'. She pointed out that I had asked her if she had ever been hit, hurt or touched in a way that she didn't like. She said she hadn't, but from the time she was seven until she was ten, she had had sexual contact of various sorts with a man, Nick, in his twenties, who was a lodger in the home, whom she really liked. Well, she said, she *thought* she liked him, but actually she was a bit terrified by his threats to her if she told anyone about what they were doing together.

I do not view the task of the individual psychotherapist as one of becoming involved in formal child sexual abuse investigations. However, I did view it as essential to inform the team social worker. I explained to Anna that I would be doing so. She did not want me to tell anyone. It was necessary to help her with her own anxiety about getting to know what she felt about her experience with Nick. The social worker on the team carried forward the child sexual abuse (CSA) investigation and was involved in managerial decisions regarding Anna's visits home. Meanwhile I continued the task of psychotherapy, which is to understand the current anxieties which emerge in the context of each session and not to take on managerial decisions with regard to the patient's life. This meant that Anna did talk about the CSA investigation, her emotional experiences in being with Nick and the people discussing the CSA issues with her. The task of providing psychotherapy did not become confused with other tasks allocated to other team members.

The tendency towards over-identification with the child and failure to identify empathetically with the parents' anxieties

When the child describes very worrying home situations such as incidents of physical, sexual or emotional abuse, there can be a tendency on the part of the therapist and other team members to become over identified with the child. Also, if the parents have a tendency to feel guilty about aspects of the child's upbringing, they can perceive questions and comments of the staff as implying criticism.

As an individual therapist for the child, I would choose to have discussion of the child done through liaison with team members who can make a good connection with the parents and convey their concerns to me. Likewise, I prefer for team members to represent my point of view in case conferences in which the parents are present. If I do meet the parents regarding the child's sessions I ask the child's permission to do so. This lack of contact with the child's parents tends to protect the confidentiality of the child's individual session. However, not meeting the parents can sometimes lead the therapist to confuse the child's internal image of the parents, at times distorted by the child's projections into the parents, with the personality characteristics of the real parents. If the child presents a picture of inadequate, neglectful or non-understanding parents, the therapist can find an attitude of criticism or superiority to the parents creeping in. Over-identification with the child's views erodes the therapeutic task of enabling the child to work on her own distortions of the parents, integrating loving and hating feelings and forgiving the parents for their inadequacies while finding a way of relating to or relinquishing them.

My recent attendance at parental support groups has provided a useful check on my emotional stance towards children's parents. I am surprised by how often the child has an intuitive, clear, but perhaps exaggerated, sense of the parent's frailties and strengths. I can see the interaction with the child which may have led to failures in parenting or diminution of the parental capacities. Also I begin to understand how the child's intolerance of the parental couple, with the pleasures of friendship and intimacy, can be a source of the child's dismissiveness of one parent or splitting of the parental union.

Anna's parents however presented a challenge to my attempts to maintain a therapeutic stance. When the social worker discussed the sexual issues, the parents insisted that what she said couldn't possibly be true. It took time for us to realise that they needed support in being able to bear the pain of knowing that their daughter had not been able to confide in them. Once the parents did acknowledge the abuse, they were ready to blame the child rather than feel the distress of how traumatised their child had been. Denial was a shared family defence.

Out of guilt they tended to be very lenient with Anna. As a therapist, it was easy to blame the parents internally for being so inadequate and ineffectual with Anna. It was more difficult to look with Anna at how she held onto 'control of others and of food' as a method of escaping from the unbearable, out-of-control feelings she was experiencing.

When I and the rest of the staff were able to understand this, we could accept in a more understanding way the parents' continual criticisms about the in-patient meals, the unhelpfulness of the therapy, the untidiness of the unit and their dislike of attitudes of particular staff members. While utilising the parents' comments to examine our own style of work and the conditions of our setting, we could also understand that Anna's parents were also projecting some of their own unbearable sense of inadequacy and guilt into us. This was an important development which shifted the staff group's defensive anger and fear of the parents' criticism into receptive listening, using their own countertransference to tune in at a deeper level to the parents' underlying anxieties (Kennedy, 1986).

Competition, conflict or co-operation with other staff members

In this middle phase of therapy, as the team's various emotional links with the child and her family deepen and intensify, the multidisciplinary team's group dynamics surrounding the child's treatment become suffused with the inner emotional dramas of both the family and the treatment team (Hinshelwood, 1987). At times the parents may feel they have lost their child to the professional team, who provide for most of the physical and emotional needs of the child on the unit. The parents may accuse the staff of being competitive and suggest that the staff members are 'taking their child over'. In parents' groups, the parents often cry about losing so many of their own roles in relation to their hospitalised child. At the same time, there is often competition and conflict between team members which re-enacts difficulties within the family and between the team and the family. This is often dealt with by projecting negative feelings back onto the parents and child. If the team does not sort out the underlying conflicts that are generated between and within team members, the child's therapeutic progress is impeded. We cannot say to parents that what is essential is that they work together in making decisions about the child without accepting that, likewise, the team members need to work co-operatively together with each other and with the parents.

Handling the child's complaints

It often feels safer to the child to make an indirect complaint. After listening carefully to the actual complaint I try to see what unconscious component in the complaint relates to a present conflict with the therapist.

> Anna told me with glee that she had done something terrible that she thinks I won't like. She had knocked over a young girl standing in the doorway of the in-patient unit. The little girl was whining and her mother was listening to her. Anna did not even look back to apologise.

After a long discussion I discovered that Anna felt that I was bored with her and had thereby hurt and rejected her in the previous session. Rather than hold onto her anger with me, Anna projectively identified with me hurting her feelings by appearing bored. In this identification with the 'rejecting me' she hurt the little girl. In the session I am then put in the role of the one complaining to her for having knocked down the little girl.

Subsequently, a ward staff member approached me asking me what I was doing with Anna because she was becoming aggressive to other children. The family therapist approached me saying that Anna was complaining about me in the family session, claiming I was bored and not speaking with her. I felt criticised by the staff for not doing my work properly.

It was only when we had the half-hour review of Anna's stay in hospital that I felt that I and the rest of the team worked together constructively in relation to Anna's complaints. We understood that it was a step forward for Anna to own her own irritation and complain about me, even though she voiced her complaints to another member of staff and her parents. We also accepted that Anna found it easier to be the source of complaints rather than make a complaint, i.e. to evoke my complaint about her hurting a child was less risky than complaining directly to me about my demeanour in the session. The staff wondered why I hadn't interpreted how the session was being drained of emotional life rather than letting it happen to me. I was too defeated to do anything, I said. In the ward meeting we had moved towards mutual understanding whereas previously, in the corridor conversations, I had felt worried that the staff might be utilising Anna's criticism of me 'to put me down' for their own purposes.

Feeling responsible for the child's progress or failure

Several months into therapy Anna said that now she could differentiate between being the right weight, wearing nice clothes, looking nice on the outside, having friends and how she felt on the inside. She said she felt more youthful and engaged more with her peer group, but she still felt a 'grey-lump-inside'. She said she was also aware of time passing and was worried about mis-spending her adolescence, her school years, and her time in therapy.

This differentiation between external reality and inner psychic reality with a healthy respect for her inner feelings and the external reality of time passing showed progress in Anna's psychological development. As I acknowledged this to myself I felt rather buoyant, as though her progress could be contributed solely to her individual therapy with me. However,I recall another moment when Anna was starving herself and losing weight on weekends at home and I attributed this simply to her parents' inadequacy in containing her anxieties about eating while firmly assisting her to eat. One day I realised that I was attributing Anna's *progress* to my work with her and her *failures* to her parents and the family therapist! I was striving to be 'the successful therapist', which did not facilitate Anna's progress. But there is in reality a whole network, consisting of parents, in-patient professionals and Anna herself, that affects her progress towards psychological health. I am just a part of this multidisciplinary team. Any understanding I can give will be used by the child for her development or to disregard or to destroy.

Working co-operatively with parents and the team members

What happens to me when I work co-operatively rather than competitively with the team members? Primarily, I have to own disowned aspects of myself lodged in various people in the network, including the patient. For example, it was easier to locate inadequacy in the parents than in my tentative, inexperienced attempts to participate in psychotherapy with Anna, my first anorectic patient. Likewise, it was much more difficult to acknowledge the projection of my own depression into Anna's 'grey-lump-inside' than to own my own depression (Magagna, in press).

By working co-operatively with the team of family and staff, a certain humility emerges. Despite all the years of professional training I have had, if I listen to the patient in individual therapy or parents in the parents' group, I become aware that insight is not solely the province of trained professionals. At times as I work co-operatively, I acknowledge, primarily to myself, that I embarked on some psychotherapeutic training to make up for some embarrassing deficiencies in my own capacity to remain emotionally alive to my feelings and develop intuitive insights about myself and my relationship to others. Knowing this is important for my own development.

ENDING PHASE

After three months of in-patient treatment Anna is discharged with the recommendation that she return to her secondary school while continuing to have outpatient psychotherapy. Anna is very angry and says she wants to stay home with her mother or in hospital. She is angry about being considered ready to go to school, but nevertheless she manages to go. Because she has reached near normal weight for height for her age, Anna fears that she will blend in with all the other students and will be forgotten about. This is a problem for the in-patient. What happens if your serious symptoms warranting in-patient admission diminish? The new patients admitted to the unit and assigned to have individual therapy, will be viewed to be more anxiety provoking and therefore absorbing more of the therapist's interest. Certainly the new patients will be allowed to stay in hospital while the child getting symptomatically better will be discharged.

I interpret that Anna is terrified that she will be dropped 'out of sight' by me if she is not a severely emaciated anorectic girl arousing my anxiety. She fears that I will not notice her internal difficulties, but simply note with little interest that she looks all right on the outside. She begins to wear very colourful clothing, a bright, peasant-girl flared skirt, different from the trendy straight skirt style. She also puts on a colourful scarf circling her hair, jangly bracelets and a bright silver necklace. Now she feels people might notice her.

Because of the primary task of in-patient units to hospitalise patients with worrying symptoms, the child's anxiety about separating from the unit and the therapist can lead to prolonging 'the symptom'. Part of this difficulty is mitigated on our unit by having a term of follow-up during which the children and parents meet in the parents' group and children's group as well as having regular meeting with their therapists.

Anna expresses the dilemma vividly in the following session just before she is about to become an outpatient:

She says that she has had a dream in which a blond-haired woman resembling me is lying on the grass. The woman is having a baby which Anna sees coming out of the woman. Somehow the baby then gets pushed back into the woman. Reflecting on the dream Anna says that pushing the baby back inside the woman hurts both the baby and the woman. She adds that she was upset when she awakened in the morning. She isn't sure she wants to be well, be an adolescent living outside the in-patient unit.

The hatred and fear of being an adolescent living with some independence outside the in-patient unit, away from the nurses, therapists and her parents, attacks Anna's hopes for her future life with peers in her school environment. Anna also hates the burden of being responsible for her newly born emotional self rather than being reliant on the less emotionally difficult obsessional intellectual control which she previously utilised. Anna also has a strong fear, a somewhat realistic one, that she still has too little internal capacity to cope with her intense feelings. There is a danger that she will resort to obsessional control or 'acting out' when the burden of her adolescent sexuality and possessive jealousy becomes too great. Her dreams at this time vividly portray her developing capacity to elaborate on psychically undigested anxieties.

She dreams of walking slowly and being hit by a car. When she arrives at the hospital the doctor discovers that she has a broken leg and he mends it.

Having linked the dream to her in-patient treatment and fear of how she is going to survive outside the unit, Anna also reports with triumph that she has embarked on a very severe diet to starve herself which will continue during her forthcoming weekend at home.

A subsequent dream gives me some assurance that this increase of anxiety and symptoms at discharge is partially a reaction of rage about separation rather than a true reflection of Anna's capacities to think about her emotional experiences and look after herself :

She says that she has had a dream in which she and I are in her house. We are sitting on chairs talking about some issues to do with her friends. These feel like important issues to her.

On hearing this dream I suggest to Anna that she has a sense that she has internalised some therapeutic capacity to hold her emotions alive and think about them, even when she is at home (Meltzer, 1983). In this sense, although she will be outside the in-patient unit, she will have taken some of the therapist's capacities home with her to use in looking after herself.

As an outpatient, Anna's need to occupy the special position of the most difficult child, the most dramatic patient, regularly threatens progress in therapy, particularly during the separation from the therapist during holidays. The establishment of a secure internal mother-therapist with whom she can identify helps, but does not resolve all of Anna's problem of wanting to be the only one and omnipresent to the mind of anyone special to her.

Figure 11.4 Being part of the group

CONCLUSION

I have delineated some particular aspects of the in-patient experience.

1) the child's feeling of incarceration and a sense of threat from both the physical and the psychological enclosure of the unit
2) the sense of being special that the severe symptom requiring in-patient treatment gives the child
3) the sense of inadequacy felt by the child and family because there is a need for admission into a psychiatric unit and a stigma attached to residing in one (Magagna, 1995)

4) the fact that discharge from the in-patient unit does not mean that the patient is ready to stop therapy, but rather arouses fear of real challenges outside the protected environment of the ward.

Inherent in in-patient psychotherapy is the likelihood that the admission will not be long enough to meet the child's requirements. In many instances, because of staff resources or travelling time for the family, it is necessary to provide psychotherapy with a different therapist when the child is discharged. I consider in-patient psychotherapy to be successful, not when all the child's problems are resolved, but when the child develops a willingness to explore her emotions and think about them (Magagna, 1994). This enhances the possibility that the child will continue developing outside the in-patient unit and that, if necessary, the child may willingly consider work with another therapist.

NOTES

1 Phantasy is spelt in this way to suggest the psychoanalytic concept of an unconscious phantasy in contrast to fantasy found in the conscious process of daydreaming.

REFERENCES

Box, S., Copley, B., Magagna, J. and Moustaky, E. (1981) *Psychotherapy with families.* London: Routledge and Kegan Paul.
Hinshelwood, R.D. (1987) *What happens in groups.* London: Free Association Books.
Janssen, P. (1994) *Psychoanalytic therapy in the hospital setting,* London: Routledge.
Kennedy, R. (1986) *The family as in-patient.* London: Free Association Books.
Lask, B., Britten, C., Kroll, L., Magagna, J. and Tranter, (1991) Pervasive refusal. *Archives of General Psychiatry,* 866–869. London: British Medical Association.
Magagna, J. (1994) Individual psychodynamic psychotherapy. In B. Lask and R. Bryant-Waugh (eds), *Childhood onset anorexia nervosa and related eating disorders.* Hove: Lawrence Erlbaum (pp. 191–208).
Magagna, J. (1995) Psychophysiologic treatment of cyclic vomiting. *Journal of Pediatric Gastroenterology and Nutrition, 21,* Supplement 1, ss31–37.
Magagna, J. (1996a) Beyond the infinite: psychotherapy with a psychotic 6 year old child. *Melanie Klein and Object Relations, 14, 2.*
Magagna, J. (1996b) Understanding the unspoken: psychotherapy with children having severe eating disorders. London: Association of Child Psychology and Psychiatry, *ACPP Occasional papers.* No. 12 *Psychosomatic problems in children.*
Magagna, J. (1996c) The eye turned inwards: working with hallucinations. (L'occhio rivolto all'interno.) *Associazione Fiorentina di Psicoterapia Psicoanalitica, Contrappunto, 17,* 61–82.
Magagna, J. (in press) The child compelled to die. In G. Williams (ed.), *Eating disorders in adolescents.* New York: Jason Aronson.
Magagna, J. and Segal, B. (1990) L'attachement et les processus psychotiques chez un adolescente anorexique. In *Psychoses and creation.* Seuil, France: GRAPP/Diffusion Navarin (pp. 121–127).

Meltzer, D. (1983) *Dreamlife*. Perthshire: Clunie Press.

Rey, H. (1994) *Universals of psychoanalysis*, ed. J. Magagna. London: Free Association Books.

Rosenfeld, H. (1987) *Impasse and interpretation*. London: Tavistock Publications.

Steinberg, D. (1986) *The adolescent unit*. London: Wiley.

Strachey, J. (1934) The nature of the therapeutic action of psychoanalysis. *International Journal of Psychoanalysis*, l5, 127–159.

12 Educational management

Wendy French and Anna Tate

INTRODUCTION

A child's education helps provide a framework for lifelong learning, the interpretation of everyday experiences and an environment in which a child's self-image can develop alongside the skills required for forming relationships. These are crucial elements of education that can sometimes be overshadowed by the more academic aims of schooling. Formal education provides a structure to a child's life, complementing that which is provided by the family. It also has a therapeutic role when aspects of the child's life are dysfunctional and when the child is emotionally or psychologically disturbed.

Graham (1991) considers that an important characteristic of child psychiatric disorders is the degree to which they affect and are affected by different aspects of the child's life. Therefore, an important task for the teacher during a child's admission is to help the multidisciplinary team understand the relationship between the child's experiences of school and their illness. A visit to the school at which the child is on roll will be helpful in discovering first hand how a child has been presenting there, and will often produce information not contained in existing reports. School issues must be addressed as part of treatment and the future educational needs of the child must be given serious consideration before discharge.

Many illnesses, both psychiatric and physical,[1] can affect cognitive ability either permanently or temporarily; some medications can affect cognitive ability and in addition some psychiatric syndromes involve specific learning difficulties or a significant discrepancy between verbal and performance IQ.

Although many psychiatric disorders are not accompanied by any fall off in either IQ or reading attainment (Maughan and Yule, 1994), some children may be functioning at a level which does not reflect their cognitive potential. For example the child's illness may involve a pervasive refusal to comply with normal expectations (Lask et al., 1991), or their behaviour may be out of control. There may be an avoidance of school work because learning has become involved in a neurotic conflict or associated in the child's mind with pain or unpleasant feelings. Depression and schizophrenia may result in underachievement and 'school-work may suffer when . . . the disorder specifically involves anxieties on conflicts over learning' (Rutter and Yule, 1977) including adverse peer pressure. While academic failure is in itself a potent cause of psychiatric disorder in children (Maughan and Yule, 1994), children suffering from eating disorders may develop obsessional and compulsive work habits which drive them to work beyond acceptable limits in order to attain perfection and academic excellence (Tate, 1993).

THE PURPOSE OF EDUCATION IN A CHILDREN'S UNIT

The Department for Education (DFE)[2] recognises the importance of providing education for children receiving in-patient treatment in psychiatric settings and suggests that without 'effective education their prognosis for a full recovery may be diminished' (DFE, 1994a, p. 18). The aim of hospital education 'is to minimise as far as possible the interruption and disruption to a child's normal schooling' (ibid., p. 10), and education in a child psychiatry setting should have the therapeutic aim of minimising pathology and capitalising on the child's strengths.

The purpose of education in a child psychiatry setting is thus twofold. Firstly it is to ensure that the educational experience is successful and rewarding for the child while challenging and working with the various educational and behavioural difficulties presented in the classroom. Secondly, as part of a comprehensive, multidisciplinary assessment, it is to try to understand the relationship between the child's performance at school and his/her illness. These two aims are inter-related and will influence both the teacher's expectations regarding the pupil's achievement during the admission and the recommendations made regarding the pupil's educational needs on discharge.

> Nicky came to hospital following a psychotic breakdown with a school history of non-compliance, stealing, hiding in the toilets and not participating in any of her school work. This behaviour had been observed in the top year of her primary school and she was described as 'delinquent'. After time participating in our small, structured but calm school with the expectation of attending each day Nicky settled well into an academic programme. She loved work and was anxious to progress in all aspects of school life except PE. Nicky's previous school difficulties were thought to be a contributing factor in her illness. She was in hospital for many months; on discharge Nicky's educational achievements were considered by the multidisciplinary team to be an important factor in her recovery which therefore determined her future placement.

Education in a child psychiatry setting has an additional function over and above its conventional one in society because it acts as a therapy in its own right. In a child psychiatry setting, education reinforces the norms of everyday existence. It provides individual educational programmes and group work within a therapeutic environment so that pupils can put aside their worries and problems to concentrate on what they can achieve. As far as possible, the children's activities will reflect those of children who are not in hospital and a continuing educational programme will help to achieve this. However, the focus in the classroom is on success and achievement even though these may appear limited in comparison with mainstream education. Apparently minor steps forward can be of major significance in this context.

> Almost two years after a cycling accident Raymond was admitted to a child psychiatry unit bedridden with unbearable pain for which no medical explanation could be found. He reported that prior to his accident he had worked with adults, including his father, in the building trade whenever he could, including all day Saturday and Sunday. He had done manual jobs as well as carpentry work and welding. He indicated that his peer group was drinking heavily and smoking as well as being involved in violence. Following his accident Raymond had rejected all school work. He had became very controlling, was fussy about whom he allowed to help him and showed obsessional traits regarding the care of his personal possessions.

> The first task for Raymond was to establish regular school attendance, which involved making room in a very small classroom for a full sized hospital bed. Apart from attendance, no expectations were placed on him to participate in planned activities, both to avoid setting up possible conflict situations and to allow him the autonomy to choose activities which he might enjoy. He first chose sewing and music; he began to learn how to play the guitar. This choice of activities surprised staff as it contrasted so sharply with the self-image Raymond had been projecting. Three months later Raymond enjoyed school and had begun to identify educational targets for himself. He was looked to for support by other children and had an established and respected position among the peer group.

In contrast to Raymond, it should be appreciated that some young people admitted to hospital are over-achievers and find it difficult to relinquish compulsive work habits; sufferers from eating disorders frequently fall into this category. If their achievements are celebrated by both parents and mainstream school, this may act as reinforcement to their unhealthy work habits. Although they may be extremely bright academically, such children may need to be relieved of the pressure that has contributed to their illness. Their needs will be different but the educational and social structure provided by the school constitutes an important aspect of their treatment.

Achievements and expectations in the child psychiatric in-patient unit classroom may not be measurable in terms of the usual norms such as chronological age and individual ability. In our society educational achievement is measured by regular formal testing, and academic competition between schools is encouraged and published in the form of league tables. Therefore it may be difficult for parents and professionals to recognise and value the progress made by pupils in a child psychiatry setting.

TEACHING CO-OPERATION

Poor peer relationships are common features of many, if not most, children who become in-patients in a child psychiatry setting. In schools, pupils are members of groups of varying sizes from class groups to year groups and beyond, with various sub-groups in each. The ability to interact within and between these groups is essential for coping with school life and therefore the curriculum must provide opportunities for co-operative and collaborative work among peers.

Children working on different tasks can work co-operatively by sharing equipment and can be encouraged to show each other their work and help each other with difficulties. Collaborative work can be planned for pairs and small groups. Removing barriers created by age and ability can enable children to begin relating to each other in new ways and to start asking for and offering each other help and encouragement. Each child will need support to change and practise their behaviour and role within the peer group and, in addition to other shared working experiences, there should be planned whole group activities as part of the curriculum in a child psychiatry setting.

A good way to provide these is through creative activities which can act as a counterbalance for the negative experiences, such as disappointment, despair, destructiveness and violence, so prevalent in a child psychiatry setting. A weekly group music session or a termly edition of a class magazine, for example, will enable all the pupils to work together while accommodating various levels of individual skill and ability.

CURRICULUM

There is no mandatory responsibility to implement the National Curriculum in child psychiatry units although the curriculum offered should be broad, balanced and both 'complementary and comparable to that in a mainstream school' (DFE, 1994a). However, for the disturbed child, formal education may seem of little relevance. What matters the history of the American Civil War or the importance of diamonds in the economy of Botswana when children's emotions have been shattered, or their grasp of reality is fragile? How relevant is French conversation to children hearing voices telling them that they are going to die? A balance has to be struck between the child's right to education and what she can learn at a particular point in her illness.

The task of the teacher is to select carefully from the curriculum that content which is suitable and appropriate for both the individual and the pupil group. Certain emotive topics may need to be avoided, for example the importance of the family, homes, size and food. Project work using several skill areas, e.g. history, maths and English, enables the child to use skills that they may have but about which they lack confidence. They may feel that they are useless at mathematics but be able to design and measure plans in a design and technology project. Creativity must be an important part of any curriculum in a child psychiatry setting as it provides a counterbalance to the destructive experience of psychiatric illness which interferes so dramatically with normal development. They may have completely lost confidence in their potential to be able to read, with accompanying very poor self-esteem.

> Ben, a nine-year-old boy who had been excluded from his mainstream school, was admitted to the hospital when his behaviour became totally out of control at home as well. Ben had experienced a difficult nine years. His mother had had a series of different partners and Ben's position in the family was constantly changing because of his mother's relationships. Ben had not been functioning well academically and his reading age was recorded at 6.4 years on the Schonell Reading Test. After an initial assessment period, Ben's Individual Education Plan concentrated on ways to raise self-esteem and establish more positive peer relationships. Ben responded to praise and attention and showed himself to be very capable in creative activities. He designed a rabbit hutch for the school's rabbit. After a three-month reading recovery programme which centred on reading and recording details of the rabbit hutch and other projects in design and technology, Ben gained in confidence. Intensive family work was initiated on the unit and after five months Ben was able to return to a new mainstream school where he continued to do well.

Teaching style and organisation will be as significant as curriculum content in order to make educational tasks meaningful, worthwhile and attainable for each pupil. The teacher must provide for the pupil a different experience of school in order to change the pupil's perception for the better (Salzberger-Wittenberg 1992, p. 36). This requires taking into account both the way in which prior experiences may be influencing the pupil's performance and the factors which may be affecting interaction between the teacher and pupils (ibid., p. 32).

Pupils should learn to work together collaboratively in a group. Thought must be given to how separation into smaller groupings may be organised according to the requirements of the task involved rather than by age and ability. This will reinforce a sense of belonging to the group and support equality of pupil worth and contribution, and result in pupils developing working relationships with all peers and adults.

The very fact that pupils are expected to participate in an educational programme requires them to concentrate their minds on external matters and provides distraction from their problems and preoccupations. Working in a group with the teacher and other children will help individuals to be aware of the needs and problems of others, thus militating against rumination and self-directed behaviours.

EDUCATIONAL STYLE

Curriculum goals will vary for individual pupils and need to be reflected in a child's Individual Education Plan. A child of very low weight may benefit from a balance which favours creative rather than academic activities as this may alleviate the pressure of striving to achieve. A child with problems of motivation and/or concentration may benefit initially from a balance in which a short period of teacher directed activity is followed by a longer period of free choice. Such a balance can be increased proportionally in favour of the former in line with the child's increased ability to manage demands and expectations.

For each child this creates a subtle shift in the relationship between the teacher and the pupil(s) from the teacher as expert, to enabler, facilitator and helper, to that of teacher as equal. Whatever the role, the teacher must retain responsibility for work and behaviour in the classroom. These changes in dynamics will allow pupils to take greater responsibility for themselves in some areas while at the same time learning how to respond to and respect the authority of the teacher as well as learning to work with and alongside peers.

It is important to recognise beginnings and endings as significant events in the school week. This is particularly pertinent because in a hospital setting admissions and discharges may not correspond with the beginnings and endings of school terms. We can celebrate the beginning of each day and each week spent in school as well as the progress made during the whole admission.

Each school day may begin with a short period of silent reflection which is aided by appropriate music. This marks the start of the school day as separate from ward activities and focuses on what may be achieved during the next few hours. Similarly the week may finish on a positive note providing children with good memories to take away for the weekend, to build on and use to anticipate the next week without a fear of immediate failure. Pupils can be encouraged to reflect on and assess the effort they have put into the week in school. Staff can comment on achievements they have observed socially, academically and emotionally while acknowledging the difficulties some youngsters may have had. Pupils should be invited to think about and make constructive comments about the work of peers in order to realise that despite problems it is worthwhile to persevere together. This process will help them focus on their work and target areas for the following week. Teaching children to reflect in this way may facilitate their confidence outside school to explore experiences which have previously been too frightening and painful to contemplate.

It is important to collect good work and encourage pupils to prepare a Record of Achievement to take away with them when they are discharged. In addition to celebrating and positively noting the achievements made by a pupil, such a record can help build a bridge between school work on the unit and school work outside it.

Francis left a child psychiatry unit having attended its school for two years. He left to go to a therapeutic community knowing that his mother did not want him at home and his father had left the country. He was clutching his Record of Achievement as he stepped into the car waiting to start his journey from London to Aberdeen.

STAFF SUPPORT

Damaged children may try to damage themselves or others. Their emotions are very powerful and can make adults feel just as inadequate as they are feeling. Teachers have a responsibility to try to minimise the hurt and pain that many youngsters are experiencing by organising curriculum content, resources and groups to deal with these emotions as part of a programme of study.

It is not enough to establish a relationship in which the pupil trusts the teacher; the relationship between the teacher and the pupil must be an appropriate one in which personal boundaries reflect professional role. Children who have experienced poor parental relationships and who have attachment difficulties may attempt to breach the boundaries of an appropriate teacher–pupil relationship by trying to intrude into the personal life of the teacher. In attempting to make the teacher feel particularly special to them, the child may create an illusion that the teacher has something to offer over and above any other adult. This behaviour is powerfully seductive and therefore both dangerous and destructive as it may split the teacher from working consistently and co-operatively with the rest of the team. It is imperative that a teacher new to this field is made aware of this dynamic through supervision and support (see also chapter 8). Colluding with the fantasies of such children may prolong or prevent the recovery of the child and damage working relationships for the teacher.

> Mary, suffering from post-viral fatigue syndrome, was following a programme which required her to finish all activities fifteen minutes before other pupils, encouraging her to control management of her own recovery and not overtax herself. However in school Mary always insisted that she was not tired and wanted to continue working with the rest of the group, while on the ward at weekends, Mary would not get up until midday and would rest in the afternoon saying that school had tired her out. Mary was aware that this caused some conflict between teaching staff and ward staff. Eventually responsibility for her management during school time was transferred to teachers who insisted that Mary complied with her programme. The ward staff, who had previously identified with Mary's criticism that school was overworking her, were then satisfied that Mary had been manipulating staff with the result that she maintained her symptoms.

Adequate support for teachers, however experienced they are, and supervision are vital, otherwise teachers tend to take powerful feelings home and can be prone to burn-out. The balance between behavioural management and under-standing of the child's plight is difficult, requiring sensitive self-examination by teachers and close liaison with ward staff who are subject to similar pressures.

Educational play is appropriate with those children for whom academic work is, as yet, beyond their cognitive developmental stage. It ranges from sensory play and various forms of model making to board games and jigsaw puzzles. These pupils may require a great deal of individual teacher attention. Some will need firm behavioural management and vigilant supervision and others will need a great deal of nurturing. The task of the teacher will be to work at an emotional and developmental level appropriate to the pupil's current level of functioning while constantly assessing whether and at what pace the pupil might be challenged to make progress. Creative work can be teacher-directed in a very structured way requiring intense concentration and self-discipline from pupils; and academic work can be planned in a semi-structured way to engage pupils in making decisions and choices such as designing and making something which involves an electrical circuit.

DISCHARGE

Good communication about the child's future educational needs must be timed to facilitate appropriate educational provision at discharge. This may need to involve professionals from outside the child psychiatry setting as well as the parents. A child may need to be formally identified and assessed for special educational needs in line with the Code of Practice (DFE, 1994c). Teachers in child psychiatry settings must be familiar with this procedure and use individual pupil educational plans to gather evidence in support of the child's special educational needs. In addition the judgement and experience of colleagues within the setting should be fully utilised to support the opinion of teachers.

The best method of initiating formal discussion about a child's educational needs is face to face in a professionals' meeting. Depending on the particular needs of the child, such a meeting could include a representative from the local educational authority, an educational psychologist from the child's home area, the child's former teacher and the Special Educational Needs Co-ordinator (SENCO) from the child's home school,[3] in addition to the parents, members of the team and representatives from the local health authority and social services department (see chapter 7).

Finding specialist educational facilities takes time and requires a great deal of determination and persistence, as fewer now exist and many obstacles will be encountered in trying to gain access to them. Most local education authorities will be reluctant to pay for education outside their own area as this depletes the amount of funding available for all their pupils. Sometimes this difficulty may be overcome by arranging for education to be funded by more than one party; social services and/or health departments may agree to contribute towards it if a sound case can justify the commitment. Otherwise, it may be necessary for the parents to battle for the education most suitable for their child, possibly with the help of supportive organisations such as ACE, the Advisory Centre for Education.[4] Such negotiations are usually painfully protracted and teachers in child psychiatry settings should acknowledge the limitations of their professional influence in them while producing all the information required to expedite a successful outcome for the child.

Not all children will require specialist placements and many pupils will be able to return to their home school. If this is the case, it is advisable to arrange a meeting at that school between their staff, the pupil's parent(s) and staff from the child psychiatry setting (a teacher sometimes together with a nurse or a doctor). It will be necessary to agree about how the pupil will be reintroduced to the school, which peers and teachers can be of support to the child and how predicted difficulties might be managed. Gradual reintegration (attending part-time while remaining an in-patient of the child psychiatry unit) allows initial difficulties to be addressed while providing support for the child. The role of the teacher from the child psychiatry setting is to facilitate the successful transfer of the child. This may require sharing those teaching and behavioural strategies helpful for that child as well as setting up a review date at a suitable time after discharge. Unit and home school teachers can then address any difficulties and mark progress for the child.

EDUCATION AND THE REST OF TREATMENT

For education to be effective in a child psychiatry setting its purpose must be agreed and supported by the whole multidisciplinary team. Teachers must be fully integrated members of this team (DFE 1994a, p. 18) and attend relevant multi-disciplinary discussions to facilitate good communication regarding the pupils' educational needs and strengths. Every opportunity must be used to further an understanding of the context for educational difficulties. Education, as part of a planned and structured daily programme, must be complementary to the treatment ethos and milieu while clearly identified as a discrete area within it.

The child's work and behaviour in the classroom must complement, rather than interfere with or intrude into, areas being tackled in therapies with other disciplines. Some children may refuse to leave the classroom for treatment such as physiotherapy or psychotherapy, expressing a wish to continue with school-work, possibly as a means to avoid working towards recovery or facing painful experiences. However, it is important that teachers challenge such non-compliance and insist that the children leave the classroom for the duration of the appointment, whether they attend it or not. This gives a clear message to the child that the intervention is necessary and that the various disciplines are working respectfully together to affect the child's recovery. There will be many occasions when children attempt to split the adults who have responsibility for their care but teachers must work collaboratively with other disciplines just as good parents will work together to support each other in the best interests of their child.

Education, while entirely separate from more formal therapies, is highly therapeutic in the child psychiatry setting. It should provide a sense of normality in the crisis of psychological (and physical) illness with clearly defined roles for pupil and teacher within a stable, purposeful and containing classroom environment. It should not be looked upon as merely a useful way of occupying patients while nothing else is happening, nor is it a cuckoo in the child psychiatry nest.

Children must not be allowed to use school attendance as an excuse to avoid treatment interventions such as psychotherapy or physiotherapy and will need to leave school to attend necessary appointments. However, the number of interventions involved in each child's treatment can encroach on schoolwork and interfere with pupil progress. Co-operation between colleagues is recognised as good practice by the DFE (1994b). Some colleagues may express concern that a system of 'protected' school times results in priority being given to schooling over and above therapies and treatment. Certainly, an attempt to create normality and continuity of daily routine will highlight the dilemma of balancing the needs of the group with the needs of the individual. Moreover it will demonstrate the necessity for all disciplines in child psychiatry to be equally valued, respected and co-ordinated in such a way that they are complementary to and not conflicting or competing with each other.

The extent to which particular child psychiatry settings are specialising in order to reflect the requirements of purchasers may mean that teachers will be able to participate in research and the development of strategies which could usefully be transferred into schools.

RANGE OF TEACHERS

While teachers who work in child psychiatry settings gain unique experience in how to engage and enable children to make use of their own abilities, there is a danger that they may become isolated and removed from developments and initiatives in mainstream education.

In the United Kingdom, Ofsted (the Office for Standards in Eduation) inspects teachers in child psychiatry settings. The inspectors use the same evaluation criteria for all mainstream and special schools. Feedback from teachers working in those child psychiatry and hospital school settings which have been inspected suggests that education within a child psychiatry setting constitutes an anomaly within the framework of the inspectorate. Although the inspectors have been sympathetic to the constraints of such settings and respectful of the work of the teachers working in them, they have been apologetic that their reports have had to be framed within the context designed for mainstream and special schools. Nonetheless, in those child psychiatry units where teachers have had the confidence to justify their aims, objectives and provision, favourable reports have been written. A coherent educational strategy for the hospital school is essential. This suggests that teachers working in child psychiatry settings should believe in what they do and be pro-active in communicating their philosophy to others in education who may denigrate work and achievements in this field.

FUNDING

In a survey of all child psychiatry in-patient settings in the UK, no two school provisions are the same (Membrey and Tait, 1997). Generally, local education authorities are responsible for employing the teaching staff but this is now becoming an area of concern as financial resources are more limited and the required high ratio of teachers to pupils means that funding a hospital school or unit is very expensive. If a hospital does not have a local catchment area, the patients may be pupils from outside the local education authority and may therefore represent a low priority for educational funding. Recoupment is an ongoing battle between authorities and it would be more satisfactory if hospital education were centrally funded.

NOTES

1 Some children suffer from both psychiatric and physical illness. Others may be admitted for psychologically-based non-compliance with physical treatments (e.g. insulin regimes for diabetes).
2 Now called the Department for Education and Employment (DFEE).
3 The school at which the child is on the roll.
4 Advisory Centre for Education, 1a, Aberdeen Studios, 22 Highbury Grove, London N5 2EA.

REFERENCES

Department for Education (DFE) (1994a) *The Education of Sick Children*, Circular number 12/94. London: DFE.

DFE (1994b) *The Education of Children with Emotional and Behavioural Difficulties*, Circular number 9/94. London: DFE.

DFE (1994c) *The Code of Practice on the Identification and Assessment of Special Educational Needs*, Circular number 6/94. London: DFE.

Graham, P. (1991) *Child Psychiatry: A Developmental Approach*, second edition, Oxford: Oxford University Press.

Lask, B., Britten, C., Kroll, L., Tranter, M. and Magagna, J. (1991) Children with pervasive refusal. *Archives of Diseases in Childhood*, 66, 866–869.

Maughan, B. and Yule, W. (1994) Reading and other learning disabilities. In Rutter, M., Taylor, E. and Hersov, L. (eds) *Child and Adolescent Psychiatry: Modern Approaches*, third edition, Oxford: Blackwell Scientific.

Membrey, H. and Tait, K. (1997) *Education for Children and Young People with Mental Health Problems: Some Preliminary Findings*, report from the National Association for the Education of Sick Children.

Rutter, M., Maughan, B., Mortimore, P. and Ouston, J. (1994) *Fifteen Thousand Hours: Secondary Schools and Their Effects on Children*. London: Paul Chapman Publishing.

Rutter, M. and Yule, W. (1977) Reading difficulties. In Rutter, M. and Hersov, L. (eds) *Child Psychiatry: Modern Approaches*, first edition, London: Blackwell Scientific Publications.

Salzberger-Wittenberg, I. (1992) Learning to understand the nature of relationships. In Salzberger-Wittenberg, I., Henry, G. and Osborne, E. *The Emotional Experience of Learning and Teaching*, London: Routledge.

Tate, A. (1993) Schooling. In Lask, B. and Bryant-Waugh, R. (eds) *Childhood Onset Anorexia Nervosa and Related Eating Disorders*, Hove: Lawrence Erlbaum Associates.

Part IV

Team organisation and dynamics

13 The in-patient team: models from management theory

Sean Maskey

INTRODUCTION

In-patient unit clinical teams are complex systems, professionally and personally, because of the genuine multi-disciplinary nature of the teams and the intense nature of the clinical work with very disturbed children. What does it mean to manage an in-patient team? Is it possible? This chapter seeks to address these questions by introducing some concepts from current management theory, and offers examples of their application to the in-patient setting.

All in-patient units are multi-agency as well as multi-disciplinary, and they are also multi-task. The team at Collingham Gardens for instance contains nurses, psychiatrists, family therapists, a psychologist, occupational therapist and speech therapist, all within the NHS (the speech therapist employed by the community rather than mental health Trust). The Local Authority employs the social worker and teaching staff. Each individual has their own professional hierarchy and line management. Despite the different perspectives of team members, we have developed and share a common objective in providing 'a broad based assessment and focused treatment, for children who have severe and complex psychiatric disorders'. Clinical activity is foremost, and sets the context for the other tasks of the service which include research and development, and training of students and staff. All of these activities have to occur within the constraints of finance, stakeholder and staff expectations, and the paramount requirement to ensure a safe therapeutic environment.

The systemic map of the Collingham Gardens team, shown in simplified form in Figure 13.1, is thus highly complex, with a multitude of connections to different agencies, both for staff and for children and families in treatment. The boundary of the team system is poorly defined. The differing priorities and expectations of the various subsystems, including the child and his family, impact directly on the individual team members and can create considerable tension and stress.

It would not be surprising if there were strong parallels between theories of mental health and management theory, given the centrality of human behaviour in both fields. Just as in psychiatry there are often several approaches to treating a disorder, each with advantages and disadvantages, opponents and proponents,

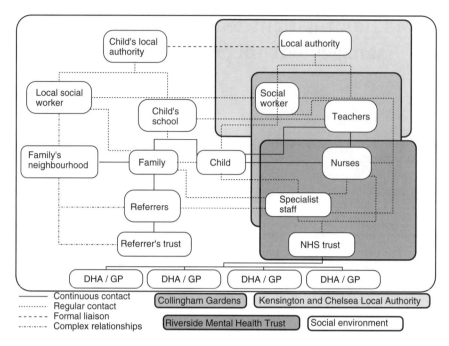

Figure 13.1 A map of the relationships and systems encompassing a child at
Collingham Gardens in-patient unit

so in management, the issues arising in organisations can be considered from a
variety of perspectives, including the behavioural, psychodynamic, systemic,
sociological and post-modernist. It is beyond the scope of this text to consider
all of these schools of thought, and the interested reader is referred to Handy's
Inside Organisations (Handy, 1990) as a starter. The same author's *Understanding
Organisations* (Handy, 1993) is a more detailed survey of the field. Gareth
Morgan's *Images of Organisations* (Morgan, 1986) advocates an eclectic approach
to the subject, applying the model that seems to offer the greatest utility in the
particular circumstance. This is particularly attractive as it is similar to the
method adopted in many in-patient services, which use several treatment models
concurrently. For a practical guide, Senge's *Fifth Discipline Fieldbook* (Senge et al.,
1994) offers a synthesis of several perspectives within a systemic framework. This
chapter will develop two themes in management theory which may shed light on
organisational management and team structure in our discipline.

The organisation as organism

The organic model of organisations, deriving from the ideas of General Systems
Theory coupled with an evolutionary perspective, describes the organisation
as an entity in a state of dynamic equilibrium with its environment. Shifts in
the environment therefore impact on the system to a greater or lesser extent

depending on the openness or otherwise of its boundary. The self-similarity of sub-systems at different levels within the wider context allows a bio-dynamic description of organisational systems regardless of scale. Relationships at different levels and between parts of the organisation are similar and so lend themselves to a general description. Thus the issues of membership and boundary control can apply to the in-patient unit, its host organisation and the group of key staff most closely associated with the child. The biological metaphor has preoccupied much management thinking following postwar studies of technology-based organisations (Burns and Stalker, 1961; Lawrence and Lorsch, 1967). These models emphasise the need for the system to be adaptive to a changing environment, rather than protected from it. One view is that a system's behaviour is entirely a product of its internal sub-units' interaction with each other and the external world (Maturana and Varela, 1980). This has been incorporated into a larger 'Learning Organisation' model (Senge, 1990). In evolutionary terms a group that is isolated from the wider environment will become increasingly specialised and, if it survives, will finally evolve into a new species.

Dawkins proposed the construct of memes, ideas that have an evolutionary life of their own, analogous to genes, but operating in a human (biological) rather than an evolutionary (geological) time scale (Dawkins, 1989). The wheel, psychoanalysis, the different religions and philosophies, and Galen's Anatomy are all example of memes that, once discovered, spread and developed rapidly across the globe, some to flourish, others to die out, and in some societies, never to be found.

A meme, like a genotype, that is isolated in a closed system becomes increasingly differentiated and may become a bizarre caricature of its original essence. Cargo cults, resulting for example in the Jonestown massacre, are an extreme example. 'Group-think', a lesser version of the same process, is regularly responsible for a great many pitfalls, from everyday misjudgements, through institutionalised discrimination, to exceptional incidents such as the Pindown and Normansfield scandals. The latter in particular are characterised by outsiders (managers, referrers, relatives and others) not knowing of, or not reflecting back to the group involved, the increasing deviance of their practice.

While hopefully not at the extremes of isolation, in-patient units operate on a spectrum of openness that is worth considering. Imagine a hypothetical in-patient service that is relatively protected from the outside influence of referrers and professional colleagues, managers and financial constraints and other pressures. It would be very comfortable to work there, in the sense that there would be little perceived conflict or tension, and, like any (genetically) isolated system, it may well become highly specialised and successful in its 'niche' environment. The staff are likely to converge in their thinking on one or two specific treatment models, e.g. biological, systemic or psychodynamic. In-patient units are stressful places to work because of the traumas that the children and families bring, and anything that serves to protect the staff from further stress, in this example the need to consider the uncertainty and threats from the outside, is going to be a very attractive solution. Such a team may well come to believe that their particular school of treatment is appropriate for all cases, and fail to recognise the filtering that goes on by the referrers so that they do not get asked to see the unsuitable cases. However such a niche can also be vulnerable to unforeseen external changes that may produce sudden 'Extinction'.

The isolation of this evolving hypothetical unit from ideas that run counter to the prevailing ethos is further increased by recruitment of staff who are already theoretically aligned with the team. Group behaviour, in the form of social inclusion or exclusion, acceptance or rejection of treatment proposals, and the type of conferences the staff 'choose' to attend, will maintain, and often strengthen, the cultural identity of the team. A very common practice in the group will be overt criticism of other (external) groups. This serves to reinforce the attachment to the group ethos. At the same time it devalues novel information and so protects the team from new possibilities.

In a service where there is one predominant treatment modality the staff are likely to have considerable role diffusion. Although the professional mix will be similar to other units, the individuals will undertake further training in, for example, behavioural psychotherapy, and new recruits will be selected for this skill. As a consequence, several people with different core training will be able to deliver the common treatment package. Because a high proportion of the team are primarily 'therapists', of whatever persuasion, the absence of one (through holiday or whatever) does not impact significantly on the treatment the team is able to deliver. Moreover because the service only works with a limited range of problems there is almost always someone available with the skills necessary to take on a new case. In the extreme form, children would be 'shoehorned' into a therapeutic programme, regardless of their particular needs. The disposition of cases in our hypothetical unit is easy, because someone with the necessary skills is always available and the unit can run to a regular timetable of sessions. This pattern of working has the effect of further closing the boundary as referrers divert 'inappropriate' cases elsewhere or resign themselves to the lack of an appropriate in-patient resource.

At the Provider (NHS Trust) level, such services are efficient to run because the children can be managed as a group, although not necessarily in groups. The clinical input offered will be very similar for each case. The use of staff resources is stable and predictable and activity is only limited by bed availability. To the Purchaser it will appear that the unit provides good 'value for money' (i.e. it is relatively cheap), since the managers in the Health Authorities often have little or no experience in the area, and are not aware of the treatment limitations being imposed. Referrers may choose to go elsewhere, which may begin to sound a warning signal to purchasers through their purses. The provision of the National Health Service and Community Care Act 1990 for money to follow patients, has helped this to some extent through Extra Contractual Referrals (ECRs). However for many children and families such a choice does not exist, since the distances involved are too great, or because the Purchasing contracts have effectively precluded choice for the referrer.

The growth in in-patient units and admissions in the USA in the last fifteen years has been attributed to attempts by the funders (i.e. the external environment) to control costs, rather than any professional evidence of their effectiveness. The contrasting reduction in in-patient services in the UK in the same time frame has not simply been a consequence of resource limitation, as the NHS investment in child mental health overall has risen significantly, as can be seen by the increase in consultant and senior registrar numbers. Rather, the boundary that enabled some of these units to operate without regard to the overall needs of their catchment and their referrers in particular, was broken down by the increasing (management) attention paid to them. This followed the 1983 and 1989 NHS reviews, and subsequent White Paper (HMSO, 1990).

> During its lifetime, the High Wick Hospital, the North West Thames Regional In-patient Unit for children, had become highly specialised as a long-term facility for the care of children with autism and pervasive developmental disorders. The education component came increasingly to the fore, and finally in the late 1980s the Regional Health Authority (RHA) withdrew its funding, and High Wick was transferred fully to the education sector. The RHA transferred the resources to central London, and Collingham Gardens was formed from a combination of the original High Wick service, and the Westminster Children's Hospital child psychiatry day unit.

At the opposite pole, the service that is open to *all* the different demands made of it from the wider environment of Health, Social Services, Education and Society, has a much more turbulent life. Each referral is unique in the network of systems in which it is located. Referring social work teams will practice in demographically and politically distinct areas, e.g. inner city and shire county. The Education Authorities' policies on Special Education Needs provision will differ in different localities, as will the treatment philosophy of the various referring consultants, and this is before we consider the differences located in the child and family. If the team tries to adapt to the wider systemic demands of each case, it has, in effect, to reinvent itself on each occasion and ceases to sustain an identity over time. An organism, or organisation, with no boundary is no organism; the biological state is that of post-mortem decay.

> Collingham was originally a Regional Service, funded directly by the RHA. Following the RHA's demise in the recent reorganisation, funding was transferred to six District Health Authorities. Each has their own set of quality standards, and for two years we were required to produce six different quality reports each quarter, a considerable investment in time and effort. As the different managers have become more secure in their knowledge and understanding of our service, and trusting of each other, we have negotiated one common set of standards and reports for the whole group.

Opening admission to all categories of problem will lead to a rapid accumulation of unmanageable children (and families), most of whom have no recognisable psychiatric disorder but have considerable unmet, and sometimes unrecognised, social and educational needs. For mainly political reasons, the professional independence of the practitioners in the NHS has been relatively protected, compared to Education and Social Services. The people in the systems and networks, of which the referrers are a part, are under pressure to find solutions to educational and social problems with diminishing facilities and resources. One consequence is an increasing demand to admit children to hospital for other than primary mental health issues. In-patient units have in response become more reluctant to take such children as the relative proportions are increasing and they would be overwhelmed by the number with severe behaviour problems.

It is interesting to observe that Social Services residential homes, which appear unable to control admissions and to have to take all comers, *do* survive. Having few places, financial constraints and fixed lengths of stay, are some of the ways in which these systems have managed their theoretically 'open' boundaries.

In contrast to the role diffusion that occurs in services with closed boundaries and a single therapy model, closer adherence to core training and more role differentiation brings another set of strengths and weaknesses. The staff are able to offer a much wider range of assessment and treatment options and so greatly increase the breadth of problems the service can accommodate. For example, a team, and the children it treats, is in a far safer and more effective position if its social worker holds a clear remit for child protection rather than acts as another 'therapist'. In the therapist role, the social worker is likely to be less aware of child protection issues with their own, and perhaps more importantly, their colleagues' cases, leading to potentially unsafe practice. Moreover when safety issues do become apparent, as a 'therapist' they may be unwilling to 'get their hands dirty' or be uncertain and anxious about the task, and over-vigorous in their intervention.

By being confident in its ability to work with these difficult issues, the service is able to treat children who present with both severe mental health problems and child protection concerns, a considerable challenge in this field, as therapists and social workers often dispute responsibility.

Sacha was a nine-year-old girl who was known to have developmental speech delay, but thought to have recovered sufficiently not to need ongoing speech therapy since school entry. One year previously she had started exhibiting sexually aggressive behaviour to her older brother. She retreated at times into infantile speech, and was reluctant to leave the home. Her mother sought help very quickly from the local child mental health service, but after a first assessment, they referred the case to social services on the grounds that she had probably been sexually abused. The social services child protection team was unable to find any evidence for this, and so closed the case. Correspondence, but no further assessment or treatment, followed. Each team thought the responsibility for further action lay with the other.

Admission was negotiated with social services and health, with the agreement that we would assess, and if sexual abuse became more apparent, social services would take up the case. It turned out that Sacha's main problem was a communication disorder, and once this was appreciated and allowed for, at home and at school, the aggressive, sexual and infantile behaviours, which had also occurred during the admission, resolved. She may, or may not, reveal abuse later on.

More importantly, in addition to variety of casemix, the increase in the range of assessments and treatments available enables the unit to work effectively with highly complex cases by providing the parallel specialist inputs that are almost never feasible in an outpatient setting (see chapter 6). The cost of this is that the availability of the specialist(s) becomes the rate limiting step in treatment, rather than the number of beds available. If there is only one psychologist in the team and they have a full caseload, or are on leave, children who need sophisticated cognitive behavioural treatment will have to wait until that person is available. Admission and case allocation is more akin to project management, with the need to plan the allocation of limited resources (the specialist staff) to the case at different stages of treatment.

Taken to extremes, this system becomes dysfunctional. No team can work well when only the social worker is allowed to consider issues of child protection, only the doctor is allowed to consider medication, or only the psychologist is able to deliver behavioural psychotherapy. In practice some crossover of skills occurs. For example, the non-medical staff working with a child who reveals a short attention span as other aspects of his behaviour improve may, through experience of other cases and internal teaching, identify the possibility of hyperkinetic disorder and so trigger a more detailed psychiatric evaluation.

Matrix management

In the classical management theory propounded by Fayol, one person has one manager, producing a continuous chain of command, from the top to the bottom, which corresponds to a root and branch diagram of an organisation. Ambiguity, dilemmas and conflict produced by different managers giving conflicting instructions to a subordinate are eliminated. The design of such systems is intended to prevent multiple lines of reporting and accountability but engenders a mechanistic and unresponsive system quite unsuited to the ability and expectations of semi-autonomous professionals. In contrast, the profession-led model with multiple specialist hierarchies, psychiatry nursing, psychology and so on, readily generates a planning and managerial log-jam because of the conflicting professional agendas and lack of overall authority.

Mintzberg (1979) coined the term 'adhocracy' for the small, highly creative and relatively unconstrained teams typical of research or advertising. Here small groups can function well without formal mechanisms for control and direction. By contrast, the sheer size, as well as external professional accountability, of health organisations make the combination of task focus and professional structure desirable. Galbraith (1971) developed an early resolution to the dilemma of machine bureaucracy or autonomous professional/specialist, in the construct of the 'matrix organisation', with task and hierarchical strands interwoven. This approach appears to embody and illuminate many of the issues that must be considered in the management of the in-patient unit and the clinical team(s) within it. Systems are primarily task (i.e. patient) driven and leaders are there to deliver on a particular task, not to head a department or professional bureaucracy.

As the size of the organisation grows, specialists are employed to undertake particular functions, which may be peripheral to the organisation's purpose (for instance in the health service, finance or estate management), or central to it. In these 'professional bureaucracies' (Pugh and Hickson, 1989: 32–7) the senior professional staff at the apex of the system often have relatively little control over the activities of the practitioners who actually deliver the service. This contrasts with, for example, a fast food outlet, where the employees work to a routine designed by the head office. Standard setting and much of the training of the staff and the fostering of professional identity and values, occurs externally to the organisation. The professional staff may have very different values from the managerial core, in contrast to most large businesses, where employees are trained and promoted within the same company.

The executive management accepts this trade off in control for the benefits that highly skilled professional staff bring. It also produces tensions between the different professional groups within the system, as there are few mechanisms available to resolve competing ideas and values. Moreover the apparatus for monitoring professional (clinical) performance and maintaining standards is located outside the organisation with the professional bodies. The economics of nationalised health care and the inclusion of teaching and training within the NHS itself has further increased the power of the professional in relation to the core management systems.

In the in-patient unit, these issues of professional accountability and hierarchies are even more complex and salient because of the multi-agency nature of the work. There are multiple sources of management authority, that may communicate little if at all, and are unlikely to share the same objectives, much less have a common understanding of the routes to them. At least within the professional bureaucracy, there is a senior management system, common to all employees, that can, if it chooses, 'knock heads together' when interdepartmental or professional disputes get out of hand. In the in-patient team, if the different professional hierarchies do not share a sufficiently congruent view of the team's aims, then the multi-disciplinary and multi-agency team whose members are actively managed by those professional hierarchies will find itself playing out those differences in its everyday work. For example:

John is a seven-year-old boy, who was referred following a sustained deterioration of epileptic control (despite a review of medication), after being bullied at, and subsequently kept away from school. Asking, after four weeks of admission 'Why is he here?' elicits a variety of responses, such as; 'To get him moved to a school for epileptic children' (teachers); 'To find out if he fakes fits' (nurses); 'To get his medication sorted out' (doctors); 'To teach him social skills and so reduce his victimisation' (psychologist) and 'Don't know!' (John).

Each discipline has focused on a particular aspect of John, relevant to their own area of expertise, and developed an interpretation of the admission gaols based on it. A weekly case discussion cannot specify in detail the separate tasks of each subset of staff, and so there is the risk of increasing drift and divergence of objectives over time, with the resultant territorial argument about the 'correct' treatment. This argument is often not really about what is the right treatment, but about different treatment objectives.

It is possible to avoid this issue in outpatient teams by simply avoiding multi-disciplinary work, either by avoiding joint working altogether, or by staff adopting a common treatment model. The psychiatrist and social worker seeing a family together using structural family therapy, are no more doing multi-disciplinary work than two family therapists delivering the same treatment, one of whom used to be a social worker, and the other a teacher. This latter solution is of course available to the in-patient unit that is isolated from external management.

The confluence of task-based activity and professional allegiance and the difficulties that arise at the interface, has been framed as a matrix, the rows and columns representing the organisational divisions and tasks (or multi-disciplinary teams) respectively. The elements of the matrix are the individuals, and the model recognises and encourages dual accountability (Figure 13.2). The professional manager, social work team leader or head occupational therapist is responsible for professional standards, training and career development, and the team leader is responsible for the project or task, in this case the delivery of the clinical service. In its fully developed state, the team leader determines the day to day workload of the team members, but this is both an unrealistic and undesirable target in a professional team where the members are competent and motivated.

In the matrix model, it is the task, in this case the child, rather than the professional hierarchy, that takes precedence. Moreover management of the task is held at the level of the team doing the work, not at some higher level of management. For this model to work effectively, the managers of the team members have to be prepared to relinquish some of their authority over their subordinates to the team leader. For this to happen, the external managers must firstly understand and support the aims of the team, and secondly they, and their staff, must trust the team leader enough to share their management responsibilities with them. A formal expression of this is the Service Level Agreement, in which the senior managers in different departments or agencies agree in writing a level of commitment and the conditions for it.

Service level agreements necessitate a dialogue between the different players

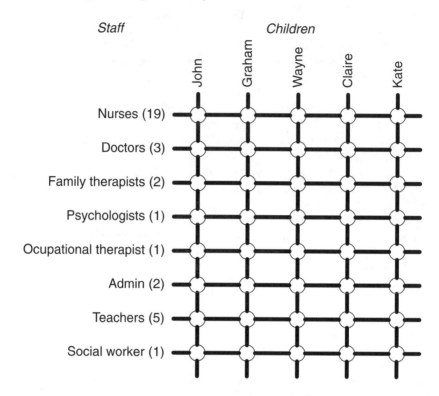

Figure 13.2   The multi-disciplinary care team (discipline/task) matrix
Note: All staff are involved, directly or indirectly, to a greater or lesser extent in each case.

in the system. The process should identify and properly locate at a managerial
level in different organisations the differences of philosophy and expectation that
underlie many of the tensions between the team members. In addition, the
written document forms a useful beginning for the new manager joining a service
and wondering what their social worker or psychologist is doing in some obscure
clinic.

Within the in-patient team, there are many small task-based teams comprising
various permutations of staff that come together for different purposes (Figure
13.3). One such is the clinical team, others for example handle referrals, negotiate with purchasers, or organise teaching or training programmes (see also
chapters 7 and 14). At Collingham Gardens, 'core teams', the key nurse, teacher,
doctor and family worker meet regularly to manage the detail of the case, track
progress and ensure that the different components of the care plan fit together
adequately. The care plan itself is devised through multi-disciplinary discussion,
at the time of admission. If the core team want to move outside the plan, based
on their developing understanding of the case, this is a request to change the task,
and so has to go back to the wider multi-disciplinary team. The core team use

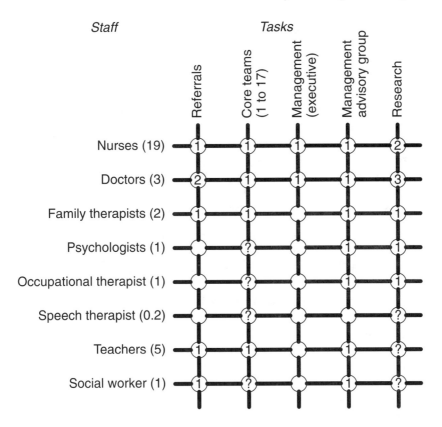

Figure 13.3 A matrix model showing some of the tasks and the Collingham 'clinical' staff group
Note: The numbers are the minimum staff allocated. ⑦: staff may be in a task/team. Note that not all tasks are shown.

their various skills and co-opt or consult other staff as necessary, in order to deliver a treatment programme that fulfils the outline care plan. Thus:

John, the seven year old with epilepsy, has a care plan that aims to help him return to school successfully, and avoid repetition of the spiral of fits and bullying that led to the original non-attendance. Physical assessment and investigation has not revealed any intercurrent infection or other reason for poor control, and medication compliance is good. John's teacher has been in contact with his school and the educational psychologist, to instigate an anti-bullying programme. His key nurse has been talking with John about positive aspects of himself and specific cognitive strategies to manage teasing, in conjunction with the psychologist. The doctor has been in contact with the school medical officer who has agreed to provide a teaching session on epilepsy for the staff at John's school. His parents have been talking with the family therapists about the origins of their shame that John is epileptic, and therefore their reluctance to bring up the issue of bullying with the school when John first mentioned it. Asking the same question, 'Why is John here?', at four weeks, elicits a similar response from the core team and from John; 'To help him return to school successfully'.

The different professional perspectives are now means to the same end, and each core team member shares and continually refocuses on the same goal. Ideas about treatment, e.g. a social skills group, are tested by the core team, against the treatment objectives, and incorporated if appropriate (and logistically practical).

The project-based organisation provides a single point of contact, authority and responsibility for the task. Core teams have been in use at Collingham Gardens for most of its eight-year life. Initially, each had a core team manager, who took responsibility for several formal aspects of the work, including the compilation of summaries, convening review meetings, and ensuring that the different staff delivered their component of the treatment. When the Unit expanded, this model was dropped in the belief that it would be too cumbersome and was re-started only recently. For a variety of reasons the staff roles have become more distinct over eight years, and the type of children seen more diverse. In re-introducing core teams, the staff group has been reluctant to accept a core team leader in a managerial role, i.e. with the power to direct other staff. This reluctance is linked with an increased sense of professional identity, and a reluctance to be 'managed' by peers in other disciplines. The consultant is however acknowledged, internally as well as externally, as the clinical head of the service. Currently the staff group meet weekly to discuss cases in a ward-round format that is open to all staff. One possible resolution of this issue that we are trying is replacing this with a weekly meeting of core team managers together with the consultant, senior nurse and teacher, which will, *de facto*, cover all professional systems involved.

The shift in authority involved in the matrix model raises the question of who decides that the system should reorganise itself in this way. Moreover the team does not usually set the task, although in a professional environment it may be highly involved in formulating it. Discussion of the nature and origins of power in teams is beyond the scope of this chapter, and the interested reader should refer to Handy (1993).

SUMMARY

Viewing an in-patient unit and the teams within it as an organism or entity draws forth ideas from evolution and biology that illuminate some of the processes and transactions that occur. It is by no means the only construction that can be placed on organisations, but it has the merit of reducing the complexity to be considered, without losing too much information. Biological, as opposed to machine, metaphors of organisations require recognition that the system is contingent on the environmental context. The matrix model extends and formalises this, linking form and purpose, professional hierarchy and clinical task.

REFERENCES

Burns, T. and Stalker, G.M. (1961) *The Management of Innovation*. London: Tavistock.

Dawkins, R. (1989) *The Selfish Gene* (2nd edn). Oxford: Oxford University Press.

Galbraith, J.K. (1971) Matrix organisation designs: how to combine functional and project forms. *Business Horizons*, 14, 29–40.

Handy, C. (1990) *Inside Organisations*. London: BBC Books.

Handy, C. (1993) *Understanding Organisations*. London: Penguin Group.

HMSO (1990) *National Health Service and Community Care Act*. London: HMSO.

HMSO (1997) *The New NHS*. London: HMSO.

Lawrence, P.R. and Lorsch, J.W. (1967) High-performing organisations in three environments. In Pugh, D.S. (ed.) (1984) *Organisational Theory* (2nd edn). Harmondsworth: Penguin.

Maturana, H. and Varela, F. (1980) *Autopoiesis and Cognition: The Realisation of Living*. London: Reidl.

Mintzberg, H. (1979) *The Structuring of Organizations*. Englewood Cliffs, NJ: Prentice-Hall.

Morgan, G. (1986) *Images of Organisation*. London: Sage.

Pugh, D.S. and Hickson, D.J. (1989) *Writers on Organisations*. London: Penguin Group.

Senge, P. (1990) *The Fifth Discipline*. London: Century Business.

Senge, P., Roberts, C., Ross, R., Smith, B. and Kleiner, A. (1994) *The Fifth Discipline Fieldbook*. London: Nicholas Brealey Publishing Ltd.

14 Team dynamics in different phases of admission

Jonathan Green and Brian Jacobs

The multiprofessional teams described in the last chapter come together in their working lives to confront complex tasks and difficult psychological realities in their patients. This chapter aims to explore some of the ways that teams organise around the demands of these tasks at different phases of the admission process – since much of the success or failure of their work will rely on the effectiveness of team functioning. Naturally, teams differ in composition and outlook: the approach in this chapter is taken primarily from systems and group dynamic theory; good references to the background of the approach can be found in Obholzer and Roberts (1994) and Hirschhorn (1990).

THE PRIMARY TASK

The 'primary task' (Rice 1963) defines the fundamental *raison d'etre* of an organisation – its core activity. In systems theory it is the basic difference made in the passage between input and output (Roberts 1994 and see chapter 13). The primary task of in-patient units is to hospitalise children with worrying symptoms. At 'input' are children and families with complex severe problems, with confusion and difficulty about their nature or a crisis in their capacity to cope; referred by professionals who similarly may be confused about the difficulty and/or finding the problem impossible to manage. At 'output' hopefully is a family clearer and more resolved about its difficulties, more empowered to cope with them, a referrer similarly clearer and supported; with a plan of ongoing management in place. During this time the child is taken into the care of the ward.

To achieve this primary task, the team has subsidiary tasks to perform, many of which alter through different phases of admission. Throughout it has to maintain its functioning by: (i) keeping reasonably intact and functional in the face of the strains and challenges put upon it by the intense nature of the work – this will include the ability to keep self-reflective; (ii) keeping effectively focused on the task without getting distracted or drawn into behaviours that are 'anti-task'; (iii) remaining open to new information and outside influences such as referral agencies, the referred family and the administrative structures that support them.

PHASES OF ADMISSION

With such overall necessities in mind, we describe ways in which a team often organises itself around the changing challenges and stresses it faces during the course of admission. Three phases are described: the admission/engagement phase, the treatment phase, and the ending/discharge phase. Naturally, these are fairly arbitrary divisions and not all the phenomena are present for all children; much depends on the nature of the presenting problem and therefore the specific tasks that the team has to perform.

Engagement and admission

Managing the boundary of the unit

Throughout the process of preadmission (see chapter 4) members of the team are preoccupied with making an engagement with various external agents such as the referring agency and the referred family. These initial engagements are crucial for what follows. Particularly important is the management of the 'boundary' of admission; how are decisions made as to whether and how a child is to be admitted? Different teams will have different solutions to this but whatever they are will have an impact on the dynamics of admission.

At Booth Hall, the decision to admit is a joint one between the nursing team after a preadmission home assessment and the psychiatrist after a psychiatric assessment, along with input from other senior team members at an open 'admissions meeting'. A sense of 'ownership' of the management of this boundary is a powerful motivator which promotes staff resilience during the work of treatment. Challenges to this systematic management of admissions inevitably arise: common ones being the pressure for acute emergency admissions and specific contractual arrangements with implications for admission priorities. It follows that there must be consensus on admission policy amongst senior staff, which is linked to wider strategic issues about the pattern of referrals that a unit wishes to accept.

Engagement

For the family, the point of admission represents a major reorientation and probably no preparation can fully prepare for its impact. The child has to engage with a startlingly new environment; parents may hover anxiously, compete, disengage with relief or engage constructively. The initial tasks of the team concern engagement with the child and family, information gathering and assessment. For other forms of treatment, the therapeutic alliance established at the beginning of treatment is an important predictor of outcome (Hougaard 1992, Green 1996); the hypothesis that this is also true for in-patient work is currently being tested in prospective research at Booth Hall. Establishing a good initial alliance with the whole family should thus be a critical foundation for the complexities of the treatment phase to follow. The ward staff and child begin to accommodate to each other, and with many behaviourally disturbed children this begins with a 'honeymoon' period of slightly unreal calm while the staff prepare for difficulties that are likely to lie ahead. A critical secondary task for both nursing staff and other members of the team at this time is the engagement of parents.

Other parts of the team establish contact with other parts of the child's life, for instance the child's school and local community support services (see also chapters 4, 5 and 6). These external communications tend to be differentiated; thus school linking to school, social worker to social worker, nurse to family, psychiatrist to psychiatrist. Through these established links early in the course of treatment the unit avoids becoming isolated or 'closed' as a system.

Assessment

The team as a whole has to process information gained from these various sources. Many of the ward assessments will be specific and structured (see chapter 6) but the overall team attention is probably best to be free floating at this point with discussions about the case wide ranging and exploratory as a variety of information is integrated. Different members of the team are engaging with different aspects of the family and external world and there is the potential already here for 'mirroring' processes to develop, potentially leading the team to reproduce *within* itself some of the external dynamics which preceded the admission. It can also be difficult to live with some uncertainty and disagreement within the diversity of information while it is being integrated in a thorough assessment. The very diversity can threaten a team's sense of coherence and purpose: 'this is just all too enormous, how can we cope with all this?'

In response to such anxieties, some teams develop highly focused goal orientations from early on. This can protect against a feeling of being over-whelmed, but too exclusive a goal orientated approach can exclude unexpected or subtle information and make it more difficult to achieve a coherent integration of the material. To avoid the opposite danger of a loss of focus, there needs to be an expectation that clear goals will emerge at the end of a defined assessment period. An important part of a team's culture, emerging over time, is the expectation of what they are able and not able to accomplish in complex situations – and what they cannot do should be made explicit.

As the team organises around assessment, recurrent issues may arise about what work should be done and by whom. How such decisions are made will go to the heart of clinical leadership in the team and can provide occasion for intra-team conflict. There are several possible approaches to the team's task of responding flexibly and appropriately to diverse presenting problems.

Firstly, defined assessment protocols can state the overall aim and methods of an assessment and define the particular contributions of different team members. A protocol of this kind for assessing parenting within the context of attachment theory is described in chapter 25. The critical feature of such protocols is that they are well operationalised and that it is apparent how individual parts of the assessment contribute to the whole. Training around such a protocol adds the general skill level of the group.

A second way in which teams can adapt to complexity of presentations is to restrict the range of admissions taken, developing a specialised unit ethos. Units specialising in eating disorders or conduct disorders are examples of this process. The difficulty that arises here is that in-patient units are a scarce resource and most will be asked to undertake many kinds of work. Greater variety and complexity of casemix leads to the need for higher staffing ratios (see chapter 9).

One contribution to a solution to this dilemma is a 'modular' approach. This aims to strike a balance between the team's needs for clear and differentiated role tasks and the purchaser/patient needs for flexibility of response. In this, separate structured assessments are available in the unit's repertoire. These can be mobilised flexibly to meet the demands of the individual case. There could be, for instance, 'modules' for assessment of parenting, assessment of a child's social functioning, assessment of neurodevelopmental status, assessment of family dynamics, all of which could be incorporated into an overall assessment.

A number of more maladaptive, 'anti-task', team solutions can develop around assessment:

1. There can be an inflexible form of assessing cases which may reduce potential intra-team conflict but increases the likelihood that the assessment will primarily serve the need for team coherence rather than be responsive to the unique needs of the presenting case (see chapter 13). In the extreme form of this, a unit offers the same assessment and treatment procedure for every case and holds to this with procrustean rigidity (and passion) in a way that is uncritical and unscientific.
2. There can be a preoccupation with internal team conflict about who assesses what that reduces effective team response.
3. There can be an unintegrated series of separate assessments which avoid potential team conflict by never being brought together into a coherent formulation (which would itself need to weigh one assessment against another). In this way, a team can preserve a 'pseudo mutuality' but at the expense of a coherent understanding and of the needs of the presenting patient and referrer.

The treatment phase

In most admissions there comes a point where the team 'takes on' a case and makes a therapeutic investment in the child and family. The team here implicitly believes it can do something about the problem. A complexity of engagements and alliances develop during the treatment phase, summarised in Figure 14.1.

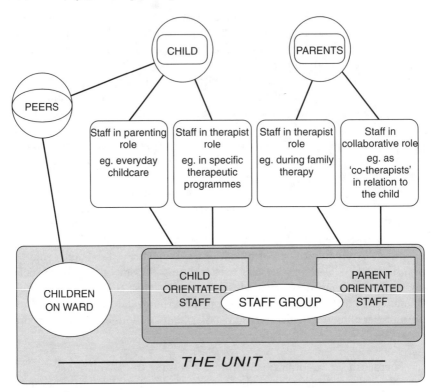

Figure 14.1 Therapeutic alliances within child in-patient psychiatry

Providing a residential environment

Firstly, the team has to organise around the fact that the child is resident with them. Just what the unit is providing in this residential aspect of treatment requires clarification.

- It is not a *substitute* for parenting and yet 'parental' concerns inevitably arise when the ward staff, for a time, have total care of the child's needs and safety. This is especially true when a child forms an intense transference to the ward environment; within this many parental expectations and projections arise.
- It can be thought of as a temporary *supplement* to family functioning, perhaps an 'extended family', but this analogy does not capture the *professional* nature of the enterprise.
- Admission is relatively short-term and cannot aim to be the 'total environment' or substitute care that can be attempted in some residential environments over a number of years (see chapter 32). It can seem more like short-term fostering; this does not capture the intensity of commitment or the sense in which the team have a long-term developmental perspective.

After discharge a child's development is often eagerly followed for years and specific children are talked about as part of a unit's shared memory.

- The task can be seen in pragmatic managerial terms; a convenient 'holding' environment for the child while specific assessments and treatments are undertaken. This approach does not utilise the potential of the ward milieu as a therapeutic agent (see chapter 8).

- It can be seen as a place for crisis management and acute behavioural alteration; the approach of 'minimal necessary change' before discharge advocated recently by some American authors (Nurcombe 1989).

- In our view it can be seen best as a place of *adapted psychological care* which is not family but which does build upon knowledge of what adult/child interactions constitute successful parenting. The adult behaviour within the institutional environment will not be exactly the same as that within a family, but it will inform and be informed by the family approach, as well as by theories of milieu dynamics (see chapter 9). In its historical context this provision of adapted psychological care for children is a constant theme (see chapter 3). There has, it seems, always been the need for society to make a residential provision for disturbed, very complex or alienated children. The in-patient psychiatry environment is part of this historical continuum adapted now for particular aims.

A unit must formulate explicit aims for the residential component of treatment that suit its ultimate purposes and provide enough nursing supervision and support to allow these to be accomplished.

Parental identification

Nursing staff aim for a relatively brief (in life span terms) but intense involvement with patients. Many children elicit a powerful need for 'rescue'. Units who admit a high proportion of children with conduct disorder or attachment difficulties may feel particularly pressured in this way: in cases where core parenting is not necessarily an issue, then the pressure may be less. This pressure often comes from the child. At a particular stage in the treatment phase, when they have adjusted to the ward, the child may make powerful attachments and go through a period of significant dependency. Typically, at this point, the child will idealise the unit and denigrate the parents, resisting going home at weekends and ignoring parents when they come to visit. Simultaneously, the unit as a whole may be discovering emerging facts of inadequacy, neglect or abuse in the home. The stage is set here for the common process of 'parent blaming' (Penfold 1991). A child's dependency can be highly reinforcing to the staff's sense of value: in subtle ways, the staff can come to act 'as if' they were parents and this can communicate itself to the child. ('Oh I'd just like to take him home in my pocket'.) Here the unit has to keep clear about what it is and is not trying to do. A good strategy to avoid over-identification is for the staff to have the child's parents constantly in mind as they go about working with the child, as well as them having regular contact with the parents themselves (see chapter 10).

The ward as dumping ground

The team may also have to cope with the impact of extreme social deprivation and chaos that may accompany a child's presenting predicament. They can easily come to feel the repository of denigrated 'rejected goods' and displaced hate and projections of the family's own sense of lack of social value. The ward can come to see itself as an end stage 'dumping ground' for impossible problems and this can be profoundly demoralising. Active support from other members of the team and active management of the admission boundary of the unit is essential to prevent this state of mind taking hold.

Mirroring and splits

On occasion, significant disagreement or splitting within the team can arise for no obvious reason. This can often be understood as a 'mirroring' of the family's conflicts within the team itself: a process classically described by Main (1955). Team conflict arising in this way can seem quite inexplicable until the connection is made. Such splitting can occur at any point within the team but is often between staff primarily concerned with the child and those primarily concerned with the rest of the family. When identified and reflected upon effectively, such intra-team dynamics can be a powerful and fascinating source of information about the structure of a family's difficulties as well as a source of potential solutions. In a reversal of this mirroring process, as the team discuss and find ways of resolving their own internal conflicts about a case, they often generate the germ of solutions that can be fed back into therapeutic work with the family.

There is also potential for related splits between the unit in its role as 'parent' and the child's real parents. A child who begins powerfully to engage therapeutically with the ward may begin to enjoy it and even idealise it, in turn denigrating parents: expressing this perhaps in increased hostility or a resistance to going home at weekends. Parents can respond by feeling demoralised, deskilled, angry or envious. This is a serious potential problem. Data in preparation from a prospective study at Booth Hall shows that *both* the child's engagement with the milieu *and* family problem solving abilities predict good outcome from in-patient care: any phase of treatment in which one of these seems to be enabled at the expense of the other is worrying. If such phenomena arise then greatly increased attention needs to be paid immediately to the alliance with parents. Parents' groups on the ward, regular parental visiting and counselling, and periods of parental residence on the ward, if facilities allow, are all useful preventative and reparative measures. Simultaneously, while work with the child must actively support their therapeutic engagement to the milieu, it must also emphasise the reality that the child's stay is temporary and that the overall purpose of admission is a preparation for a return to the realities of life outside the ward. In this context, attendance at the unit's school promotes a valuable reality orientation since it is an aspect of the child's admission experience that is very clearly connected with outside functioning (see chapter 12).

The children themselves can get triangulated within team splits.

A young child who was resident on the ward 'escaped' into the outpatient section of the unit and caused havoc. A senior nurse commented that she found herself feeling glad that the staff in the 'protected' outpatient area had been made to feel the impact of the difficulties the ward staff were currently experiencing and so be more sensitive to nursing concerns.

Repairing splits

Difficulties of this kind inevitably arise during the treatment phase of in-patient work and a team, for its survival, needs to feel that it is able to repair splits reasonably well and gain satisfaction from doing so. When the process is going well it can seem as though the concentrated power of group thinking in the team is focused productively towards the health of the patient. This can be an exceptionally satisfying as well as effective clinical experience which plays a major part in sustaining clinicians (including ourselves) through the demands of in-patient work. When things are going badly on the other hand, the team can feel it is pulling itself apart and the patient can feel neglected and out of control. During a difficult case the team usually goes through both sensations several times!

What characteristics of team functioning allow repairs in splits to be made? General factors are clearly important, such as overall organisation, communication, clinical support, leadership and a mutual valuing stemming from working and training together. Many of these have been discussed in the previous chapter. A key specific factor in addition is the management of diverse staff roles. Role diversity is generated in two main ways. Firstly by the demands of the task, so that different subgroups of the team will be involved in different activities (an example would be the 'child orientated' team members and the 'family orientated' team members). Secondly, some roles are generated by the team dynamic itself. Examples of these might be the 'neutral arbitrator' between disputes; the 'reflector' of group functioning; the person urging completion of tasks; the professional who reflects the 'inner world' or development of the child.

It is likely that certain members of staff will gravitate to certain roles but, at the richest level, role diversity will develop from the personality, training and experience of individuals interacting with the particular requirements of the group. When understood and mutually valued this can act as a series of counterbalancing forces and a varied resource to deal with problems. It is probably good for team health that a particular group role and a particular person do not become rigidly locked together. The 'neutral arbitrator' role may often fall to the consultant in the team, particularly since that person carries the final clinical responsibility for the case. Equally, it is likely there will be times during the team process where the consultant him or herself is deeply involved in a piece of clinical work and unable to be neutral. Then it is helpful if another senior member of the team has the confidence to be able to hold the neutral ground. Similarly, it is a quality of good team functioning if different members of the team, even very junior members, can at times hold the reflective functioning of the group and be valued for doing so.

Task roles in relation to child work or family work can be varied according to the skills of the individuals and professional training. A key sign of healthy functioning in the team is when all these roles are valued in their different contexts and there is a sense of lightness and flexibility: humour and laughter during team meetings are a good sign. It is also useful to have formal occasions during the ward routine where the team can present a whole case to itself, 'tell the story of the case' in a way that integrates and values different contributions.

Some teams are keen to open themselves up to other collaborations during admission, for instance having a referring professional come in and do joint work around the case. Such moves can be extremely helpful to keep the system open but they can sometimes reflect 'anti-task' behaviour by not taking on the appropriate responsibility that the staff team has for its own coherence and responsibility in relation to an admission. An opposite form of 'anti-task' behaviour can be the occasional denigration of other agencies and a sense of embattled isolation of the team as the only functioning system in the area. Since the child is often going to be dependent on other agencies during after care the in-patient team needs to have collaborative engagement with other agencies throughout the admission and particularly during the ending phase.

Ending and discharge

The shift towards an ending phase is marked by the emergence of other themes. Typically, the ward's engagement with the child moves towards closure and there is a feeling of resolution within the team. The impression of a complex mixture of alliances between different *parts* of the team and different *parts* of the family is replaced by a sense of a simpler pattern of alliance between the *whole* team and a *whole* family: family systemic work begins to take precedence in the treatment. This shift is also marked, both practically and symbolically, by discharge planning meetings during which the role of the parents as 'consumer' (in terms of plans for ongoing care) and as 'collaborator' (in terms of continuing progress after admission and generalising it to other environments) is emphasised. The disengagement of the child from the unit is marked in a number of ways with 'summing up' sessions and leaving parties.

As with any ending phase this process will be often complicated by feelings of loss and anxiety. There may be an intensification of the child/ward alliance with hyper-vigilance or protectiveness towards the child from the ward group and an escalation of symptoms from the child. Problems in the unit/family alliance can arise, particularly if the 'treatment' phase has not been wholly successful. Families may swing between hope and despair about the future, the rest of the family may not have made as much progress as the child or perhaps underlying rejection may become increasingly evident. The staff team may become concerned about post-discharge child protection issues (indeed for a minority of cases the admission proves to be a stepping stone to alternative care). Alternatively the ward staff may be exhausted or angry with a child and have to struggle with a desire to push them away back into the family (in a mirroring of many families' expelling of the child into the ward at admission). Such intensification of issues in the ward/family alliance around discharge points up the need for post-discharge work. Precipitate discharge is sometimes necessary – this never feels like good practice but is sometimes an essential protective measure for the milieu.

Post-discharge

Attention to aftercare is known to be important for good treatment outcome (Pfieffer and Strzelecki 1990). There can be a consolidation of the unit's alliance with the family as a whole, reinforcing the restoration of whole family functioning after the major adjustments within the in-patient phase. At the right time steps need to be taken to then hand back care effectively to local services, ending the in-patient task.

DISRUPTIONS

In addition to the primary clinical task, many teams will have a number of parallel tasks which at best complement and at worst compete with and confuse the clinical work. Typically these will include teaching and research. It is demanding to introduce a research culture into a team and to use in-patient units as a locus of research; but research will be crucial to the future of in-patient care (see chapter 27). Training covers both the training function of a teaching institution and the in-service training for any unit. Since the latter is primarily focused towards the primary task of the unit, this should be easier to integrate.

Other disruptions can arise at any time from forces within and without. Challenge from within to authority or leadership in the team may come out of personal or professional rivalry or represent fundamental difficulties in the team functioning. Such conflict can be used subliminally by other team members for their own purposes. 'The dynamic of the institution is then one in which leader and attacker are pushed into a deadlocked fight, while the remainder of the staff take on the role of distressed and helpless onlookers' (Obholzer 1994). A related problem can come from inadequate leadership. Leadership of an in-patient team is complex and demanding. The role may usually fall to a consultant psychiatrist and/or ward manager in the UK but not all clinicians have either the aptitude or the appropriate training in management or group skills to do this well. A further source of acute and painful disruption is allegations of abuse within a unit, against children or members of staff. A response to this serious problem is presented in chapter 17.

Disruptions can come from external factors such as the absence of institutional support or financial pressure. The management of these 'external boundaries' is a crucial leadership role. 'Like the two-faced Roman God Janus, the leader must always be looking both inwards and outwards, a difficult position which carries the risk of being criticised by people both inside and outside the system for neglecting their interests' (Obholzer 1996). The need for in-patient units to adapt to various forms of external managerial and financial constraint is reflected in other sections of this book.

CONCLUSION

In-patient treatment is a dynamic group activity which will vary considerably from unit to unit and also within a unit from time to time as staff come and go and different patient demands are felt. Team organisation has to adapt to these changes. Key issues within team dynamics are:

1. *Clarity* of the whole team with respect to the primary task of the unit and within that the strategic tasks that need to be accomplished at different phases of admission.
2. *Roles* should be well differentiated with respect to these tasks and operationalised in such a way that it is clear how each role task relates to the whole enterprise. Teams that deny role differentiation operate on an assumption that everyone can do anything – which usually leads team members paradoxically to feel that they are capable of nothing.
3. *Protocols* can be valuable, to define role tasks and their integration in a common purpose. The generation of these is a matter of training and clinical leadership.
4. *Boundary management*; great care must be given to the decision about who manages the key boundary events around the in-patient process, i.e. admission, discharge, treatment choice, negotiation with external management.
5. A *sense of humour* in working through of role conflicts, and a feeling ultimately of great satisfaction in the corporate pursuit of difficult tasks; these are both markers and rewards of healthy team functioning in a complex environment.

REFERENCES

Green, J.M. (1996) Engagement and Empathy: A Pilot Study of the Therapeutic Alliance in Outpatient Child Psychiatry. *Child Psychology and Psychiatry Review*, 1 (4), 130–138.

Hirschhorn, L. (1990) *The Workplace Within*. Cambridge, MA: MIT Press.

Hougaard, E. (1994) The Therapeutic Alliance: A Conceptual Analysis. *Scandanavian Journal of Psychology*, 35 (1), 67–85.

Main, T.E. (1957) The Ailment. *British Journal of Medical Psychology*, 30 (1), 129–145.

Nurcombe, B. (1989) Goal Directed Treatment Planning and the Principles of Brief Hospitalisation. *Journal of the American Academy of Child and Adolescent Psychiatry*, 28 (1), 26–30.

Obholzer, A. (1994) Authority, Power and Leadership. In: A. Obholzer and V.Z. Roberts (eds), *The Unconscious at Work*. London: Routledge.

Obholzer, A. and Roberts, V.Z. (eds) (1994) *The Unconscious at Work: Individual and Organisational Stress in the Human Services*. London: Routledge.

Penfold, P.S. (1991) *Mother Blaming on a Child Psychiatry In-patient Unit*. Presentation to the 9th Congress of the European Society for Child and Adolescent Psychiatry: London.

Pfeiffer, S.I. and Strzelecki, S.C. (1990) Inpatient Psychiatric Treatment of Children and Adolescents: A Review of Outcome Studies. *Journal of the American Academy of Child and Adolescent Psychiatry*, 29 (6), 847–853.

Rice, A.K. (1963) *The Enterprise and its Environment*. London: Tavistock Publications.

Roberts, V.Z. (1994) The Organisation of Work: Contributions of Open Systems Theory. In: A. Obholzer and V.Z. Roberts (eds), *The Unconscious at Work*. London: Routledge.

15 Staff supervision and support

Jonathan Green

Large amounts of time and energy are expended within milieu teams on supervision and support. Since expensive senior staff often provide this time, it is a critical question as to whether the structure and degree of supervision and support in a team is efficient and effective.

The importance of supervision can be highlighted by its absence: a caricature of a staff member working in an environment which is poorly supervised and supported. This staff member will be fairly junior in rank with a moderate level of previous academic and clinical training. Although working in a team of others, they will typically feel isolated and often bewildered by the complex and unpredictable behaviour that they are faced with from the children in their care. They are unsure of their ability to handle these challenges and often unsure of exactly what is expected of them by others, particularly senior members of staff. They are unclear about the general ethos of the unit and the expectations both of them professionally and of the children behaviourally in the unit. They are equally unclear about plans of treatment and management for particular children. Under stress they may well become less communicative with other members of the team and less willing to share their anxieties. They will often feel or anticipate feeling criticised by other team members who are similarly isolated. If a difficult period occurs on the ward, they may feel that the best policy is to become sick. They will not look forward to coming to work.

Failure to provide support can also have a detrimental effect on the whole staff team. Unresolved conflicts between members of the staff group can be enacted in relationships with the children (Bonier 1982).

The breakdown of any milieu can be recognised in several ways:

- observations of the children are discussed negatively;
- there is no detailed analysis of any events involving the children;
- staff use social frameworks to provide care, i.e. 'I am a parent so I know about children';
- there is a punitive culture towards the children;
- there are increased absconsion rates;
- there will be increased violence and aggression from the children;
- care planning loses its child centred approach;

- the experience of living and working in the environment will be damaging;
- there will be high levels of sickness and absence of staff.

Effective supervision and support must aim to avoid or at least minimise these phenomena. Three main areas of need can be identified.

PSYCHOLOGICAL SUPPORT AND SUPERVISION OF THE SELF IN TREATMENT

Staff in the milieu inevitably use themselves in the treatment process. Experience brings the capacity for regulating the use of self and the capacity to refresh oneself outside work. Failure to do this leads to burn out. The consequences of not opening up these issues, in a constructive way, are grave: 'The emotional investment required to suppress true feelings and continue to care comes at personal cost' (Smith 1992). The use of the self as an instrument of therapy is complex in the milieu since milieu staff are usually acting in a complex of roles involving quasi parenting, professional containment and specific treatments. The disturbed children in their care can elicit complex personal and counter-transference reactions and present staff with unpredictable challenges during which staff have to think on their feet.

Supervision structures must provide an environment which feels safe and supportive to staff and allows them to explore their feeling reactions to the work, understand their countertransference to particular patients (which will often involve the stirring up of difficult personal affects including aggression and sexuality). Some of this self-examination needs to happen in private supervision, some needs to be shared with other staff members to create a culture of understanding in the team. There *must* be a way for staff to feel that their efforts are valued by important figures on the unit and by their peers.

Through this process, talented staff will learn to deepen their insight and capacities to empathise with the world of the children. This will greatly increase their potential effectiveness. This knowledge can however be used positively or negatively: the capacity to 'mind read' the patients can be used, when staff feel threatened or insecure, as a method of attempting to control children. If this happens, the children are likely to feel exposed, frightened and even violated by the insights. On the other hand, if insight is used at the service of understanding, support and emotional contact, the child is likely to feel understood, valued and recognised in a way that usually represents significant therapeutic advance. For staff to use psychological insight in this way, *they need themselves to feel safe and contained* in an atmosphere that supports them psychologically and is committed to a high quality of work, while recognising that all professionals will have moments of error and regret.

How should such a climate of support and psychological supervision be provided? One critical decision is whether external or internal supervisors are recruited. External supervision from a psychotherapist or consultant is commonly used and can be most effective as long as the supervisor is essentially promoting values congruent with the unit philosophy. Combination of the supervision role with that of unit director (or consultant) has implications that have been well documented within therapeutic residential environments of various kinds. An advantage to the arrangement is the opportunity it gives for integrated supervision and leadership – leading to a powerful opportunity to reinforce a unit culture. Many charismatic unit leaders have achieved this. The process is not without dangers. For example, the climate of psychological support can get confused with the presence of managerial authority, potentially reducing the feeling of safety and thus the effectiveness of the supervision.

CASE SUPERVISION

The purpose of case supervision is to make a bridge between a formulated care plan and its implementation day to day in the unit, in all the micro interactions which provide the fabric of the child's real experience of treatment. The most successful case management occurs where aims and objectives are agreed, clearly operationalised, recorded and shared, both between senior and junior staff and between staff and patients. The process begins with good care planning (see chapter 5); the organisational question is how such care plans are initiated, reviewed and supervised. Large group 'team meetings' provide a good forum for care planning and review at a general level but usually do not have enough time for detailed operational reviewing, and many staff find large group forums difficult. The dynamics of the large team meeting can lead to a dominance by senior staff and silencing of juniors. At worst it is ineffective in transmitting information. The inverse care law applies here: the important outcome is that *junior staff* leave the meeting with refreshed ideas and increased confidence.

The use of small staff groups for planning and supervision is effective. The system is often referred to as one of 'mini teams' or 'working groups'. These working groups can be formed around particular patients or around particular pieces or styles of work: for instance groups around the planning and implementation of behaviour programmes for specific symptoms which could be led by a clinical psychologist.

The third useful element of case supervision is a programme of case reviews where the staff team can review cases, identify and celebrate success and learn from the problems. This is a form of audit.

CLARIFYING AND REINFORCING UNIT ETHOS AND CULTURE

This area of work is essentially where the ward culture is generated. Much is done implicitly and by example but there clearly needs to be an interlocking series of strategies to promote and sustain the unit culture.

a) *Forums for strategic thinking and review.* These can be forums involving the whole unit and at different times a senior management group. The overall strategy of the unit, its relationships with external agencies and response to new developments need to be discussed and decisions made about how such strategic aims are translated into practice. Some units involve 'consumers' in such meetings, in the form of either parents, purchasers or external management. This seems sensible and creative.

b) *Critical incident reviews.* There should be a swift and well co-ordinated senior staff response to critical incidents: immediate crisis management followed by a debriefing for those staff involved and then a more general review of the immediate and longer term implications of the incident.

c) *In-service training, unit reviews and open days.* These are all valuable. There could be a good case for an annual three-day unit review for staff, when clinical work is suspended and the staff meet together to undertake in-depth review of the unit's functioning.

d) *Specific training and supervision initiatives.* These should articulate and exemplify the unit ethos. Having the unit director or senior staff undertake staff supervision is a useful means of promoting this. Also programmes of assessment and treatment delineated with a clear rationale and aims, operationalised so that all staff have a specific function that interlocks to the overall task, can be very productive.

e) Various forms of *team building* activities are relevant here, including celebrations, welcoming, leave taking and the involvement of staff in social and relaxation activities. Bendicsen and Carlton (1990) recommend the establishment of what they call 'clinical team building': 'clinical team building recognises and provides a vehicle for correcting the powerful counter-transference reactions elicited in staff through their work with children and adolescents and acted out in staff relationships'.

OTHER OPPORTUNITIES FOR SUPERVISION AND SUPPORT

Delegation of supervision

Supervision should not be seen as an activity conducted only by senior staff. A good principle could be that of 'supervision by the least senior colleague able to undertake the task'. This leads to a pattern of supervision exchange between colleagues, between senior registrars and registrars, between F grade nurses and D grade nurses, between teachers in charge and classroom teachers. The position of senior staff should also not be forgotten, since provision is often not made for their own support and the tradition, certainly in medicine, is slightly against seniors having their needs met in this way.

Informal 'corridor' supervision

Many people particularly value informal contacts around coffee in corridors and over mealtimes. In such informal settings staff can seek out those who may choose to give them support.

CONCLUSION

In conclusion, one might characterise junior staff members in a well supported team. They will recognise that the work is complex and demanding and they will often not be clear how to proceed. However, they will feel that they are engaged in a corporate and exciting undertaking and that there is a network of support around them with which to share their difficulties. They will gain confidence by being able reciprocally to share others' difficulties. The general expectations of the institution will be clear to them, as they will to the group of children patients. There will be a clear culture of how to act in emergencies and crises and senior staff will be responsive and available at difficult moments. In amongst the difficulties they will be lucky enough to see some moving moments of psychological change and feel privileged to share the experiences of the children they treat. Somewhere on the ward will be an album of photographs of children treated and grown whom they won't know personally, but who will form part of the unit's memory and its sense of worth to the community it serves.

REFERENCES

Bendicsen, H. and Carlton, S. (1990) *Residential Treatment for Children and Youth*, Vol. 8 (1). The Haworth Press, Inc.

Bonier, R.J. (1982) Staff Countertransferences in an Adolescent Milieu Treatment Setting. *Adolescent Psychiatry* (Vol. 10) *Developmental and Clinical Studies*.

Smith, P. (1992) *The Emotional Labour of Nursing: How Nurses Care*. Hong Kong: Macmillan.

ACKNOWLEDGEMENT

The author would like to acknowledge the contribution of Maureen Burke to this chapter.

Part V

Critical areas of management

16 Managing oppositional and aggressive behaviour

Ian Higgins and Maureen Burke

INTRODUCTION

For many professionals, especially nursing staff, this will be one of the first chapters they turn to. This is not, we should hasten to add, due to the notoriety of the authors! The safe and successful management of oppositional and aggressive behaviour is one of the most discussed aspects of care on in-patient units.

This chapter will discuss common approaches, problems and the way management has developed since the introduction of the Children Act. As well as highlighting the various strategies and practices used, it will endeavour to look at these behaviours from the young person's perspective. This is vital if we are to explore this element of treatment fully.

There has been increasing debate over the last two to three years around whether in-patient units should be managing severe oppositional and/or aggressive behaviours. Some units have made a decision that they will not admit children with conduct disorder as their primary diagnosis. The majority appear to be prepared at least to assess these children and use local guidelines to decide what is a safe number of mixed emotional and conduct disordered children to have on the unit at any one time. To date there has not been an open debate over this issue, but it appears that individual units are beginning to look more closely at the question (see chapter 2). Such a debate needs to be actively encouraged by managers and clinicians, as this is more likely to lead to clearer strategies and management.

The Children Act (1989) had a significant effect on the management of oppositional and aggressive behaviours. The act provided the stimulus for a more open and honest appraisal of approaches and interventions used up to that time. Children's units had to take stock, and question whether their practices truly met the individual needs of the children being cared for. The Act posed as many questions as it answered and with hindsight it has had a major impact.

CREATING A CONTAINING ENVIRONMENT

The team

Before young people can feel contained and safely managed it is very important that the staff feel that they are similarly held. Thus it is vital to discuss the type and levels of oppositional and aggressive behaviour that the unit might be able to manage. This means creating time for the team to look at the issues and their implications. It is well worth investing in an outside facilitator to support this process. The aim is to give staff the opportunity to look at the wide-ranging aspects both for the service team and for individuals. One of the major difficulties for in-patient units is that they sometimes tend to react to rather than plan for situations. The safe and successful management of challenging and aggressive behaviour is dependent on an approach that is open to scrutiny. Appropriate policies, procedures and clinical responses need to have as high a priority as any other therapeutic intervention. The approach of the unit needs regular and consistent review, not simply in response to a particularly challenging episode. Reactive responses lead to staff feeling criticised and isolated. Invariably it is the nursing staff, responsible for the day to day running of the unit, who feel most vulnerable.

Many nurses report that they do not feel that other members of the team fully understand the complexities of managing severe oppositional and aggressive behaviour. They are concerned that the wider team only becomes involved if there is a complaint or if a child or member of staff is injured. Staff managing the behaviour may feel unsupported and that their practices are being questioned.

The aim for managers and lead clinicians is to create an environment where all aspects of managing and responding are open to discussion. The team has to understand that this is an area that will always be a potential risk for staff and children. Policies and clear management strategies provide a framework but cannot cover every eventuality. The aim is to provide as safe a practice as possible, but not create a 'sterile field' where challenging behaviours are avoided.

Staff self-awareness

This is a complex and ongoing process and needs investment from clinicians and managers if it is to be successful. To achieve an open and honest understanding of oneself requires support, training and commitment from the unit involved. This can be provided through study days, workshops, support groups and clinical supervision. The aim is to increase the personal awareness of stressors, attitudes, motivators and anxiety and develop an understanding of how these impact on therapeutic effectiveness. This highlights key questions such as 'What am I bringing to this situation? How does this child make me feel? What does this remind me of?' Developing self-awareness can create stress and tension in its own right and needs to be discussed and planned. The introduction of formal, individual, clinical supervision at Stepping Stones took nine months of planning, discussion, arguments, research and risk taking before a structure was agreed. To have implemented this process more quickly could have created greater problems and been extremely threatening for some staff. The strategy that most helped was to use outside trainers to encourage staff to look beyond the unit and learn from others' experiences. This made the change less personal for a close knit staff group and allowed a model to develop that uses supervisors from within and outside the unit. This level of awareness is important in debriefing after stressful situations. Staff responses will vary in complex ways to slightly differing situations.

After an incident staff must have an opportunity to share and explore the emotional impact the situation had on them. Physical restraint, for example, will affect staff and children in a variety of ways. Sometimes staff may feel that a healthy resolution has been reached by keeping a child safe through holding.

> Ben, a 10-year-old boy, became abusive and violent when 'grounded' for leaving the unit without permission. He required physical restraint owing to his level of aggression.
>
> When calm Ben was clear that his anger was about not being allowed out which he knew was his fault. This made him frustrated and angry with himself but once his anger was out, he accepted the sanction.
>
> The staff involved felt positive about this intervention, as there had been a clear resolution from the situation. Ben understood the process although it was not necessarily the approach or outcome he had been hoping for.

> Alan, a 12 year old, refuses to accept that he has to make reparation following damage to furniture. He tries to leave the room saying staff are picking on him and he cannot be forced to comply. He is stopped from leaving the lounge as he is agitated and has a history of absconding.
>
> Alan becomes increasingly angry and distressed and unable to cope with staying in the room. Staff give Alan space and options to avoid the conflict escalating. Staff are also aware of how distressed Alan becomes if he has to be physically held and how he projects these feelings onto staff.
>
> When Alan tries to leave the room he becomes violent and has to be physically held. (There are reports that he may well have been sexually abused.) During restraint there is a great deal of pleading and accusations towards the staff.
>
> This incident left the staff with strong emotions and uncertainty about whether they had achieved anything. One staff member remarked that they could not remember what had led to restraint being required.

Managing such situations is complex and requires detailed insight and strong managerial support. Strategies may include:

- De-briefing after the situation
- Formal individual clinical supervision

- Group supervision – this can provide the opportunity to discuss a specific child in detail and share feelings and ideas
- Training opportunities outside the ward environment
- A comfortable, well-situated room where staff can unwind
- A culture that encourages support, awareness, openness and sharing of feelings.

Creating the culture

Creating a culture involves constantly revisiting the subject. One of the major problems for in-patient units has been the ease with which they can encourage rather than dissipate conflict. The units themselves may often mirror the conflict that the young person is experiencing (Dockar-Drysdale, 1953). The efforts made to manage the challenging behaviour can in themselves lead to confrontation. The units can be drawn into a position of believing they have to be in control. The young people exhibiting the behaviour want to retain control as this is often their only way of managing their circumstances.

Aggressive behaviour is often a coping mechanism. The children have not learnt or experienced other, more effective coping strategies. Rather than being powerful or in control they have few skills and resources for managing emotions and conflict. The chemistry is ripe for conflict and it is on this critical point that any unit needs to focus. The challenge is to use the potential for conflict as a therapeutic tool rather than simply react to it.

Staff often assume responsibility for controlling and managing the patient's anger. This can allow the child to avoid responsibility and blame the staff for their situation. The environment should aim to provide the opportunity for change rather than replicating what has already occurred. The young people need to see that there are different ways and better responses. All too often the expectation of the young person is that they will have little alternative but to continue their challenging response to authority. The task is to break this cycle and create an opportunity for the young person to take responsibility and ultimately, control themselves. The basis for this is not how to change the young person, but how to adapt the approaches and attitudes of staff.

The undoubted strength of feeling about the problems of managing highly challenging behaviour has not led to new, innovative styles. For some staff it is easier and requires less personal change to continue reacting to the behaviour. In many cases jumping in and taking control has been one of the earlier interventions rather than a later more radical response. Therapeutically it is far more difficult to stay with the emotions rather than intervene when oppositional and aggressive behaviours are to the fore. This requires confidence and a high level of self-awareness. Staff need to be able to explore their own responses to aggression and manage them. The problem with taking control too quickly is that the young person is able to deflect their own feelings on to the staff. They can then be used as a reason for the young person to stop looking at themselves and to focus on the 'authority figure'. Staff require training and support to allow the young person to own their feelings. Staff may not acknowledge that the feelings are an integral part of the process. The young person needs to be given permission to experience the strong feelings and struggle with how to manage them.

This remains an important approach and can be very effective in managing challenging behaviour. The problem can be that unless the young person is helped to become aware of the predisposing factors for themselves, they are dependent on and can react against the staff around them.

Teaching understanding

There are symptoms and signs that, if not responded to, may well lead to an aggressive outburst. Children cannot be expected to find these for themselves and staff are responsible for educating young people about them.

These signs may be general and common to most people when they lose their temper. They are predominantly physiological and can be a less emotive introduction to anger management. They include:

- A rise in temperature – feeling hot and looking flushed
- Increased heart rate
- Clammy, sweaty hands
- Verbally unresponsive
- Poor eye contact
- Increased restlessness
- Feeling tense and 'enclosed'.

These factors can be learnt by both staff and children and provide general cues to which to respond. They allow a rationale for action to be applied and explored, as highlighted in these examples: 'You seem to have stopped talking to me', 'You look hot and restless, how can I help?' 'This could be a sign that you might lose your temper'. Responding to these signs may allow the child the opportunity to regain control. The responses are *general* and do not assume that the child is about to lose their temper or become violent.

The second aspect in teaching understanding is more personal and centres around the child's own anger. The task is to explore the individual cues for this child together with the circumstances and building awareness of them. It can be tackled individually or in a group setting. The aim is to help the child identify what could trigger an aggressive outburst. Simple examples may include:

- Feeling let down: 'They said they would ring at 6.00' or, 'I'm afraid football is out as it's raining'
- 'They are making fun of me'
- 'I always get the blame'
- 'You can't make me do it'
- 'I can't manage that, it's too difficult.'

The building of this awareness can be used in tandem with the physical symptoms to help the staff and child learn what happens to them. The anger becomes more identifiable and 'real', as emotion linked to thought, rather than intangible. This linkage also provides staff with a framework in which to work and a clearer reference point. This can reduce the level of inconsistency as all staff have a clearer focus.

The approach reduces the variables but allows for individual and therapeutic interventions based on the specific child. It also provides a yardstick for staff as they will have a rationale for their responses. This is vital as staff are able to appraise their own and others' practices against specific behaviours.

Policies

Most in-patient units now have a policy for managing challenging behaviours. Many of these were written in response to the Children Act (1989) which highlighted this area as an issue requiring legal guidelines. The Act has itself suffered criticism from various quarters and many professionals have felt that in this particular area it was not definite enough. However, the Children Act was probably pitched at the right level: it created an environment for residential settings to look at their practice in more detail. It is important that any policy is owned by the team and shared with all those who use the particular service. This creates an environment of openness and avoids insularity and a defensive approach. The policy should take into account the views of both children and families with regard to the safe and therapeutic management of oppositional and aggressive behaviour. An example of creating policy from the recommendations from the Act can be found in the Stepping Stones Restriction of Liberty Policy. This broadens the definition of restriction and directs staff to record any incidents to which they child has not clearly consented. This type of policy clearly identifies restriction as an integral part of treatment.

The problem has been that the management of violence and aggression is often part of the daily routine and may not be given the same therapeutic priority as other interventions: what clinician would prescribe medication without assessment, discussion and accurate recording?

Pre-admission planning

In addition to the strategy used to manage a particular incident or behaviour, the work carried out prior to admission is a key area (see chapters 4 and 5). The pre-admission period gives all those involved time to assess and plan their strategies. The unit can discuss previous interventions and what has been successful or not. This period also allows the unit and young person to begin the work of how they are going to manage the problem together. The role of the unit is to begin the process of helping the young person to take responsibility for their behaviour. The sooner this dialogue begins, the clearer it will be whether a working relationship can be established. The unit can explain their approach and attitude towards oppositional and aggressive behaviour. The therapeutic work starts at this point as the young person is already being given options and decisions to make. The unit is making a clear statement that they are looking t o create change in a different way. The young person will probably be expecting conflict with the unit and may well use oppositional behaviour to assert themselves and take some control. They may also believe that if they raise the level of their behaviour they will prevent an admission. The unit needs to reflect this back to the young person by taking a more neutral position. At this point there is no contract between the two parties. The unit can remain impartial by explaining what is available, the opportunities they can offer and the benefits they believe can follow. Many young people displaying these sorts of behaviours will often fall back to the position of the conflict they have been used to. This does not mean that if they consent to treatment the work from then on is plain sailing. Far from it! There is, however, a form of contract that can be used as part of the framework when conflict inevitably arises.

The pre-admission period also allows for practical issues to be discussed with the young person and their carers. The strategies used for managing challenging behaviour must be discussed and agreed before admission. It is most important that the young person is prepared for the approaches they will be faced with: the type of sanctions; the response of staff; the use of physical restraint; the role of time out or seclusion. All of these must be discussed in detail and their use laid out clearly in the unit policy. The young person should be as fully prepared as possible for the range of interventions to be used. It is important that the unit does not become drawn into a battle, as it cannot be won. Rather than seeing this as a situation of potential conflict it should be regarded as an opportunity for therapeutic interventions. The focus should be to help the young person look at and find ways of managing the conflict they are having themselves. This also allows choice and an opportunity for the young person to experience adults in authority respecting their views. This approach also allows consent to be obtained.

One of the key questions for in-patient units is their response to a referral where the young person is clearly opposed to admission or working with the unit. It is not enough to simply give general statements regarding the management that will be used; the use of physical restraint, for example, must be explained in great detail, together with the reasons for its use and what behaviour or situation will lead to its implementation. Most of these young people do not enjoy being physically held, but the most common complaint is not the restraint itself but the inconsistent reasons for its use. This is where the guidelines must be clear so that the young people concerned know where they stand. This principle runs through all of the strategies that may be used. The guidelines are literally to 'guide staff along a particular route'.

Management strategies

Therapeutic reviews play an integral part in the overall management. The behaviours highlighted in this chapter will have an impact on the unit as a whole. They will affect not only staff but also the other residents and anybody using the unit on a regular basis. The unit needs to be seen as part of the wider community rather than totally isolated. If the pre-admission work has been well managed, the young people will be aware of the culture and expectations of the unit. This can be used to reinforce standards and norms. This may be achieved by holding meetings for the whole community when certain types of behaviour occur such as bullying or racism. These may be in the form of 'crisis community meetings' involving the whole of the unit. These affect the whole of the community and require skilled management by the staff involved. The reasons for calling the meeting must be clear, as must its aims. The intent should not be to humiliate the individual concerned but to highlight that they have expressed their feelings in an unacceptable way.

This approach maintains the ethos that individuals have choices and responsibilities for how they manage and that their behaviour has an impact on others. The danger is that in certain circumstances the response of the peer group towards a certain level of behaviour can have a powerful effect on some young people. It is important, however, not to labour this approach or use it at every turn. That can lead to a loss of impact or possibly conflict if the group do not take the situation seriously or feel they are being used by staff. A possible alternative to this approach is to use the community to reinforce positive behaviour. A 'positive' meeting could be called to highlight how an individual managed appropriately and deserves credit from the rest of the community.

Another important aim of in-patient units is that they try to remain realistic. One of the problems units have is that they are often very intense places. Behaviour that in other areas could be missed or strategically overlooked is often picked up on. For example, a fight is hard to ignore on a small in-patient unit, whereas in an average secondary school it might not even come to the attention of staff. It is important, therefore, that staff are able to look at situations in perspective and respond appropriately. This is one of the many grey areas highlighted previously and successful management requires an environment that encourages openness and honesty and opportunities for sharing and discussing situations and responses.

Mistakes will inevitably be made but these are also a key element of the therapeutic process. It is important that we can acknowledge our mistakes to the young people we are working with. This allows them to make mistakes themselves and learn from them. They also see adults in authority in a different perspective. It again emphasises that in-patient units are trying to provide a different type of experience that allows opportunity for change.

The 'realistic approach' is also pertinent to allowing a certain level of conflict to occur. All young people need opportunities to test boundaries and learn from the experience. The in-patient unit can provide an environment where more vulnerable young people can test adults and authority. The difficulty for staff is to tease out 'healthy' as opposed to extreme and potentially aggressive oppositional behaviour . What then is the most effective framework to support this approach?

Know your patient

Oppositional and aggressive behaviour is usually one of the reasons why a young person might be referred to an in-patient unit. There is often a history of challenging behaviour of some nature. The unit therefore has ample opportunity to make this a specific area for treatment. Often the energy is used in looking for strategies once the young person is admitted and the difficulties are already happening.

Knowing the patient is an evolving process that requires a high level of skill in observing, assessing and understanding behaviour. This also needs training and support to develop acute skills so that small changes can be detected and understood. Staff may find this deskilling and possibly threatening if they feel their judgement is being questioned. It is important that this detailed knowledge of the patient is seen as a vital skill and not simply as a day to day task. The emphasis needs to be on the importance of knowledge and understanding in the process of successful management. The reward for the staff can be that there is less crisis management of violence and aggression. Staff need to be made aware that their increased skills will lead to a more therapeutic, safer and satisfying environment.

Research

There have been a number of studies in recent years focusing on the management of aggression and violence in health care settings. Few of these studies have highlighted child and adolescent units, but some helpful themes can be detailed. There is now greater emphasis on educating staff about aggression, providing support and teaching new types of intervention (Ryan and Poster, 1993). Training during the 1980s and early 1990s introduced physical methods of control and restraint, but crucially failed to develop skills required to prevent violent incidents occurring in the first place. By increasing the understanding of violence and the processes that create and maintain it there is opportunity for more creative, patient-centred interventions. Theoretical training aims to look at broader issues that affect violence and aggression whilst clinical training aims to provide staff with a variety of skills to enhance care. The term de-escalation has been applied to this process. Stevenson (1991) describes this as a 'complex, interactive process' aiming to reduce anxiety, maintain personal space and control and prevent acting out. There are a number of vital factors that need to be taken into account if these aims are to be achieved.

Understanding methods of de-escalation

The theme of investing in training continues in this section as the skills of listening and communicating effectively need to be developed and honed.

Language

The way we talk to the children is a vital tool in the therapeutic process. Cotton (1993) describes this as 'helpful talking' as it requires the correct phrases, pitch, tone, information and ideas to help the child respond and move on.

The opportunities for staff to provide this experience are rich and varied but need constant assessing and reviewing. Take these two responses to the same situation as an example:

> John, aged 8, has been playing in the garden and needs to wash his dirty hands before lunch. He refuses:
>
> *Staff 'A'*: John, I know you don't want to wash your hands, how can I help? Don't worry, your lunch is safe and as soon as we finish we can go and have some.
>
> *Staff 'B'*: John, I know you don't want to wash your hands, but unless you hurry up you might miss your lunch and I know you wouldn't want that.

The key here is that in the first example there is a sense of empathy and working together. Note the use of the word 'we' as opposed to 'you'. In the second example the responsibility lies with the child and there is a veiled sanction that could be imposed if John does not speed up.

Listening skills

As with language, effective listening is a skill that can be assessed and developed. When working with the extreme emotions and behaviours found on in-patient units, listening and maintaining empathy is not a simple task.

There is often an overwhelming desire to either respond or to try and 'make the situation better'. The struggle is to stay with and understand the *child's* experience rather than attempt to solve it. This can lead to increased anger and emotions as children may feel patronised, misunderstood or threatened by the 'helpful' approach.

The angry child often wants their anger acknowledged, not quashed or avoided.

> Adam, an 8-year-old boy, was told by his mother that he could choose the unit video. The rota had not reached Adam so that he was not allowed to do so. He responded by swearing and kicking out. Staff responded as follows:
>
> 'Adam you are right to be angry because you feel disappointed and let down. It doesn't feel fair, does it. Can we help you to be angry in a safe way?'

This may appear straightforward but the nurse may have wanted to say 'Adam, I know you are angry, but it's not our fault. You can still watch the video but we have to stick to the rota'. This approach is reasonable but puts some responsibility onto Adam for how the nurse is feeling, i.e. 'Don't blame me, its your mum's fault for saying you could choose!'

This is an understandable sentiment but it belongs to the nurse, not to Adam, who had his own confused feelings about his mother's role.

Non-verbal cues

These can be as important as verbal language and can convey a variety of messages. Increased awareness and understanding can be taught and developed. Key areas include:

- Posture – this can be supportive or challenging
- Personal space – when to respect the child's space and when to go into support the child
- Coming down to the child's level by kneeling or squatting
- Awareness of space, quietness, time, heat, light and privacy are essential. All of these elements contribute to the successful management of violence.

Safety

To communicate and develop a therapeutic relationship both the nurse and patient must feel safe in the environment. This includes awareness of:

- Staffing levels and the appropriate skill mix to provide the best management
- Where staff are situated and who they are with
- What is planned for the shift and what is expected of patients and staff
- Relevant information from earlier in the day, e.g. unresolved incidents or continued tension.

Group work

Anger management groups can allow children to discuss and explore their own and other's response to anger and its predisposing factors. These groups provide an opportunity to 'practise' in a safer environment where support and structure make learning safe. The style of these groups can vary but can provide a therapeutic setting for young people to develop new strategies. They can also build confidence and self-esteem as there are opportunities to help and support others in the group. This approach can also be fun and innovative and may include use of camera and video; role-play; relaxation; art and music. The secondary task for the groups is to provide opportunities for staff to share and discuss situations and allow them to learn from mistakes and misjudgements.

CONCLUSION

As previously stated, this chapter does not set out to teach specific management skills for oppositional and/or aggressive behaviour. The intention is to look at the attitudes and conditioning that in-patients and staff have towards this particularly emotive area. For some readers this approach may be frustrating as they look for more concrete, practical advice. The answer is that there are no quick fixes and that the methods of managing aggression have to evolve over time. It cannot be a short-term approach but a process that develops through continually discussing and reviewing approaches and strategy. What was regarded as good practice five years ago may not be so now.

Without exploring the emotions, fears and therapeutic value of treating these problems, they remain a response rather than a treatment in their own right. When the unit has fully gauged its own responses, attitudes and level of containment it can then apply them to the treatment of young people.

REFERENCES

The Children Act (1989), London: HMSO.

Cotton, N. (1993) *Lessons from the Lion's Den*. San Francisco, CA: Jossey-Bass Publications.

Dockar-Drysdale, B. (1953), Some aspects of damage and restitution. *British Journal of Delinquency, 4 (1)*.

McHugh, A., Wain, I. and West, N. (1995) Handle with care. *Nursing Times,* 6, (91), 62–63.

Ryan, J. and Poster, E.C. (1993), At risk of assault, *Nursing Times*

Stevenson, S. (1991), Heading off violence with de-escalation. *Journal of Psychosocial Nursing and Mental Health Services, 29 (9)*, 6–10.

17 Child maltreatment and in-patient units

Caroline Newbold and David Jones

There are several reasons why child psychiatric in-patient units need to be highly attuned to child maltreatment issues. First, a sizeable proportion of their child patients will have been abused or neglected. Second, there will be a strong tendency for staff, who often take over the parental role and commonly feel critical about the quality of parenting which the child has received, to perceive the child's carers as abusive or neglectful. Finally, children may be abused within the unit itself, by other children or by staff. In this chapter we contend that the unit's ethos, its policies and consequently its atmosphere will lead to a setting within which disclosure of any maltreatment will be possible. The atmosphere of safety, containment and respect for children, as persons in their own right will, we believe, inevitably lead to children disclosing sensitive information of many kinds. Existing suspicion may become clarified during the admission or, alternatively, new and surprising information revealed. We first discuss our approach to making the institution as safe as possible before turning to any abuse revealed during the child's stay.

MAKING THE INSTITUTION AS SAFE AS POSSIBLE

We begin from the premise that child psychiatric in-patient units have the potential to be unsafe. It would be short sighted and arrogant to presume differently, especially in the light of the numerous instances of institutional abuse within residential children's homes which have come to light in recent years (Utting, 1991). Children's psychiatric units are not usually such long stay institutions, but nonetheless, because of the intensity of emotion and the relative vulnerability of the children, we feel that the institution must do everything possible to make itself safe.

There are various dimensions to this potential lack of safety: child to child, staff abuse to children, staff abusing other staff and possibly children being abusive to staff. We are concerned here with situations where children are the victims. The abuse or trauma may be an individual problem, or may represent a collective deviance, perhaps associated with charismatic yet misguided leadership, as occurred in the Pindown affair (Levy and Kahan, 1991). All forms of maltreatment occur, including physical, sexual and psychological. There may also be frank neglect of adequate care.

In our view the problem of institutional abuse is best approached through the unit espousing a clear set of principles and practice concerning child welfare and children's individual rights. The UN Convention on Children's Rights (UNICEF, 1995) and the Children Act 1989 (White et al., 1990), provide us with useful guidance. We can utililise these legal frameworks in order to embed the issue of prevention of institutional abuse within a series of *positive* initiatives which emphasise child welfare principles. Such an approach may strike some practitioners as unnecessarily grandiose or moralistic. However, we have found that it enables a series of clear principles to be laid down, from which practical outcomes can flow. Children should benefit from the following rights:

1.   To have the highest quality psychiatric assessment and treatment.
2.   To receive high quality care, of a type appropriate to their age and developmental level.
3.   To be safe from harm, abuse and neglect.
4.   To have their voice heard and to contribute to those decisions made about them, to a degree commensurate with their developmental and health status (including issues of consent to have treatment or not).
5.   All children, regardless of race, gender, disability or any specific vulnerability, should expect the same high standard of care, to have any special needs attended to, and to be protected from stigma and prejudice.

Based upon this culture of child welfare and rights to fundamental aspects of care, safety and protection, we can develop a procedure with which to respond to any concerns about maltreatment occurring within the institution (Figure 17.1). The approach will need to be predicated by the question 'how will we handle abusive situations when they occur?', rather than *if* they occur. It should be self-evident that the assumption that the unit is too safe or that 'it could never happen here' would, in our view, be dangerous.

Figure 17.1 represents the procedural aspect of the policy for responding to child welfare concerns. This type of procedural response will need to be matched with a programme of awareness raising for all the unit's staff about the potential for institutional abuse. This allows for difficult issues to be discussed and thought about by all staff members (e.g. gender of staff involved in the intimate care of children, especially those with disability). Also, issues such as who to go to when maltreatment is suspected, and what kind of response could be expected, can be rehearsed and discussed. The confidentiality and employment position of anyone who notifies possible maltreatment must be assured, as well as their safety from stigmatisation or loss of job opportunity and advancement. All staff must feel that issues will be explored thoroughly and objectively without either over-reaction or under-reaction, but with balance (Nunno and Motz, 1989). They should know that the institution intends to commit itself to enhancing children's welfare and will be subjecting itself to a continuing process of audit and review.

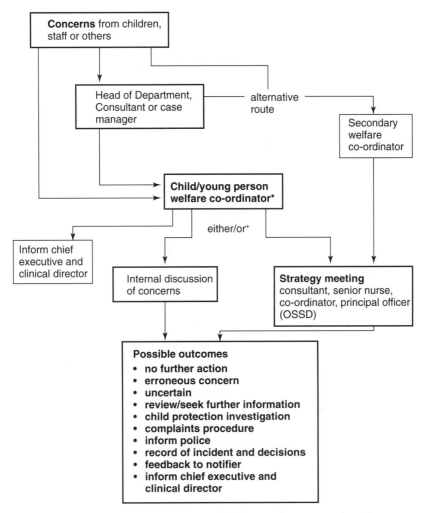

Figure 17.1 Responses to welfare concerns of children and young people within psychiatric in-patient units

This review might be local, or be undertaken through review from outside, perhaps by another unit or agency.

This approach will not only encompass institutional abuse, but also involve a review of consent to treatment within the institution, the nature of psychological treatments, policies on restraint, etc. We predict that the process will inevitably bring with it an increasing ethos of openness and discussion about all matters to do with the rights and welfare of the child. It should also make the unit unattractive to potential paedophiles.

Development of these unit policies and procedures would be refined in partnership with the local Social Services Department, and local Area Child

Protection Committee. The latter can then become conversant with the difficulties and dilemmas which a psychiatric unit faces, as well as the unit's intended response. This can be important for understanding the context of any concern about institutional maltreatment. The procedural approach outlined can respond to overt abuse or suspicions, as well as erroneous allegations, including concocted, malicious and misinterpreted suspicions of maltreatment. Our experience has been that this has led to staff feeling increased confidence in the way in which concerns will be handled, and that, in fact, repeated erroneous allegations of maltreatment have become less frequent as a result.

The welfare co-ordinator's role is crucial, bringing together all efforts made to enhance and assure children's welfare, and is the central cog in the system of response to any concerns about child welfare. This is likely to be a senior member of staff, appointed by the unit's Management Group and answerable to both the Unit Management and the Trust Management. They keep a log of all incidents and the decisions made about them which is open to audit. The co-ordinator would be informed about all concerns arising within the unit and would delegate responsibility when unavailable. The co-ordinator gathers information by private interview and/or case note examination .

Having one welfare co-ordinator in a unit removes potential confusion as to who to inform, and establishes where the responsibility for assessing mal-treatment concerns finally resides. The Clothier Report concerning the actions of Beverley Allitt (DoH, 1994a) demonstrated the danger posed by having several senior nurses and doctors and not one named responsible person. The welfare co-ordinator is, in part, a response to this tragedy, though we have taken the opportunity to expand the role.

There is a secondary welfare co-ordinator appointed, intended to provide a fail safe mechanism if the principal co-ordinator is considered unresponsive or unable to take an objective view because he or she is the subject of complaint.

If there is a possibility of child maltreatment, the co-ordinator gathers sufficient information to decide whether the concern falls within the criteria agreed by the local area child protection committee for initiating an investigation. Generally this will involve deciding whether the child has suffered or is at risk of suffering significant harm (for further discussion see Oxon ACPC, 1996a, pp. 16–17 and DoH, 1994, pp. 5–7). If so, a *strategy meeting* is called within twenty-four hours involving the consultant, senior nurse, the welfare co-ordinator and the principal officer from the local Social Services Department. They meet to discuss how the matter will be taken forward and investigated. Various outcomes are possible – ranging from no further action if the concern is discovered to be spurious or insubstantial, through to continuing review, and, finally, formal child protection investigation procedures. Serious cases could require police involvement alongside continuing care of the children involved. Staff members may need to be placed on leave pending disciplinary procedures if it seems likely that a child has been abused by a member of staff and the unit's managers will be involved. A complaint may be lodged, and a child protection investigation commenced. We have found that the strategy meeting has enabled the several aspects of such cases to be held together and repetition avoided. Previously, each discipline from within the unit, as well as outside police and social service units, worked separately, often duplicating each other's work and leading to unacceptable delay and confusion. The strategy group can also ensure that child psychiatric care is continued, whether the child is suspected to be a victim or a perpetrator of maltreatment.

Figure 17.1 also indicates a process of *internal review* for some types of concern. These will be instances which are not sufficiently serious to trigger a strategy meeting or where the concern is unclear. An internal review would normally involve a consultant, senior nurse and child welfare co-ordinator, together with any other involved professional. A full record will be kept of these, as of the more serious ones, to facilitate external review and audit. The outcomes of internal review could be either no further action, gaining further information or, if concerns are raised, a decision to call a strategy meeting. The co-ordinator will keep the unit's managers informed as necessary, and certainly about all those concerns which trigger a strategy meeting. At the end of the process, regardless of outcome and the level of response which is undertaken, the notifier is informed about the review process and the measures which have been taken.

Policy and procedure is worthless without a determined attempt to make such a procedure visible throughout the unit. All staff need to be made aware of the policy, regardless of their standing within the institution. Cleaners and domestic staff may well be in possession of vital information and their concerns must be able to be properly evaluated. The procedure will need to be part of the induction process for any new staff. It will be necessary to have a programme of awareness raising about all matters to do with abuse and maltreatment for all the staff, especially those involved in direct care. The Chailey Heritage programme has provided a useful model which could be adapted from the field of learning disabilities to our own units (Chailey Heritage, 1992).

MANAGING THE DISCOVERY OF EXTERNAL ABUSE DURING ADMISSION

Children are admitted to psychiatric in-patient units suffering a complex range of emotional or behavioural symptoms which have persisted despite outpatient treatment. The possibility of maltreatment being a significant part of the final diagnosis is always present, although staff need to maintain a discipline of open-mindedness by raising alternative diagnoses or aetiological factors to account for any particular presentation. We see abuse disclosures made by children and, on occasion, by their parents, in the context of either current suffering or past abuse which has stopped.

Staff members who are involved in the daily care of these vulnerable children and who effectively take on a temporary parental role may feel critical and angry towards parents who have contributed to the child's psychological difficulties. This in itself may lead to an atmosphere in which it is presumed that a child with a particular range of problems must have been abused. The child in turn may come to believe that revelations of maltreatment are expected as part of their therapy. There is fine balance here between creating a caring atmosphere within the unit which enables children to feel safe to explore their difficulties and ensuring that any disclosure of abuse is received in a way that fulfils the exacting evidential requirements of the law. The aim must be the maintenance of an atmosphere of open-mindedness with an avoidance of both leading questioning and the idea that a history of abuse is expected, no matter how suggestive of such a history the child's behaviour and emotional state may be. It can be extremely distressing for staff to realise that disclosures made by children in their care are unsatisfactory for the purposes of future case decision making.

Staff at all levels who face the task of responding to unexpected disclosures need guidance and personal support. A fear expressed by many abused children concerns what will happen once their secret is out. Junior nurses and those who are involved in the daily care routine are likely to be the people to whom a child will come to feel particularly close and may be identified by the child as being removed from the authority structure of the institution and therefore 'safe' to talk to. Children may decide to 'test the water' in this way in the hope of retaining some control of their situation. They may communicate their whole experience at one time or more gradually over several sessions. In adolescent units it is typical for young people to disclose to staff of a similar age or apparent disposition; while our observation with young children is that they may have most confidence in those staff members who fulfil the more nurturing roles (night staff are often chosen). There needs to be extreme care and a well defined and communicated policy as to the response to tentative disclosures made by children at times of intimate care such as bathing and bedtimes so that a way is found to ensure that staff report children's communications through the established professional hierarchy, while reassuring the child that it is safe to talk. All staff should be aware of a duty to make a written record immediately following discussion with the child or the discovery of physical injury and report allegations to their professional line manager. It then becomes the responsibility of that manager to inform a designated child protection specialist in their own professional hierarchy and the clinical team responsible for the child's care. It may be that children are seen to be injured on return from temporary stays at home. Any visible signs of harm should be accurately described and combined with explanations which children give at these times. All staff should be familiar with the guidelines associated with the need for evidentially sound recording of information about the child's situation. If staff feel confidence in the policies of the unit and are appropriately supported within the team they will be best prepared to respond to disclosures in an empathic and responsible way.

Decisions as to how to proceed to an appropriate investigation can then be made by a small multidisciplinary group of senior staff members, possibly with the involvement of colleagues from police and social service departments. There may be differences between the area within which the unit is situated and that which serves the child's geographical home and these must be clarified urgently. This procedure mirrors guidance for Area Child Protection Committees (DoH, 1991 and 1994b).

During this process a tension may develop between the unit's commitment to confidentiality to the child and the necessity for reporting abuse to outside statutory agencies. There can be a need for the unit to contain developing information whilst clarifying it, before sharing it with outside agencies. While the unit should generally embrace a policy of open working with statutory agencies this may need to be carefully modified, perhaps when a child's account is initially unclear or if their mental state is precarious and the therapeutic alliance fragile – situations requiring especially sensitive management. The unit must guard against over protection and the attempt to manage cases single-handedly but equally colleagues in outside statutory agencies may have to accept a degree of risk management in order that appropriate long term decisions can be made in the interests of the child. In order for such managment decisions not to seem to be in breach of guidelines regarding interagency working, it is crucial that a unit's policy towards such matters is discussed with the local area child protection team. Of course this will vary according to the authority of origin of the child. Such discussions will inevitably be easier for a unit which already actively liaising with local agencies throughout the admission. Interagency working is inevitably more difficult with distant agencies because mutual confidence derived from shared past experience will not have been established.

Some important forms of abuse will not be recognised by direct disclosure and may be poorly identified within an in-patient unit. Neglect in its various forms is generally long-standing and its assessment is most appropriately the prerogative of community-based services. An in-patient unit may have a limited contribution to make in this area, perhaps in the form of developmental assessment or observation of parent/child interaction, but the essential integrating of information from a variety of sources to produce an overall picture of neglect remains the role of local agencies. It is unfortunate in such cases that the legal process has come to expect the weight of opinion about a child's predicament to rest within the specialist unit.

The identification of psychological maltreatment however is an area in which a child psychiatric in-patient unit does have a significant role to play. Even here there will need to be close liaison between the unit and locality-based services in order that a comprehensive assessment can be achieved. Children may not complain directly of neglect or psychological maltreatment and so diagnostic weight will have to be placed on observation and history. Some children do of course describe, directly or indirectly, experiences of insufficient love and affection and can talk quite clearly about feelings of rejection and terror, for example being shut in cupboards, persistent threatening with harm, being placed outside in the cold. It is clear that these kinds of disclosures are just as important and relevant to an overall conclusion as more overt reports of physical or sexual assault.

Having described the framework within which disclosures of abuse are handled by the unit staff, we will use two case examples to illustrate some of the benefits of a clearly defined system. Both are complex cases of long-standing abuse which were clarified during in-patient care. Jane was our patient some years ago, when child protection policies in the unit were in their infancy, while Colin's case is much more recent and shows how well established multiprofessional working can best serve the child's interests.

Case 1

Jane, aged 13 years, was admitted for investigation of medical symptoms associated with epilepsy. She did not come from the local area and had not previously been the subject of child protection concerns at home. She did however have a poor record of school attendance and was known to have been behaviourally difficult both at home and at school. She displayed acute and very worrying symptoms although an exact diagnosis had been difficult to establish.

Within the unit she was initially uncommunicative and difficult to manage. Staff were immediately concerned by her attempts at self-harm and apparent disregard for her own safety. There was little known of her home circumstances but her presentation led to much speculation among the team at all levels.

During the course of Jane's admission she began, very tentatively, to trust individual staff members sufficiently to intimate that she had been the victim of incest. She was extremely controlling of the people in whom she confided and demanded guarantees of confidentiality from them. Such was the severity of her disturbance that staff found it extremely difficult to remain objective in their professional roles. Jane's own intense fears about her situation led to a paralysing of the unit's normal responses.

As Jane's story unfolded over a period of some weeks the staff team struggled for an effective way of managing her disclosures. We were not initially able to reassure her about sharing information with child protection agencies in her home area and by the time this became essential it took considerable effort to build their trust and co-operation. Discussion with Jane's extended family was undertaken by the local workers who were met with categorical denial of the allegations. Poor recording and imprecise information from the unit made it difficult for statutory agencies to form a clear care plan and the case was beset with professional wranglings and insecurity.

Care Proceedings were initiated after much discussion, and a series of interim orders initially ensured Jane's safety within the in-patient unit. She was finally discharged, the subject of a full Care Order, and placed in a specialist residential setting offering both care and education on site. Contact between Jane and members of her extended family remained a very difficult issue throughout, as established family loyalties were severely strained following the disclosure of abuse.

Within our own unit this case highlighted some fundamental difficulties in our practice at the time and provided the impetus for a review of internal procedures for handling allegations or suspicions of abuse. Most significantly, we identified the need for comprehensive recording of concerns and the establishment of professional support and reporting guidelines within and between disciplines.

We also became acutely aware of the necessity for positive professional communication with outside child protection agencies. This needed to be established at a much earlier stage than was achieved in Jane's case so that an open atmosphere of trust and understanding could develop between agencies with the aim of working together in her best interests. We have, more recently, been able to set up professional links which have recognised the need to move through the process of disclosure at the child's pace (assuming that his/her safety is assured) within an atmosphere of co-operation between agencies. This inevitably requires a commitment on all sides to respect each other's different perspectives in the child protection system.

Case 2

Colin, aged 5 years, was admitted recently from the local area following significant medical and social concerns about his failure to thrive. It was suspected that this condition was psychological rather than physical in origin but community-based social work intervention had done little to improve his situation. Once he had settled in the unit and felt safe Colin began to disclose details of his life at home. This was not done in the form of direct allegations of abuse but more as an indirect expression of how uncaring and punitive life was for him at home. Added to this, the observations of his family relationships made by staff at contact times helped to build up a comprehensive picture of neglect and psychological abuse of long standing. Liaison with colleagues in the local social work team confirmed our assessment and enabled us jointly to establish the severity of the problem.

In order to understand the origins of Colin's abuse individual work was undertaken with his mother during the admission. This enabled us to formulate the nature of the severe parenting failure which had occurred within this family. While she was aware of the high level of professional concern around Colin's situation and the ongoing process of investigation, it was possible to respect the mother's request for personal confidentiality in respect of the detail of her own history of childhood and current sexual assault. Inter-agency agreement was established to the effect that it was sufficient to indicate that there were personal reasons why this mother could not offer appropriate parenting to this particular child, without disclosing detailed explanations for this breakdown. It was the clinical judgement of the unit staff that Colin should continue to have time at home during his admission although there was a clear acknowledgement of the continuing harm within the family. It was imperative to maintain a working relationship with the mother as the assessment continued and colleagues in statutory agencies outside the unit agreed that a recognised degree of risk-taking at an early stage had the best chance of enabling a comprehensive diagnosis to be made. Members of the nursing team who were most closely involved in caring for Colin and who therefore were most attuned to his distress felt supported by their nominated line managers as well as by the clear case planning of which they were an integral part. Open discussion with local colleagues, as well as agreed patterns of documenting the work, led to a multi-agency care plan being presented to the Court in respect of Colin's future safety.

As in Jane's case care proceedings led to the making of a full Care Order for Colin with a care plan which secured his long-term future within the extended family. He continues to have contact with his mother and siblings although his placement is geographically distant from his original home. Our most recent contact with the family indicated that Colin is well integrated into his new home and community. He is doing well at school after a difficult introduction which established that he had considerable 'catching up' to do academically and he is now growing well both physically and emotionally.

Colin's successful placement within the extended family highlights the benefits of establishing a respectful link with parents even within the context of adversarial legal proceedings. By clearly discussing our serious concerns with his mother alongside offering her some control over the disclosure of her own difficult past history, we feel we have contributed in some way to her being able to recognise Colin's dilemma and 'give him permission' to move on to a more secure and nurturing base.

The specialist work of an in-patient unit is most helpfully seen in terms of its contribution to the overall assessment of a child's difficulties and it is only when the professional system responds in a clear and agreed manner that the best interests of the child can be served. The two case illustrations above are good examples of the pitfalls and benefits which surround this complex area of child protection work.

PRACTICE POINTS

1.   An ethos of care and security should be established within the unit. This will help both children and staff to feel supported.
2.   The unit should be fully committed to the enhancement of children's welfare and fundamental rights, such as to have their safety assured, to be listened to and to have any special needs attended to.
3.   Recognition of the potential within all residential institutions for abuse to occur.
4.   Staff are encouraged to have open and frank discussions about child abuse, and for these to inform their working practice.
5.   Each unit needs a clear policy for responding to concerns about maltreatment of its residents, which is co-ordinated with the local ACPC and national Working Together arrangements (DoH, 1991), and which is open to audit and review.
6.   Maintenance of good working relationships with colleagues outside the unit. Respect for each other's role and statutory responsibilities.
7.   Initial open-minded attitude about diagnostic formulations. Abuse is only one of several possibilities.

8. Appropriate training must be available for staff at all levels about how to manage disclosure of maltreatment.

REFERENCES

Chailey Heritage Child Protection Working Group (1992) *Guidelines and Policies Relating to Child Protection.* Child Care Office, Chailey Heritage, East Sussex, BN8 4EF.

Department of Health (DoH) (1991) *Working Together under the Children Act 1989.* London: HMSO.

Department of Health (1994a) *The Allitt Inquiry: Report of the Independent Inquiry relating to the Deaths and Injuries on the Children's Ward at Grantham and Kesteven Hospital during the Period February to April 1991 (The Clothier Report).* London: HMSO.

Department of Health (1994b) *Child Protection: Medical Responsibilities.* London: HMSO.

Levy, A. and Kahan, B. (1991) *The Pindown Experience and the Protection of Children.* Staffordshire County Council.

Nunno, M.A. and Motz, J.K. (1989) The development of an effective response to the abuse of children in out-of-home care. *Child Abuse and Neglect, 12,* 521–529.

Oxfordshire Area Child Protection Committee (Oxon ACPC) (1996) *Child Protection Procedures.* Oxford: Oxfordshire Social Services Department.

United Nations Children Fund (UNICEF) (1995) *The Convention on the Rights of the Child.* London: UNICEF.

Utting, W. (1991) *Children in the Public Care: A Review of Residential Child Care.* London: HMSO.

White, R., Carr, P. and Lowe, N. (1990) *A Guide to the Children Act 1989.* London: Butterworth.

18 Unwanted effects of in-patient treatment: anticipation, prevention, repair

Jonathan Green and David Jones

As with any powerful intervention, there are potential adverse effects associated with in-patient treatment. It is particularly important to think explicitly about these since many, both within the child mental health professions and beyond, have significant concerns about residential treatment for young children and a number of non-psychiatric residential care programmes have been associated with well documented disaster. Although there have been none of these to our knowledge in child psychiatry units in the UK, it would be short sighted and arrogant to assume that this could never happen (see chapter 17)

The intention of this chapter is to describe counter-therapeutic processes that may arise during the course of in-patient care and to describe appropriate professional responses. An overall strategy could be framed in four parts:

- *Anticipation* of potential problems
- *Primary preventative* action
- *Recognition* of problems at an early stage
- Early measures towards *alleviation*.

Many of the elements of good practice described elsewhere in this book do implicitly contain these steps and reference to this will be made in the discussion that follows. The purpose here is not to reiterate all the points made elsewhere but to take a systematic approach to the anticipation of potential difficulties, with particular emphasis on areas that in-patient staff might tend to be blind to, given their own participation in the process.

The defining aspect of in-patient care is that, for a time, it radically changes the child's social context. The child moves from the familiar and local environment of family, school and social life into an institutional environment which becomes the child's temporary social, psychological and educational world. This change of context underlies the potential benefits and power of this form of treatment but equally provides the major potential source for unwanted effects for child and family. We thus consider potential unwanted effects of admission in terms of:

(1) the loss of elements within the child's local environment
(2) the presence of adverse effects within the in-patient environment
(3) the effect of admission on family life.

LOSS OF LOCAL ENVIRONMENTAL SUPPORTS

The child

Anticipation

It can be tempting during admission to idealise the child's local support network while forgetting that it is often in fact the exhaustion of the child's capacity to function within family, school or social environment which has led to the admission. Such breakdown in functioning will be presented strongly to the in-patient team by referrers and will often constitute the 'problem' that is presented (see chapter 4). The key need here is to anticipate that there may be an inevitable negative biasing in the reporting of problems and that significant *hidden sources of support* may be present in the child's life that could be compromised or lost by admission. These could include: important members of the extended family such as grandparents, uncles or pets; the presence of familiar surroundings at home; the presence of key friendships or relationships in the community and the child's experience at school.

Prevention

A crucial part of the preadmission assessment and of the discussion around decision to admit lies in the identification of any significant supports of this kind and the balancing of the impact of the loss of these against the benefits to be gained by admission. Preadmission procedures, such as those described in chapter 4, should provide an opportunity to identify such factors, as long as they are specifically asked for and the conversation does not become dominated by deficits or problems. A preadmission visit to the home by the in-patient nursing team can be very useful. During this the nurses can see the child's home environment (including, importantly, and with permission, the child's bedroom) and assess the local social environment as well as family functioning. Crucial pets, teddies, pictures and other movable items can be selected for the child to bring in to the ward (subject to ward policies on valuable items) to help the child create a personal space in the institution. Also, during the preadmission phase, the unit teachers should make contact with the child's local school and obtain a full report covering both difficulties and strengths, *prior to any decision to admit.* The break with normal education can be a loss for some children, since the social and academic environments of the school can be major supports – even though, more commonly, the school experience has been negative (see chapter 11).

Recognition and repair

After admission, a sense of loss can become apparent which perhaps could not have been anticipated, even by the child. The separation may throw crucial attachments and supports into relief (such as with grandparents or friends) and this can be useful learning for the child and the team. Of course, the loss is not absolute and much can be done by weekday visiting and weekends at home, and in many other ways to minimise the impact of important separations.

Losses more subtle to identify may relate to the loss of healthy adaptations or defences, by virtue of the containing function of the in-patient environment. While this can be a therapeutic benefit, it can also potentially contribute to a poorly adaptive regression and the beginnings of institutionalisation (see below). Once recognised, an increase in family based work and visits home, at the early stages of such loss, can help.

The family

There can also be hidden costs for the rest of the family in admission. Difficulties with time off work and the expense of travel can be a real practical problem. Given the hidden cost benefits that may accrue to local agencies following an admission (see chapter 30) it would seem perfectly reasonable that travel costs in many cases could be recouped from local social services. There can be a hidden cost of stigma for the family within their community and, for siblings (and parents), the loss of the presence of the child in their family.

Professional involvement

There may also be losses in relation to local professional involvement. Local social services and educational support may be withdrawn during hospitalisation. Local professionals may take the admission as a cue to withdraw completely from involvement in a case. Naturally, these problems can be ameliorated by good communication between in-patient units and local resources. Local agencies (particularly schools) need to hear about a child's improvements during admission so that they can prepare for the child's return – in part this means adapting their expectations, rather than continuing to treat him on the basis of how he was before.

The balance of these potential losses may vary depending on the nature of the case. For many children who present with emotional and behavioural difficulties, admission is likely to have been preceded by multiple difficulties in their local environment. For a child who presents with more discrete psychological illness or developmental disorder, it may be more likely that there are positive strengths in the local community which might risk being undermined by the admission. All these factors, balanced with the indications for the admission, should be discussed with child and family and agreed on, prior to the admission.

The issues here may need particularly careful attention from in-patient clinicians because they are likely to be less visible to them, compared with issues arising within the in-patient clinical environment.

UNWANTED EFFECTS ARISING WITHIN THE IN-PATIENT ENVIRONMENT

Anticipation

Whilst a number of children may enter the ward with a profound sense of relief to have some respite from external events in their lives, others will find it, at least initially, a frightening and bewildering experience (see chapter 11). For a child, the milieu is always intense and challenging; and units would be foolish not to recognise the possibility that the environment can at times become frightening and hostile or even abusive. Newbold and Jones (chapter 17) describe the establishment of ward practices to act against such institutional difficulties, particularly the appointment of a child welfare co-ordinator for the ward to have special responsibility for any matters of this kind.

Parents are frequently and naturally concerned before admission that their child may be negatively affected by other patients, learn bad habits or bad language or be 'contaminated' by more severe versions of their own problem. It is foolish and misleading to maintain that this never happens. It can help to communicate clear house rules about behaviour – explicit and developmentally couched for children of all ages – to parents before admissions.

Aggression between peers can arise, just as in any child group setting but with the potential added intensity of the residential experience. A particular danger in the clinical setting is the potential for an explosive and adverse mixture of cases (usually a 'critical mass' of aggressive acting out) which escalates in the group. Certain children, whose underlying problems may implicitly or explicitly resonate with each other, can pair off in escalating disturbance. Some very disturbed children have the capacity to powerfully stir and lead a peer culture. Staff need to know exactly how to manage escalating problems of this sort: usually by an early and focused meeting to analyse the dynamics of the problem and definitive early action either to separate groups of children, call a meeting between children to reflect on the difficulty, or special measures to protect or isolate vulnerable children. There needs to be a clear and explicit anti-bullying culture shared between children and all staff, across ward and school. Sometimes one child's acting out is a critical factor (although scapegoating always needs to be carefully excluded) and we will on occasion exclude such children for a time, for the safety of others. The anti-bullying culture needs to include exploitation of all kinds: emotional threats and terrorising or sexualising behaviour and unwanted sexual coercion, as well as physical bullying.

Particular concerns, given the high rates of likely sexual abuse among children admitted, are forms of sexual acting out or exploitation (see chapter 17). If confidently and carefully handled, the extremely delicate dynamics generated by different children's experience of sexual exploitation or other forms of abuse can be turned into therapeutic benefit. Discussion groups, 'keeping safe' groups (Cotton 1993) and specific staff training can help.

Since the dynamics of the peer group and the staff group are closely linked, it is not surprising that the professional atmosphere of the milieu can shift quite rapidly between a therapeutic and an anti-therapeutic, containing stance. At the extremes, the culture can become more than temporarily anti-therapeutic and sometimes potentially dangerous (see chapters 17 and 9). Staff have to constantly strive to keep the peer culture therapeutic and to avoid what can be rapid shifts into anti-therapeutic dynamics. The dynamics of a unit can become unhelpful in a number of ways. Especially working with deprived groups, there is a tendency to become introverted and self-contained, preoccupied with 'rescuing' children from an external environment that is increasingly seen to be harsh and uncaring. Attitudes can drift into 'parent blaming', longer admissions, and anxious over-protection of the children; in effect, a substitute care (see chapter 14). We work against this tendency by involving ward staff in community visiting and home visits, and active engagement of families in treatment alongside the child.

The 'parental care' of the unit can fail under stress, leading to serious unwanted effects: demoralisation and disintegration of care; the emphasis switching from care and therapy to custodial control; the fabric of the unit deteriorating. Here the stage is set for the excesses of institutional abuse, which have been at times associated with residential environments. Prevention lies in leadership, a clear unit ethos, supervision and support from experienced staff, and in good staff recruitment.

In-patient units can sometimes be denigrated along with their patients, seen as places of 'last resort', and become overloaded with 'impossible' intractable problems. This obviously promotes demoralisation. The answer lies in patient selection, and a more active approach to the use of intensive therapy earlier in the course of psychopathology. The in-patient unit should not be seen as the end of the line, but rather an 'intensive therapy unit', where work can be undertaken at any stage in the development of psychiatric disorder.

Recognition and repair

Recognising impending difficulties in the milieu is crucial, and an important area of research and development could be the development of instruments to monitor these process variables in clinical practice. Adaptation of the Ward Atmosphere Scale (Moos et al., 1973) for children's units may help to achieve such monitoring and to identify early warning signs of a change in therapeutic culture (see chapter 27). Good clinical supervision is also crucial (chapter 9).

There must be explicit routes whereby individual children can regularly tell staff about how the admission is going, how they are feeling about the milieu and about their treatment: this is probably best accomplished through a key nurse system. Similarly, there needs to be regular opportunity for discussion and feedback with parents. If the therapeutic alliance with either child or parent deteriorates then this should be a matter of review to make sure it is not due to adverse effects of the treatment itself. An open, rolling parent group for parents of children on the ward can also act as very useful feedback.

Audit in this area can be initially done using child and family satisfaction questionnaires at the end of admissions.

ADVERSE EFFECTS OF ADMISSION ON FAMILIES

The cultural discordance between many referred families and the professional environment and assumptions of the residential unit may be easily forgotten. Professionals on units who are striving to act according to their best abilities, within their understanding, may often not be in the best position to see this (chapter 8).

A frequent concern is that admission will reinforce a covert rejection or scapegoating of that child from the family. This must be carefully assessed since the presence of scapegoating is a relative contraindication to admission. However a 'scapegoated' child should *not* be denied the benefit of admission, if this is necessary. There should be careful preparatory work with child and family (and other agencies if necessary) in order to create the best circumstances for an admission. Written agreements or fully open and shared formulations of the problem are vital, so that all (including the child) understand the objectives of the admission. Also central to this is listening to the child's perspective, active involvement of the family in the in-patient work, during which the scapegoating is actively addressed. Whether or not there is overt scapegoating, the child often perceives the admission as a punishment (see chapter 11). Careful screening and preadmission work with the child in person should alert staff to this.

It is common for parents to feel deskilled at some stages of an admission (see chapter 14). This can be covertly or overtly reinforced by communication and attitudes of ward staff if they become preoccupied with substitute parenting, 'rescuing' the child and distancing or blaming the parents. As in any intensive psychological treatment, there can be the potential for dependency from either child or parent. In the context of admitting children or families in which a parent is showing Munchausen by Proxy behaviour, there is the risk of reinforcing a hospital addictive behaviour in the parent through the admission (chapter 24). A key preventative measure here is the framing of the problem directly in psychological terms, in contrast to an approach via the metaphor of physical illness.

There is no doubt that admission can be stressful for families in a number of different ways. Families who are extremely fragile may not be able to use the treatment well and may become disrupted by it (Green 1994). In general, however, many of these problems can be minimised by a committed family orientation from the unit (see chapter 8).

Researching unwanted effects

Unwanted effects of in-patient care are often closely linked to the potentially therapeutic aspects of the treatment. While attention needs to be paid to procedures for anticipating, preventing, recognising and repairing difficulties, there also needs to be empirical research into the actual incidence of unwanted effects rather than a reliance solely on theoretical or anecdotal concerns. There has been very little systematic work in this area. Research strategies could include:

- Investigation of family functioning, pre- and post-admission.
- Family expectations prior to admission and satisfaction and comments following it.
- Children's expectations and post-treatment comments.
- Investigation of ward process variables such as ward atmosphere (both as a trait measure of general institutional style and a state measure of fluctuating ward dynamics), or therapeutic alliance with the unit.
- Referrer and local agency expectation and satisfaction measures.
- The close examination of premature discharges or cases that 'go wrong'.

Table 18.1 Key clinical points: anticipation, prevention, recognition and management of adverse impacts of in-patient care

---

Preadmission
- Contact with all agencies involved.

- Evaluation of any *strengths and supports* in the community, including extended family.

- Admission decision based on thorough preadmission assessment; balancing benefits against costs of admission.

- Preparation and caution when the family dynamics are overwhelmingly scapegoating/rejecting.

- Is the anticipated case mix following admission potentially problematic?

During admission
- Continuous assessment of anti-therapeutic elements in current peer dynamics, staff dynamics, unit dynamics.

- Is there bullying of any kind?

- How good is child/family engagement and alliance?

- Is there demoralisation in the family?

- Regular reviews.

Post-admission
- Audit of patient/family/referrer satisfaction.

- Investigate cases that go wrong.

REFERENCES

Cotton, N.S., (1993) *Lessons from the Lion's Den: therapeutic management of children in psychiatric hospitals and treatment centres.* San Francisco, CA: Jossey-Bass.

Green, J.M. (1994). Child in-patient treatment and family relationships. *Psychiatric Bulletin, 18, 12,* 744–747.

Moos, R., Shelton, R. and Petty, C. (1973) Perceived ward climate and treatment outcome. *Journal of Abnormal Psychology, 82,* 291–298.

19 Externalising disorders: conduct disorder and hyperkinetic disorder

Brian Jacobs

CONDUCT DISORDER

There is controversy about admitting children with conduct disorder to children's in-patient psychiatric units. The published evidence for the successful outcome of such treatment is not very good (Pfeiffer and Strzelecki, 1990). This may be associated with treating such youngsters in a group setting (Kazdin, 1997). Nevertheless, about 25 per cent of admissions have this diagnosis (see chapter 28). This may conceal sub-populations where the prognosis has been improved. A poor prognosis is associated with a younger age of onset and presentation (Patterson, 1982; Loeber, Brinthaupt and Green, 1990), probably reflecting the number and severity of adverse influences operating when conduct disorder occurs at a younger age. There is great pressure on children's in-patient psychiatric units to admit such children because they worry child psychiatrists and other services. Many other appropriate residential service provisions have been closed over the past two decades.

What then are the roles of in-patient units for these children? There are several. Firstly, there is a diagnostic one. Many of these children have multiple diagnoses that have gone unrecognised by outpatient services. In some instances this happens because of a lack of resources to those services – often it requires continuous observation of the child for the difficulties to be dissected. A child might have Tourette's syndrome but their tics have not been regarded as significant elsewhere and have not been reported. Careful assessment of comorbid features or diagnoses, of psychosocial influences, of organic features such as head injury epilepsy and toxic exposure (e.g. lead) and of causal mechanisms should be sought (chapter 6). Small-scale audit has indicated meeting diagnostic solutions when there has been uncertainty in 90 per cent or more of cases.

> For example, AB, referred at the age of 10, had severe behaviour problems and a diagnosis of conduct disorder only. He had been excluded from two primary schools and was causing placement difficulties for his education authority. He also posed major difficulties for his father, chronically ill, and his mother with whom he had an intense and often mutually abusive relationship. Though she loved him she was repeatedly scapegoating him;

she had taken to sending him to stay with his grandmother each weekend. Outpatient treatment had been attempted twice without significant change.

Admission led to the recognition that this boy had multiple comorbidity meeting research diagnostic criteria for conduct disorder, attention deficit disorder with hyperactivity, depression and anxiety disorder. He also had mild learning difficulties with reading difficulties superimposed. He showed a range of psychosomatic symptoms. Mostly, these difficulties had not been specifically addressed in the past.

Another situation occurs when a complex case has been misdiagnosed because of the surface behaviour of the child.

EF, aged 7, was referred from another teaching hospital department of child psychiatry with a diagnosis of severe conduct disorder and mild learning difficulties. His behaviour led to his exclusion from a primary school. His single mother refused admission because he had just been given a place at a school for emotionally and behaviourally disturbed children. She said that he was manageable at home. He was re-referred some months later having been excluded from the EBD School. Early observation indicated a high degree of arousal and some apparently autistic features, with very poor language and play skills. He would jump up and grab people's hair and hang on with all his weight, seeming to think that this was funny. He had pulled out clumps of hair leading to adults becoming very wary of him.

Ward observations suggested that he was having absence seizures. Investigation confirmed EF's epilepsy together with evidence of right frontal lobe brain dysfunction. This area of the brain contributes to socially appropriate behaviour, amongst other functions. It also emerged that his mother, who was herself depressed, was physically and emotionally abusing him. She refused all offers of treatment by the unit. Her behaviour led to a care order being granted. EF was treated with carbamazepine medication for his epilepsy. This medicine may also have helped his behaviour directly. He was taught some basic social problem-solving skills and began to learn in our hospital school. He was transferred to a therapeutic children's home after six months' admission where he has improved further but he remains a disinhibited and difficult child.

The second indication for admission is to provide a coherent analysis of needs for the child. Often these children have made it very difficult for adults to get a close overall view of them and their families. Admission can rectify this. The nursing team can provide clear observations of how the child reacts to certain situations. Does he show aggression? In what circumstances? What precipitates it? How can it be overcome? Does the child need restraint or seclusion? Is he able to talk about the difficulties afterwards? Observations of his social skills in different situations and of his social problem-solving skills and deficits (Lochman, White and Wayland, 1991) are valuable.

Negotiating the purposes of the admission with the family and the referrers is a crucial process, as described in chapters 4 and 5.

Usually these children have given up on learning in school as a result of repeated failure. The admission gives an opportunity for a skilled specialist school staff group to delineate the child's levels of attainment and his learning strengths, and also provide a detailed picture of his difficulties (see chapter 11).

Family relationships and other psychosocial variables form important parts of this needs analysis (see chapter 12). Often there is a pattern of distorted attachments and confused relationships, with poor boundary setting; this contributes to maintaining the behaviours in the child. Surprisingly often one or both parents are clinically depressed. Frequently, this has not been addressed effectively. Abuse in the background of the parents can affect their parenting styles either by repetition or by a determined avoidance of setting appropriate boundaries with fears of repeating their own upbringing. We consider there to be an overlap between children with conduct disorder, children who have suffered abuse and those with attachment difficulties and disorders. They are not coterminous (Figure 19.1).

During a six-week assessment admission such cases can be examined carefully. Tentative treatment approaches for the child and often for the parents can be explored to gauge whether they are likely to be acceptable and whether they may offer change for the family. Sometimes it becomes apparent through intervention

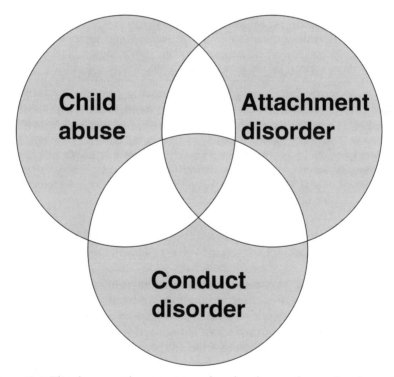

Figure 19.1 The phenomenology seen in conduct disorder, attachment disorders and child abuse

that the admission should be extended for further treatment (see chapters 7 and Part III). At other times advice can be given to the referring clinicians, bearing in mind the more limited treatment resources that they are likely to have available.

An assessment admission of this sort can lead to the conclusion that the child needs the twenty-four-hour consistency of a residential school, often with special resources and sometimes outside therapeutic interventions (see Part VIII). It is the assessment of need, comorbidity and treatment where appropriate that will make an in-patient admission worthwhile in selected cases before transfer to such boarding schools. Sometimes admission can prevent such longer-term family separations.

Unfortunately, it occasionally becomes obvious during assessment admissions that the child should not return to live with his parents because there is a pattern of abuse that is not susceptible to change. More commonly this process can take longer than the admission to resolve. Advice from social services and the calling of a child protection conference may be necessary. This can be difficult, particularly if the family is previously unknown to the social services department. Those units that still have a social worker are greatly helped in negotiating a careful approach in such cases. In all cases the social services department will need to carry out their own assessment. They will rely to a greater or lesser extent on observations made by the in-patient psychiatric service.

TREATMENT

Psychological treatments

There is some uncertainty about the efficacy of admitting young people for treatment of pure conduct disorder. Often there are comorbid diagnoses that require treatment and attempts to treat the conduct disorder are undertaken at the same time. Impressionistically, we have been able to intervene effectively with younger children rather than when they present later even though the research, as indicated earlier, suggests a worse prognosis statistically for the younger onset children. Having several children with conduct disorder on the ward at the same time leads to worse outcomes.

Treatment for children with conduct disorder often requires a careful behavioural intervention. This must encourage the child to learn positive behaviours and discourage outbursts of rage. The child often needs help with relaxation techniques so that he can begin to feel more in control of himself. Anger management programmes are useful for children of about seven years and older. They help the child to notice the physiological and emotional signals of increasing irritation and anger and then to interrupt the cycle. They will be taught to problem-solve by brainstorming for possible ways to behave and to think about the consequences of each thing they might do including violent and non-violent solutions. There are programmes for younger children based on puppet approaches; these are embedded in social skills programmes such as Dinosaur School (Webster-Stratton and Hammond, 1997).

In this programme, which was developed for outpatient groups of children aged 4–7, they first learn the rules of behaviour towards each other during the two-hour treatment groups. Throughout the programme, large puppets are used as social problem-solving detectives. Through the use of trigger cards, videotape vignettes and role-play the children learn to recognise a broader range of emotions and gradually learn social problem-solving skills. This leads to work on anger management, accompanied by the efforts of a turtle puppet, followed by sessions that concentrate on making friendships and sustaining them and then self-management in a classroom setting. Throughout the programme a behavioural regime to encourage good behaviour in the therapy settings is used. Between sessions, children are expected to practise the skills they are learning with the help of their parents and teachers.

The programme has to be adapted for use in an in-patient setting and we find that taking particular elements from it, tailored to the needs of two or three children with social difficulties, not all of whom may be conduct disordered, works best. Ward staff augment the work done by parents as the child is away from home for a part of the week. Staff of different disciplines can carry this work. It is often offered in parallel to elements of the Webster-Stratton parent training programme.

An important component of the psychological processing deficits seen in these children is their very poor recognition of their own emotions. For the most part it seems that they only notice the intensity of the emotion and its coarse quality. They recognise anger and happiness but often have difficulty with other emotions, mislabelling them and reacting with confusion. This is unsurprising, as their parents often have similar difficulties (Patterson, Reid and Dishion, 1992).

The milieu of the in-patient unit can provide a corrective influence by giving children the opportunity to have a variety of interchanges with their peers and adults but then having the opportunity to review these quietly afterwards with a sympathetic adult. It also gives them experience in negotiating more effectively and being rewarded socially (and initially materially) for this. The social skills training available in an in-patient setting is crucially dependent on the mix of children admitted; if there are more than a small number of children with the conduct disorder pattern of social skills deficits at any one time then there are insufficient peer role models for them. Rather, they tend to follow the leadership of dysfunctional role models. Sometimes a child's liberty has to be restricted in maintaining his safety and that of others. In these circumstances, the considerations carefully discussed in chapter 16 and the Children Act (see chapter 29) need to be applied with care.

When attachment difficulties are diagnosed, remedial work can help the child and parent change their patterns of interaction. Joint sessions using tasks such as cooking can be helpful. Individual work with the parent, usually the mother, and with the child are often necessary; it may be brief but often needs to be long-term treatment which cannot be carried out in the time scale of an admission to most units. However, prolonged assessment for such work can be helpful in opening the parent and child to the possibility of undertaking subsequent treatment. Whilst not sufficient it may be a necessary component of a treatment package.

Medication

The use of medication for the treatment of a behaviour disorder is at first sight controversial. Some might regard its use as an assault on a child. Clearly, where there is comorbid hyperactivity it should be treated by a combination of behavioural treatment and medication as appropriate. Medication does have a limited role in the treatment of children with conduct disorder (Campbell, Gonzalez and Silva, 1992).

The biochemical rationale for its use in conduct disorder is still uncertain. Many conduct-disordered children that are referred to our service have accompanying elements of behaviour that suggest an organic component as well as environmental difficulties. For these highly aggressive children, medication can be useful. For that subgroup that can be described as having the episodic dyscontrol syndrome, Nunn has discussed management, in this volume (see chapter 22) and elsewhere. For some children, their volatility and aggressive responses are catastrophic both in their speed of onset and in the consequences for them in the home and at school. They are quickly excluded from the mainstream and progressively marginalised. This is associated with a very poor self-esteem. In these circumstances we will try to intervene using behavioural and cognitive social learning approaches but sometimes it is insufficient. Using medication can create a window of opportunity in which psychological treatments can work.

Sometimes such children are very aroused. In these circumstances I have used chlorpromazine in 25mg doses (up to three times daily) or less as an 'emergency' measure. It is not suitable for longer-term use for this indication, in my view, so that I will try to reduce the medication within a week. I do not use benzodiazepines because of the reported disinhibiton of aggression that can sometimes occur. Nonetheless, others do use them with success.

If there are longer-term indications for the use of medication, several alternatives have been used. I would start with carbamazepine (slowly increasing divided doses to a total of 400–800 mg per day). There is no certain guide to blood levels of carbamazepine for conduct disorder. Whilst for epilepsy norms range from approximately 4.0 to 12.0 µg/ml, higher doses are associated with toxicity; they should be regarded as an upper limit. Drowsiness, poor co-ordination and leukopaenia are sometimes seen. They are usually transient. Using a slow-release version of carbamazepine may help the former two side effects. Leukopaenia can be worrying because of the rare complication of agranulocytosis. There is uncertainty as to whether regular monitoring of blood counts is necessary after stabilising a young person on carbamazepine but initial measurement of a full blood count and of liver function tests is wise. Agranulocytosis is thought to be an idiosyncratic response to the drug, without a prodrome; it is rare. Allergic skin responses are more common in children.

Both lithium carbonate and haloperidol have been shown to be effective treatments (Campbell et al., 1984). Haloperidol has strong extrapyramidal side effects. These may be particularly troublesome in children; it is generally avoided in British practice. Lithium carbonate may be used as a mood stabilising drug (Nunn, 1986; Campbell, Katantanis and Cueva, 1995). It has fewer side effects than haloperidol but it is associated with weight gain, stomach aches, headache and a tremor on occasion. These can limit its acceptability to the child. A biochemical screen including thyroid function, creatinine, electrolytes and ECG must be performed. Adequate fluid and salt balance is essential during therapy. A good fluid intake must be encouraged and monitored particularly in hot weather. During the initial stages lithium levels should be monitored twice weekly and subsequently monthly. Dosage regimes have been tried at between 500 to 2000 mg per day producing serum levels 0.32 to 1.79 mMoles/L (Campbell et al., 1984; Campbell, Katantanis and Cueva, 1995). However, this is not recommended as in adult practice, levels in excess of 1.0 mMoles/L have been associated with renal damage and occasionally with reduced glomerular filtration rates, particularly with intercurrent illness. Caution should prevail but should not prevent use of the drug in appropriate cases. Monitoring of thyroid and renal function is essential.

CHILDREN WITH HYPERKINETIC DISORDER

A steady number of children are referred to the child psychiatric in-patient service with a presumptive primary diagnosis of hyperkinetic disorder. Mild cases are not seen. Usually there are particular complications in addition to severity. For some of these children there has been a question about the diagnosis. For others there have been difficulties with medication that need to be solved in a controlled setting; there may be special factors such as concurrent epilepsy with the clinician wanting medication to be started in hospital under specialist observation. The request may be for a programmatic intervention to help the child's social skills or the treatment of a comorbid disorder such as anxiety or aggression associated with conduct disorder or oppositional defiant disorder. There may be a question of parental attitudes with high levels of expressed emotion and critical commenting. Critical commenting seems to be detrimental to the child's outcome in hyperactivity.

Most of these situations could be addressed on an outpatient basis. It is usually the number of difficulties, their complexity or a wariness about relying on non-professional observations because of previous inconsistencies, that lead to admission.

When there are questions about psychostimulant medication, it is often an opportune time to wean the child from it. This commonly leads to a few days of increased behavioural difficulties. For some children it is the first time that they have been medication free for some time. With the child stabilised, observations are carried out on the ward and in the hospital school. Conners' scales (Conners, 1982) are used as a guide to quantify these results. However, caution is appropriate. The scales depend on the expectations of the observer. A teacher in the hospital school used to seeing many such children may well have a higher threshold for scoring the child than a colleague in the home school. There, the child stands out more and is one of many more charges on the teacher's time. The stable milieu of the ward can lead to an underestimate of problems shown elsewhere.

It is important to carry out a full diagnostic assessment of the child (chapter 6). A careful history for neurological difficulties and epilepsy should be taken (chapter 22). This has sometimes been neglected, leading to observations of minor seizures or complex partial seizures on the unit in the absence of any apparent history. Assessment of comorbid psychiatric difficulties is imperative. Frequently hyperkinesis is accompanied by oppositional defiant disorder or conduct disorder, less commonly but importantly by anxiety or other emotional disorders. The child's social skills repertoire and social problem-solving need examination. Family attitudes towards the child as well as the mental health of each parent will also need to be assessed.

A full assessment will lead to a plan of intervention that is likely to include serial introduction of behavioural approaches and medication. It is preferable not to introduce both simultaneously; it can then be difficult to disentangle which intervention produces what effect.

Often a programme to help the parents learn the behavioural approach is necessary. Depending on the child's age and previous interventions, etc., there are several approaches to increasing specific parenting skills. These include the parent–child game (Jenner, 1997), the group approach to parent training (Webster-Stratton, 1994) and video trainer approaches to encouraging effective parenting. For children with hyperkinetic disorder it is often necessary to adopt quite an intensive reward scheme initially for the child. This can be wearisome for the parents. They are helped by coaching from the nursing staff and through practising work with the child at home at weekends.

Family therapy sessions are important as elsewhere (see chapter 12). There may be a history of antisocial behaviour, usually in the father's past, and a tendency on his part to behave indulgently, 'a chip off the old block', or with unpredictable anger. Neither style is helpful for the child. Family work alongside parent training can help parents spot these patterns and interrupt them.

Parental depression is also quite a common concomitant of the disorder. This may be a result of parental exhaustion. Treatment may be required for this separately or brief focussed counselling may be arranged on the unit. The child's relationship with his siblings will need to be explored. The latter have often borne much of the effects of the child's behaviour, especially if he is also aggressive.

The child may have been placed on medication elsewhere which does not seem to have been effective or which has been limited by the appearance of side effects such as tics.

GH, aged 10, was referred for assessment and treatment by a child psychiatrist. He had been known to that service for two years having been referred with serious behavioural difficulties at school and at home including suspension on several occasions. He was treated in the outpatient service with play therapy and couple therapy for his parents without a significant change of his behaviour. The mother requested a second opinion because she thought that the treatment had led to greater understanding but that the core of her son's problems had not changed. His private school had more or less excluded him unless there was a change in the boy. On assessment it was thought that he might have hyperkinetic conduct disorder. He was upset, had a low mood, poor self-esteem and some clumsiness amounting to developmental dyspraxia. An admission was recommended because outpatient treatment had failed and the case was regarded as complex, needing detailed observation in the hospital school and in a peer context. His home environment was quite fraught by this stage.

On admission he was found to function reasonably well in quiet settings but in complex or more stimulating settings he became highly overactive, aggressive, chaotic in his behaviour and overaroused. When he was taken out to a sweet shop and then to a teashop he became impossible to manage and the outing had to be curtailed. Psychometry showed that he had specific learning difficulties including difficulties with short-term memory and sequencing together with visiospatial difficulties. He had high average general intelligence with verbal scores higher than his performance scores. An occupational therapy assessment confirmed his dyspraxia and sequencing difficulties.

Educationally, he was failing significantly and his classroom skills were poor. He tried very hard. He was over-polite, as if always wary that something would go wrong. His attachments and family representations suggested denial of negative feelings. Little positive was perceived as coming from his mother and his hostility was directed towards his younger sister. Play assessment using semi-structured vignettes showed an avoidant relationship with his mother and he played out hostility and criticism from her. His father was felt as more supportive.

He was treated with a trial of methylphenidate. His parents undertook parenting work and a review of how their behaviour had been shaped by the child. His mother revealed her own hostility towards her own mother through an adult attachment interview. An educational approach to the parents and to the child himself was taken about his difficulties. In our school his needs assessment led to a programme of remedial work. The school's advice was that he should manage in a mainstream junior school but that he was misplaced in his private preparatory school. The hospital school liased with the school to which he would be discharged. His admission was extended for four weeks as a day patient to allow him to build his self-confidence.

A repeat outing to the sweet shop and other stimulating environments was successful. Follow-up included outpatient occupational therapy to help him with his perceptual difficulties; his parents had ongoing work on their parenting and oversight of his medication was be maintained.

This case illustrates how an admission of ten weeks can take a child through an intensive multifaceted assessment. It can elucidate the developmental processes underlying severe behavioural difficulties. This can lead to a trial of treatment and to reorientating his educational provision. It can make a different sort of engagement with parents and can interrupt a coercive, critical parenting style through parent management training. This total package would be very difficult to achieve as an outpatient. It requires a rhythm and momentum that can best be achieved in an in-patient setting.

Medication

The use of methylphenidate is well described elsewhere (Greenhill, 1992; Wilens and Biederman, 1992). Dosage of methylphenidate depends on age and physical size but usually falls towards the lower end of a range from 0.2 to 1.5 mg/kg/day in divided doses during the daytime. Each dose usually takes effect within thirty minutes and lasts up to about three hours. The aim is to improve concentration during school hours without major rebound in the evening or side effects such as tics.

There are often transient side effects on starting the medicine, which sometimes recur briefly with a change of dose. These include loss of appetite, tearfulness, or a rash. Occasionally, the latter is more serious and can lead to exfoliative dermatitis. Tics may be more persistent, requiring a change of medication if their severity increases. At higher doses than those recommended, ECG monitoring may be advisable. High doses can produce a restriction on the child's ability to move from one focus of attention to another, so-called 'cognitive constriction'; reduction of dosage abolishes this.

Dexamphetamine (approximately half the dose of methylphenidate) may be preferred. In some cases one is effective when the other is not. Dexamphetamine raises the threshold for fits whilst methylphenidate can lower it. Clonidine, an $\alpha 2$ noradrenergic agonist, has been shown to act on presynaptic receptors, decreasing neuronal discharge rates in the locus coeruleus. This area is linked to hyperarousal states. Clonidine has been used as an adjunct to methylphenidate towards the end of the day if rebound loss of appetite or sleeplessness is a problem with methylphenidate. Doses recommended start at 50µg each day, increasing every three days until improvement with a maximum dose 3–4 µg/kg/day (Hunt, Minderaa and Cohen, 1985). Some cardiac problems of intraventricular conduction delay have been reported so ECG is advised.

Tricyclic antidepressants such as imipramine are also used to treat hyperkinetic disorder. This can be an effective treatment but it must be approached with caution. Several children have died unexpectedly on undertaking mild exercise.

This is thought to be due to cardiac dysrhythmias (Riddle et al., 1991; Varley and McClellan, 1997). Tricyclic antidepressants have been shown to be an effective treatment for hyperkinesis. Careful review before treatment including ECG with expert opinion of the record and continuing monitoring with slowly increasing doses and blood level monitoring of the medication is justified. Dosage should start at 0.5 mg/kg/day and increase slowly to therapeutic doses. Whilst an absolute maximum dose of 5mg/kg/day is recommended in the USA (Greenhill, 1992), I would tend to limit this to a maximum of 2 mg/kg/day. There have been no reported deaths at this dosage, whilst there is definite benefit in some cases.

As ever, medication is not the sole treatment for hyperkinesis. It offers the opportunity for behavioural and other approaches to help the child and family alter their interactional patterns and to become less driven by the disorder.

SUMMARY

This chapter has described approaches taken towards externalising disorders in an in-patient setting. It has emphasised the multifaceted approach that is often needed. Whilst less emphasis has been placed on experiential therapies, they also have their place with these children. They can help a child to feel less alone in their plight and can aid a reworking of the anxiety and low self-esteem that often accompanies these disorders. A holistic approach, which carefully dissects the contributing factors including learning difficulties and appropriateness of school provision as well as other comorbidity, can markedly change the outlook for these children and their families. On occasion, more limited goals need to be sought, with appropriate placement of the child in a residential school setting where longer-term work can be undertaken. Some of these children will settle best in a warm, structured setting that emphasises a behavioural approach; they will have shown in the in-patient setting their inability or unwillingness to participate in more reflective therapies. Other children will thrive in a therapeutic school (see chapter 33) or therapeutic children's home (see chapter 32).

REFERENCES

Campbell, M., Gonzalez, N.M. and Silva, R.R. (1992). The pharmacologic treatment of conduct disorders and rage outbursts. In D. Shaffer (ed.), *Pediatric Psychopharmacology*, vol. 15 (1). Philadelphia, PA: W.B. Saunders Company.

Campbell, M., Katantanis, V. and Cueva, J.E. (1995). An update on the use of lithium carbonate in aggressive children and adolescents with conduct disorder. *Psychopharmacology Bulletin, 31*, 93–102.

Campbell, M., Small, A.M., Green, W.H., Jennings, S.J., Perry, R., Bennett, W.G. and Anderson, L. (1984). Behavioral efficacy of haloperidol and lithium carbonate: a comparison in hospitalised aggressive children with conduct disorder. *Archives of General Psychiatry, 41*, 650–656.

Conners, C.K. (1982). Parent and teacher rating forms for the assessment of hyperkinesis in children. In P.A. Keller and L.G. Ritt (eds), *Innovations in Clinical Practice: a source book*, vol. 1. Sarasota, FL: Professional Resource Exchange.

Greenhill, L. (1992). Pharmacologic treatment of attention deficit hyperactivity disorder. In D. Shaffer (ed.), *Pediatric Psychopharmacology*, vol. 15 (1). Philadelphia, PA: W.B. Saunders Company.

Hunt, R., Mindera, R. and Cohen, D. (1985). Clonidine benefits children with attttention deficit disorder and hyperactivity: report of a double-blind placebo-crossover therapeutic trial. *American Journal of Child and Adolescent Psychiatry*, 24, 617–629.

Jenner, S. (1997). Assessment of parenting in the context of child protection using the parent/child game. *Child Psychology and Psychiatry Review*, 2, 58–62.

Kazdin, A.E. (1997). Practitioner review: psycosocial treatments for conduct disorder in children. *Journal of Child Psychology and Psychiatry and Allied Disciplines*, 38, 161–178.

Lochman, J.E., White, K.J., and Wayland, K.K. (1991). Cognitive-behavioural assessment and treatment with aggressive children. In Kendall P.C. (ed.), *Child and Adolescent Therapy: cognitive behavioural procedures*. New York: Guilford.

Loeber, R., Brinthaupt, V.P. and Green, S.M. (1990). Attention deficits, impulsivity and hyperactivity with and without conduct problems: relationships to delinquency and unique contextual factors. In R.J. McMahon and R.D. Peters (eds), *Behaviour Disorders of Adolescence: research, intervention and policy in clinical and school settings*. New York: Plenum Press.

Nunn, K. (1986). The episodic dyscontrol syndrome in childhood – annotation. *Journal of Child Psychology, Psychiatry and Other Disciplines*, 27, 439–446.

Patterson, G.R. (1982). *Coercive Family Process*. Eugene, OR: Castalia Publishing.

Patterson, G.R., Reid, J.B. and Dishion, T.J. (1992). *Antisocial Boys*. Eugene, OR: Castalia Publishing.

Pfeiffer, S.I. and Strzelecki, S.C. (1990). In-patient psychiatric treatment of children and adolescents: a review of outcome studies. *Journal of the American Academy of Child and Adoelscent Psychiatry*, 29, 847–853.

Riddle, M.A., Nelson, J.C., Kleinman, C.S., Rasmusson, A., Leckman, J.F., King, R.A. and Cohen, D.J. (1991). Case study: sudden death in children receiving Norpromin: a review of three reported cases and commentary. *Journal of the American Academy of Child and Adolescent Psychiatry*, 30, 104–108.

Varley, C.K. and McClellan, J. (1997). Case study: two additional sudden deaths with tricyclic antidepressants. *Journal of the American Academy of Child and Adolescent Psychiatry*, 36, 390–394.

Webster-Stratton, C. (1994). Advancing videotape parent training: a comparison study. *Journal of Consulting and Clinical Psychology*, 62, 583–593.

Webster-Stratton, C. and Hammond, M. (1997). Treating children with early onset conduct problems: a comparison of child and parent training interventions. *Journal on Consulting and Clinical Psychology*, 65, 93–109.

Wilens, T.E. and Biederman, J. (1992). The stimulants. In D. Shaffer (ed.), *Pediatric Psychopharmacology*, vol. 15 (1). Philadelphia, PA: W.B. Saunders Company.

20 Affective disorders and psychosis

Brian Jacobs

INTRODUCTION

Childhood depression historically has been under-diagnosed. Development of DSMIII and IV alongside the development of ICD-10 diagnostic criteria has improved understanding of this area of childhood psychopathology. Application of adult criteria has been helpful in beginning to clarify the nosology of depression in children but they have to be adapted for the developmental stage of the child. School refusal and social withdrawal have frequently been found among depressed children (Goodyer and Cooper, 1993; Harrington, 1992). In the preadolescent age group depression is as common in boys as in girls. It begins to increase in prevalence from about 10 years with a disproportionate increase amongst girls possibly because of hormonal changes, greater social pressures and poorer social support systems.

There has been an increasing realisation that the co-occurrence of multiple psychiatric diagnosis (comorbidity) is quite common among children and adolescents (Caron and Rutter, 1991; Hill-Smith, Spender, Glaser and Jacobs, 1994). Depression is no exception. Kolvin and colleagues (Kolvin et al., 1991) found that 1:4 of children referred to a child psychiatric outpatient department met criteria for major depression. Comorbid depression is common with conduct disorder, after sexual abuse and accompanying intractable school refusal.

Admissions for depression to children's in-patient units are uncommon. Rather more frequent are admissions for other reasons where the child turns out to have a comorbid diagnosis of depression or a severely depressed mood. Among the latter group are commonly youngsters admitted with anorexia nervosa. The frequency of a comorbid diagnosis of depression among child psychiatric in-patients, using modern criteria, is not known.

ASSESSMENT

A detailed clinical history of depressive symptomatology is required. This needs to be taken from the child on their own in addition to that from the parents as parents have been found to have a relatively poor knowledge of their child's internalising symptoms. (Barrett et al., 1991). In addition, some units may use questionnaires for rating depression with the child, such as the Birleson Depression Inventory (Birleson, 1981) or may use semi-structured interviews to obtain a better-defined diagnosis. Issues of assessment are well summarised in Harrington (Harrington, 1992, pp. 336–7). However, a note of caution is required. If structured assessments are not used regularly, then they will be poorly applied and the information obtained from them of dubious reliability and validity.

The history should ask about feelings of low mood, poor concentration, irritability and a lack of energy. A history of anhedonia (loss of enjoyment of activities and interests), which may be quite variable in children should be sought. Feelings of worthlessness may appear from middle childhood; guilt is seen rather later. Thoughts of self-harm tend to occur from later childhood (age 10–12) but may be seen in some children rather earlier if they have been exposed to patterns of self-harm in those around them. There may be accompanying biological features, such as a change in appetite, which can increase or decrease, sleep disturbance and motor agitation. A history of psychosocial impairment is crucial to the diagnosis. Such impairment may result in loss of friends, loss of schooling and dropping out of other previously enjoyed activities.

The assessment should include obtaining information from any other possible sources including outpatient/community child mental health services, general practitioner, school, and sometimes social services. Educational failure is common and may be chronic. A family history of mental illness will be sought, as will any suggestion of past or current child abuse or other adverse life events. The history should also explore other possible comorbid child psychiatric disorder.

The mental state examination will be based a psychiatric interview but it also relies substantially on the observations of other ward staff (see also chapter 6). They will give valuable observations about the child's fluctuation in mental state and their ability to concentrate and to enjoy themselves. Similarly, observations by others such as the hospital school's teachers can provide a valuable enriching of the information available in this condition. At times mood will be found to vary across situations. This may reflect the child's self-view as somebody who can cope or not in particular social situations.

Staff must be trained to observe the alterations in attention characteristic of the hallucinating child. They learn to make accurate observations of emotion, affect and behaviours. They are asked to elicit gently from the child what they have been paying attention to, then or later. To integrate the various observations leading to an accurate assessment of fluctuating mental states it is essential that staff provide detailed observations separate from their interpretation of what these states might mean. At times, charting particular unusual behaviours will help to clarify the diagnosis.

Formal mental state examinations should elicit evidence of current affect, coherence and speed of thinking, and concentration. Self-worth and negative thinking should be assessed as well as any evidence for depressive or other hallucinations and delusional thinking. Simple cognitive testing may be appropriate at this stage, though a clinical psychologist will carry out a more detailed cognitive assessment at a later point. It will be important to assess any suicidal ideation and whether the child has thought of practical plans to harm themselves in any way or to kill themselves. As elsewhere, interviewers must be sensitive to possible hints of childhood sexual abuse. These interviews will supplement the detailed observations taken elsewhere on the unit and will allow the psychiatrist to produce summary assessments of changing situations.

Family interview will explore the resources to help the child with their difficulties as well as possible aetiological factors. It is important to establish the meaning of the child's condition and behaviour to other family members. This colours their behaviour towards the child. Similarly, the family members' understanding of the proposed admission to hospital is crucial. Unless the parents accept the need for admission and that depression may not be all that is amiss, then the admission may well fail. Siblings need to understand what is happening at a level appropriate to their age and stage of development.

Physical investigations are, in the main, not very helpful in childhood depression. Thyroid function tests are appropriate, together with electrolytes if the child has not been drinking adequately.

MANAGEMENT

The treatment of children with depression in an in-patient setting uses a combination of psychological approaches and, often, medication. The child may be chronically depressed by the time they are admitted. Illness behaviour and secondary gains of being depressed may be helping to maintain the illness. The ward milieu needs to be careful to encourage participation in ward activities by the child. Staff must do this sensitively, acknowledging the difficulties for the child. A helpful approach can encourage the child, express hope that they will feel well enough to take part in interesting activities (as with children showing refusal syndromes), but it avoids criticising him or giving additional attention for non-participation. This can set in train the beginning of healthier and less ruminative behaviour. Specific psychological interventions can include relaxation work with the child. Sometimes a cognitive behavioural programme, such as that devised by Harrington (1993), has a place. These children often need individual counselling of some form.

When depression is found as a comorbid diagnosis, each clinical diagnosis will need to be treated. For example, a conduct disordered child found to have elements of depression or a separate diagnosis of depressive disorder: treating the depression will not stop the conduct disorder whilst reducing the behavioural difficulties may not relieve the depression.

PSYCHOLOGICAL TREATMENTS

There are many important aspects to the treatment of depression apart from drug treatment. Psychological treatments of depression in childhood fall into various groups. Cognitive behaviour therapy approaches have been developed for children by Harrington and others (Harrington, 1993). For younger children, they focus on helping the child to develop a problem list, move on to recognising emotions, the activities they associate with those feelings and the thoughts accompanying them. For example, a child may feel content when stroking his cat and thinking about how the cat particularly chooses to sit on his lap. The work moves to self-monitoring, helping the child to learn self-observation and the recurring links between type of mood, activity and thought. This shows the child how he tends to pay greater attention to negative thoughts and feelings. In subsequent sessions the child rewards himself for small tasks that he feels good about. Such rewards may be material ones initially but soon become self-praise. He will learn the components of successful interpersonal skills such as listening and tracking, asking nicely, following instructions and ways to continue conversations. This work continues as social problem-solving.

If the child can grasp these concepts and apply them, the treatment moves to help the child with cognitive restructuring. Here the therapist works with the child to interrupt his automatic negative thoughts, over-extension and producing catastrophic scenarios in his mind. Reattribution aims to enable the child to look for alternative explanations and solutions. As an outpatient homework is carried out between sessions. This can easily be adapted in the in-patient setting to allow homework and discussion between sessions with the child's key nurse and increasing application at home during weekend leave.

Interpersonal therapy has been tried with adolescent patients (Mufson et al., 1994). It has not yet been adapted for use with younger children. Nevertheless, some aspects of its counselling and cognitive approach are already used with middle childhood patients who are depressed on in-patient units. It is an area that could well be explored further as a treatment for younger children in this setting.

Usually children are in-patients for insufficient time to consider that individual psychotherapy can be completed during their stay. Nonetheless useful work can be done. Such work is best regarded as a prolonged assessment for future psychotherapeutic treatment. It can contribute to the assessment of the child's internal world and its relationship to his mental state. It also will help to decide whether this style of working will be useful for a particular child. For some children, a therapy that is based on language jars or just seems to miss the point. Such children sometimes respond instead to art therapy or to music therapy (see chapter 7).

Occupational therapy will work with the social skill deficits of the child using practical tasks such as model making and cooking. Working with other children practises co-operation in a setting with focused tasks and one in which difficulties can be discussed at the time or through later debriefing. This will be an opportunity for potential enjoyment, for taking their thoughts away from depressive rumination. It can improve a depressed child's self-esteem. Other activities such as swimming and horse riding can allow depressed children to lift their mood and to feel positive emotions towards others.

Activities with peers arise from the communal living. The child's key nurse will also spend individual time with the child to talk and take part in games. Sometimes, the child is better able to explore their feelings towards others here rather than in a formal therapy setting. As such, it is important that the activities are properly supervised. The milieu has an important part to play in the treatment programme (see chapter 8).

In the hospital school depressed children are observed for any evidence of psychotic behaviour. Their academic work is supported, having frequently fallen behind that of their peers at their home school. Other remedial work helps them with skill deficits, such as reading, that may have chronically interfered with their learning and reduced self-esteem. The aim is for them to see themselves as children who can learn successfully at school.

Work with the child's family will focus, in part, on comorbid difficulties and relationships between the child and others in the family. Often dysfunctional communication patterns have appeared. The family will be helped to encourage the child to take part in positive family activities in the room. Plans for time spent at home at weekends or other times will be discussed. One aim will be for the child to have some enjoyable activities with others.

In addition, there may be depression or other psychiatric illness in a parent that needs attention in its own right. Here liaison with the General Practitioner and adult psychiatric services is important. Sometimes the issues are more specifically connected with separation and fears of abandonment. They merge at times into attachment difficulties (see chapter 25). These may be addressed partly in family meetings and partly through separate work with one parent or the couple.

Medication

Medication is commonly used as part of the treatment, despite the uncertain efficacy of antidepressants in children. The choice is essentially between the use of a tricyclic antidepressant such as imipramine or amitriptyline and one of the newer serotonin specific re-uptake inhibitors. Monoamine oxidase inhibitors have been used more rarely in childhood.

The evidence for the use of tricyclic antidepressants in children and younger adolescents is not good. There have been a few controlled trials but they do not show an improvement over the use of placebo (Hazell et al., 1995). Nevertheless, these trials have been small, using populations with substantial comorbidity, so that it is possible that there are sub-samples of depressed children who will respond. It is in that context that tricyclic antidepressants are used on an in-patient unit. The greatest danger is that of cardiotoxicity. A medical history and family history should elicit any of cardiac symptoms or disease. Physical examination including pulse and blood pressure is essential as is a baseline ECG. Ryan (1992), with colleagues at the University of Pittsburgh, recommends a detailed protocol for monitoring cardiac status during tricyclic administration. There have been deaths from the use of tricyclic antidepressants in children (Varley and McClellan, 1997).

- Obtain an ECG at baseline before beginning cyclic antidepressants. Then obtain an ECG rhythm strip after each dosage increase and after reaching steady state on medication.
- Reduce or discontinue cyclic antidepressants if the PR interval is greater than 0.18 seconds in patients under 10 years of age, or greater than 0.20 seconds in patients over 10 years of age.
- Reduce or discontinue medication if the QRS interval is greater than 0.12 seconds or widens more than 50 per cent over the baseline QRS interval.
- Reduce or discontinue medication if the corrected QT interval (QTc) is greater than 0.48 seconds.
- Reduce or discontinue medication if the resting heart rate is greater than 110 beats per minute in children aged less than 10 years, or if the resting heart rate is greater than 100 beats per minute in children 10 years or over.
- Reduce or discontinue medication if the resting blood pressure is greater than 140/90 or persistently greater than 130/85 in children under 10 years, and if the blood pressure is greater than 150/95 or persistently greater than 140/85 in children aged 10 years or older.

ECGs and blood levels should be monitored at least forty-eight hours after any change in dosage. There is experience with amitriptyline and imipramine working effectively for some children who are depressed. Tricyclic medication should be started at a low dosage and increased gradually. There is great genetic variability in the rate at which the body metabolises and excretes these drugs. Some authors have produced algorithms for calculating the appropriate dosage from single test dose responses but careful monitoring through blood estimation is probably best. For most children dosage of amitriptyline will work up to a range of 50–75 mg per day (or the equivalent of another drug).

Selective serotonin re-uptake inhibitors (SSRIs) are increasingly popular, with lower cardiotoxicity in overdose and fewer side effects, but deaths have occurred when they have been combined with other psychotropic drugs. Fluoxetine may be started at 5mg per day and increased every seven to ten days up to 20–30mg. Above this range, side effects (headaches, nausea, nervousness insomnia, vivid dreams, motor restlessness, gastrointestinal upset, reduced appetite and occasional allergic skin reactions) become more troublesome, with little increase in efficacy. There are a few reports beginning to appear supporting their effectiveness (Emslie, Kowatch, Costello and Pierce, 1995).

Electroconvulsive therapy

ECT is used rarely in children under the age of 13. Nonetheless, there have been situations in which a child in a catatonic stupor has benefited from ECT. Before considering this treatment it is wise to seek several independent consultant opinions. The Royal College of Psychiatrists recommends that two such opinions should be obtained for young people under the age of 16 years (Freeman, 1995) – one more than legally required if a patient is under a section of the Mental Health Act. The report recommends that this should happen for voluntary patients as well as those protected by the Act. If ECT is to be used, modern equipment delivering brief pulse shock to the non-dominant hemisphere has been shown to produce less memory impairment in adults (Weiner and Coffey, 1991). Like other physical treatments, ECT is only one part of any treatment programme.

The overall aim of the admission is to return the child to the family as soon as safely possible. Careful timing is necessary. Discharge too early can result in relapse with accompanying disappointment for the family and child together with loss of confidence and self esteem.

Follow-up must be negotiated between the in-patient unit and the referring service (see chapter 7). In addition to the usual issues, there may need to be periodic review of any medication by the in-patient service. Often community child mental health clinics have limited experience of prescribing anti-depressants to younger children and welcome this support.

The prognosis for childhood depression is generally good for the index episode but there is quite a high likelihood of recurrence. Kovacs et al. (1984) found that 70 per cent of children with major depressive disorder had a recurrence within five years. This was not a selected in-patient population, so it is unclear if admission would alter that result. Similarly, Harrington and colleagues (Harrington et al., 1990) following a depressed child cohort into adulthood found a fourfold increase of depression in adulthood compared with a non-depressed child psychiatric control group.

MANIA

Manic episodes in childhood are rarely seen on child psychiatric in-patient units. They increase in frequency during adolescence and can be a cause throughout childhood of confusion between affective disorders and schizophrenic spectrum illnesses. It is likely that this represents a truly low prevalence of the disorder among prepubertal children. When mania does present, the child is quite likely to be floridly disturbed and such cases will normally be quickly referred to specialist centres and in-patient services.

Admission is necessary for the child's protection from their lack of vigilance and often because their parents are exhausted. There may be little time for observing the child before intervention is necessary. However a few days without medication may allow the child's mental state to settle.

Often medication with neuroleptics is necessary. Careful observation of the child's response to medication is helped by an admission. Other drugs including carbamazepine and sodium valproate have been used to treat mania in childhood. Lithium has been effective on occasion though there is at least one study that questions its efficacy in prepubertal children (Strober et al., 1988) Lithium is not a first line treatment; the usual precautions concerning hydration and monitoring must be observed (Fetner and Geller, 1992). (See also chapter 19.)

SCHIZOPHRENIA AND RELATED DISORDERS

Schizophrenia can be a difficult diagnosis to make in this age range. Very early onset schizophrenia, with an onset before 13 years old (VEOS) is often characterised by an insidious prodrome (Asarnow and Ben, 1988), though some youngsters will show a clear change in behaviour over weeks or months. Difficulties may be first recognised in the child's school with increasing in-attention and preoccupation as well as social withdrawal. Three studies of VEOS have established the diagnosis in their earliest cases from 4.9 years to 6.7 years old (Kolvin, Ounsted, Humphrey and McNay, 1971; Green et al., 1984; Russell, Bott and Sammons, 1989). A good general account of the assessment and treatment of schizophrenia in this age range is provided by McClellan and Werry (1994).

The history

This should obtain a detailed account of the onset of the disorder and of the child's premorbid functioning. Any relevant family history of psychiatric disorder should be sought. It may include a relative with a psychotic disorder or with affective disorder. A history of prenatal or perinatal difficulties should be sought, as there is an increased frequency of such difficulties.

Often (54 per cent to 90 per cent of cases) there is a premorbid history of other child psychiatric difficulties (McClellan and Werry, 1992). In one study (Russell, Bott and Sammons, 1989) these ranged from attention deficit disorder (40 per cent), conduct disorder (17 per cent), to 'a variety of developmental abnormalities seen in children with pervasive developmental disorder' but not meeting criteria for diagnosis of either autism or other pervasive developmental disorder (26 per cent).

The current history often reveals comorbid child psychiatric diagnoses; the most common are conduct disorder and atypical depression.

Mental state

The child usually has auditory hallucinations (about 80 per cent of cases). Care must be taken to distinguish true hallucinations from illusions, fantasy and eidetic images. Hallucinations may arise in other disorders such as depression, intense anxiety states and in organic conditions. Given the possible sources of confusion, hallucinations, by themselves, do not form sufficient grounds for the diagnosis. Observations of the ward and school staff are essential here to supplement interviews (see above, depression).

Inappropriate affect is common in VEOS and may be seen before affect becomes flattened. This can lead to confusion with mixed affective states. Hypomanic and depressed states are also quite common in the early stages of VEOS and are reasons to be wary of jumping to diagnostic conclusions.

Formal thought disorder is quite common and tends to show itself as illogical thinking and loosened associations (Garralda, 1985; Werry, 1992). It can be difficult to be certain of thought disorder in younger children.

Delusions are often transient and ill-formed in the early stages of the illness though they can be bizarre and quite florid. They may appear as a confused state of mind initially crystallising only slowly. Russell, Bott and Sammons (1989) found 63 per cent of cases had clear evidence of delusions. Systematic delusions, poverty of thinking and catatonic symptoms are less frequently seen in VEOS (Werry, McClellan and Chard, 1991).

Diagnosis

The diagnosis of schizophrenia in childhood is made on the same grounds as that in adulthood using the criteria of ICD-10 or DSM-IV. In DSM-IV (see DSM-IV manual for precise criteria) two or more of the category A symptoms are required to be present for one month or longer unless removed by successful treatment, i.e. delusions, hallucinations, disorganised speech, grossly disorganised or catatonic behaviour, negative symptoms. If the delusions are bizarre or the hallucinations consist of a running commentary or two voices conversing then one symptom from this category is sufficient.

Other necessary criteria include:

- social dysfunction
- a continuous duration from onset of six months
- exclusion of schizoaffective and mood disorders (see manual for details)
- exclusion of substance abuse or organic conditions
- a high threshold for diagnosing schizophrenia in the presence of pervasive developmental disorder.

Differential diagnosis

The differential diagnosis for VEOS includes autism and pervasive developmental disorders. These disorders can be difficult to distinguish if there is a marked behavioural change in a non-verbal child with pervasive developmental disorder (PDD). The onset of VEOS can be quite insidious so leading to further confusion. Acutely, major depression or mania presents problems in differential diagnosis at this age when it is accompanied by thought disorder, hallucinations or delusions. In one study there was clear evidence of a tendency to misdiagnose bipolar affective disorder as schizophrenia during the first episode (Werry, McClellan and Chard, 1991). This problem is not isolated to one centre and seems to be a feature of the disorders of early onset (Carlson, 1990; Bashir, Russell and Johnson, 1987). At times it is only possible to distinguish these disorders and schizoaffective disorder from schizophrenia with time and careful follow-up.

Dementias of childhood may cause confusion but they are typically characterised by intellectual stasis with subsequent deterioration and positive neurological findings. Delirium requires careful exclusion of physical illness and substance abuse. On occasion careful neuropsychological assessment will show disorientation in delirium whilst it is absent in schizophrenia (Caplan, Perdue, Tanguay and Fish, 1990).

There is a mixed group of other psychotic disorders, the so-called reactive psychoses. They are difficult to diagnose because they are associated with strong environmental stressors, and may produce brief psychotic episodes. There are also cases where the symptomatology changes rather rapidly and the presentation is unstable. Many of these cases will eventually be diagnosed as schizophrenic.

Treatment

The treatment of schizophrenia in childhood consists of pharmacological intervention and psychosocial treatments.

Medication

There are few studies of neuroleptic medication in children. Most of the evidence for clinical practice is based on double-blind trials in adults. With the advent of the new generation of 'atypical' antipsychotics, practice is like to change in the next few years. There has been a view that current neuroleptics may be less effective in children and adolescents than in adults (Campbell and Spencer, 1988) but more recently a controlled trial (Spencer et al., 1992) suggests this may be untrue. Campbell suggests that none of the current antipsychotics have any marked advantage over the others apart from clozapine (Campbell et al., 1993).

Generally, recommendations are to become familiar with a few neuroleptics. We avoid the use of haloperidol because of the greater risk of extrapyramidal effects. Our current practice is to use chlorpromazine acutely as a first line drug (recommended daily doses 0.5 to 3.5 mg/kg/day normally but occasionally higher). This has greater anticholinergic effects but less risk of the unpleasant extrapyramidal ones. We use sulpiride, a substituted benzamide, once the acute phase is over or occasionally as a first line drug. It has fewer side effects than many of the neuroleptics. The dose is slowly increased using a regime 1mg to 6mg/kg/day in a divided dose. In drug resistant cases we use clozapine in doses up to 5mg/kg/day commencing with 12.5mg/day. The precaution of regular blood count monitoring is required because of the rare (1:6000) risk of agranulocytosis. Munro and Pipe (1997) have found that if side effects appear then initially lowering the dose and then raising the dosage very slowly allows therapeutic doses to be achieved in adolescent patients.

There is some experience beginning to accumulate in the literature for risperidone for adolescents but not yet for children (Armenteros et al., 1997). However, note should be taken of reports of hepatotoxicity so that liver function tests and weight should be carefully monitored during therapy (Kumra et al., 1997).

Untoward effects

The same range of adverse treatment effects is seen in children as in adults.
Acutely these include (Werry and Aman, 1993):

- irritability and worsening of behavioural difficulties
- extrapyramidal effects
- sedation
- endocrine effects such as weight gain and galactorrhea
- orthostatic hypotension and other cardiovascular system effects
- skin reactions and photosensitivity
- liver dysfunction
- lens opacities
- blood dyscrasias
- seizures
- neuroleptic malignant syndrome

More chronically, abnormal involuntary movement disorders including tardive dyskinesia occur.

Psychosocial interventions

Psychosocial interventions aim to help the child and their family accommodate to the illness and to minimise its consequences. There are some direct interventions that can help the patient. These include the use of social skills training (Liberman, 1988) which has been developed for schizophrenic adults but which may be adapted for children and cognitive behavioural therapy approaches (Tarrier et al., 1993). The latter may not be suitable for younger children. Interfering stimuli such as a portable tape machine and headphones to distract from auditory hallucinations have been used.

Individual work to support the child who has a very frightening experience is important. He will need help to cope with family and peers, to manage social situations and to realise that his thoughts are not transparent to others. Equally, the child must be kept informed about the various treatment interventions, including the use of medication and common side effects. Through this it is possible to retain the child's confidence. Careful assessment and education that is geared to the fluctuating ability of the child to cope with academic and related work is crucial. It helps the child retain some sense of normality in a bewildering world. One might think that children with schizophrenia would be frightening to other children on the unit. This is not so and in most cases they are very caring towards them. However, they do need some explanation about the child's difficulties. This will include discussion, as elsewhere, that each child is different, having specific needs, and will not be managed in the same way.

Work with the family is to help them come to terms with the illness. Work is also directed to help families adopt a style of interaction that has a low expressed emotional content and that is not critical of the child.

DISCHARGE AND FOLLOW-UP

Very early onset schizophrenia is worthy of admission for careful diagnostic work-up and to begin a treatment regime. Good links must be established with the community child mental health team for continuing treatment, but there is a strong case for continuing oversight from the in-patient child mental health service because cases are rare and will tend to be referred to in-patient centres. This allows the development of specialist skills. It is also important because development of research series. Their tracking is likely to aid the understanding of schizophrenia in the very young.

In-patient units should develop ways of working directly with these youngsters and with their families to try to minimise the toll of the illness using psychological approaches. These could then be taught to community clinics as expertise is developed. Unfortunately, there is little evidence as yet of such developments.

PROGNOSIS

The prognosis of schizophrenia presenting in childhood is poor. However, there may be diagnostic uncertainties. Additionally, a first episode may be relatively brief, not meeting the time criteria for ICD-10 (an active phase of at least one month's duration) or DSM-IV (six months for a complete episode). In such children a tentative diagnosis only can be made and the case should be reviewed regularly.

REFERENCES

Armenteros, J.L., Whitaker, A.H., Welikson, M., Stedge, D.J. and Gorman, J. (1997). Risperidone in adolescents with schizophrenia: an open pilot study. *Journal of the American Academy of Child and Adolescent Psychiatry*, 36, 694–700.

Asarnow, J.R. and Ben, M.S. (1988). Children with schizophrenia spectrum and depressive disorders: a comparative study of premorbid adjustment, onset pattern and severity of impairment. *Journal of Child Psychology and Psychiatry*, 29, 477–488.

Barrett, M.L., Berney, T.P., Bhate, S., Famuyima, O., Fundudis, T., Kolvin, I. and Tyrer, S. (1991). Diagnosing childhood depression: who should be interviewed – parent or child? The Newcastle Depression Project. *British Journal of Psychiatry, 159,* 22–27.

Bashir, M., Russell, J. and Johnson, G. (1987). Bipolar affective disorder in adolescence: a ten year study. *Australian and New Zealand Journal of Psychiatry, 21,* 36–43.

Birleson, P. (1981). The validity of depressive disorder in childhood and the development of a self-rating scale: a research report. *Journal of Child Psychology and Psychiatry, 22,* 73–88.

Campbell, M. and Spencer, E.K. (1988). Psychopharmacology in child and adolescent psychiatry: a review of the past five years. *Journal of the American Academy of Child and Adolescent Psychiaty, 27,* 269–279.

Campbell, M., Gonzales, N.M., Ernst, M., Silva, R.R. and Werry, J. (1993). Antipsychotics (neuroleptics). In J.S. Werry and M.G. Aman (ed.), *Practitioner's Guide to Psychoactive Drugs for Children and Adolescents* (pp. 269–296). New York: Plenum Medical.

Caplan, R., Perdue, S., Tanguay, P.E. and Fish, B. (1990). Formal thought disorder in childhood onset schizophrenia and schizotypal personality disorder. *Journal of Child Psychology and Psychiatry, 31 (7),* 1103–1114.

Carlson, G.A. (1990). Child and adolescent mania: diagnostic considerations. *Journal of Child Psychology and Psychiatry, 31,* 331–342.

Caron, C. and Rutter, M. (1991). Comorbidity in child psychopathology: concepts, issues and research strategies. *Journal of Child Psychology and Psychiatry, 32,* 1064–1080.

Emslie, G.J., Kowatch, R., Costello, L. and Pierce, L. (1995). Double-blind study of fluoxetine in depressed children and adolescents. *42nd Annual Meeting of the American Academy of Child and Adolescent Psychiatrists.* New Orleans: AACAP, Washington DC.

Fetner, H.H. and Geller, B.R. (1992). Lithium and tricyclic antidepressants. In D. Shaffer (ed.), *Pediatric Psychopharmacology* (vol. 15:1, pp. 223–241). Philadelphia: W.B. Saunders.

Freeman, C.P. (1995). *The ECT Handbook. The second report of the Royal College of Psychiatrists Special Committee on ECT* (CR39). Royal College of Psychiatrists.

Garralda, M.E. (1985). Characteristics of the psychoses of late onset in children and adolescence (a comparative study of hallucinating children). *Journal of Adolescence, 8,* 195–207.

Goodyer, I.M. and Cooper, P. (1993). A community study of depression in adolescent girls: II. The clinical features of identified disorder. *British Journal of Psychiatry, 163,* 374–380.

Green, W.H., Campbell, M., Hardesty, A.S., Grega, D.M., Padron, G.M., Shell, J., and Erlenmeyer, K.L. (1984). A comparison of schizophrenic and autistic children. *Journal of the American Academy of Child and Adolescent Psychiatry, 23,* 399–409.

Harrington, R.C. (1992). The natural history and treatment of child and adolescent affective disorders. *Journal of Child Psychology and Psychiatry, 33,* 1287–1302.

Harrington, R.C. (1993). *Cognitive–Behavioural Manual for Use with Child Patients with Depressive Disorders.* University Department of Child and Adolescent Psychiatry, Manchester University.

Harrington, R.C. (1994). Affective disorders. In M. Rutter, E. Taylor, and L. Hersov (ed.), *Child and Adolescent Psychiatry* (pp. 330–350). Oxford: Blackwell Scientific.

Harrington, R.C., Fudge, H., Rutter, M., Pickles, A. and Hill, J. (1990). Adult outcomes of childhood and adolescent depression: I. Psychiatric status. *Archives of General Psychiatry*, *47*, 465–473.

Hazell, P., O'Connell, D., Heathcote, D., Robertson, J. and Henry, D. (1995). Efficacy of tricyclic drugs in treating child and adolescent depression: a meta-analysis. *British Medical Journal*, *310*, 897–901.

Hill-Smith, A., Spender, Q., Glaser, D. and Jacobs, B.W. (1994). Comorbidity found in recruits to the pilot phase of a treatment trial for conduct disorder. *Royal College of Psychiatry, Child and Adolescent Section Annual Meeting*. Isle of Wight, September.

Kolvin, I., Ounsted, C., Humphrey, M. and McNay, A. (1971). Studies in the childhood psychoses: II The phenomenology of childhood psychoses. *British Journal of Psychiatry*, *118*, 385–395.

Kolvin, I., Barrett, L.M., Bhate, S.R., Berney, T.P., Famuyiwa, O., Fundudis, T. and Tyrer, S. (1991). The Newcastle Child Depression Project: diagnosis and classification of depression. *British Journal of Psychiatry*, *159*, 9–21.

Kovacs, M., Feinberg, T.L., Crouse-Novak, M.A., Paulauskas, S.L., Pollock, M. and Finkelstein, R. (1984). Depressive disorders in childhood II. A longitudinal study for the risk of subsequent major depression. *Archives of General Psychiatry*, *41*, 643–649.

Kumra, S., Herion, D., Jacobsen, L.K., Briguglia, C. and Grothe, D. (1997). Case study: Risperidone-induced hepatotoxicity in pediatric patients. *Journal of the American Academy of Child and Adolescent Psychiatry*, *36*, 701–705.

Liberman, R.P. (1988). *Psychiatric Rehabilitation of Chronic Mental Patients*. Washington DC: American Psychiatric Association Press.

McClellan, J.M. and Werry, J.S. (1992). Schizophrenia. *Psychiatric Clinics of North America*, *15*, 131–148.

McClellan, J. and Werry, J. (1994). Practice parameters for the assessment and treatment of children and adolescents with schizophrenia. *Journal of the American Academy of Child and Adolescent Psychiatry*, *33*, 616–635.

Mufson, L., Moreau, D., Weissman, M.M., Wickramaratne, P., Martin, J. and Samoilov, A. (1994). Modification of interpersonal psychotherapy and depressed adolescents (IPT-A): Phase I and II Studies. *Journal of the American Academy of Child and Adolescent Psychiatry*, *33*, 695–705.

Munro, J. and Pipe, R. (1997). Minimising side effects of Clozapine [unpublished].

Russell, A.T., Bott, L. and Sammons, C. (1989). The phenomenology of schizophrenia occurring in childhood. *Journal of the American Academy of Child and Adolescent Psychiatry*, *28*, 399–407.

Ryan, N.D. (1992). The pharmacologic treatment of child and adolescent depression. In D. Shaffer (ed.), *Pediatric Psychopharmacology* (vol. 15:1, pp. 29–40). Philadelphia: W.B. Saunders.

Spencer, E.K., Kafantaris, V., Padron-Gayol, M.V., Rosenberg, C. and Campbell, M. (1992). Haloperidol in schizophrenic children: early findings from a study in progress. *Psychopharmacology Bulletin*, *28*, 183–186.

Strober, M., Morrell, W., Burroughs, J., Lampert, C., Danforth, H. and Freeman, R. (1988). A family study of bipolar I disorder in adolescence: early onset of symptoms linked to increased familial loading and lithium resistance. *Journal of Affective Disorders*, *15*, 255–168.

Tarrier, N., Beckett, R., Harwood, S., Baker, A., Yusupoff, L. and Ugarteburu, I. (1993). A trial of two cognitive behavioural methods of treating drug-resistant residual psychotic symptoms in schizophrenic patients: I. Outcome. *British Journal of Psychiatry*, *162*, 524–532.

Varley, C.K. and McClellan, J. (1997). Case study: two additional sudden deaths with tricyclic antidepressants. *Journal of the American Academy of Child and Adolescent Psychiatry*, 36, 390–394.

Weiner, R.D. and Coffey, C.E. (1991). Electroconvulsive therapy in the United States. *Psychopharmacology Bulletin*, 27, 9–15.

Werry, J.S. (1992). Child and adolescent (early onset) schizophrenia: a review in light of DSM-III-R. *Journal of Autism and Developmental Disorders*, 22, 601–624.

Werry, J.S. and Aman, M.G. (1993). *Practitioner's Guide to Psychoactive Drugs for Children and Adolescents*. New York: Plenum Medical Books.

Werry, J.S., McClellan, J.M. and Chard, L. (1991). Childhood and adolescent schizophrenic, bipolar, and schizoaffective disorders: a clinical and outcome study. *Journal of the Academy of Child and Adolescent Psychiatry*, 30, 457–465.

21 Obsessive compulsive disorder

Chris Wever

INTRODUCTION

Juvenile obsessive compulsive disorder (OCD) is a disabling condition that affects about 1 per cent of children and adolescents (Flament et al., 1988, Valleni-Basile et al., 1994). It often follows a chronic course and has a poor long-term prognosis (Allsop and Verduyn, 1988). Many young people with OCD do not receive treatment (Flament et al. 1988) and this is of particular concern since there are effective treatments available.

Pharmacotherapy is effective in OCD and evidence for this is well reviewed by March and Leonard (1996). Clomipramine and the newer selective serotonin reuptake inhibitors (SSRIs) will reduce OCD symptoms, yet the majority of patients have an increase of symptoms on withdrawal of medication (Thomsen and Mikkelson, 1995; Leonard et al., 1993).

Clinical and emerging empirical evidence suggests that cognitive behaviour therapy (CBT) is also an effective treatment for OCD in children and adolescents (March, Mulle and Herbel, 1994; Bolton, Luckie and Steinberg, 1995; March and Leonard 1996; Wever and Rey, 1997). March (1995) critically reviewed the published literature on CBT for OCD in juveniles. Thirty-two studies describing OCD in children and adolescents using non-pharmacological treatment interventions were identified. The majority of studies demonstrated the effectiveness of cognitive–behavioural interventions despite vast differences in terminology and theoretical orientation. However, all but one were single case reports. Given that a well-designed treatment-outcome study relies on systematic assessment, these earlier studies, although providing valuable information on treatment, cannot be generalised.

Clinically, experience suggests that pharmacotherapy and CBT work well together and many authors consider that the combined use of CBT and pharmacotherapy is the treatment of choice in adult OCD patients (Griest, 1992; Piacentini et al., 1992; Rapoport, Swedo and Leonard, 1992). To date however only two studies (March, Mulle and Herbet, 1994; Wever and Rey, 1997) have examined the effectiveness of a combination of pharmacotherapy and CBT in obsessive compulsive disorder in children and adolescents. In the first systematic prospective follow-up study, Wever and Rey (1997) examined the effectiveness of a combined CBT and pharmacological treatment package with a group of 57 juveniles diagnosed with OCD. Following treatment over a four week period, there was a 68 per cent remission rate. Of the 43 cases followed up over an average of two years, 79 per cent remained in remission. The findings indicate that the combined OCD treatment programme produces durable results which may continue beyond a two year period. Residential treatment was used in 20 per cent of this sample. Factors leading to admission, singly or in combination, included the severity or type of OCD symptoms, failure of past therapy, comorbidity, family factors or geographical isolation. This in-patient subgroup had double the rate of comorbid diagnoses compared with the outpatient group. They had a poorer outcome. The usual length of residential treatment was 8–20 weeks.

RESIDENTIAL TREATMENT

General issues

As most patients with OCD can be treated as outpatients there has to be a clear rationale and justification for the choice of the more expensive and potentially riskier residential option. Advantages and disadvantages are listed in Table 21.1.

Common reasons for residential treatment

Severity of symptoms

Some patients have such severe OCD symptoms that they are functioning poorly in their environment and have not responded to outpatient treatment. Residential treatment may provide an environment to manage the condition more intensively.

Type of symptoms

The treatment of symptoms such as obsessional slowness is very labour intensive and may require the admission of patients to a residential unit.

Comorbid diagnoses

Other comorbid diagnoses may be more easily and safely managed in a residential setting.

Family issues interfering with outpatient treatment

Some families may undermine treatment as a result of family dynamics or psychopathology of one or both of the parents. Residential treatment can help observe the patient in an environment away from their family and offer treatment not possible if the patient stayed in the family environment.

Table 21.1 Advantages and disadvantages of residential treatment

Disadvantages of residential treatment	Benefits of residential treatment
• Residential treatment is stressful for the patient and family. • Puts the patient in contact with other disturbed patients. There is then the risk of learning maladaptive behaviours from them. • Dislocates a child from their family, school and social supports. • Many OCD symptoms are exclusive or more prevalent in the context of the patient's immediate family and environment. CBT may be difficult to conduct if the patient does not have access to their family and home. • From a public health perspective residential treatment is a more costly option.	• The ability to observe symptoms more closely. • The opportunity to implement treatments which may be more labour intensive. • The use of educational personnel to assess educational difficulties and to work in parallel with health staff in therapy. • A safer and more controlled environment to trial other medication.

Geographical isolation

Some patients have no access to clinicians proficient in pharmacotherapy and CBT.

Diagnostic clarification

Rarely, some patients have unusual presentations of OCD that may be difficult to differentiate from psychoses, developmental disability or other organic disturbances.

If outpatient treatment failure is the reason for residential treatment, one needs to review the reasons why it was not successful. Were the outpatient pharmacological and cognitive behavioural treatments adequate? If comorbidity factors complicate the presentation, one needs to assess whether residential treatment will be able to address them any better than outpatient treatment. If family factors interfere with treatment, will admission benefit the patient by dislocating them from their family? If geographical isolation prevents outpatient treatment, could the patient's local health professionals implement the treatment if appropriate support and education is provided? Could the patient be accommodated with family members close to the residential treatment centre and be treated as an outpatient?

Assessment

It is best practice to interview all family members on the initial assessment. One not only gains better information and insights about the functioning of the family but it is also an opportunity to educate all family members about OCD. Education in the neurobiological nature of OCD and the lack of control that the patient has over their symptoms will frequently relieve guilty feelings in parents and decrease conflict between family members and the patient. The potential of the other family members as co-therapists can also be evaluated.

A standard family and individual interview suited to the age of the patient is conducted though there is an emphasis on clearly delineating the OCD symptoms. The Children's Yale-Brown Obsessive Compulsive Scale (CYBOCS) (Goodman et al., 1989a) should be used in this first assessment. It is both a clinical aid in elucidating the many obsessions and compulsions which may be present, and a record of baseline symptom severity which can be used in the assessment of progress. The CYBOCS is a clinician administered measure that lists a range of OCD symptoms, rating each separately in terms of time taken, interference with functioning, distress, resistance and degree of control over these symptoms.

During this initial interview it is important to assess comorbidity since this is often the major determinant of outcome (Wever and Rey, 1997; Fuller and Wever, unpublished). Patients who have comorbid oppositional behaviours, difficult personalities, attention or poor impulse control problems or poor insight, make poor candidates for CBT but are frequently the patients who are candidates for residential treatment. Not only are they poor candidates for CBT, but they may also be difficult to manage in a residential setting.

Admission

Prior to admission, the patient and family need to understand and agree to treatment and their role as active participants in the treatment process (see Part II and chapter 8). To conduct a course of CBT with no agreement to the process is doomed to fail. Many units formalise this in a treatment contract signed by the patient, family and therapist clearly delineating their respective roles and responsibilities. It is also useful to clarify a projected timeframe and outline the treatment plan. This information is useful for both the family and other residential staff. This may initially prove to be difficult with patients with oppositional symptoms. Development of a trusting and cooperative therapeutic relationship may then have to be the first step in treatment.

The key to successful management is to have staff that are familiar with OCD and its treatment. This includes a psychiatrist who is experienced in OCD psychopharmacology and staff proficient and experienced in use of CBT with sufficient time to implement this in the setting. Neither are extremely complex skills to learn. Many times patients with OCD are admitted to residential units for intensive treatment but languish as no appropriate CBT is provided because of ignorance, lack of experience or lack of time staff have available to do CBT. An OCD treatment manual that can be referred to by other staff members is useful. A treatment plan for patients clearly documented in the case notes and updated to describe patient homework tasks for all staff to read is also important.

All staff in direct care of these patients must know the expectations placed on the patient and themselves, and the roles of other staff. Without this coordination and role delineation inconsistency of management will occur.

Patients admitted to a residential unit run the risk of being influenced in a negative manner by other patients with different problems. Patients with OCD admitted to a unit frequently have comorbid disruptive behaviour disorders. In order to avoid adverse effects from the other patients one should endeavour to keep the admission focussed on the OCD treatment and keep it as short as is practical.

Cognitive behaviour therapy (CBT)

It is best that one therapist takes responsibility for the CBT process. They work with the patient developing a hierarchy of symptoms that the patient will steadily address, usually in the form of graded exposure and response prevention (see chapter 10). It is best to let the patient dictate the pace of the exposure rather than being too confronting. In this population in particular the patient frequently may become angry if the symptoms are too rapidly challenged and anxiety raised too high in the early phase of treatment. The patient is encouraged to use cognitive strategies to help in the exposure/response prevention process, for example:

Is this sensible or silly?
Is this OCD?
If it is silly and OCD I should be able to stop doing it.
I'm the boss today, not the OCD.

A workbook for the patient is useful for the encouragement of their active involvement in treatment.

Table 21.2 Contents of an OCD workbook

- instructions on use
- fact sheet on OCD
- outline and rationale for the management approach
- practical strategies to cope with anxiety
- self-talk strategies useful in fighting the OCD
- diary for the patient and family to log symptoms over a week (probably best done prior to admission)
- space for a hierarchy of symptoms to be generated by the patient and therapist as targets for treatment in exposure/response prevention
- space for the patient to record progress in the CBT sessions and homework exercises

---

A useful way of describing the relationship between patient and therapist is that the therapist acts like a coach for the patient, to help the patient become psychologically fitter and better able to control the OCD symptoms. An analogy for the treatment process is that of a sporting activity the patient may be interested in; to become good at the skills required and to become physically fitter the patient needs to train at their sport. The patient similarly needs to train at controlling the symptoms of OCD, and the CBT is the training process. The OCD is also externalised, given a nasty nickname, and the child is encouraged to 'boss back' the OCD. Reading material about OCD appropriate to the developmental age of the patient is also useful to make available at this stage (Wever and Phillips, 1994). Most OCD symptoms are usually worst in their home environment, and during the first few days of admission fewer OCD symptoms may be present. This should be kept in mind in the early stages of admission.

It is important to remain focussed on the OCD treatment unless comorbidity factors prevent the specific OCD treatments. One hour of specific CBT in the form of exposure/response prevention needs to be done daily and the patient encouraged to complete homework exercises in the ward and on any home leave they may have. It is important, if possible, to give the patients opportunities to practise their CBT skills in the home environment so that what they have done while in residence can be generalised to the home situation. Some ingenuity is required to give appropriate experiences in treatment to approximate home based OCD symptoms in a residential setting. The patient needs to record in their workbook the work done with the therapist and their homework exercises. The homework needs to be reviewed by the therapist at the beginning of each CBT session. Parents should be kept informed on treatment progress and included as co-therapists if appropriate and possible.

Unusual presentations of OCD may require different approaches. Most young patients with OCD have both obsessions and compulsions. If the patient has primarily obsessions, treatment includes the use of a thirty-second continuous tape on which the patient verbally records their obsessional thoughts. The patient is instructed to listen to this tape for fifteen minutes twice a day and not avoid situations which precipitate these thoughts. If there are a number of obsessions then each needs to be dealt with in a similar fashion in a hierarchical manner similar in approach to the exposure/response prevention. In cases where the patient has obsessional slowness, 'pacing' is the treatment of choice. Here therapist and frequently the nursing staff/residential care workers limit the time allowed for tasks which are done slowly. This is an extremely labour intensive task and requires close observation and record keeping.

Educational staff involvement

In residential treatment facilities educational support is usually provided. It is important to instruct the educational staff both to monitor the impact of the OCD on learning and to help the patient deal with OCD in the school environment. Response prevention in the classroom, pacing techniques and encouragement of appropriate goals through cognitive work can all be very useful in helping the patient in this area of functioning. The educational staff can also liaise with the patient's home school prior to discharge to prepare appropriate school support.

Family work

Appropriate family or carer work needs to parallel the individual treatment process. Much of the family work is primarily focussed in the neurobiological nature of OCD providing information about progress in treatment, supporting the parents as co-therapists and teaching them skills to manage the patient at home (see chapter 8). For example, it can be extremely valuable to instruct the family members to disentangle themselves from the OCD, by not performing the patient's rituals or not answering reassuring questions. The family can tell the patient that their non-response to these OCD requests and questions is under instruction of the therapist, with statements such as: 'Dr X has told me not to answer OCD questions and that sounds like an OCD question to me' or, 'Nurse Y has told me not to do those OCD things for you any more'.

This may reduce angry responses to the parent, as the patient perceives this as part of the treatment process, not a parent thwarting their desire for anxiety reduction. Family dysfunction usually settles as the patient's OCD comes under control. The therapist of course needs to use their clinical judgement on the level of family pathology present and the amount of family work needed in each case.

Medication issues

Once a decision to admit a patient is made most patients will usually have been trialled on one or more medications. An early review of pharmacotherapy is important as medications used in the treatment of OCD have a lag time of several weeks before any resultant clinical changes are seen. Changes in medication must have sufficient time to take effect. Medications are often too frequently changed because of perceived ineffectiveness. There is often pressure to change things quickly because of the expensive nature of residential treatment and pressure on places in those settings. Yet sufficient time needs to be given to observe the effects of any medication changes. Because of this delay many changes of medication should perhaps be performed prior to admission unless safety issues require closer observation, particularly if combination pharmacotherapy is trialled.

Generally either an SSRI or clomipramine is the first line of pharmacological treatment. With the SSRIs the main side-effects are gastrointestinal disturbance and agitation. The gastrointestinal symptoms often settle and the agitation is usually dose dependent and responds to a decrease in dose. Occasionally an elated or slightly hypomanic presentation may occur after the prescription of an SSRI and this too responds to a decrease in dose. Clomipramine causes a variety of anticholinergic side effects, drowsiness and has a cardiovascular risk. If one medication is not effective at a therapeutic dose for a sufficient duration (twelve weeks) then an alternative agent should be tried. If an SSRI is ineffective it may be prudent to try clomipramine or vice versa. If one SSRI is ineffective another may be effective. Trials of monotherapy should be of sufficient dose and duration with the trial of at least two medications before more complex augmenting treatment is started.

Some presentations of OCD require the addition of an augmenting agent. Neuroleptics such as haloperidol and risperidone are often needed for patients with tics, Tourette's Disorder and schizotypal personality disorder. There is also some emerging evidence (mainly case reports) in the adult OCD literature that other agents such as buspirone, lithium, fenfluramine and clonazepam may be adjunctive agents for treatment resistant OCD. There is little evidence of their use in younger patients but they should perhaps be kept in mind for intractable cases where standard treatments have failed to significantly improve symptoms.

Comorbidity

If patients have other problems requiring specific treatments this needs to be done before, in parallel or after the bulk of the OCD CBT has been conducted. For example if a patient is observed to be suffering from panic disorder with symptoms of hyperventilation this may need to be addressed prior to the exposure and response prevention with appropriate education, breath control and relaxation. Patients suffering from Tourette's Disorder may require the addition of haloperidol or risperidone before much improvement is gained from CBT. Occasionally patients with severe attention deficit hyperactivity disorder may need to be prescribed stimulants, despite the risk of making their OCD worse, as their poor impulse control severely impedes their CBT and general everyday functioning. Similarly, psychodynamic or family issues such as the patient's adoption of a pathological sick role or maintenance of pathological behaviours by relatives, may need to be addressed in both individual psychotherapy and family sessions.

Discharge and follow-up

Realistic goals need to have been delineated either before or in the early stages of admission. Usual periods of residential treatment fall between eight and twenty weeks. When the residential treatment episode is concluded, active follow-up needs to be organised. Discharge is usually dependent on sufficient symptom reduction for the patient to return to normal activities, or if no further progress is being made, or the condition is deteriorating. Prolonged residential treatments may become counterproductive for the patient, as they may become dislocated from their family and social support system.

Follow-up is usually best done by staff who have been involved with the in-patient care. They know the individual patient's strengths and weaknesses and have a knowledge of OCD treatment. They are in a position to monitor more closely relapse in patients well known to them and use strategies they know work with that individual patient. Of course this may not be possible in some cases, for administrative or geographical reasons.

Review of medication and booster CBT sessions should be regularly scheduled to prevent relapse. One follow-up study (Fuller and Wever, unpublished) strongly suggests that regular contact is an important part of ongoing treatment to prevent relapse. Withdrawal of medication should be attempted slowly after at least six months of reasonable symptom control. In one study (Wever and Rey, 1997) about half of the patients were successfully withdrawn from medication during the two-year follow-up period. This of course needs to be negotiated with the patient and family. Many patients choose not to have medications withdrawn as they experience few side effects and do not wish to run the risk of relapse.

Common problems with treatment in a residential setting

Historically, many residential treatment facilities for younger people have had a psychodynamic treatment approach. This may lead to paradigm clashes, inconsistencies and even conflict amongst staff about the use of an approach primarily based on medication and CBT. If this matter is not resolved then patients will suffer as a result of this systems problem.

- Many of the patients admitted have had previous therapy failures. This may undermine their confidence in getting help and may wrongly be interpreted as poor motivation by staff. Consistent, appropriate and calm treatment and an optimistic therapeutic attitude emphasising progress no matter how small is required.
- Staff are often poorly trained in CBT. Without staff experienced in OCD treatment then residential treatment of these patients is often fruitless. A training programme is needed to teach at least a few members of the staff appropriate treatment for OCD.

SUMMARY

Most patients with OCD can be treated as outpatients. Treatment should include appropriate medication, usually an SSRI or clomipramine, and appropriate CBT, usually exposure/response prevention. For a patient to be admitted to a residential unit staff need experience in these areas if treatment is to be effective. Previous treatment failure or complicating factors in the patient's presentation are usually the reason for admission. Such in-patients are a poor outcome group compared to an outpatient sample. Goals of treatment need to be realistic. Compared to outpatient work, treatment usually requires more intense and longer input. Staff need to be patient and any small gains encouraged and positively reinforced. Yet prolonged admission may also be detrimental as the patient may lose contact with family and important social supports within their environment. Therefore if no progress is being made, despite intensive and appropriate treatment, benefits of admission need to be evaluated and ongoing outpatient treatment considered.

REFERENCES

Allsopp, M. and Verduyn, C. (1988). A follow-up of adolescents with obsessive compulsive disorder. *British Journal of Psychiatry, 154,* 829–834.

Bolton, D., Collins, J. and Steinberg, D. (1983). The treatment of obsessive compulsive disorder in adolescence: a report of fifteen cases. *British Journal of Psychiatry, 142,* 456–464.

Bolton, D., Luckie, M. and Steinberg, D. (1995). Long-term course of obsessive-compulsive disorder treated in adolescence. *Journal of the American Academy of Child and Adolescent Psychiatry, 34,* 1441–1450.

Flament, M. F., Whitaker, A., Rapoport, J. L., Davies, M., Berg, C. Z., Kalikow, K., Sceery, W. and Shaffer, D. (1988). Obsessive-compulsive disorder in adolescence: an epidemiological study. *Journal of the American Academy of Child and Adolescent Psychiatry, 27,* 764–771.

Flament, M. F, Koby, E., Rapoport, J. L., Berg, C. J., Zahn, T., Cox, C., Denckla, M. and Lenane, M. (1990). Childhood obsessive-compulsive disorder: a prospective follow-up study. *Journal of Child Psychology and Psychiatry, 31,* 361–380.

Goodman, W. K., Price, L. H., Rasmussen, S. A., Mazure, C., Heischmann, R. L., Hill, C. L., Heninger, G. R. and Charney, D. S. (1989a). The Yale-Brown Obsessive Compulsive Scale. *Archives of General Psychiatry, 46,* 1006–1011.

Goodman, W. K., Price, L. H., Rasmussen, S. A., Mazure, C., Delgado, P., Heninger, G. R. and Charney, D. S. (1989b). The Yale-Brown Obsessive Compulsive Scale. *Archives of General Psychiatry, 46,* 1012–1026.

Griest, J. H. (1992). An integrated approach to treatment of obsessive compulsive disorder. *Journal of Clinical Psychiatry, 53,* 38–41.

Leonard, H. L., Swedo, S. E., Lenane, M. C., Rettew, D. C., Hamburger, S. D., Bartko, J. J. and Rapoport, J. L. (1993). A 2- to 7-year follow-up study of 54 obsessive-compulsive children and adolescents. *Archives of General Psychiatry, 50,* 429–439.

March, J.S. (1995). Cognitive-behaviour therapy for children and adolescents with OCD: a review and recommendations for treatment. *Journal of the American Academy of Child and Adolescent Psychiatry, 34,* 7–18.

March, J. S. and Leonard, H. L. (1996) Obsessive compulsive disorder in children and adolescents: a review of the last ten years. *Journal of the American Academy of Child and Adolescent Psychiatry, 34,* 1265–1273.

March, J. S., Mulle, K. and Herbel, B. (1994). Behavioural psychotherapy for children and adolescents with obsessive compulsive disorder: an open trial of a new protocol-driven treatment package. *Journal of the American Academy of Child and Adolescent Psychiatry, 33,* 333–341.

Piancentini, J., Jaffer, M. and Gitow, A. (1992). Psychopharmacologic treatment of child and adolescent obsessive compulsive disorder. *Psychiatric Clinics of North America, 15,* 87–107.

Rapoport, J. L., Swedo, S. E. and Leonard, H. L. (1992). Childhood obsessive-compulsive disorder. *Journal of Clinical Psychiatry, 53* (supp. 4), 11–16.

Thomsen, P. H. and Mikkelsen, H. U. (1995). Course of obsessive-compulsive disorder in children and adolescents: a prospective follow-up study of 23 Danish cases. *Journal of the American Academy of Child and Adolescent Psychiatry, 34*, 1432–1440.

Valleni-Basile, L. A., Garrison, C. Z., Jackson, K. L., Waller, J. L., McKeowan, R. E., Addy, C. L. and Cuffe, S. P. (1994). Frequency of obsessive-compulsive disorder in a community sample of young adolescents. *Journal of the American Academy of Child and Adolescent Psychiatry, 33*, 782–791.

Wever, C and Phillips, N. (1994). *The secret problem*. Sydney: Shrink-Rap Press.

Wever, C. and Rey, J. (1997). Outcome of a combined treatment in juvenile obsessive compulsive disorder. *Australian and New Zealand Journal of Psychiatry, 31*, 105–113.

22 Neuropsychiatry in childhood: residential treatment

Kenneth Nunn

HISTORICAL BACKGROUND

Lauretta Bender, at the Bellevue Hospital in New York (Bender, 1956) and Mildred Creak (Creak, 1963) at Great Ormond Street Hospital for Children in London both had a commitment to residential treatment and the organic investigation of psychiatric disorder. Sara Williams at Arndell Children's Unit in Sydney, Australia, was among the first to introduce CT Scanning, metabolic and neuroendocrine screening of children with psychotic and autistic disorders (Williams and Harper, 1973). These women pioneered the medical investigation and treatment of psychiatric disorder arising from cerebral dysfunction in residential treatment settings. Christopher Ounstead and others sustained a dual interest in child psychiatry and epilepsy at The Park Hospital in Oxford. The emergence of the scientific study of neuropsychiatry within an epidemiological framework was marked by the publication of *A Neuropsychiatric Study in Childhood* by Rutter, Graham and Yule (1970). It would be another fourteen years before this was followed up by *Developmental Neuropsychiatry*, an elaboration and extension by Rutter and others (1984) of the earlier work. However, none of these works purported to be clinical compendia offering a coherent body of experience to the practising clinician. Important works on particular clinical problems appeared from time to time, including Gualtieri's (1990) *Neuropsychiatry and Behavioural Pharmacology*, and Taylor's (1986) *The Overactive Child*. It was not until Gillberg (1995) produced his book *Clinical Child Neuropsychiatry* and the publication of *Developmental Neuropsychiatry* by John Harris (1995) that the clinical domain was defined. Those desiring a detailed review should refer to these latter two books. Unfortunately neither of these addresses common clinical problems of delirium, dementia and the somatoform disorders with neurological presentation. This chapter aims to provide a clinician's synopsis of neuropsychiatry in childhood with special reference to those problems and conditions that are managed on in-patient units.

ASSESSMENT

Neuropsychiatry works across the divide between physical and psychological medicine. The request for neuropsychiatric assessment, especially assessment for residential treatment, is usually a request of last resort. Most frequently safety cannot be maintained and behaviour is intolerably disruptive, distressing to the carers or to other medical facilities.

Examining the context: what can and cannot be done?

Why is the family presenting with this child, in this way, at this time? What can they manage realistically? How much can they change and adapt to their child's problem and how amenable is their child's problem to change? Context interacts with the disorder. Where the brain fails in some way, the demands of the environment are often more critical than in conditions where the neural substrate is intact. Contrary to what is often thought, environmental and contextual therapies are therefore of special significance in these disorders.

Defining the symptomatic presentation

Neuropsychiatry in childhood is a new speciality. The nosology remains tentative and the natural history of these disorders is far from clear. Relational phenomena, the child's ability to adapt to naturalistic tasks and the more demanding processes of planning and organising the future are critical elements of the assessment. Describing what is impossible or what is absent in the inter-action between examiner and child, or examiner and family, often illuminates as much as the *presence* of abilities or phenomena. Establishing direct cause and effect between brain dysfunction and psychiatric presentation is often problem-atic. The childhood neuropsychiatrist has to manage uncertainty.

Neuropsychological assessment

A neuropsychological assessment can make an important contribution to the neuropsychiatric evaluation and subsequent management of in-patient children. The identification of underlying cognitive ability very discrepant from a child's social presentation, of previously undetected specific learning difficulty or of neurodevelopmental abnormalities may influence formulation and treatment (Rourke, Fisk and Strang, 1987). To take only one of many examples, children with very impaired verbal memory may constantly appear to ignore requests or instructions, though may comply better with visual prompting of acceptable behaviours.

Delirium

Delirium is the widely fluctuating impairment of a child's capacity to respond appropriately and accurately to the moment by moment demands of the environment. This is secondary to a pervasive disruption in arousal and the capacity to attend. The difficulties are not solely explained by the presence of seizures, dementia or amnestic disorders. The patient's level of arousal is not sufficiently reduced to warrant the term stupor or coma.

There is normally evidence from the history, physical examination or laboratory tests that the patient's delirium is a direct physiological consequence of a general medical condition, substance intoxication or withdrawal, use of a medication, or toxin exposure or a combination of these factors (DSM-IV). Many other analogous and related terms are used, such as confusional state, encephalopathic state, acute brain syndrome and toxic encephalopathy.

Most delirium occurs with children in the family home who never present for treatment and do not appear to suffer subsequent difficulties. Delirium that presents in its own right to medical practitioners is much less common and may have grave outcomes. It must be emphasised that delirium is a clinical state and not a causal diagnosis.

Differential diagnosis

Delirium can be confused with other fluctuating clinical states arising from psychiatric illness and other specific syndromes (see below and Table 22.3).

Aetiology

The possible causes of delirium are protean. Identifying a cause can be aided by considering the source of referral, the nature of the presentation and the longitudinal course of the delirium.

THE SOURCE OF REFERRAL

The majority of referrals will come from neurological, general child psychiatric and general paediatric sources. The closer the affiliation of a psychiatric residential service with paediatric facilities, the more likely are referrals to come from neurology, oncology, renal, respiratory, infectious diseases and intensive care facilities. However, most cases of delirium will never be referred to a psychiatric in-patient unit. This is highlighted by the different profile of cases in Tables 22.1 and 22.2. Referred cases are more likely to be aggressive, psychotic, overactive or to have an unusual presentation. The quieter, less aggressive, hypoactive and clearly systemically ill are less likely to be referred to psychiatrists. General paediatric referrals are, by definition, extremely diverse, but encephalitis and idiopathic delirium remain the most common findings. Idiopathic delirium is

Table 22.1 Neurological causes of delirium in a consultation–liaison setting

- Encephalitis
- Anticonvulsant toxicity
- Complex partial seizures
- Neurodegenerative disorders
- Meningitis
- Non-convulsive status epilepticus
- Acute head injury
- Chronically multiply shunted child
- Intracranial tumour (often infra-tentorial in children)
- Neuroleptic malignant syndrome.

that form of delirium which is indistinguishable from other forms of deliria except that, even after very extensive investigation, no aetiological factor is identified which is sufficient to explain the disorder.

General child psychiatric referrers will usually recognise that the delirious child does not have a functional psychosis but may be unsure what is wrong. Encephalitis, disintegrative psychosis (progressive or non-progressive), acute drug toxicity, catatonia, akinetic mutism, neuroleptic malignant syndrome and dementia may all present in this way. However, even the functional psychoses, especially the bipolar affective disorders and the disorders of excessive sleep, may be mistaken in the early stages for a delirium.

Functional psychoses with brief alterations in consciousness ('*Benommenheit*') are more prominent clinically in childhood. The classic distinctions between schizophrenia and delirium are much more confused, especially in the peri-pubertal period. *Bipolar disorder with mixed mood states* may appear agitated, confused and disoriented. *Catatonia* may be indistinguishable from idiopathic hypoactive delirium with mutism. *Kleine-Levin* (Pike and Stores, 1994), *peri-pubertal psychosis* (Abe and Ohta, 1995) and *menstrually-related hypersomnia* (Billiard, Guillmenault and Derwent, 1975) are all sleep disorders which have altered levels of consciousness, confusion and disorientation but have no

Table 22.2 Neurological causes and drug toxicity presenting to a residential child psychiatry unit as delirium

- Encephalitis
- Psychotropic toxicity (including NMS and anticholinergic delirium and psychosis)
- Disintegrative psychosis
- Brain tumour
- Idiopathic delirium (differential diagnosis is NMS)

Table 22.3 Psychiatric differential diagnoses of delirium presenting to a residential child psychiatry unit

---

- Major affective disorders (especially bipolar)
- Hypersomnias
- Schizophrenia
- Disintegrative psychosis
- Dementia
- Akinetic mutism

---

demonstrable organic aetiology. Some have been linked with mood disorders over time but look much more like organic brain syndromes. Children who have episodes of acute cognitive decline may be delirious initially. These children may have delusions, hallucinations and thought disorder, in which case they will be diagnosed as acute disintegrative psychosis. If they remain intellectually impaired but not psychotic they are often treated 'as if' they have had encephalitis. If the outcome is autistic they are now referred to as having a disintegrative disorder (Volkmar, 1996; DSM-IV). Each of these groups may have a delirious presage to their final outcome state. Even when the decline is progressive, acute delirious episodes may occur upon chronic intellectual and social decline.

The florid, hyperactive hallucinosis (including vivid visual and tactile hallucinations) of anticholinergic psychosis may be characterised by hyperarousal, staccato motor movement and fine tremor. Dilated pupils, tachycardia and rapid response to physostigmine are all characteristic. Seizures, cardiac dysrhythmia and volatile reactions, which can be violent, are recognised complications.

Neuroleptic malignant syndrome (NMS)

Those who have NMS may be delirious with hyperthermia, muscular rigidity and dysautonomia. However, those who have 'idiopathic delirium', or delirium of the sort found in encephalitis lethargica, may have many of the features of neuroleptic malignant syndrome. This confusing picture is confounded by the fact that many may have had exposure to dopamine antagonists in the initial phase of the illness. One is left wondering which came first.

Hypoactive delirium versus hyperactive delirium

Impairment of consciousness is often associated with a lack of modulation of motor movement. The hyperactive–hypoactive distinction is the most prevalent sub-typing used in North America (Trzepacz, 1994). The more the picture is one of hypoactivity, proneness to mutism, social withdrawal and adverse sensitivity to dopamine antagonists, the more likely will night time sedation with benzodiazepines or even activating medications and dopamine agonists (such as bromocryptine) have to be considered (Gualtieri, 1990; pp.49–51, 212–213).

The more hyperactive, garrulous, interactionally inept, intrusive and disruptive with socially inappropriate behaviour, the more likely dopamine antagonists will be required (Ross and Stewart, 1991). For most, the picture is a mixed one (Trzepacz, 1994) with one or other picture predominant at any one time. The experienced clinician's task is to titrate regulation of activity and sedation, while at the same time ensuring a comprehensive medical investigation.

Recurrent/intermittent delirium

Subacute chronic infections with neurotoxic viruses such as coxsackie, herpes and mycoplasma may give rise to recurrent episodes of delirium. The delirious conditions associated with sleep disorders, predominantly hypersomnias, raise issues about the definition of delirium. Is recurrent intermittent idiopathic delirium best understood as a diffuse, acute organic brain syndrome or a primary disorder of arousal? Should we introduce the notion of primary and secondary delirium? However, the practitioner in a residential setting will mainly be concerned with three issues. How far should investigations be taken? How are the episodes to be managed? How are future episodes to be prevented?

Chronic delirium

Although delirium is usually acute, florid and episodic, it may be subacute or chronic, insidious and have a low-grade continuous course. This is usually in children with chronic serious medical illnesses that do not come to residential settings.

Adults versus children

The difficulties of distinguishing functional psychoses in childhood and adolescence from delirium have already been mentioned. This is especially true in the peripubertal period. In general, adult delirium is much more associated with dementia and withdrawal syndromes. Dependency phenomena are almost totally absent from childhood and rare in adolescence as a cause of delirium. Encephalitis, sleep disorder and idiopathic delirium are much more prominent in childhood and adolescence. If delirium occurs in adulthood with a malignancy, it is much more likely to be metastatic and in the cerebral cortex. In childhood it is much more likely to be a primary central nervous system tumour in an infratentorial location with extension and associated with infection following intensive immunosuppressive therapy.

Investigation and treatment

Symptomatic treatment of delirium often has to precede full investigation to find its cause. The child is too agitated to co-operate. The investigation of delirium requires the active collaboration of a paediatric neurologist. Cerebrospinal fluid microscopy and culture for viruses, the cerebral SPECT scan and the EEG are usually the three most useful investigations while CT and MRI, though necessary, generally yield less.

The treatment of delirium involves a judgement as to whether the delirium is mild and/or predominantly hypoactive or severe and/or predominantly hyperactive. The milder the delirium and the more hypoactive the more helpful is the increase in sensory stimulation, reality orienting information and consideration of dopamine agonist medications. The basic strategy is to increase arousal. The more severe and the more predominant the hyperactivity the more likely is the child or teenager to benefit from increasing the depth of the delirium by sedation and using dopamine antagonists. The presence of mutism, extrapyramidal signs and dysautonomia will also favour dopamine agonists, while hallucinations, delusions and incoherence of thought will favour dopamine antagonists.

Where the picture is mixed with hyperactive and hypoactive elements and severe, it is best to proceed with a sedating dopamine antagonist initially. Extreme sensitivity to even atypical antipsychotics, such as risperidone (0.025–0.05 mg/kg/day), with mutism, extrapyramidal reactions, hypoactivity or even catatonia, may suggest the need to move to dopamine agonists such as bromocryptine (0.5–1mg/kg/day) with sedation, such as diazepam. Starting at relatively low doses and proceeding slowly is critical, despite the desire to obtain a satisfactory behavioural outcome. If benzodiazapines are required in addition to dopamine agonists or antagonists for sedation and/or anticonvulsant purposes, a stable airway must be maintained. If this is particularly difficult, transfer to an Intensive Care Unit may be necessary. The vast majority of cases will be maintained with special nursing and frequent, repeated nursing observations.

Reassuring the parents that chronic psychosis is a less common outcome but warning that long-term intellectual deficit is a likely outcome, is part of the preparation of expectations in family consultation.

Dementia in childhood

Definition of dementia

> Dementia in childhood involves the pervasive and progressive loss of already attained developmental skills. This usually reduces the child's subsequent developmental trajectory and generally but not always leads to death. The condition is not explicable in terms of acute drug toxicity or the other causes of delirium.

In older children, this will include those with a loss of at least 15 IQ points with a final outcome below 70 IQ points. In younger children, the loss of previously acquired skills of walking, speech and fine motor function is more pronounced. In infants, there is a loss of responsiveness, feeding difficulties and even a failure to develop these skills, along with more traditionally neurological difficulties such as seizures. Those children that are referred to a residential facility are usually seen from mid-childhood to adolescence. They have major emotional and behavioural accompaniments to their deterioration. They may be frankly psychotic, profoundly depressed or elated, aggressively disruptive or quietly amnestic and manageably disinhibited. All of these pictures are seen and can be managed within a residential child psychiatric setting once diagnostic issues have been clarified.

Problems of definition

PROGRESSIVE, DECELERATED OR STATIC?

Not all dementia leads inexorably to a rapid death, although life will be foreshortened in almost all cases to some degree owing to the complications of intellectual impairment and seizures. Paediatric neurologists prefer the term dementia to be reserved for those who relentlessly progress towards death, though this makes classification difficult, except in retrospect. There needs to be a clear requirement of absolute loss of function and skills, not merely a loss of trajectory. However, following the loss, three pathways need to be distinguished: the decelerated trajectory, the developmental plateau (static dementia) and the pathway of progressive loss. Complete return to normal is rare.

Developmental pathways following cognitive loss

(See Figure 22.1). An example of decelerated dementia will include non-progressive disintegrative psychosis (Corbett et al., 1977). Static dementia may include conditions such as the child who has had a severe encephalitic process. Progressive dementia includes conditions such as subacute sclerosing panencephalitis. Again, it is important to emphasise that when paediatric neurologists refer to dementia, they mean those who have a progressive and absolute decline in development and skills.

Reversible or irreversible

Hypothyroidism, vitamin B12 deficiency, hydrocephalus and the hyper-phenylalanaemias are all conditions potentially capable of resulting in dementia. Timely treatment prevents this and can on occasion produce an apparent reversal of a dementing illness. Many of the neurometabolic disorders that now result in dementia may, in time, be treatable.

Presentation

The varieties of presentation will depend upon the developmental stage of the child, the nature of the neuropathology and the course of the disease. In terms of residential treatment facilities, most of the children will present with depression,

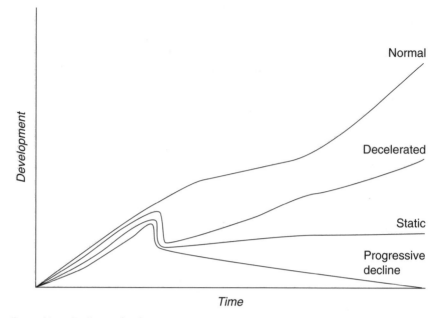

Figure 22.1 Differing developmental trajectories in dementia

aggression or psychosis. Occasionally, the first inkling that the child has a dementing illness may occur in a psychiatric treatment setting where antidepressants or antipsychotics are used and the child has a seizure or becomes confused. Lowered seizure threshold and a more permeable blood brain barrier will make seizures, adverse drug reactions and drug toxicity more likely.

Recognition

The group of conditions in childhood associated with pervasive neurocognitive decline has not received the consideration or been associated with the service development that dementia has received among the elderly. Paradoxically, there are many more conditions than in adulthood, over 600 in all (Nunn, 1993), that have been identified as 'causes' of dementia. For some, there is a neuropathological or neurometabolic characterisation of the lesion. For others only the syndromal pattern is recognised but the underlying mechanisms are unknown. Research and service developments have been fragmented. Estimations of the incidence of childhood dementia, excluding cases which have a reduced or static trajectory only, suffer from serious under-ascertainment (Nunn et al., 1997). Despite the very real needs of this group, child psychiatry has not generally advocated for their needs in the way that geriatric psychiatry has for the elderly. These children and adolescents find themselves in acute hospital beds where there is often no appropriate surrounding milieu of acceptance of the chronic, non-curative nature of the disorder. Child psychiatrists have traditionally not had patients with terminal illness in their care. The task has been left to general paediatricians, neurologists and oncologists. Dementia in childhood offers the possibility of developing a wider concept of child psychiatry's role. In doing so, each of these professions is likely to work more closely with us in the curative, diagnostic and general treatment roles.

The pervasive uncertainty surrounding these conditions, the progressive disintegration of the child and the prolonged impending bereavement have a cumulative impact that is perhaps one of the most poignantly distressing in paediatric medicine. Added to this is the possibility of sibling involvement, for example the mitochondrial disorders such as Leigh Disease which have a greater than 1 in 2 chance of sibling involvement (depending on the degree of the heteroplasmy), autosomal dominant disorders with a 1 in 2 probability such as Tuberous Sclerosis (with degeneration) and conditions like Batten Disease with a 1 in 4 probability.

Management

First and foremost one must treat the psychiatric symptoms and manage the parental and sibling uncertainty. Second, working in collaboration with a paediatric neurologist, clarify what can be known in terms of aetiology, treatment and prognosis. Third, assisting the family with regular and crisis respite care occurs alongside management of the changing clinical picture as time goes on. It is helpful if some of the nursing staff in residential units have not only psychiatric expertise but paediatric neurological expertise. The progressive decline in educational attainment will require changes in educational placement. However, the school provides valuable respite for the parents and social and recreational contact for the child. Academic demands should be gradually, rather than suddenly, relinquished. Parents gain reassurance from clear explanations of the relationship between brain function and behaviour. It is surprising how often parents fear the child's condition is due to some inadequacy of their parenting skills. Post-mortem family sessions are often appreciated. Reviewing the autopsy findings and the scans of the child's brain which demonstrate tissue damage can be very therapeutic. Parents will frequently be relieved over the long-term by these findings, albeit distressed in the shorter-term, especially where there has been an absence of structural findings till late in the disease and where the early manifestations of the dementia were predominantly behavioural. The special needs of siblings, their fears and concerns, need hardly be emphasised.

Epilepsy

The association of psychiatric disorder and epilepsy has a long and productive history. Residential units for psychiatric disorder and epilepsy have provided valuable insights into both conditions. For most residential units there will be several case scenarios that are referred with some frequency and that present the greatest challenges.

The child with psychiatric disorder who happens to have epilepsy

There is compelling evidence that children with epilepsy have a lower threshold to all psychiatric disorders (Rutter et al., 1970) and that this exceeds the vulnerability created by chronic medical disorder not involving the central nervous system. In general, where the epilepsy has been stabilised this should be managed by ignoring the epilepsy in the first instance and establishing the psychiatric treatment and then recalibrating the anticonvulsants. It is important once reasonable precautions have been taken not to allow the epilepsy to dominate the clinical management.

The child whose principal problem is epilepsy but who has associated psychiatric disorder

There are several forms of association.

ICTAL PSYCHOSIS

Although uncommon, this can be very dramatic with sudden onset, intense paranoia, automatisms and even violence or self-injury. Consciousness is clouded, emotions fearful or angry and thoughts are inaccessible. This picture may last for seconds to minutes though it may be prolonged into hours or even, rarely, days. It can be profoundly modified with antipsychotics that do not lower seizure threshold, such as risperidone, but will also require anticonvulsants such as carbamazepine or valproate. Such seizures are usually fronto-temporal in origin.

ICTAL BEHAVIOUR ABNORMALITY

The important feature of these seizures is the prominent psychiatric features. Behaviourally bizarre seizures with complicated behavioural sequences usually involving the frontal lobes may be misdiagnosed as hysteria (Stores, Zaiwalla and Bergel, 1991). They may last for extended periods of time; usually minutes, occasionally in excess of an hour. Again treatment may require combined psychotropics and anticonvulsants. These episodes are characterised by complex behaviours rather than ideational or perceptual distortion.

INTER-ICTAL BEHAVIOUR DISORDER

Disinhibited, overactive, easily distractible behaviour which is aggressive and disruptive is common. While the anticonvulsant medication must be rationalised, environmental changes to school and home will be crucial. The need for small classes, one-to-one attention, slowing down progression through school as early as possible in infant or primary school and the inclusion of special classes in mainstream school for the more impaired children will all help. The child's stay in a residential unit is often the first time all the issues can be addressed 'all of a piece'.

PSEUDOAUTISM

Occasionally a child may present with an acquired autistic picture and as part of the work up in a residential setting the EEG reveals a Landau-Kleffner Syndrome or non-convulsive status epilepticus.

PSEUDO SEIZURES

The most likely child to have pseudoseizures is one who has epileptic seizures. A child's fears, wishes and predicaments are apt to become entangled in their medical disorders. The more prolonged the episode, the more people enlisted to manage it, the more school missed because of it, the less medication affects it, the more clarity of consciousness within it and the less injury because of it, the more likely it is to be a pseudo seizure. A post-ictal rise in prolactin may be helpful (Bye, Nunn and Wilson, 1985) in distinguishing seizures from pseudo seizures.

The single most important dictum with epilepsy is to be open in mind to multiple contributors to behaviour while being decisive in practice. Dogmatic distinctions between epileptic and non-epileptic behaviour are usually wrong. Equally, allowing seizures to dominate behavioural managment is usually wrong as well. Striking the balance will only come with staff being familiar with both behaviour disorder and epilepsy and managing both in a firm, non-punitive manner.

Tourette's syndrome

Tic disorders are relatively common and vary greatly in their severity and comorbidity. Presentation to a residential psychiatric unit will depend upon these two factors together with the coping style of the family. Rarely, the tics will be so severe, especially those of the cervical and lumbar spine, that general hospitalisation will be required to rest the patient, to place the child in a non-stigmatising environment and, rarely, to ensure stability of the atlanto-axial joint. For the most part, however, admission to a child psychiatric residential unit will be for associated comorbidity of depression, attention deficit, obsessive compulsive disorder or disruptive behaviour.

The disorder is a long-term syndrome without a definitive cure and is extremely variable and unpredictable in its course. Exacerbations do not always occur with stress and amelioration does not always occur with benign life events. Tics come and go, not only in severity but also in type. A significant minority will improve spontaneously. To add further to these uncertainties, neuroadaptation to medication is sometimes encountered requiring rotation, elevation and sometimes cessation of medications. Further, the growing child is reducing their relative dosage over time.

Residential treatment requires a clear decision as to the target symptoms and signs for treatment. The comorbidity of obsessional symptoms, attentional difficulties, disruptive behaviour and the impact of tics on mood and social relationships, all need to be considered. Occasionally parents show a tendency to 'hyperattribution' in which all of the child's personality difficulties are attributed to Tourettes.

Treatment

Milder cases rarely come to residential units with only 30–40 per cent requiring medication (Leckman, 1992). More difficult cases may need dopamine antagonists and serotonin agonists and occasionally one of the benzodiazapines such as clonazapam. More recently, the serotonin and dopamine antagonist, risperidone, has been used and sometimes, because of exacerbation of obsessional symptoms, in conjunction with an SSRI. Clonidine is rarely helpful in severe cases in our experience. The individual management of the teenager needs to take into account the ridicule or disdain they suffer, their tendency to utilise the symptoms aggressively or in a care-eliciting manner and the impact on their social life. The medication benefit-to-toxicity ratio may be reduced so significantly that 'the treatment is worse than the disease'.

The family management needs to reduce the attribution of blame while encouraging the taking of responsibility for managing the disorder. Any tendency to see the family as 'causing' the illness is to be discouraged (Nunn, 1985). Keeping expectations down about the possible benefits of medication while fuelling long-term optimism about learning to live with tics, is likely to prevent disappointment and promote trust.

Sleep disorders

The sleep disorders are a relatively newly defined group of problems characterised by alterations in arousal and the day–night cycle (Kryger, Roth and Dement, 1994). Those that most commonly present to residential units will present as psychotic, hypersomnic or manifest bizarre behaviour which is taken to be behavioural in origin and nature. Both the hypersomnic and the psychotic young people will usually have alterations in consciousness and therefore much of what has been said about delirium applies. What impresses the clinician is the absence of demonstrable medical pathology, the persistence or recurrence of the problem, the extremity of the sleep disruption, the frequent amnesia for the episodes, the associated alterations to eating and social mores and, finally, the almost total inter-episodic recovery.

This description is true for Kleine-Levin which, though said to predominate in boys, is at least as frequently being seen now in girls in residential treatment units. It is also true for familial hypersomnia, sporadic hypersomnia and menstrually related hypersomnia (Billard, Guillmenault and Derwent 1975). The idiopathic hypothalamic syndrome (Nunn et al., 1997) may also show these same features except that, where brainstem features such as central hypoventilation pre-dominate, deterioration and death are likely. This condition is characterised by alteration in salt and water regulation, more extensive pituitary dysfunction with multiple endocrine abnormalities, sleep and respiratory difficulties suggestive of impaired brainstem mechanisms and behavioural disorders in which aggressive features predominate. These conditions are referred to residential units because of the combination of behaviour disorder and diagnostic perplexity. The salt and water regulation and endocrine difficulties may not be immediately apparent. Most of the cases present between three and nine years with sleep and behaviour difficulties.

Management

Symptomatic management during the episodes is largely that of the presenting behaviours but follows the lines of the management of delirium. If antipsychotic and sedative medication do not suffice the therapeutic, as opposed to prophylactic, use of lithium may be necessary.

The investigation of sleep architecture and advice from a sleep physician and consultation with a paediatric neurologist are likely to be helpful in excluding other disorders including non-convulsive seizure disorders. Again, the investigation will follow the line of the work-up for delirium. A primary idiopathic hypothalamic syndrome will require exclusion of a neural crest tumour and exquisite titration of psychotropics and sedatives. Even tiny doses may be lethal (Nunn, 1994)

The concern about recurrences and long term prognosis may become intense, especially where the episodes are frequent. Defining the exact nature of the sleep disorder will be important. If there is a narcoleptic component, dopamine agonists will be most appropriate. If cataplexy is more prominent a serotonergic agonist will be more helpful. Where the episodes are recurrent and florid, with periods of marked overactivity, a history of affective disorder, especially bipolar disorder, should be sought. Lithium is usually helpful. In the menstrually related hypersomnias hormonal regulation of the menstrual cycle can be helpful.

The sleep disorders will continue to baffle and fascinate. It is likely that some of the disorders represent quite specific primary disruptions of the median raphe (serotonergic systems) and the locus ceruleus (noradrenergic systems) even though the clinical picture is one of diffuse or global cerebral presentation.

Episodic dyscontrol

Definition

> The intermittent loss of control of aggressive feelings in which the nature of the response is overwhelming in comparison to the provoking stimulus (or where provocation is absent), is known as episodic dyscontrol.

In its most familiar form there may be a threat to the physical safety and/or survival of the victim, remorse is common and between episodes there is a stark contrast with the often normal behaviour of the child (Nunn, 1986).

These children are brought to residential units because of the severity of their attacks. They are often accepted by residential units because they do not display the antisocial disregard for social norms of conduct disordered children. However, their picture is rarely explained by central nervous system disorder alone. The usual picture is of an organically vulnerable child living in a high expressed emotion family where explosive outbursts of anger from otherwise over-controlled members occur intermittently. Marital discord is the rule and only the extremity of the child's difficulty and the failure of previous agencies to help masks the family's underlying troubles. Admission to the residential unit transfers the distress to the milieu and not infrequently the child becomes the total pre-occupation of the unit. The safety of staff and the other children emerges as the central issue. The alternation between the intimidation by the child and the overwhelming distress of staff in identifying with the child's plight, matches the child's over-empowerment and remorse associated with attacking behaviour.

Management

All that has been written in the chapter by Jacobs (chapter 19) on the psychological management of conduct disorders in this volume is also pertinent here. There are a few specific comments which must be added. Frightened staff should not be assigned to these children. Initial close proximity with particularly provocative children should be avoided. Staff need to be warned ahead of time of the dangers of over-identification and becoming punitive in the face of intimidation. Individual cognitive strategies and family therapy focussing on open acknowledgment of affect and affect regulation may help. Medication trials of SSRIs (sertraline; 12.5mg initially, then increasing slowly up to 2.5mg/kg/day), amitriptyline, beta blockers (especially where autonomic accompaniments are prominent), risperidone (0.25mg initially, increasing up to 0.04mg/kg/day) and lithium may also be considered. One should beware of introducing SSRIs too quickly as this may exacerbate aggressive behaviour.

Children with episodic dyscontrol associated with frontal disinhibition are a particularly dangerous subgroup. If they have no remorse and little conscience they are potentially homicidal. These children – the 'frontal sociopath' with dyscontrol – should not be accepted in anything but a forensic unit or gaol.

Frontal lobe syndromes

Head injury, infarction of brain tissue, infection, neoplasm and degenerative disorder may all give rise to a frontal lobe syndrome. Frontal lobe disorder can manifest as motorically inert, event indifferent, socially inappropriate, emotionally incontinent, task distractible and interpersonally unempathic children. Some children have difficulties with initiation behaviours ('starter motor activities'), others have trouble with controlling and censoring their own thoughts, feelings and behaviour ('steering and brakes problems') while still others have aggression and/or overactivity ('accelerator difficulties') often arising outside of the frontal lobe. Clearly increased drive states with decreased inhibitory capacities, in the presence of poor judgement, is a formula for problems with the law.

Children with frontal lobe difficulties who have little response to social disapprobation will appear conduct disordered or antisocial. They may be indistinguishable at presentation. (Nunn, 1994). Children who have planning and other executive difficulties, and who are overactive and have problems with working memory, may appear identical to those with attention deficit disorder and hyperactivity. Those who are apathetic, uninterested, emotionally labile and more or less mute, may look depressed.

Neuropsychology of frontal lobe syndrome

Children with disruptive or disinhibited behaviour may be understood best from a perspective that takes into account their executive functioning ability (Pennington and Ozonoff, 1996). Although the relationship between frontal lobe and dysexecutive syndromes in adults with acquired brain damage has been extensively explored, for children and young people it is important for a developmental neuropsychological perspective to take account of the normal emergence of self-regulatory and task management skills (Welsh, Pennington and Groisser, 1991). Within this framework, tests such as the Tower of London task (Krikorian, Bartok and Gay, 1994) for impulsivity and task planning, or verbal fluency tasks (Levin et al., 1991) can help to clarify how neuropsychological factors might be contributing to psychiatric disorder.

Diagnosis of frontal lobe syndrome rests on the combination of the characteristic clinical picture backed with investigations which will nclude neuropsychological assessment, EEG and sleep records and MRI scans where there is the suspicion of a structural lesion.

Management

Treatment involves, above all else, explanation. Dopamine agonists, tricyclics and the antipsychotics may all be considered. However, the appropriate school and placement setting will be the most critical interventions. Contraception for the frontally damaged teenage girl, together with protection from sexual exploitation, will be necessary. Mood disturbances are common and antidepressant dosage must be low if hypomanic episodes are not to be precipitated. Where pregnancy does occur, and impulsive aggression is part of the picture, the child will require alternative care. Surprisingly this is often accepted better than would be anticipated because of difficulties of attachment in this group. The prognosis is poor and social adjustment and judgement, not intellect, should be the guide.

Psychiatric disorder in the intellectually impaired

Mild to moderate intellectual impairment is associated with increased level of psychiatric disorder. Occasionally, especially in adolescents, this is beyond the coping resources of the family and respite or admission to a psychiatric residential unit is sought. If the latter, aggression, disruptive behaviour, non-specific distress or self-injury are proffered as target problems. Evaluations by a paediatrician to exclude occult infection, foreign body in ear or nose, constipation, bowel obstruction or peritonitis, are all sometimes necessary because of the child's inability to localise and articulate distress and discomfort. There is also a difficulty in discriminating between psychic and a somatic discomfort or indeed between internal distress and family/school tension. The intellectually impaired may be very sensitive to environmental stressors and yet completely uncomprehending or inarticulate. The inchoate nature of distress means that environmental stressors and developmental strain need to be disentangled carefully.

Much that is an enigma behaviourally becomes clear when examined in a developmental framework (Dossetor, 1997). Residential units enable respite for parents, examination of interaction with the child and opportunities to assess the adaptive capacities of the child and the family. Medications can be helpful. In the absence of very clear indications of which is most helpful systematic drug trials are necessary and careful psychotropic usage is required (Dossetor, 1997). Intellectual impairment cannot be treated per se. Defining the target phenomena is essential. Although the changes to be made are modest in this area, the appreciation of the parents and the impact on the child or teenager make it one of the most satisfying areas of practice for the paediatric neuropsychiatrist.

The somatoform disorders

The cardinal characteristic of the somatoform disorders is the presence of medical symptoms or signs without adequate evidence of an underlying medical condition. While these are extremely diverse and may involve all organ systems, they have been dealt with in this chapter because the most complex involve confusions with neurological disorder. Further, an understanding of the principles of managing two of the most problematic areas – conversion disorder and the pervasive refusal syndrome – is likely to be informative for the management of the broader conditions. These two are also much more likely to be referred to a residential psychiatric unit once diagnostic issues have been resolved.

Conversion disorder

Definition

> Conversion disorder involves symptoms or deficits of voluntary motor or sensory function which may be confused with neurological or other medical

conditions. Medical explanations for the condition are inadequate, psychological explanations are contributory and there is no factitious production of symptoms.

Conversion disorder in childhood is commonplace in consultation–liaison psychiatry. Those children with conversion disorder who are referred to residential units usually have chronic disorder, in deeply troubled families with very disrupted histories of education and help-seeking (Grattan Smith, Fairly and Procopis, 1988).

Diagnosis

Normally the diagnostic problems of conversion disorder have been resolved by the time they come to a residential unit. However, there are a number of principles guiding investigations and diagnosis worth reiterating. Firstly, there is no pathognomonic sign of conversion disorder. Secondly, the most likely children to have conversion disorder are previously or currently ill children. In childhood, the question is rarely 'Is this conversion disorder or organic?' It is more often 'How much do psychological factors and how much do medical factors contribute?' Thirdly, inconsistency and variability, though helpful, are common with many organic disorders. Sometimes, a child psychiatrist will have to exclude a conversion illness as the major explanation of a complex symptom presentation in an in-patient unit, before paediatricians will re-investigate a case and sometimes find the organic explanation which has been obscure. A surprisingly high proportion of conversion disorders is eventually found to have an organic basis. Child psychiatric practice differs as to whether an admission to an in-patient unit to facilitate this distinction is thought useful or unhelpful. Some families will spend much needed energy fighting over the inappropriateness of the admission. Others finally accept the psychological nature of the disorder.

The transition of parental understanding

The skill of the clinician in the consultation–liaison setting is the capacity to help the family reconceptualise the disorder and to negotiate the transfer of care. The task for the residential child psychiatrist and team is usually creating an atmosphere that enables the dissolution of a well-established and 'organised' illness. Usually this will involve addressing longstanding relational alliances in the family.

Family therapy

Families often have nagging doubts about possible organic contributors even after improvements have been established and sustained. There is little point in attempting to demonstrate a greater wisdom or trying to confront with the 'facts'. Agnosticism about aetiological information is sometimes not only the wisest path

Table 22.4 The principles of managing chronic somatoform illness in a residential
setting

---

1   Re-assess the evidence for conversion disorder, prior to admission where possible:
    i)   The evidence that there is no medical disorder
    ii)   The evidence that there are psychological contributors.
2   Always assess *before* agreeing to admit.
3   Establish clear expectations about the goals of treatment and what treatment will
    require by way of consent, *prior to admission.*
4   Parental restriction to no more than two hours' visiting can be helpful to assess
    alliances and to treat enmeshment. Where this is accomplished easily, consider
    covert rejection and abandonment. Enmeshment is the rule and extrusion is the
    exception.
5   A physical rehabilitation approach is usually the most helpful, especially with
    motor deficit.
6   The least affected parts are rehabilitated first. Keep that which is well, well. The
    most impaired functions such as paralysed limbs should be focussed on least to
    begin with and only recruited passively or by default such as in hydrotherapy.
7   Move from passive to active with school involvement, physical rehabilitation and
    social encounter; school attendance without expectation of academic activity,
    physical rehabilitation without expectation of performance and social encounter
    without demand to interact.
8   Focus on what they *can* do rather than on what they *cannot* do.
9   Keep short-term expectations low and long-term expectations high. When things
    go well emphasise potential complications. When things go badly emphasise the
    long-term positives. This smooths out 'roller coaster' reactions.
10 Keep communications centralised and highlight the dangers of the team becoming
    split or fragmented.
11 Do not rush and do not allow programme drift. Allow more time at the
    beginning of each new phase of treatment so that small achievements can lead
    to positive generalisation. Avoid becoming clinically *becalmed* with no
    short-term plans
12 Avoid termination phenomenon. Long-term follow-up even if widely spaced is
    more desirable than intensive therapy followed by abrupt terminations.

---

but the most honest. The general finding by clinicians is that if aetiological
information is to emerge it will often do so well into the treatment and sometimes
after recovery is complete. Intellectual openness is therapeutic at every point but
must be matched by clinical decisiveness about the pathway of action. Families
need to be discouraged from 'make or break solutions'.

Individual therapy

The person who knows least about what is happening to them is the patient.
Attempts to engage in in-depth discussion early on are usually frustratingly
unproductive. Permission not to talk about their troubles until later in the course
of therapy is helpful. The physiotherapist and nurse will usually hear much more
than the psychiatrist or psychotherapist. These children present their complaints
through their bodies and often they relate their difficulties and accept their

solutions through their bodies. Nevertheless, educational sessions aimed at addressing psychological and medical issues may be very productive.

Conclusion

Conversion disorder may lead to chronic impairment (Grattan Smith, Fairley and Procopis, 1988). Even, chronically disabled young people may find benefit from the care a residential in-patient unit provides. The skills and approaches used are of value in all the somatoform disorders and may be generalised to other disorders as well. In particular, they highlight the discrepancy between the family's formulation and the clinician's. Further, they remind us of how dependent we are upon the spoken word for our therapies.

The pervasive refusal syndrome

Definition

> This syndrome, first described by Lask et al. (1991), is a combination of whole body impairment, an absence of medical explanation for the disorder and help rejection by the young person. The children do not eat, walk, talk or co-operate with self-care.

Subsequent papers have described other cases. Aetiological models have been proposed by various groups (Graham and Foreman, 1995; Thompson and Nunn, 1997; Nunn and Thompson, 1996) and proposed comprehensive management strategies (Nunn et al., 1998). There may or may not be other associated somatoform comorbid disorders such as conversion disorder, psychogenic pain disorder. An atypical eating disorder akin to anorexia nervosa is a common feature in the illness. Many of the disorders will eventually be dealt with in a residential treatment setting.

Diagnosis

Haunting concerns about underlying medical disorder have often been laid to one side, even though not entirely abandoned, by the time residential treatment is sought. However, disquiet about major depression, undetected abuse and psychosis assume the same haunting quality with psychiatric staff. The discrepancy between the degree of impairment and the apparent level of family difficulties creates concern that something has been missed.

Management

All of the principles in relation to managing conversion are especially pertinent to managing pervasive refusal syndrome. However, because help-rejection is such a dominant theme, staff will need extra support, encouragement and advice on how to walk the fine divide between benign coercion and punitive attempts to obtain compliance. The most important elements of information to establish with the treatment team are: the disastrous results if nothing is done, the benefit of effective treatment, the futility of punitive measures and the success of an incrementally rehabilitative approach. Often the single most therapeutic measure is getting the psychiatric staff into their swimming costumes and helping the physiotherapist to do their job in the hydrotherapy pool. This work is detailed in a recent paper (Nunn et al., 1998).

It is sufficient to say that to date the results have been encouraging. The disorder is one which tests the unity of the team and the patience and commitment of our resolve.

Conclusion

The pervasive refusal syndrome is a rare syndrome which represents an extreme of severity among somatoform disorders. Residential treatment is often needed because of the intensity of rehabilitation needed. There is almost always a history of adverse medical experience from which the underlying disorder must be extricated. Treatment is difficult, fraught with staff complications but also potentially very productive. Skills gained in managing pervasive refusal syndrome are generalised to many other chronically impaired children and families where help-rejection and a fragile consent are involved.

TREATMENT PRINCIPLES IN RESIDENTIAL NEUROPSYCHIATRY

There are few areas in child psychiatry where the principles of treatment are so consistently misunderstood. Table 22.5 offers some examples of misconceptions.

Table 22.5 Some common misunderstandings in the treatment of neuropsychiatric disorders of childhood

---

- *Neuropsychiatric disorders are less amenable to treatment than other psychiatric disorders.* While this can be true for particular disorders, it is by no means the rule. There are many neuropsychiatric disorders that greatly benefit from intervention and there are many emotional and behavioural disorders arising as a result of social and family difficulties that do not.

- *The modality of therapy must match the modality of aetiology.* In complex interacting systems it will be evident that intervening with environmental demands may improve the child's neurological function or using biological treatments may improve the availability of the child to psychological therapies.

- *Children with neuropsychiatric disorder are less environmentally responsive, emotionally inaccessible, verbally inarticulate and socially comprehending.* Many children do not know what it is that is happening or why, but they are aware that something is amiss. This non-specific registration of family or school tension may be more acute in those children who rely on non-verbal cues rather than verbal cues.

THE MANAGMENT OF UNCERTAINTY

Irrespective of the neuropsychiatric condition being treated, we are likely to be managing uncertainty. It is helpful to outline the broad strategy of management, namely, the movement from symptomatic management to systematic investigation to long-term definitive treatment options. This is usually much more evident to the clinician than to the family and child. Even outlining this process and the possibilities of not coming to any definitive conclusion can reduce the perceived chaos and sense of isolation. Defining the principal fears and expectations and the most salient uncertainties from the family's and child's perspective will reduce anxiety. The uncertainties of the child and the family take precedence over the clinician's uncertainties. However, a judgement may need to be made on whether, or to what degree, the clinicians' uncertainties should be weighed against the need for consent and co-operation.

Table 22.6 The use of psychotropic medication in child psychiatry: general principles

1	Start the dosage low and increase slowly.
2	Attempt mono-therapy to begin with wherever possible
3	In general avoid agonists and antagonists of the same neurotransmitter group.
4	Do not use the reversible inhibitors of mono-oxidase A (RIMAs) and the selective serotonin re-uptake inhibitor (SSRIs) together.
5	Do not use combined agonists lightly, e.g. amitriptyline and thioridazine together are powerful anti-cholinergic synergists.
6	If poly-therapy is being considered, discuss with a colleague and document the discussion.
7	Do not use stimulants in psychosis.
8	Keep expectations of the outcome of medication low with benefits over weeks to months rather than days to weeks.
9	Side effects are minimised by making changes slowly.
10	Do not allow chaotic families to lead to chaotic prescribing.
11	The parents who provide the pressure to prescribe that cannot be resisted are the parents who will take you to court if things go wrong.
12	Wherever possible review, audit and share your practice with a peer group.

In general the question is not whether to tell, but when and how and in what detail. The level of explanation should match the level of uncertainty. The answer to 'What is happening to our little girl?' may not be a request for the precise metabolic pathway. If the clinician says 'I don't know' when it is quite clear that a dementing process is involved then a disservice has been done to the family. In general describing how the condition affects children, with the particular child in mind, helps the parent link the syndromal picture together.

Initially, dicussing the available evidence, with the weaknesses as well as the strengths, provides gentle help in managing their anxiety. Words, patterns of dysfunction and the presence of a medical familiarity, give support and some cognitive mastery. Describing the current medical theories with basic descriptions of neuroanatomy, neuropsychology, neurophysiology and neuropathology are often appreciated. Finally, discussing prognosis is the most difficult and most necessary element in managing uncertainty. The outcomes that parents fear are often quite different from those of the clinicians. Distinguish between prognosis for the symptom versus prognosis for the episode and prognosis for the episodes versus prognosis for the condition. Parents need know the prognosis for the illness with and without intervention.

Hope and despair

Sometimes there is no hopeful counsel to give except the willingness and the commitment to remain involved. This is particularly so where several children from the same family have a dementing disorder. Nevertheless, for most of the children, however modest our interventions, more hopeful scenarios can be proffered. The residential unit can provide a symbol of that commitment. The fear of leaving the unit for both the child and family may be the first test of their independence. It is always best to predict that they will be anxious and that there will be difficulties so that they are not subject to disappointment or unrealistic expectations. If times of success are tempered with warnings of major disappointments or unrealistic expectations, and times of difficulty with long term prospects of success the 'roller coaster' of rising and falling expectations is avoided.

CONCLUSION

The move to address neuropsychiatric need in the residential setting is fraught with problems. There will be a need for close medical collaboration which is not always available or comfortable. Children with intellectual impairment, sensory deficit or specific central nervous system damage put huge adaptational demands on staff. The problems of this group are long term, complex and shot through with interpretational difficulties.

Nevertheless this there is evidence (Gillberg, 1995) that this represents a very substantial group within the population. Many of them are poorly dealt with in community settings. Finally, they represent an important frontier for understanding the rest of psychiatric disorders in childhood more generally. However, if we are to move in this direction there is one inevitable corollary. We will have to take the role of the brain more seriously in child psychiatry and we will have to remind ourselves, albeit belatedly, that child psychiatrists are part of the medical profession.

ACKNOWLEDGEMENT

We are grateful for a short contribution on neuropsychological assessment by Dr Ian Frampton, Clinical neuropsychologist, The Children's Department, The Maudsley Hospital UK.

REFERENCES

Abe, K. and Ohta, M. (1995) Recurrent Brief Episodes with Psychotic Features in Adolescence: Periodic Psychosis of Puberty Revisited. *British Journal of Psychiatry*, 167, 507–513.

American Psychiatric Association (1994) *Diagnostic and Statistical Manual of Mental Disorders*, Fourth Edition. Washington, DC: American Psychiatric Association.

Bender, L. (1956) *Psychopathology of Children with Organic Brain Disorders*. Springfield, IL: Charles C. Thomas.

Billiard, M., Guillmenault, C. and Derwent, W.C. (1975) A Menstruation-linked Periodic Hypersomnia. *Neurology*, 25, 436–443.

Bye, A. M. E., Nunn, K. P. and Wilson, J. (1985) Prolactin and Seizure Activity. *Archives of Disease in Childhood*, 60, 848–851.

Corbett, J., Harris, R., Taylor, E. and Trimble, M. (1977) Progressive Disintegrative Psychosis of Childhood. *Journal of Child Psychology and Psychiatry*, 18, 211–219.

Creak, M. (1963) Childhood Psychosis: A Review of 100 Cases. *British Journal of Psychiatry*, 109, 84–89.

Dossetor, D.R. (1997) The Hit and Miss of Magic Bullets: A Guide to Psychotropic Medication for Young People with Intellectual Handicap. *Clinical Child Psychology and Psychiatry*, 2 (1), 65–93

Gillberg, C. (1995) *Clinical Child Neuropsychiatry*. Cambridge: Cambridge University Press.

Graham, P.J. and Foreman, D.M. (1995). An Ethical Dilemma in Child and Adolescent Psychiatry. *Psychiatric Bulletin*, 19, 84–86.

Grattan Smith, P., Fairley, M. and Procopis, P. (1988) Clinical Features of Conversion Disorders. *Archives of Disease in Childhood*, 63, 408–414.

Gualtieri, C.T. (1990) *Neuropsychiatry and Behavioural Pharmacology*. New York: Springer-Verlag.

Hamilton, M. (1976) *Fish's Schizophrenia*. Bristol: John Wright and Sons Ltd.

Harper, J. and Williams, S. (1974) Early Environmental Stress and Infantile Autism. *Medical Journal of Australia*, 1, 341–346.

Harris, J. (1995) *Developmental Neuropsychiatry*. Oxford: Oxford University Press. Volumes 1 and 2.

Krikorian, R., Bartok, J. and Gay, N. (1994). Tower of London Procedure: A Standard Method and Developmental Data. *Journal of Clinical and Experimental Neuropsychology*, 16 (6), 840–850.

Kryger, M.H., Roth, T. and Dement, W.C. (1994). *Principles and Practice of Sleep Medicine*. London: W.B. Saunders Co.

Lask, B., Britten, C., Kroll, L., Magagna, J. and Tranter, M. (1991). Children with Pervasive Refusal. *Archives of Disease of Childhood*, 66, 866–869.

Leckman, J. F. (1992). Tourette's syndrome. In Peschel, E., Peschel, R., Howe, C.W. and Howe, J. W. (eds). *Neurobiological Disorders in Children and Adolescents. New Directions for Mental Health Services*. San Francisco: Jossey-Bass.

Le Doux, J. (1996) *The Emotional Brain. The Mysterious Underpinnings of Emotional Life.* New York: Simon and Schuster.

Levin, H.S., Culhane, K.A., Hartmann, J., Evankovich, K., Mattson, A.J., Harward, H., Ringholz, G., Ewing-Cobbs, L. and Flectcher, J.M. (1991). Developmental Changes in Performance on Tests of Purported Frontal Lobe Functioning. *Developmental Neuropsychology*, 7 (3), 377–395.

Nunn, K.P. (1985) Beyond Orthodoxy – A Commentrary on Prata and Masson. *Journal of Family Therapy*, 7, 333–339

Nunn, K.P. (1986) The Episodic Dyscontrol Syndrome in Childhood. *Journal of Child Psychology and Psychiatry*, 27 (4), 439–446.

Nunn, K.P (1993) Dementia in Childhood. *Canadian Child Psychiatric Bulletin*, 2 (3), 45–51.

Nunn, K.P. (1994) Neuropsychiatric Aspects of Conduct Disorder with Special Reference to Frontal Lobes. *Annals of The Australian Society for Adolescent Psychiatry*, 2, 21–24.

Nunn, K.P. and Thompson, S.L. (1996) The Pervasive Refusal Syndrome: Learned Helplessness and Hopelessness. *Clinical Child Psychology and Psychiatry* 1 (1), 121–132.

Nunn, K.P, Lask, B.L and Cohen, M. (1986) Viruses, Neurodevelopmental Disorder and Childhood Psychosis. *Journal of Child Psychology and Psychiatry*, 27 (1), 55–64.

Nunn, K.P., Ouvrier, R., Sprague, T., Arbuckle, S. and Docker, M. (1997) Idiopathic Hypothalamic Dysfunction: A Paraneoplastic Syndrome? *Journal of Child Neurology*, 12 (4), 276–280

Nunn, K.P., Thompson, S.L., Moore, S.G., English, M., Burke, E.A. and Burne, N. (1998) Managing Pervasive Refusal Syndrome: Strategies of Hope. *Clinical Child Psychology and Psychiatry*, 3(2), 1359–1405.

Pennington, B.F. and Ozonoff, S. (1996). Executive Functioning and Developmental Psychopathology. *Journal of Child Psychology and Psychiatry*, 37 (1), 51–87.

Pike, M. and Stores, G. (1994) Kleine-Levin Syndrome: A Cause of Diagnostic Confusion. *Archives of Disease in Childhood* 71, 355–357.

Prugh, D.G., Wagonfeld, S., Metcalf, D. and Jordan, K. (1980) A Clinical Study of Delirium in Children and Adolescents. *Psychosomatic Medicine*, 2 4(1), 11.

Ross, E.D. and Stewart, R.M. (1991) Akinetic Mutism from Hypothalamic Damage: Successful Treatment with Dopamine Agonists. *Neurology*, 31, 1435–1493.

Rourke, B.P., Fisk, J.L. and Strang, J.D. (1987). *Neuropsychological Assessment of Children: A Treatment-Oriented Approach.* New York: Guilford.

Rutter, M.L. (1984) *Developmental Neuropsychiatry.* London: Churchill Livingstone.

Rutter, M. L., Graham, P. and Yule, W. (1970) *A Neuropsychiatric Study in Childhood. Clinics in Developmental Medicine*, Nos 35/36. London: SIMP/Heinemann.

Stores, G., Zaiwalla, Z. and Bergel, N. (1991) Frontal Lobe Complex Partial Seizures in Children: A Form of Epilepsy at Particular Risk of Misdiagnosis. *Developmental Medicine and Child Neurology*, 33, 998–1009.

Taylor, E. (1986) *The Overactive Child. Clinics in Developmental Medicine.* No. 97. Oxford: Blackwell.

Thompson, S.L. and Nunn, K.P. (1997) The Pervasive Refusal Syndrome *Clinical Psychology and Psychiatry*, 2 (1), 145–166.

Trzepacz, P.T. (1994) The Neuropathogenesis of Delirium. A Need to Focus our Research. *Psychosomatics* 35, 374–391.

Volkmar, F. (1996) *Psychoses and Pervasive Developmental Disorders in Childhood and*

Adolescence. Washington, DC. American Psychiatric Press, Inc. and American Academy of Child and Adolescent Psychiatry.

Welsh, M.C., Pennington, B.F. and Groisser, D.B. (1991). A Normative-Developmental Study of Executive Function: A Window on Prefrontal Function in Children. *Developmental Neuropsychology*, 7 (2), 131–149.

Williams, S. and Harper, J. (1973) Aetiological Factors at Critical Periods of Development in Infantile Autism. *Australian and New Zealand Journal of Psychiatry*, 7, 163–168.

23 Pervasive developmental disorder

Jonathan Green

INTRODUCTION

A wide range of disorders within the autistic spectrum may present themselves to in-patient services. Children with classical autism, especially those with significant mental handicap, are much more likely to be treated by mental handicap or specialist autistic than generic child in-patient services. Nevertheless, general procedures in relation to this work will be considered in this chapter for two reasons; firstly some units may choose to specialise in this area and secondly the assessment of more atypical autistic states rests most securely in familiarity with prototypical autistic presentations and uses adaptations of techniques developed in work with classical autism.

More likely to present to child in-patient units are cases within the spectrum of atypical autistic impairments or the 'extended phenotype' (Bailey, Philips and Rutter 1996); this will include many cases with complex, severe or mixed pictures for whom in-patient assessment and management comes into its own. Because of their singularity and relevance to in-patient units, work with these groups of children will be discussed in particular detail in this chapter.

A third group of problems presenting to in-patient units is essentially diagnostic: either the functional assessment of complex autistic spectrum cases or the identification of autistic spectrum comorbidity underlying other severe presentations. Thus a minority of children presenting apparently with severe conduct disorder, attention deficit disorder, dyspraxia, bizarre behaviour or severe neglect or maltreatment can prove to have social impairment within the autistic spectrum. In-patient assessment can be invaluable for such diagnoses; which can literally transform the perception and management of the problem.

GENERIC IN-PATIENT ASSESSMENT OF AUTISTIC IMPAIRMENTS

Assessment of children with autism and related disorders presenting in in-patient care builds on assessments of these children developed in other contexts. A summary is provided here and readers requiring more detail should refer to standard texts (for instance Lord and Rutter 1994). Attention has to be paid to defining the nature and extent of the handicap in different areas and to identifying any underlying aetiological causes. An assessment starts with taking a structured developmental and family history and collating information from other professionals who know the child. The Autism Diagnostic Interview (ADI) provides a standardised structured history but it is lengthy and requires training. Its algorithm is only designed to diagnose core autism but information from the interview used with clinical discernment can be valuable for the wider spectrum of disorder in conjunction with other evidence. Clinical present state examination will cover examination of the nature of the child's communication skills, social reciprocity, play skills and behaviour. The Autism Diagnostic Observation Schedule (ADOS) (Lord et al. 1989) is a valuable standardised clinical examination which allows recording of these features. Physical examination will focus particularly on dysmorphic features and neurocutaneous abnormalities. Neurodevelopmental examination is essential. It may identify the need for further neurological investigations as well as identifying associated problems such as dyspraxia. Certain biological investigations are important although significant positive findings are not excessively common in the absence of neurological abnormality. Detailed chromosome analysis is essential, not only for fragile X sites but also for a number of other trisomies and deletions which may present with atypical autistic states. A brain scan may be more productive than EEG (Scott 1997), but EEG investigation should be performed if there are clinical indications. Thyroid function and white cell enzymes are useful screens. Other investigations can be used as indicated by clinical examination. Psychometric assessment is very useful, firstly because all developmental phenomena need to be interpreted in the light of the child's basic cognitive level, and secondly for the light it throws on the child's profile of abilities. Children with autism commonly show peaks of ability in WISC subtests such as block design, and troughs in others such as picture completion and verbal comprehension (Frith 1991). Other psychological tests can be discriminating, especially in subtle cases; autistic children show above average performance on the embedded figures test (Frith 1991) and poor functioning on tests of first or second order theory of mind. Complex cases should have a full language assessment. Age appropriate tests that may discriminate subtle impairments in social cognition and executive functioning in the 'extended phenotype' are currently being developed in research settings and may help soon in clinical assessment. This will be a significant advance.

Ward assessment should focus on a functional assessment of developmental skills, social reciprocity and behaviour. Very important information can be gained in difficult cases by such observations in naturalistic settings over time; subtle social impairments which may not be apparent in the one to one context of clinic assessment can become clear in everyday group settings with peers. Ward assessments need to be practicable but yet make best use of the rich opportunities for observation presented by admission. I have found the Childhood Autism Rating Scale (CARS) (Schopler et al. 1980) and the Vineland Adaptive functioning scales (Sparrow and Cicchetti 1985) to be useful for this purpose.

Ward staff observe the subtleties of children's interactions during group life and their empathic responses to other children's feelings. Details of children's behaviours can be observed: obsessional routines or subtle behavioural change that are markers for non-convulsive epileptic episodes, stereotypies and over-activity. School staff will be able to observe classroom behaviour, motivation towards learning and the ability to cope with structured social settings. Social behaviour observed in these real life settings complements information gained from structured clinical assessments such as the Autism Diagnostic Observation Schedule.

A different kind of diagnostic problem is the assessment of possible functional psychiatric disorder in a communicatively impaired child whose behaviour has shown a bizarre deterioration. The differential diagnosis may be between an onset of psychotic illness, an organic disorder such as the onset of complex seizures, a mood disorder, typically depression, or a reactive disorder to environmental stresses, about which the child is finding it very difficult to communicate.

> Stephen was a 10-year-old child with severe learning disability and some autistic social impairment. He was admitted with a possible psychosis after the death of his grandfather. His behaviour had become bizarre and withdrawn and he had become increasingly uncommunicative. His limited existing language had regressed. The admission was difficult because of trying to nurse this learning disabled child alongside other children of normal intelligence. Careful assessment of his reactions and behaviour in naturalistic settings over a number of weeks suggested that psychosis illness was unlikely and that Stephen was probably showing a mood disorder in relation to his bereavement. He was placed on antidepressants and showed a significant clinical improvement.

IN-PATIENT MANAGEMENT OF AUTISTIC DISORDERS

The mainstay of the management of children with typical autism is appropriate educational provision (Jordan and Powell 1996; Trevarthen et al. 1996). The use of a psychiatric in-patient unit in management is likely to be needed for two main purposes: firstly the management of acute behaviour disturbance and secondly a trial of medication.

Behavioural treatments

Behavioural treatment is the best described and researched intervention for autism. Behavioural analysis and contingency management can be applied to minimising unwanted behaviour and support the development of wanted skills (Howlin and Rutter 1987; Clements 1987; Lovaas 1987). These techniques in broad outline are discussed in chapter 10. There has been specific work in autism on common problems such as aggressive outbursts (Clements 1987), stereotypy and self-injury (Murphy and Wilson 1985) and obsessional behaviour (Marchant et al. 1974). Because of the communication problems, understanding the antecedents and meaning of behaviours can be a challenge requiring careful assessment and insight into the autistic world. Behaviour management is also complicated by the strong tendencies towards rigidity and routinised behaviours in autism which tend to result in over-learning and obsessive elaboration of new skills. Some apparently unwanted behaviours may just be the result of a limited behavioural repertoire (Jordan and Powell 1996) but it is at times possible to identify factors underlying behavioural change, such as physical discomfort, uncommunicated pain, illness, frustration, anxiety or uncommunicable need. Autistic children without language can particularly benefit from programmes that emphasise pre-linguistic and interpersonal communication (Hermelin and O'Connor 1985). The TEACCH programmes (Schopler et al. 1980) are particularly systematic and eclectic in utilising children's skills at the service of communication and learning. The most effective use of in-patient units in this context can probably be for specific investigation of perplexing behaviours, particularly for biological causes, and the setting up of well designed but short-term behavioural programmes for the management of particular difficulties, with the aim of generalising them to other settings. This kind of work does require an adapted milieu which can be difficult to combine with more generic in-patient work.

Pharmacological treatments

The in-patient setting can be useful for establishing pharmacological treatments. Autistic children who develop epilepsy may well be best stabilised within a psychiatry in-patient setting (see chapter 22). Haloperidol shows a significant improvement over placebo in reducing motor stereotypies, motor restlessness and aggression (Campbell et al. 1978; Cohen et al. 1980). Unfortunately frequent unwanted effects include drug-related dystonias even with low doses. Stimulants can produce useful changes in the behaviour of some autistic children, particularly in improved attention span, reduction in motor restlessness and some improved social behaviour (Campbell et al. 1988; Sloman 1991) – although Fenfluramine is not now recommended due to recent concerns about its safety. There has been interest in the use of naloxone and naltrexone, particularly in self-injury (Campbell et al. 1988). The possibility of comorbid psychiatric disorder should be considered for treatment; perhaps especially in higher functioning autistic individuals since comorbidity rates are high (Gilchrist and Green submitted). Treatment here should follow the diagnosis.

ATYPICAL, COMPLEX AND 'BORDERLINE' PRESENTATIONS: MULTIPLEX DEVELOPMENTAL DISORDER

A particular group of children within the autistic spectrum for whom in-patient units can be crucial in both diagnosis and management are those young children

Table 23.1 Criteria for multiplex developmental disorder

Disordered arousal

At least two of:

- intense generalised anxiety or tension

- fears and phobias (often unusual)

- panic episodes

- episodes of behavioural disorganisation showing immature, primitive or unpredictable explosive aggressiveness

- wide emotional variability and bizarre anxiety reactions

Disordered thinking

At least two of:

- irrationality, intrusions into normal thought process, bizarre magical ideas

- confusion between reality and inner fantasy life

- perplexity and confusion

- apparent delusional or overvalued ideas including paranoid and self-referential ideation (sustained and solid delusions will shift diagnostic thinking towards psychosis)

Social impairment

At least two of:

- impaired empathy and understanding

- high degree of ambivalence to adults

- impaired peer relationships

- lack of interest, detachment and withdrawal

Onset in first few years of life

Child not suffering from autism or schizophrenia

Source: after Cohen et al. 1991

who present often extreme behavioural disturbance coupled with fluctuating and bizarre mental states. Such children have fascinated clinicians for many years and have attracted different labels and theoretical formulations. Early formulations were of 'infantile psychosis' or 'childhood schizophrenia' (Bender 1971) but studies in the seventies made clear the epidemiological distinction between these early onset developmental disorders and schizophrenic-like illness presenting in middle childhood (Kolvin 1971). Psychoanalytically orientated clinicians described infantile psychotic states (Mahler and Fuhrer 1960) and the concept of 'borderline disorder' in children was used by analogy with adult borderline disorders (Pine 1974). Previous UK approaches to the in-patient management of such children have been described (Stroh 1974). I have found a most useful recent formulation within this area to be that of 'multiplex complex developmental disorder' (Cohen, Paul and Volkmar 1987; Cohen et al. 1991; Van der Gaag 1993). In this formulation, such disorders are brought within the autistic spectrum: children showing atypical autistic social impairments along with profound disorder of the regulation of affective states and disordered thinking (Table 23.1).

Using the generic assessment approach described above, we can generally elucidate a pattern of underlying autistic like social impairment despite the fluctuations in mood, arousal and thinking which may mask the underlying developmental disorder. The child is often described as grossly immature, but the mixture of delay and deviations in the development are complex.

Family factors

Primary difficulties in family environment in these disorders have been described (Van der Gaag 1993). Even when there are not primary family adversities, the strains of caring for a child with such a severe and complex disorder make it common for the child to be subject to high intensity interactions at home. Not only do the parents have to cope with the perplexities of the lack of consistent social response in their child, they have to constantly adapt to rapidly changing swings of mood and behaviour, abnormal thoughts (which may be of delusional intensity) and aggression. The children also frequently show paradoxical clinging and rejecting behaviour, especially towards those most familiar to them (Van der Gaag 1993).

At the time of admission parenting is often marked by extreme distress, with desperate efforts to control that can often become punitive. The whole interaction can be characterised by extremely high expressed emotion. This amplifies the child's disturbance.

MANAGEMENT STRATEGIES IN MULTIPLEX DISORDERS

Respite

One of the first benefits of admission can be to remove the child from the crisis at home, into an environment that can promote a reduction in arousal. Here the stress-diathesis model of the disorder, applied usefully to adult schizophrenia by writers such as Falloon (e.g. Shepherd, Watt, Falloon and Smeeton 1989) is a useful guiding principle. In this way, admission is often followed by a reduction of arousal and overt symptomatology.

Adapted communication

On the ward great attention has to be paid to simple and clear social communication that takes account of the cognitive and language development of the child. Their social abilities are usually much lower than expected. One-to-one communication taken slowly can establish rapport and generate coping strategies. We work then to generalise this into more complex social situations in which the child is likely to have greater difficulty, such as group settings with peers. If unable to handle the more complex situations, the children can rapidly show increased arousal and then behavioural disturbance.

Psychopharmacology

Neuroleptics can be effective and crucial in management, helping to reduce arousal, organise thinking patterns and reduce distress, and allowing the child to be more available for other therapies. Thioridazine, Haloperidol and Stelazine can all be useful (Cohen et al. 1991). Dosages should be titrated up from a low level and may need to be continued over a long term.

Empirically, stimulant medication has sometimes proved effective, perhaps through the improvement in reflective thinking and planning and thereby the reduction of anxiety produced by disorientation (though stimulants can para-doxically increase anxiety in other cases). With some children I have used the (unusual) combination of stimulants and neuroleptics with greater success than either alone, and other clinicians (Van der Gaag personal communication) have had similar success. In the older child I have used beta blockers with benefit in the manner described for use in episodic dyscontrol syndromes (see chapter 22). These pharmacological treatments are combined with psychological therapies.

Psychological treatments

Insight orientated forms of psychotherapy tend to increase fragmentation and arousal and are usually contra-indicated. More cognitive behavioural approaches to therapy however can make progress in organising the child's understanding of their own functioning and development of coping strategies. Children with this disorder seem to have an extremely fragmented sense of the continuity of their experience, and this lack of a stable basis for perception and action increases and intensifies anxious reactions. When the child is available for communication, we can work through play and language to help them understand their own predicament, make sense of their thinking and help them feel more in control of their thoughts and behaviour. The ABC (antecedents, behaviour, consequences) schema can be used:

> *Nurse:* All right Joanne, I can see that you are very angry indeed. Now tell me what happened. What happened first? What did you see? What did you feel? What did you think? Then what did you do? Then what happened next? Let's make a picture of this.

By sitting alongside one another (rather than face to face) and writing down what happened in such an ABC scheme, arousal reduction can be attempted and alternative behaviours proposed. Written or drawn information can be referred to repeatedly. Cognitive methods to master delusional and hallucinatory thinking can also be tried. However, the limitations of such approaches must be recognised. Children with these difficulties usually have great difficulty in assimilating strategies flexibly and fail to generalise. They remain relatively dependent on adults.

Neuromotor integration

Neuromotor development is often as fragmented as cognitive development. Occupational therapy assessment usually reveals gross difficulties in sensory motor integration, co-ordination, spatial perception and motor planning. We have found that specific work with all these areas in the occupational therapy department is extremely useful to help the child orientate himself and develop confidence. We find these skills can on occasion show generalisation to planning cognitive, behavioural and relational tasks.

Family work

A central part of treatment is to help families understand the nature of the disorder and the cause of exacerbation in symptoms. Central to this is the understanding of the primary impairments in social functioning, arousal and thinking, which can make sense of much about the child's behaviour and reactions. Parents have often formulated the problem for themselves very differently or had other diagnoses from professionals. Much can follow from this in terms of a more realistic orientation to the child's behaviour and experience and in the generation of coping and management strategies. One treatment goal is to reduce parental expressed emotion to the child. Often there are also implications for the child's school placement.

FOLLOW-UP

The in-patient admission is merely a phase in the management of these children. The aims are for precise diagnostic formulation and assessment to guide future treatment, to manage the acute crisis and to stabilise the child on longer-term therapies. Further aims are to establish the child in the correct long-term educational placement and to put in place necessary therapy and support for the family. Admission may have to be repeated at times of crisis, and families usually need respite arrangements – a weekly residential school environment can be a good solution. The longer-term management aims to maintain as stable a state as possible; to foster development, using, if necessary, low dose neuroleptics. The parents need to have as good an understanding as possible of their child's difficulty and ongoing therapeutic support.

SUMMARY

Diagnosis is the first task: these presentations can be extremely confusing. Often it is the social impairments that are masked and the key to unravelling the problem. I advocate a multi-faceted approach to treatment. This firstly uses the ward as a therapeutic environment to modulate the sensory input to the child – in the context of a stress diathesis model of the disorder. We then selectively combine medication and psychological treatments to modulate arousal and improve cognitive functioning and to help them gain a sense of coherence in their experience. High expressed emotion in the family – common initially – is extremely disruptive to the child's functioning, and family work is pursued to reduce this. With this kind of treatment many of the presenting symptoms usually reduce, revealing beneath the more pervasive developmental difficulties. This has further implications for prognosis and educational provision.

The complex problems that these children present are probably under-diagnosed and may be relevant to a number of children with severe psychopathology (for instance involving conduct disorder), the complexity of whose true difficulties are not appreciated. As a related issue, at least two false allegations of severe and complex abuse ('satanic abuse' in one case) have been made in relation to such children, in my clinical experience, on the basis of their bizarre and extreme fantasy material; and with disastrous consequences. The facilities provided by an in-patient unit come into their own with these cases: to allow assessment, containment and properly planned therapeutic work.

Richard was a 6-year-old boy referred by a Community Psychiatric Nurse following increasing worries at his school. His behaviour had changed and become more and more bizarre in class, where he would act completely without restraint, crouching under desks, throwing books around, attacking other children and shouting out. The teachers were particularly worried by deterioration in his thinking, with unusual language and thinking patterns. He was increasingly socially isolated. Richard's mother had had a probable schizophrenic breakdown in late adolescence and remained a brittle and sensitive personality, traits exacerbated when she took marijuana. Richard's father was not known, but her long-time partner in the household was a chronic heroin abuser, who also took other street drugs. Richard had experienced drug induced adult behaviour and had witnessed unpredictable emotion and aggression. Despite this, the mother and partner were protective of Richard and generally tried to do their best for his welfare, albeit (for the partner) through periods of drug addiction and attempted detoxification.

On admission, Richard was nursed to provide low arousal, consistency and predictability in adult behaviour. Care was taken to communicate very clearly and simply; to structure his environment and not to over-stimulate him. Within a few days Richard's bizarre symptomatology (initially seen on the ward) diminished, as his arousal reduced. He began to engage in school and ward life. As the behavioural symptoms decreased, Richard's underlying developmental difficulties became more apparent: his developmental language disorder (containing both pragmatic and semantic deficits), his impairment of age-appropriate social skills and his rigidity. The admission enabled his subtle pervasive developmental disorder to be elucidated and after discharge he was placed in a specialist speech and language school, which gave him the ongoing learning environment that he needed. Therapeutic work with mother and partner aimed to provide them with adequate social support and help in developing a child centred consistent environment at home. Following discharge Richard's symptoms occasionally returned, although less severely, and he adapted well in his new school. At five-year follow up he has continued to make good progress, and as his language and communicative ability have improved his episodes of psychological disintegration psychologically have reduced. He never required medication.

Sarah was a 7-year-old girl referred from a neighbouring day unit for further assessment, after they found it impossible to understand her disorder. She had been a day patient for seven months and had attracted a number of different diagnoses, including attention deficit disorder, conduct disorder and psychosis. Because of her presenting symptomatology, there had also been concern about the possibility of sexual abuse. Sarah had presented with a severe oppositional disorder from the age of three years, which had led to her exclusion from a number of primary schools. She was extremely and unpredictably aggressive in school, but also at home towards her parents. Sarah had abnormal beliefs and anxieties: one that a boy in the neighbourhood, whom she did not know, was trying to poison her. She had a number of obsessional routines which dominated the family. At its height, Sarah would entrain the family into enacting episodes of a TV soap opera for hours a day, and would control the way her parents ate because of her sensitivity to chewing sounds. When aroused she would develop a frenzy of agitation, with fragmented, distractible and aggressive behaviour, and could hardly be settled. Her play reflected her high-arousal, apparently delusional states, and intense fears of objects and people in her family.

Mother had been a psychiatric care assistant and father a salesman. Sarah was a long awaited child, an early adoption after many miscarriages. Detailed developmental history showed the early emergence of resistance to change, unusual use of language, over-activity and poor social relating. At the time of admission both parents were at breaking point and freely admitted there were times when they screamed and shouted and hit Sarah, to try and keep in control. They were on the other hand, devoted to her care and in their attempts to find some understanding of her problems.

Following admission Sarah was an extremely difficult management problem, but, gradually, over a number of weeks, her arousal levels reduced, her thinking became clearer, and her fragmented behaviour lessened. Assessment on the Autism Diagnostic Interview algorithm showed a score of 8 (clinical cut-off for autism 10) on the social domain, 10 (8) on the communication domain, 3 (3) on the abnormal behaviour domain, with abnormality emerging before 3 years. Score on the Childhood Autism Rating Scale showed 35.5 ('mild–moderate autism'): Autism Diagnostic Observation Schedule showed a similar result. WISC showed full scale IQ of

86 with no Verbal Performance discrepancy. Language assessment showed no semantic deficits in language but significant deficits in pragmatic use of language and higher order perceptual processing. Occupational Therapy assessment showed very significant dyspraxic and visuo-perceptual deficits – confirmed on neurodevelopmental examination. Chromosomes, CT scan and biochemical screens were normal. Clinically, she could at times be behaviourally almost appropriate for her age, but at other times was extremely bizarre in thinking and behaviour. The abnormal thoughts waxed and waned. However admission did undoubtedly quieten and reduced her symptoms. When returned home at the end of admission her arousal levels increased again and her behaviour worsened, eventually necessitating a second admission, which again calmed her.

The ward team were initially perplexed by her presentation and unsure how to proceed. Over time it became clear that despite normal intelligence, a significant pattern of pervasive developmental disorder was present; apparent in her impairments of social cognition, difficulties in rapport, misunderstanding of social communication and rigidity of thought and behaviour. When we were able to make a diagnostic formulation of multiplex developmental disorder, a way ahead for treatment looked clearer. We had initially begun a trial of methylphenidate. This clearly improved her cognitive functioning, lowered her activity levels, and had some benefit on social rapport. However, she was still prone to massive swings in arousal and the emergence of abnormal ideas and possibly auditory hallucinations. Low dose haloperidol was added and the combination of neuroleptic and stimulant was effective in improving her functioning. On trial of reduction of methylphenidate her behaviour rapidly worsened. In the improved state we began psychological treatments using play materials but focused around structured cognitive tasks, as we engaged her in talking about her experience and tried to make sense of it. She played out extreme and sadistic fantasies in relation to her family. Sarah's heightened feeling towards her parents waxed and waned and there was never any evidence to support a notion of abuse. We tried to work towards helping her find a language for her experience and her perceptions of family members and other people in her environment. She began to engage on the unit and developed close ties with many of the staff (as well as intense aversions to others). Regular occupational therapy focused on sensory integration techniques with benefit. Increasingly the staff were able to develop more normal capacities in her behaviour and thinking and by the time of her discharge she had made immense progress, both socially and at school, even though pervasive developmental problems remained. Intensive work was undertaken with the family to help their understanding and reduce expressed emotion. She was placed in a weekly residential school and remains now after two years fairly stable on neuroleptic treatment. Attempts to reduce medication have led to acute deterioration.

REFERENCES

Bailey, A., Philips, W. and Rutter, M. (1996) Autism: Towards an Integration of Clinical, Genetic, Neuropsychological, and Neurobiological Perspectives. *Journal of Child Psychology and Psychiatry, 37 (1)*, 89–126.

Bender, L. (1971) Alpha and Omega of Childhood Schizophrenia. *Journal of Autism and Childhood Schizophrenia*, 1 (2), 115–118.

Campbell, M., Anderson, L.T., Meier, M., Cohen, I.L., Small, A.M., Samit, C. and Sachar, E.J. (1978) A Comparison of Haloperidol, Behaviour Therapy and Their Interaction in Autistic Children. *Journal of the American Academy of Child Psychiatry*, *17*, 640–655.

Campbell, M., Adams, P., Small, A.M., Tesch, L., McVie and Curren, E.L. (1988) Naltrexone in Infantile Autism. *Psychopharmacology Bulletin*, *24*, 135–139.

Clements, J. (1987) *Severe Learning Disability and Psychological Handicap*. Chichester: John Wiley and Sons.

Cohen, D.J., Paul, R. and Volkmar, F. (1987) Issues in the Classification of Pervasive Developmental Disorders and Associated Conditions. In Cohen, D.J., Donnellan, A.M. and Rhea, P. (eds) *Handbook of Autism and Pervasive Developmental Disorders*. New York: Wiley and Sons.

Cohen, D.J., Towbin, K.E., Mayes, L. and Volkmar, F. (1991) Developmental Psychopathology of Multiplex Developmental Disorder. In Friedman, S.L. and Haywood, H.C. (eds), *Developmental Follow-Up: Concepts Genres Domains and Methods*. Academic Press.

Cohen, I.L., Campbell, M., Posner, D., Small, A.M., Triebel, D. and Anderson, L.T. (1980) Behavioural Effects of Haloperidol in Young Autistic Children. *Journal of the American Academy of Child Psychiatry*, *19*, 655–677.

Donnellan, A.M., and Rhea, P. (eds), *Handbook of Autism and Pervasive Developmental Disorders*. New York: Wiley and Sons.

Frith, U. (1991) *Autism and Asperger Syndrome*. Cambridge: Cambridge University Press

Hermelin, B. and O'Connor, N. (1985) Logico Affective States and Non Verbal Language. In Schopler, E. and Mesibov, G. (eds), *Communication Problems in Autism*. New York: Plenum Press.

Howlin, P. and Rutter, M. (1987) *Treatment of Autistic Children*. Chichester: John Wiley and Sons.

Jordan, R. and Powell, S. (1996) *Understanding and Teaching Children with Autism*. Chichester: John Wiley and Sons.

Kolvin, I. (1971) Studies in the Childhood Psychoses: Diagnostic Criteria and Classification. *British Journal of Psychiatry*, *118*, 381–384.

Lord, C. and Rutter, M.R. (1994) Autism and Pervasive Developmental Disorders. In Rutter, M. R., Taylor, E. and Hersov, L. (eds) *Child and Adolescent Psychiatry Modern Approaches*. 3rd Edition. Oxford: Blackwell.

Lord, C., Rutter, M., Goode, S., Heemsbergen, J., Jordan, H., Mawhood, L. and Schopler, E. (1989) Autism Diagnostic Observation Schedule: A Standardised Observation of Communicative and Social Behaviour. *Journal of Autism and Developmental Disorders*, *19*, 185–212.

Lovaas, O.I. (1987) Behavioural Treatment and Normal Educational and Intellectual Functioning in Young Autistic Children. *Journal of Consulting and Clinical Psychology*, *55*, *1*, 3–9.

Mahler, M.S. and Fuhrer, M. (1960) Observations on Research Regarding the Symbiotic Syndrome of Infantile Psychosis. *Psychoanalytic Quarterly*, 297, 317–327.

Marchant, R., Howlin, P., Yule, W. and Rutter, M. (1974) Graded Change in the Treatment of Behaviour of Autistic Children. *Journal of Child Psychology and Psychiatry*, 15, 221–227.

Murphy, G. and Wilson, B. (1985) *Self Injurious Behaviour*. London: British Institute for Mental Handicap.

Pine, F. (1974) On the Concept 'Borderline' in Children. A Clinical Essay. *Psychoanalytic Study of the Child*, 29, 341–368.

Schopler, E. and Olley, J.G. (1982) *Comprehensive Educational Services for Autistic Children: The TEACCH Model*. In Reynolds, C.R. and Gutkin, T.R. (eds), Handbook of Social Psychology. New York: John Wiley and Sons.

Schopler, E., Reichler, R.J., De Vellis, R.F. and Kock, K. (1980) Towards Objective Classification of Childhood Autism: Childhood Autism Rating Scale (CARS). *Journal of Autism and Developmental Disorders*, 10, 91–103.

Scott, S. (1997) How Useful are Medical Investigations in Assessing Learning Disability? *Presentation to the Annual Residential Meeting of the Child and Adolescent Faculty of the Royal College of Psychiatrists*. Edinburgh, September.

Shepherd, M., Watt, D., Falloon, I. and Smeeton, N. (1989) The Natural History of Schizophrenia: A Five Year Follow Up Study of Outcome and Prediction on a Representative Sample of Schizophrenics. *Psychological Medicine Monograph Supplement 15*, 1–46

Sloman, L. (1991) Use of Medication in Pervasive Developmental Disorders. *Psychiatric Clinics of North America*, 14, 1, 165–182.

Sparrow S., S. and Cicchetti, D., V. (1985) Diagnostic Use of the Vineland Adaptive Behaviour Scales. *Journal of Paediatric Psychology*, 10, 215–225.

Stroh, G. (1974) *Psychotic Children*. In Barker, B. (ed.), *The Residential Psychiatric Treatment of Children*. London: Crosby Lockwood Staples.

Trevarthen, C., Aitken, K., Papoudi, D. and Robarts, J. (1996) *Children with Autism. Diagnosis and Interventions to Meet Their Needs*. London: Jessica Kingsley.

Van der Gaag, R.J. (1993) Multiplex Developmental Disorder: An Exploration of Borderlines on the Autistic Spectrum. (*Unpublished thesis*) University of Utrecht, Netherlands.

24 Severe breakdown in the parenting of infants

Gerry Byrne and David Jones

DESCRIPTION OF THE UNIT

The residential family unit at the Park Hospital for Children was established by Dr Christopher Ounsted in 1967. Then, as now, the unit specialised in providing psychiatric treatment for families in which there had been a severe breakdown in parenting. The unit's pioneering work with abusing families has been described in previous publications (Lynch, Steinberg and Ounsted, 1975; Roberts, 1978). This work has continued over the last thirty years and currently the unit is engaged in a programme of assessment of risk, treatment and management of families in which severe abuse has occurred, or is likely to occur. All forms of abuse are referred, amongst which Battered Child Syndrome and Factitious Illness by Proxy (Munchausen Syndrome by Proxy) feature prominently. In all cases we aim to assess both the risk of abuse or neglect recurring (or occurring) and the treatability of the family. Two families can be accommodated; they will be at different stages in the assessment and treatment process.

APPROACH TO ASSESSMENT AND TREATMENT

The team's approach to assessment and treatment is grounded in an ecological/developmental perspective on severe parenting breakdown, including child abuse and neglect (Jones, 1996, 1997). This incorporates concepts from the psychoanalytic, child development and attachment fields. A biopsychosocial approach is used, which recognises the changing developmental and family propensities through time. Pathological development contrasts with normal development in that it is conceived of as a lack of integration of the individual's competence in social, emotional and/or cognitive fields of functioning. That is, disorder is perceived as developmental deviation. Psychoanalytic and child development thinkers such as Anna Freud (1976) and Alan Sroufe (1996) have described how dissimilar deviant pathways can arrive at similar destinations in terms of psychopathology, and, conversely, how similar pathways can have quite dissimilar destinations. This perspective holds that while prior adaptation constrains change, change *is* possible at many points on the pathway.

At the centre of the model is the child himself and his immediate caretaking context. Surrounding this are family influences and, moving outwards in circles of increasing social complexity, are school factors, the quality of the child's neighbourhood, his friendships and social contacts and the family's social adaptation versus isolation within the community. Finally, surrounding this level of organisation is the influence of the culture within which the family live.

As Belsky emphasised, both child and parent bring their own history to bear upon this contextualised setting, which, via their personality and social functioning, affects the child's appeal and the parent's competence (Belsky, 1993). Fraiberg also stressed the importance of the child's environment and developed a model of parent–infant psychotherapy which aims to free the infant from parental neurosis. Fraiberg wrote eloquently of this in her seminal paper, 'Ghosts in the nursery', in which she describes the parents' projections into the infant and transference from the past onto the infant as ghosts (Fraiberg et al., 1975). Recent research in the allied fields of attachment and child development have shown that it is not so much the nature of a parent's past experiences that influence parenting behaviour as their capacity for subsequent appreciation and understanding of past experiences (Fonagy, 1994).

This ecological/developmental perspective complements the theoretical and clinical interests, trainings and experiences of the multidisciplinary team and integrates these into a comprehensive assessment and treatment approach. The team's approach to understanding severe parenting breakdown and the factors which contribute to the risk of occurrence or recurrence of abuse is informed by psychoanalytic, child development, attachment, systems and group analytic theories.

SETTING UP THE WORK

The assessment and treatment of a family with severe parenting breakdown begins before admission and continues long past discharge. Following referral, a first interprofessionals meeting is arranged. Aims and objectives of assessment and treatment are clarified with all agencies, including, as is often necessary, the court. At this stage it is usually possible to lay some foundations for future liaison with the local primary care teams (such as GPs or health visitors) and mental health teams (whether adult and/or child and family); and thus to gauge the level of professional support likely to be available to the family after in-patient treatment has ended. This is followed with an extensive review of medical records in which all family members' medical records are scrutinised for evidence of prior difficulties/somatisation and/or psychiatric disturbance. The family is then seen for an initial outpatient assessment including risk assessment and search for signs of parental acknowledgement, and possibilities for engagement in psychological treatments. At this point the team decides whether to proceed with an in-patient, residential phase, which may last from two to six weeks (a two week assessment, followed, in selected cases, by a four week treatment phase).

DOMAINS OF ASSESSMENT

The team follows the risk management process outlined by Jones (1997) in which the risk matrix is described and broken down into more manageable components or domains. The **parental domain** includes parental mental health, state of mind with regard to attachment, degree of acknowledgement of responsibility for the abuse, its effects upon the child, and their capacity to benefit from psychological treatment. Key factors in the **parent–child domain** are: parental sensitivity to the child, parental perceptions of the child, the parent's capacity for empathy and parenting competency, the pattern and quality of the child's attachment to the parent and the history of the parent–child relationship. Factors within the **child domain** include the child's development, functioning and constitutional factors. The **family domain** includes all areas of family functioning, with particular emphasis on the distribution of power within the family, family violence, and the expression of affect. The nature, severity and frequency of the **abuse act(s)** constitute a further domain. The ABC (antecedent, behaviour, consequence) of the abusive act is examined. The assessment identifies the parent's state of mind and the nature of interaction between child and parent as well as the family and social context prior to the abuse, particularly that which existed immediately prior to the abusive act. Similarly, what happened during the abuse and what followed is closely explored. Support versus isolation are key factors within the **social setting domain** and finally the **professional system domain** includes both the resources available to the family and the nature, quantity and quality of the professional response to the family's needs.

The identification of both positive and negative features within each of these domains is considered critical to risk assessment and treatment planning, and permits the many factors to be weighed and counterbalanced during decision making and risk management. The approach described has also proved a useful framework for communication and liaison with other professionals.

THE PROCESS OF ASSESSMENT AND TREATMENT

The unit's ethos and milieu is designed to support the child and parent(s) in an optimum and non-judgmental way, while maintaining a clear focus on the primacy of the child's welfare. Almost invariably, these families hold the view that the unit represents their last hope for possible reunification with their children. Thus, some families are very keen to engage with staff, and are likely to project their most hopeful and ideal selves into the team and individual team members, with someone else holding the split off 'bad' feelings (often the family's social worker). Other families may come with considerable denial and underlying resistance. Beneath a superficial commitment, they perceive unit staff as intent on gathering evidence to facilitate the removal of their children. Such projections can be located in one or more team members and the family may, unconsciously, seek to split the team. It is critical that the team is able to address the different perspectives and counter-transference feelings of its members and demonstrate to the family a team capacity to overcome divisions (see also chapter 14). This facilitates the vitally important process that enables the parents to move towards a full acknowledgement of their responsibility for the reality of the abuse and its impact upon the child, and accept back their split-off, 'bad' parts into their perceptions of themselves.

Abuse can result from a parent's acute failure to contain his/her response to the child's distress, with projection into the child. For instance, a father battered his baby son when he vomited, causing skull fractures. He had lost his own mother when he was one year old and his father blamed him for her death and physically abused him. The father was anxious his baby would choke on his vomit and felt helpless, infuriated and persecuted by his rejection of food. Momentarily, the baby became the projected dying mother and abusing father. In other cases the failure to contain is chronic and the parent has little capacity for understanding or tolerating emotional states in the child. In both cases the admission to an in-patient unit was helpful in providing the family with respectful, thoughtful containment by a wide range of professionals during stressful situations.

Containment does not mean an invitation to regress and in fact this is discouraged. With the child in central focus, the parents are firmly but gently encouraged to continue to parent their children appropriately, while exploring their own very painful and difficult childhood experiences. Containment does mean that the previously unmentionable thoughts of harming a child and accounts of actual harm can be voiced and met with respectful understanding. The team's emphasis upon the safety and primacy of the child's needs makes their moral position explicit. We have found that many parents have said that their experience of us as respectful, notwithstanding severe abuse of their children, permitted them to entertain hope for a way through, not just to reunification with their children but to a way of living with the guilt for their actions.

In all cases we are also mindful of the need for us to contain some of the anxiety and projections of professionals involved with the family. In severe abuse cases, especially where the parents initially deny responsibility, the professional network is frequently driven into a polarised view in which 'evil intent' is attributed to the abusing parent, thereby precluding the possibility of rehabilitation. It is then important for these professionals to know we do understand and appreciate the full extent of the injuries and often it is only when this is evident to them that they feel they can trust us sufficiently to work in partnership on assessment and treatment of the family.

Observing, nursing and intervening on a daily basis in a grossly dysfunctional parent–child relationship can be excruciating for the parent–child therapist and other members of the team. Being a witness to the emotional abuse or neglect of a child is painful. Staff who are in daily contact with the child in these circumstances will be attuned to the child and identify with his experience. In this way one member of a team can feel as though only they hold a 'true' perspective on the danger to the child, because it is felt so acutely by them. The team considers it crucial to retain a clear image of the child and all maltreatment which has occurred. This is achieved through making available to all therapists complete descriptions of harm to the child, supplemented by photographs and X-rays etc. so that the abuse is not 'sanitised', or staff minimise severity or avert their gaze. When families are in denial we often find ourselves returning to the court reports to assure ourselves that abuse did in fact happen, so convincing are some of the parent's initial stories. There is a weekly forum for the staff's counter-transference feelings to be explored and understood and this contributes greatly to our understanding of the family's functioning. Any splits between team members emanating from the family can be integrated through sharing and thinking together.

Parent–child domain

Two parent–child therapists, the clinical nurse specialist in psychotherapy, the occupational therapist, and the psychologist are all involved in a thorough assessment of the parent–child relationship. Perspectives from the psychoanalytic, developmental and attachment fields on the parent–child relationship are taken and the team seeks to empathise with a child's experiences within his family, that is; to maintain a 'child's eye view' (Jones, 1997). Sessional, structured observations and interviews are used alongside informal, unstructured observations which take place throughout the day, every day. In all observations key foci of assessment include: the parent's sensitivity and responsiveness to the child's cues; the pattern and quality of the attachment relationship; the parent's capacity for empathy with the child; parental competency in all other aspects of parenting; the history of the parent–child relationship (which may extend to the time before conception); the parent's perception of the child, encompassing the conscious attributions and the unconscious fantasy bestowed upon the child through the mechanisms of projection and projective identification (Fraiberg, Adelson and Shapiro 1975); the child's developmental age, his state of mind, disposition and his capacity to engage with a caregiver.

Parent–child therapists[1] are with the family throughout the day, run nursery sessions twice daily, and are present at all meals, bathtimes and bedtimes. Their daily observations are recorded in a standardised way. Of primary importance is the therapist's sensitivity to the fine nuances of the parent–child relationship and her intuitive feelings about particular observations are considered very carefully. In one assessment a mother was observed responding to her baby's cues with apparent sensitivity and appropriate modulation but it was felt, intuitively, that she was somehow not truly in an empathic relationship with him. This was later confirmed when it came to light that the mother avoided eye contact with her baby, by focusing on a point in the centre of the baby's forehead. The parent–child therapists receive weekly supervision which is at once an opportunity for emotional and psychological support, a distillation process for refining the assessments, and a process of exploration of the dynamics of the parent–child relationship, as evidenced both in the use the parents make of the child and of the therapists, and in the therapist's counter-transference.

Structured assessments include video recording and analysing a mealtime and a playtime, a developmental assessment of the child and an interview with the parent, focusing on the evolution of the parent–child relationship. This interview explores the development of the conscious and unconscious meanings the child holds for the parent from conception through pregnancy, birth, early infancy, and up until the episode of abuse.

Parent domain

Normally, an individual therapist will see each parent twice weekly during the assessment period. In many cases, one parent has abused the child, so individual therapy with the abusing and non-abusing parent will differ. The non-abusive parent will require much support in order to face the many dilemmas at precisely the time when they have been shattered by the shock of discovery of mal-treatment (Sharland et al., 1996). At this point in the assessment phase, we will also be attempting to gauge the commitment the non-abusing parent has to the child and to their partner. Assessment of the abusing parent differs, in that the overall aim is to help reduce abusing behaviour and improve the child's predicament, the adult's needs being secondary. Therefore, the therapist always has the 'child in mind' and it is of interest to note that Fraiberg (1980) suggested that individual psychotherapy with abusing mothers should occur with the child in the room. This approach acknowledges, we feel, that the abusing parent was not in an empathic relationship with the child at the time of the abuse, and that adult progress must be anchored to the needs of the child. Exploring the parent's own early experience can encourage appreciation of their own children's needs, and increase their sensitivity and empathy for their children. The therapist is also careful to monitor any indication that the parent is consciously or unconsciously using their own prior victimisation as a means of excusing their abusive behaviour. A significant number of parents are significantly damaged individuals, with difficulties in forming complex, reciprocal relationships and often report long-standing feelings of intense loneliness. In these cases we have often found that there has indeed been a failure in the most important early relationships and their current relationship with their child(ren) is similarly affected (Fonagy, 1994). Both psychoanalytical and social learning theory based explanations can be invoked to explain this cycle.

In addition, a number of standardised assessments are used to enhance the clinical picture. An adult mental state examination is done in all cases by a psychiatrist. Each parent is given an Adult Attachment Interview (Main, 1991) designed to explore their own attachment experiences and to facilitate under-standing of their internal working model of parenting and attachment. Further analysis of the interview has been useful in some cases and the interview has also provided a springboard for therapy in a number of cases. Currently, the Park group uses a number of standardised assessments to complement clinical observations in the following areas: parental mental state; personality; hostility; empathy; and risk of child abuse. Parent assessment is therefore a combination of informal observation, semi-structured assessment and standardised tests.

Timing

Ordinarily, in severe abuse cases, the family will reside as in-patients for a two to three week period to complete a comprehensive assessment. In this period there is a graded increase in the amount of unsupervised contact with the child, providing risk of abuse permits it. The family unit has the facility to move from a situation in which the family is under twenty-four hour observation, to one in which the family can be unsupervised for long periods during the day and overnight, while remaining on site. Following a promising assessment period, and after full discussion with all agencies and the court, a further four to six weeks of intensive treatment can proceed. Initially the accent is upon assessment, and later on treatment, though of course elements of each are present at all stages.

Integration

Throughout the assessment period the team meets regularly to collate information and to direct the foci of the work. Towards the end of the assessment period the team meets with the local professionals to communicate the findings of the integrated risk analysis and to formulate a plan of treatment, should this be indicated and agreed. Often there is a court report to be filed and one senior member of the team collates all relevant information from the many dimensions of assessment into a coherent account, with recommendations for future management/placement of the child and family.

Establishing a treatment plan

Following assessment the family may continue as in-patients for treatment prior to discharge to locality based social work and health care teams. A treatment plan is drawn up, in liaison with all other professionals involved with the family. Broadly speaking we identify three phases to the treatment process (Jones, 1997):

- acknowledgement
- increased sensitivity and parental competence
- and finally, resolution.

Acknowledgement phase

This is not a cathartic one-time confession of guilt, but rather a gradual unfolding of the various elements involved in the abuse, combined with an appreciation of its impact and meaning. Throughout this process the abuser will be encouraged to re-evaluate his/her feelings about the abuse act and particularly about his/her perception of the child's experience of the abuse. It is anticipated that as parental sensitivity to the child increases and they notice and reduce their projections onto their child, the burden of guilt and remorse will grow.

Development of increased parental competence and sensitivity

The aim of this second stage of treatment is to increase parents' sensitivity, emotional responsiveness and overall parental competence with respect to their children, and to improve the degree to which parents can meet their children's needs. A useful starting point for this phase of treatment grows out of the parents' acknowledgement of the impact of abuse on their child. The essential qualities which it is hoped to increase in the parents are those of empathy and emotional availability for their children. The therapists need to maintain a 'child's eye view' to assess and monitor the level of progress. Therapeutic approaches include individual psychotherapy or cognitive behavioural therapy for one or both parents, intensive formal and informal parent–child therapy, family therapy and couple work.

Resolution phase

Two principal options are available at this stage: return home, completing the process of family reunification, or placement of the child in alternative care. It is to be hoped that, if the family have progressed this far, full return will be feasible. The challenge facing the team is to ensure that progress made by the family is maintained on return to their locality, including the continuation of therapeutic work. Comprehensive arrangements for continuing supervision, assessments and review will be essential. A great strain is placed on the strength of the professional networks, which will have been established, for it through these that effective aftercare is organised.

Disadvantages of family admission

There are some potential disadvantages of admitting a family to an in-patient setting. It is arguable that the in-patient environment provides a false situation for the family and cannot truly accord to an accurate picture of the family's functioning within the home environment. It may be possible either for a family to 'fake good', or for the stressful environment to put undue pressure upon the family and they may under-perform. The family can feel safely encapsulated from the real world, shielded from the wider family and neighbourhood influences and stresses and, feeling dependent upon the hospital, experience difficulty in separating. Professionals in the community may be resistant to resuming a high level of contact and support for the family, following discharge.

If borne in mind, the impact of these factors on the quality of the assessment and treatment can be minimised. It is true that every clinical assessment situation, even in the home, creates something of a false atmosphere, but one can be reassured by, for example, Ainsworth's demonstration that the relationship that has evolved between the parent and child *is* evident in both naturalistic and false laboratory settings and cannot be hidden by a sudden change, say, in the parent's responsivity to the child. Therefore a parent faking availability will not entice an insecure, avoidant child. Equally, a mother failing to respond under stress will not prevent her secure child from seeking the support he has grown to expect from her.

The process of separation from the in-patient setting and team can be handled with knowledge of the issues involved for the family. It can be exploited as an event in the family's life which offers them an opportunity for an appropriate leave taking and transition, contrasting with their previous experiences of loss and separation.

Advantages

Where there is severe parenting breakdown, including child abuse, it is difficult to conceive how these families could be assessed, while ensuring the safety of the child, without recourse to an in-patient facility, without placing either the family or the professionals at a great disadvantage. The in-patient family unit, with graded levels of supervision, allows for minimum risk to be taken with regard to the child's safety. This is not only a consequence of the supervision itself, but the fact that the infant resides with the family and is seen in many settings with the family, allows clinicians ample opportunity to perceive progress or otherwise, from the 'child's eye view'.

There are distinct economic and clinical advantages to having a clinical team with training and experience concentrated in one assessment and treatment centre. There is the opportunity for intensive assessment, in a wide range of settings, by clinicians from different theoretical backgrounds. This enables the team to more accurately draw conclusions about the nature and quality of the parent–child interaction and to plan effective treatment approaches. The therapeutic milieu created by cohesive and well-supported teamwork enhances treatment. The close contact between the parent–child therapists and the family members offers unrivalled opportunities for observation of the parent–child relationship, both in what they observe objectively and in what they are made to feel in response to each family member's projections.

NOTES

1   Currently these are qualified and experienced nursery nurses who have completed our certificated training in *Parent–child observation and assessment in the clinical setting* (Brookes University, Oxford).

REFERENCES

Belsky, J. (1993) Etiology of child maltreatment; a developmental and ecological analysis. *Psychological Bulletin*, 114, 413–434.

Bion, W.R. (1962) A theory of thinking. *International Journal of Psychoanalysis*, 43, 306–310.

Fonagy, P. (1994). Mental representations from an intergenerational cognitive science perspective. *Infant Mental Health Journal*, 15 (1), Special Issue, 57–68.

Fraiberg, S., Adelson, E. and Shapiro, V. (1975). Ghosts in the nursery: A psychoanalytic approach to the problems of impaired infant–mother relationships. *Journal of the American Academy of Child Psychiatry*, 14, 387–421.

Freud, A. (1976) Psychopathology seen against the background of normal development. *British Journal of Psychiatry*, 129, 401–406.

Jones, D.P.H. (1996) Management of the sexually abused child. *Advances in Psychiatric Treatment*, 2, 39–45.

Jones, D.P.H. (1997) Treatment of the child and the family where child abuse or neglect has occurred. In Helfer, R., Kempe, R. and Krugman, R. (eds), *The Battered Child*, 5th edn (pp. 521–542). Chicago: University of Chicago Press.

Lynch, M., Steinberg, D. and Ounsted, C. (1975) Family unit in a children's psychiatric hospital. *British Medical Journal*, 2, 127–129.

Main, M. (1991) Metacognitive knowledge, metacognitive monitoring, and singular (coherent) versus multiple (incoherent) models of attachment: Findings and directions for future research. In Parkes, C., Stevenson-Hinde, J. and Marris, P. (eds) *Attachment Across the Life Cycle* (pp. 127–159). London: Routledge.

Roberts, J. (1978) There's more to child abuse than spotting bruises. *Community Care*, June 28, 29–30.

Sharland, E., Seale, H., Croucher, M., Aldgate, J. and Jones, D. P. H. (1996). *Professional Intervention in Child Sexual Abuse*. London: Her Majesty's Stationery Office.

Sroufe, A. (1996) *Psychopathology as Development: Implications of Attachment Theory and Research for Developmental Psychopathology*. London: St George's Hospital.

Steele, B. (1987). Reflections on the therapy of those who maltreat children. In Helfer, R.E. and Kempe, R. (eds) *The Battered Child*. Chicago and London: University of Chicago Press.

25 Attachment disorders

Jonathan Green

THE CONCEPT OF ATTACHMENT DISORDER

Research over two decades has established attachment theory as a key concept within developmental psychopathology, although much remains to be understood about the specificity of attachment patterns and their interaction with other aspects of cognitive and social functioning in later development. Early attachment relationships are understood to arise out of an infant's need for proximity to an adult when in distress. Ainsworth and her colleagues found that the character of these relationships varied systematically in the general population (Ainsworth et al., 1978). These patterns of attachment have shown stability in the early years (Bretherton, 1985; Lamb, 1984; Van Ijzendoorn and Kroonenberg, 1988) – although there are counter findings (Belsky et al., 1996). The 'insecure' attachment patterns act as vulnerability factors for later social and psychological problems (Bretherton, 1985; Crockenberg, 1981; Crittenden, 1995). This is found for psychosocial adjustment (Cassidy, 1988) and psychiatric disorder, particularly in the presence of other stressors such as family dysfunction and social disadvantage (Lewis et al., 1984; Lyons-Ruth, 1996; Warren et al., 1997). Thus insecure or disorganised attachment patterns will inevitably be revealed as aetiological factors in many clinical presentations in early childhood. It is doubtful whether such insecure attachments (which could be thought of as a trait insecurity) should be considered as 'disorders' as such, but further research is needed to clarify their relationship to psychopathology (e.g. chapter 19). Zeanah (1996) has suggested that 'attachment problems become psychiatric disorders when emotions and behaviours displayed in attachment relationships are so disturbed as to indicate or substantially to increase the risk of, persistent distress or disability'.

ICD-10 currently identifies two such forms of severe disorder of attachment. 'Reactive attachment disorder' is thought to result from the child's experience of developing early attachment relationships in the context of parental neglect, abuse or serious mishandling. There is a pervasive difficulty in social functioning, combining high levels of arousal with a resistance to comforting. The children are often behaviourally disorganised, inattentive and aggressive to others or self. Their resistance to normal social rewards and motivations can thwart conventional parenting strategies. In 'disinhibited attachment disorder' there is by contrast a shallow and indiscriminate sociability, with some short-term adjustment but a lack of capacity for intimacy and difficulty adapting to stress or change. The disorder is described as in 'most cases' consequent on care which has frustrated the child's attempts to form specific early attachments, say because of multiple care giving or institutional upbringing (World Health Organisation, 1992).

What role can in-patient units have in the assessment and treatment of this wide variety of difficulties in attachment relationships?

ASSESSMENT

1. A generic in-patient assessment of attachment dynamics

Several key aspects of attachment in theory are relevant to the design of this assessment

Modularity

Bowlby hypothesised that there was a discrete 'attachment behavioural system' which had developed through evolution as the infant adapted to distress and anxiety by proximity seeking and contact maintenance with selected adults. There has been concern (Bowlby, 1988; Bretherton, 1985) that if the attachment construct lost this focus and became synonymous with the total parent/ infant relationship, then much of the conceptual advance in the theory would be threatened. Attachment dynamics should thus be assessed specifically, in distinction from other developmental processes.

Covariance with other factors

Attachment dynamics will nevertheless certainly interact with other factors, and assessment should not *restrict* itself to attachment issues.

Linking of internal states of mind and behaviour

Attachment theory and research combines behavioural observation in the tradition of developmental psychology and ethology, with analysis of states of mind and 'internal representations' (Main, Kaplan and Cassidy, 1985). The structure of day-patient or in-patient assessment is well suited to this, since the unit's great strength is the opportunity for sustained clinical observation of children and families within a controlled environment.

Attachment is dyadic

Assessment must address itself to the child, caregiver and the interaction between them.

Using separations and reunions

The paradox of using admission to assess family relationships has been noted elsewhere (chapter 18), but this can be turned to advantage when assessing attachment relationships. Firstly, the observation of reunion after separation is of particular value in assessing attachment dynamics (Ainsworth et al., 1978), and the in-patient setting provides many naturally occurring instances of this. Secondly, admission can provide a break from self-sustaining cycles of coercion and oppositional interaction at home and hence clarify underlying relationship issues that may have become masked.

An assessment of parent–child relationships emphasising the attachment dynamic has been developed at Booth Hall Hospital (Green, 1996). In outline, this takes a 'diagnostic' approach; assuming that there are different pathways to parenting dysfunction and considering factors in addition to attachment dynamics that predict parenting dysfunction.

Assessment of parents

Internal attachment representation

Research has shown a significant linkage between the 'internal representation' of attachment relationships that forms in the adult on the basis of past experience and the pattern of attachment relationship that the adult forms with a child (Main et al., 1985; Grossman and Grossman, 1988; Fonagy, Steele and Steele 1991). This internal attachment representation can be investigated using the Adult Attachment Interview (AAI) (George, Kaplan and Main, 1985). The long research coding of the interview is impractical for use in clinical practice, but its format gives excellent clinical data which can be used to inform assessment (see also chapter 24). A reliable clinical adaptation of the research rating would be a useful advance.

This assessment also considers other areas of adult functioning, known to affect parenting effectiveness, which might interact with or confound the delineation of attachment difficulties.

Personality functioning

Personality difficulties can have an adverse effect on parenting (Quinton and Rutter, 1988; Cox, 1993). Personality variables may relate to attachment dynamics (Fonagy et al., 1995), but in the absence of more knowledge about the linkage between the two, it seems appropriate to assess them as independent dimensions. Standard clinical assessment can be supplemented if necessary by the Personality Assessment Schedule (Tyrer, Alexander and Ferguson, 1988).

Current mental state

A number of studies have shown how maternal depression can have a profound effect on mother–child interaction, parenting abilities and child development

(Mills et al., 1985; Pound et al., 1985; Murray, 1992). It is also possible that it will bias parental attitudes within the assessment.

Social stress and support

The presence or absence of effective social supports can alter parental functioning, particularly at times of stress (Werner and Smith, 1982; Crnic et al., 1983). Lack of social support can compromise attachment relationships (Crockenberg, 1981). Clinical assessment of this area can be supplemented by the Social Stress and Support Interview (Bailey and Garralda, 1987).

Assessment of the child

As in the adult, the assessment firstly addresses the *child's internal representation of attachment relationships* (Main, Kaplan and Cassidy, 1985). The Bene–Anthony Family Relations Test (Bene and Anthony, 1994) provides related information but is not attachment specific. Indirect techniques have been described for evaluating aspects of attachment representation in young children using pictures, dolls and puppets (Cassidy, 1988; Wright, Binney and Smith, 1995). The 'Child Attachment Interview', developed by the author and colleagues, is a doll interview allowing assessment of attachment status in 4–7 year-olds. Using a vignette completion technique it aims to activate the child's representation of attachment by drawing them into stories containing a degree of hurt, distress, or anxiety. The rating of the interview allows a classification of attachment representation analogous to the strange situation and adult attachment interviews (see case study). Similar methodology in relation to the MacArthur story stems have been published (Oppenheim, Emde and Warren, 1997).

Other important developmental variables which may determine the expression of attachment should also be assessed.

Cognitive and neurodevelopmental assessment

This identifies behavioural profiles related primarily to language disorder, general and specific learning disability or pervasive developmental disorder (see chapters 6 and 23). There is evidence of the pathoplastic effect of developmental disorder on attachment behaviour (e.g. Rogers, Ozonoff and Maslin-Cole, 1993; Sigman and Ungerer, 1995). These are distinctions that will often preoccupy in-patient clinicians. The relationship of temperamental variables to attachment behaviour has also been the subject of debate (Vaughn and Lefever, 1989; Kagan, 1997) and temperamental variables should be considered.

Physical examination

Physical examination aims to assess for any dysmorphology that suggests a behavioural phenotype or neurodevelopmental disorder (see chapter 22).

Child mental state examination

This needs to delineate the effect of current environmental stressors and related adjustment reactions from long term adaptive phenomena pertaining to the parent–child relationship. This can be a difficult area of assessment, especially in children in acute crisis, such as in acute family breakdown and foster placement. Yet significant decisions and recommendation may follow from the assessment.

Social interactions

The in-patient milieu is an effective place for assessing peer and adult interactions. Attachment difficulties may not be immediately apparent in ordinary social relating, but may emerge under conditions of distress. Life on an in-patient ward is likely to present such conditions in the course of things.

Assessment of parent–child interaction

Clinicians on the in-patient units have the opportunity to observe directly the parent–child interactions linked in research to attachment relationships (Ainsworth et al., 1978). Of course much of this research relates to younger

Table 25.1 Ward based assessment of caregiver–child interaction

Contexts

- (i) reunions
- (ii) separations
- (iii) unstructured play
- (iv) structured play in which the adult has to get the child to accomplish a task
- (v) mealtimes
- (vi) bedtime and bathtime

Dimensions of rating

- (a) proximity seeking (appropriate for the age of the child): reunion following separation
- (b) quality of caregiving:

  - (i) responsiveness to the child's needs
  - (ii) consistency
  - (iii) capacity to nurture appropriately in distress
  - (iv) patterns of 'reversal' of caregiving
  - (v) quality of communication with the child

- (c) limit-setting/guidance: observations are made here of:

  - (i) parents' capacity to make appropriate limits and keep the child safe
  - (ii) presence of coercive cycles of interaction
  - (iii) capacity to negotiate with the child
  - (iv) child's response to limit-setting

- (d) parental relationship (if there are two parents involved on the assessment): how well the parents work together and use each other as support in their parenting tasks

children and no assumptions should be made that interactional behaviour seen between early school age children and their parents has equivalent meaning. For instance older children do not usually show the reunion proximity behaviour of toddlers; their social referencing and discourse with the parent on reunion does, however, seem an equivalent behaviour (Strage and Main, 1985; Cassidy, 1988; Grossman and Grossman, 1991, pp. 93–114). This is an area where in-patient units could contribute to research. At Booth Hall the nursing team undertake this assessment during day visits by the parent to the child; often it will be undertaken during one or more intensive weekend admissions in the middle of the assessment. Observations are made within the framework of attachment theory and social learning theory in situations which occur during the course of the assessment (Table 25.1)

Compiling the assessment

The team integrates information from these different viewpoints. Appraisal of parenting phenomena from a number of different angles in this way is more reliable and minimises halo effects (Cox, 1993). Parent's and child's representations of attachment may mirror each other. Observations made in a specialised setting over a short time are always prone to error and need evaluating in relation to information and observations obtained elsewhere. Discrepancies here, and also between the three areas of the assessment, always need investigating. Conversely, agreement confers convergent validity.

2. Assessing severe attachment disorders with complex presentations

In-patient units are commonly asked to assess very disturbed young children who have a mixture of developmental vulnerability and adverse life experience. The question commonly posed by referrers is whether such presentations represent primarily an attachment disorder or an intrinsic developmental disorder such as Pervasive Developmental Disorder (PDD), Attention Deficit Disorder (ADD) or psychosis (see chapter 20). Some developmentalists have argued that such 'nature/nurture' questions represent a false dichotomy (Zeanah, 1996), but the balance of interactional effects often have important implications for subsequent placement (in social service cases), treatment and prognosis and there is good clinical and research evidence that distinctions are both possible and crucial. Children with developmental disorders characteristic of the 'extended phenotype' of the autistic spectrum are suffering from a genetic disorder of high heritability (Bailey et al., 1996). There is evidence that autistic children show normal attachment patterns when the unusual nature of their communication strategies is taken into account (Capps, Sigman and Mundy, 1994). Moreover, the developmental deviations in cognition, attention and communication which are found in children with severe attachment disorder (see Richters and Volkmar, 1994) are qualitatively different from PDD. The use of intensive

Table 25.2 The differential diagnosis of severe attachment disorders in early childhood

- pervasive developmental disorder
- developmental language disorder – especially semantic pragmatic disorders
- attention deficit disorder, especially with secondary social impairments
- stress and adjustment disorders, including post-traumatic disorders

observation on the in-patient ward and specific assessment strategies can be invaluable for clarifying such diagnoses (Table 25.2).

A detailed development and family history is vital, since the diagnosis of ICD-10 attachment disorder depends on the presence of abnormal caregiving in the history (although some clinicians have challenged the relevance of this, given how often the history is unavailable or distorted (Richters and Volkmar, 1994). On the ward, behaviour in specific contexts provides evidence to distinguish between the *pervasive* social communication and processing difficulties in PDD (see chapter 23) and the *contextual and specifically relational* difficulties characteristic of attachment problems. Additionally in attachment disorder one is looking for critical *social competencies* not found in PDD; typically including the integration of verbal and non-verbal communication, normal prosody, normal use of eye gaze, as well as a lack of the characteristic rigidities of thinking and abnormalities of behaviour which characterise PDD.

A full range of investigations and assessments for the different disorders being considered will usually need to be mobilised. For example, 1) the assessment of attachment described above; 2) generic assessment of autistic impairment (chapter 23); 3) speech pathology assessment.

Commonly in practice there is a mixed picture, with the interaction of intrinsic developmental/genetic vulnerability and abnormal experience. In severe attachment disorders particularly, a discrete assessment is often made difficult by interacting effects of traumatisation, deprivation and abnormal social learning. Nevertheless, assessment can at the minimum provide a thorough delineation of the different functional impairments presenting in the child. These assessments are fascinating and challenging; they raise fundamental conceptual issues and have important consequences for the prognostic and advisory formulation. They also provide good opportunities for in-patient units to contribute to clinical research.

TREATMENT

The child's engagement with the milieu

During admission the child experiences basic care in a different environment. This is a crucial component. Times of ordinary physical care such as bedtimes, bathtimes and naturally occurring times of distress and anxiety can generate gradual intimacy. If handled well, this therapeutic provision can begin to be experienced as a 'secure base' (Bowlby, 1988) and form a basis for trust and reparative experience. Through this, children with attachment disorders can form powerful and complex relationships with the ward, evoking and reworking early experience (see chapter 9). Staff need good supervision and support to ensure that the sensitive work of psychological containment and empathy can continue amongst the difficult, bruising, everyday realities of the group and behavioural control. The effect of disturbed attachment relationships on the child's internal mental representations causes skewed cognitive processing, affecting the child's appraisal and response in current social situations (Crittenden, 1992). Unsurprisingly, after a variable period of inhibited conformity, the child usually starts to reproduce behavioural responses reflecting these distortions. The aim of the milieu here is to open up other possibilities for the child by patiently presenting them with consistent responses adapted to their needs and different from those they are used to – in the hope that their representational model is responsive to this new experience. Both peer and adult–child reactions are relevant. Individual psychotherapy or cognitive therapy can be crucial in facilitating and reinforcing these changes (chapters 9 and 10). The aim is to generate a positive cycle involving therapists, children and adults in the milieu and the school to obtain a momentum of mutually reinforcing change in different settings.

The most severely disturbed children find it extremely difficult to tolerate sharing with other children's need for care and can be intensely jealous and destructive in the peer group. Towards the end of admission, as primary child–adult needs feel less pressing, they may begin to be able to tackle peer relating in the milieu more constructively. This is important for future outcome because of the increasing impact of peer relationships as the school-age child develops. Cicchetti and Toth (1995) describe various interventions including 'peer–pair counselling' in which peers work in pairs with a therapist to develop and practise different interactions – much of the group work on the ward can be adapted to a similar end.

For children who have made important attachments, it is essential that for a period some post-admission follow-up be undertaken by the key nursing staff. This is an extra burden to take on but a necessary accompaniment of work at this level.

Engagement of parents with the ward

In attachment disorders the engagement of caregivers with ward staff is particularly important. Parents in these circumstances will usually have unresolved attachment issues of their own and these will affect engagement. There is often a dilemma about whether to undertake quite substantial treatment of adults on the unit or to refer them to adult therapeutic services. The decision here is likely to be based on both resources and the severity of the problems in the adult. The dynamics of the treatment can seem more coherent if the parent is engaged in at least some treatment with the in-patient unit team. Undertaking this work is a crucial pre-condition for the third phase. An important current issue is whether specific therapeutic programmes can be devised for the particular purpose of helping modify parental attachment representations in the service of good parenting .

Parent and child work

Usually, direct parent–child work is best introduced after there has been some movement within the individual work with both parent and child separately. The individual work aims to work on feelings, memories and attitudes rooted in attachment representations, so that new possibilities for different patterns of relationship are opened up. On the other hand, there are times where behavioural or practical joint work, such as through cooking together, craftwork etc. on the unit, with the help of occupational therapists or nurses, can unlock a previously mutually critical and uncaring mental set between parent and child. This can then allow them to work on their internal representations of each other and of past carers.

As parent and child come to see each other and possibilities of relationship with each other differently, then it is possible successfully to introduce behavioural interventions, such as the parent–child game, or parent management strategies, and also re-awaken the possibility of play and mutual enjoyment between the pair. This increases warmth, closeness and interaction. This phase can be difficult since the opening up of interaction can often involve the increasing expression of anger, hostility and resentment. This situation can need skilled holding from the therapist involved, otherwise it can feel frightening and uncontainable (Crittenden, 1992). This work can sometimes be helped by the strategic admission of parent with child.

Group work

The 'relationship play group' developed by Binney and Wright (Binney, McKnight and Broughton, 1994) is a specific group process for addressing attachment disorders, involving a group for mothers and a parallel group for children, followed by an interactional play group that introduces intimate interactions in a graded way. This is an example of a powerful format, the principles of which can be incorporated into in-patient programmes.

Disturbed attachment as an aetiological factor in other presentations

The foregoing elements of treatment addressing attachment issues will of course be combined with other aspects of treatment when attachment problems are embedded inside other symptoms – this could include psychopharmacology or behavioural work for instance. The critical thing for the team is to be clear about what aspects of the disorder are being treated with what treatments at any particular time.

> Tom was a 6-year-old child referred for assessment of chronic, treatment resistant constipation and encopresis. Over four years he had had multiple paediatric and clinical psychology interventions and investigations, including a paediatric in-patient admission. Copious soiling continued on a daily basis. There was no family history of encopresis. Father was a policeman training to be a lay Methodist preacher and mother a school teacher. Tom had an older brother of 8 years who was noted to show behavioural difficulties including aggressiveness. Tom himself generally showed quiet, conformist behaviour.
>
> Early developmental history was unremarkable: mother had fluctuating low mood during his infancy but did not report other early difficulties. When Tom was 2 years old, his maternal grandmother died. Mother remembered brief upset around the funeral but then completely put her mother's death 'out of my mind' and had not thought about it since. She was reluctant for the children to take part in the funeral and there was disagreement over this with father. It seemed likely that mother had had significant depression during this time. Tom went to nursery school at 3 years but failed to achieve continence. The parents first sought help when he was 3½. When Tom was 5 years mother lost her aunt, who had substituted for her mother after her death. Mother's reaction to this bereavement was similar to the previous major loss. The family soon suffered the further bereavement of father's mother.
>
> On admission, Tom presented as a pleasant, quiet but socially slightly unusual child with an active fantasy life. Aspects of the history and presentation suggested that we investigate the attachment dynamic within the family. Mother was interviewed using the Adult Attachment Interview. Her responses showed high levels of idealisation of parenting, dismissal and derogation of the relevance of attachment issues and restriction of affect in relation to them. There was evidence of anxious ambivalence underlying feelings about her parents. Analysis of the AAI showed a classification of Ds3 – a 'dismissing stance' towards attachment relationships, with a low coherence of mind (score of 3). She showed current depressed mood and was on antidepressants. Father was also interviewed about his early development. He had more ready access to attachment issues but had had relatively little involvement with parenting while the children were young. Tom was assessed using the Child Attachment Interview. He showed a mixture of angry, ambivalent and avoidant responses towards caregiving. He played out irritability and angry dismissiveness in the maternal caregiving behaviour. In the 'hurt' vignette, he came to mother with his hurt knee but she had nothing to give him. 'There's nothing in the cupboard.' There was no plaster or water or cloth in the house. He represented them facing each other helplessly. Later, he caused mother to have an accident and fall into a pond. Tom was assigned to a mixed category of C1/A2: a hostile ambivalent attachment style mixed with avoidance which belied his superficially compliant behaviour. Coherence of mind during the interview was rated moderately low at 5.5. Assessment showed no other development disorder

in physical or cognitive functioning. Observation of mother and child on the ward showed that although the superficial rapport was positive, mother tended to avoid details of intimate care such as bathing, dressing and feeding and toileting.

Assessment had thus indicated significant attachment difficulties underlying Tom's chronic symptomatology. Our formulation was that Tom's insecure pattern of attachment had acted as a vulnerability factor in infancy and that the time of maternal grandmother's death coincided with a critical period in his developing continence. Mother's reaction at this time was in keeping with her avoidant representation and she had been depressed; her responses to him became unpredictably irritable and unavailable. Tom's reactions became organised around angry inhibition and his bowel dysfunction became entrenched.

This assessment informed the treatment programme. We undertook therapeutic work with parents to revisit attachment issues and promote more interaction and support between them around parenting. The experience of the AAI interview was a good preparation for this therapeutic work. The aim was to increase emotional responsiveness and availability, particularly of the mother. We began individual therapeutic work with Tom, aimed again at reworking some of his ambivalent conflicts, particularly in relation to aggressiveness. Gradually increased and structured caregiving between mother and child was programmed into the ward visits. Simultaneously a cognitive behavioural programme of toilet training was pursued on the ward using graded desensitisation to toileting and the 'sneaky pooh' techniques. Parents were encouraged to introduce this programming at home once established on the ward. Medical treatment of the constipation included surgical evacuation at one point and maintenance on laxative medication. Compliance with medication was good and further constipation avoided.

Gradually Tom began to use the toilet appropriately for elimination although soiling continued. As the psychological therapy proceeded his behaviour at home and to some extent on the ward did become more oppositional but the social oddities noted at the beginning normalised. Mother found the work around attachment relationships difficult but we were able to recruit father actively into helping with the support and increasing sensitivity. Her distress became more apparent. The parents remained well engaged with the programme. After a few months the staff were beginning to worry at the slow progress: a change of laxative was made and a change to day patient status was imminent. At this point, Tom unexpectedly said 'my body is working again now' and the constipation and soiling dramatically stopped. Over the next two months the therapeutic programme continued and he remained asymptomatic. Mother's mood and responsiveness had improved. He was transferred to outpatient care. Tom was reviewed with a repeat CAI six months after the first. This showed a mixed picture again but this time with more secure patterns predominating – the attachment classification was B2/C1. He was making progress in his ability to express himself freely and securely, increased communication was noted at home with parents and he remained continent.

Severe attachment disorder

For many severe attachment disorders, the current length of treatment offered by in-patient units will not provide enough time for critical therapeutic change to take place. This can present difficult clinical dilemmas. If severe attachment disorders are recognised as the key issue pre-admission, and family based approaches look unlikely to be successful, then it might be that the child would be better off from the outset in a longer term residential environment such as a therapeutic community (chapter 32). The ethos of such communities is usually well adapted to working with children with attachment disorders (Dockar Drysdale, 1968). There are also schemes of residential prefostering placement for attachment disordered children whose family of origin has broken down. In-patient units need to have access to facilities of this sort which are relevant for many children who are referred to the service.

A more tractable form of the problem may be the attachment disordered/ maltreated child who is in adequate foster care but is presenting problems of relationship and behaviour in the new home. Here the focus of the work will be the foster parent–child relationship and a brief period of intensive work can be valuable. Many foster parents are ill prepared for the complexities of parenting the child with very distorted early attachment experience; careful evaluation and explanation with supportive therapeutic work can be beneficial, and psychotherapeutic work with the child to help their adjustment to the new caregiving environment and the integration of this with older memories can be vital.

Even though admission may not be able to undertake definitive treatment in some cases of severe attachment disorder, it can still nevertheless make an important contribution. This can be in the treatment of associated psychiatric morbidity, a trial of treatment for the attachment difficulties in child or family or the organisation of longer term placement if necessary. There is little research available on these clinical aspects of severe attachment disorder (Crittenden 1992). While there is some evidence of the value of early preventative programmes in modifying insecure attachment patterns (e.g. Lieberman, Weston and Pawl, 1991), there is little on the success of treatments in established and severe disorder. These more severe difficulties are difficult to engage in treatment, difficult to help and often have a poor prognosis. This author is not aware of formal research treatment in this area; clinical experience suggests that work with the existing parent–child relationship is often disappointing but that appropriate alternative or supplementary care, coupled with a period of residential treatment for the child, can result in moving and gratifying change. The intensity and focus offered by the in-patient environment can be a means properly to get hold of these problems and create a significant intervention, often at a critical stage of a child's development, which will have lasting impact on the future. One of the most effective ways to do this can be to draw attention to such children's long term needs for very specialised reparative caregiving.

REFERENCES

Ainsworth, M.D.S., Blehar, M.C., Waters, W. and Wall, S. (1978). *Patterns of Attachment.* Hillsdale, NJ: Lawrence Erlbaum Associates.

Bailey, A., Phillips, W. and Rutter, M. (1996) Autism: towards an integration of clinical, genetic, neuropsychological, and neurobiological perspectives. *Journal of Child Psychology and Psychiatry, 37,* 1, 89–126.

Bailey, D. and Garralda, E. (1987) The use of the social stress and support interview in families with deviant children – methodological issues. *Social Psychiatry, 22,* 209–215.

Belsky, J., Cambell, S.B., Cohn, J.F. and Moore, F. (1996) Instability of infant–parent attachment security. *Developmental Psychology, 32,* 5, 921–924.

Bene, E. and Anthony, J. (1994). *Family Relations Test: Children's Version.* NFER-Nelson.

Binney, V., McKnight, I. and Broughton, S. (1994) Relationship play therapy for attachment disturbances in four to seven year old children. In J. Richer (ed.) *The Clinical Applications of Ethology and Attachment Theory. Journal of Child Psychology and Psychiatry* Occasional paper No 9. London: Association for Child Psychology and Psychiatry.

Bowlby. J. (1988) *A Secure Base.* New York: Basic Books.

Bretherton, I. and Waters, E. (1985) *Growing points in attachment theory and research.* Society of Research in Child Development Monograph, 50, (1–2, Serial no. 209).

Capps, L., Sigman, M. and Mundy, P. (1994) Attachment security in children with autism. *Development and Psychopathology, 6,* 249–265.

Cassidy, J. (1988): Child mother attachment and the self in six year olds. *Child Development, 59,* 121–134.

Cicchetti, D. and Toth, S.L. (1995) Child maltreatment and attachment organisation, implications for intervention. In Goldberg, S., Muir, R. and Kerr, J. (eds) *Attachment Theory: Social, Developmental and Clinical Perspectives.* New York: The Analytic Press.

Cox, A.D. (1993) Befriending Young Mothers. (Annotation.) *British Journal of Psychiatry,* 163, 6–18.

Crittenden, P.M. (1992) Treatment of anxious attachment in infancy and early childhood. *Development and Psychopathology, 4,* 575–602

Crittenden, P.M. (1995) Attachment and psychopathology. In Goldberg, S., Muir, R. and Kerr, J. (eds) *Attachment Theory: Social, Developmental and Clinical Perspectives.* New York: The Analytic Press.

Crnic, K., Grenbert, M.T., Ragozin, A., Robinson, N. and Basham, R. (1983) Effects of stress and social support on mothers and premature and full term infants. *Child Development, 54,* 209–217.

Crockenberg, S. (1981) Infant irritability: mother's responsiveness and social support: influences on the security of infant mother attachment. *Child Development, 52,* 857–865.

Dockar Drysdale, B. (1968) *Papers on Residential Work: Therapy in Child Care.* London: Longman.

Fonagy, P., Steele, H. and Steel, M. (1991) Maternal representations of attachment during pregnancy predict the organisation of infant mother attachment and 1 year of age. *Child Development, 62,* 891–905.

Fonagy, P., Steele, M., Steele, H., Leigh, T., Kennedy, R., Matton, G. and Target, M. (1995) Attachment, the reflective self, and borderline states: the predictive specificity of the adult attachment interview and pathological emotional development. In

Goldberg, S., Muir, R. and Kerr, J. (eds) *Attachment Theory: Social, Developmental and Clinical Perspectives.* New York: The Analytic Press.

George, C., Kaplan, N. and Main, M. (1985) *The Adult Attachment Interview.* Unpublished Ms., Dept of Psychology, UCLA Berkley.

Green, J.M. (1996) An assessment of parenting based on attachment theory: theoretical background, description and initial clinical experience. *European Journal of Child and Adolescent Psychiatry, 5,* 133–138.

Grossman, K.E. and Grossman, K. (1991) Attachment quality as an organizer of emotional and behavioural responses in a longitudinal perspective. In Murray Parkes, C., Stevenson-Hinde, J. and Marris, P. (eds) *Attachment Across the Life Cycle.*

Jenkins, R., Mann, A.H. and Belsy, E. (1981). Background, design and use of a short interview to assess social stress and support in research and clinical settings. *Social Science and Medicine, 15,* 195–203.

Kagan, J. (1997) Temperament and the reactions to unfamiliarity. *Child Development, 68,* 1, 139–143.

Kroll, L. and Green, J. (1997) Therapeutic alliance in child inpatient treatment: development and initial validation of a family engagement questionnaire. *Clinical Child Psychology and Psychiatry, 2, 3,* 431–447.

Lamb, M.E. (1984). Security of infantile attachment as assessed in the strange situation: its study and biological interpretation. *Behavioural Brain Sciences, 7,* 127–171.

Lewis, M., Feiring, C., McGaffog, C. and Jaskir, J. (1984) Predicting psychopathology in six year olds from early social relations. *Child Development, 55,* 123–136.

Lieberman, A.F., Weston, D.R. and Pawl, J.H. (1991) Preventive intervention and outcome with anxiously attached dyads. *Child Development, 62,* 199–209.

Lyons-Ruth, K. (1996) Attachment relationships among children with aggressive behaviour problems: the role of disorganised early attachment patterns. *Journal of Consulting and Clinical Psychology, 64, 1,* 64–73.

Main, M., Kaplan, W. and Cassidy, J. (1985) Security in infancy, childhood and adulthood – a move to the level of representation. In Bretherton, I. and Waters, E. (eds) *Growing Points in Attachment Theory and Research.* SRCD Monographs 50 (1–2, Serial No 209).

Mills, M., Puckering, C., Pound, A. and Cox, A. (1985) What is it about depressed mothers that influences their children's functioning? In Stevenson, J. (ed.) *Recent Research in Developmental Psychopathology Journal of Child Psychology and Psychiatry,* Monograph supplement No. 4, Oxford: Oxford University Press.

Murray, L. (1992) The impact of post natal depression on infant development. *Journal of Child Psychology and Psychiatry, 33,* 543–561.

Oppenheim, D., Emde, R.N. and Warren, S. (1997) Children's narrative representations of mothers: their development and associations with child and mother adaptation. *Child Development, 68, 1,* 127–138.

Pound, A., Cox, A., Puckering, C. and Mills, M. (1985) The impact of maternal depression on young children. In Stevenson, J. (ed.) *Recent Research in Developmental Pyschopathology Journal of Child Psychology and Psychiatry,* Monograph supplement No. 4, Oxford: Oxford University Press.

Quinton, D. and Rutter, M. (1988) The assessment of parenting: some interactional considerations. *Psychiatry Bulletin, 15,* 347–348.

Richters, M. and Volkmar, F. R. (1994) Reactive attachment disorder of infancy or early childhood. *Journal of the American Academy of Child and Adolescent Psychiatry 33, 3,* 328–332.

Rogers, S.J., Ozonoff, S. and Maslin-Cole, C. (1993) Developmental aspects of attachment behavior in young children with pervasive development disorders. *Journal of the American Academy of Child and Adolescent Psychiatry, 32, 6, 1274–1282.*

Sigman, M. and Ungerer, J. (1984) Attachment disorders in autistic children *Journal of Autism and Developmental Disorders, 14, 3, 231–244.*

Strage, A. and Main, M. (1985) Attachment and parent–child discourse patterns. Paper presented at the biennial meeting of the Society for Research in Child Development, Toronto.

Tyrer, P., Alexander, J. and Ferguson, B. (1988) Personality assessment schedule. In Tyrer, P. (ed.) *Personality Disorder: Diagnosis, Management and Course.* Bristol: John Wright.

Van Ijzendoorn, M.H. and Kroonenberg, P.M. (1988). Cross cultural patterns of attachment: a meta analysis of the strange situation. *Child Development, 59, 147–156.*

Vaughn, B.E. and Lefever, G.B. (1989) Attachment behaviour, attachment security and temperament during infancy. *Child Development, 60, 728–737.*

Warren, S.L., Huston, L., Egeland, B. and Sroufe, L.A. (1997) Child and adolescent anxiety disorders and early attachment. *Journal of the American Academy of Child and Adolescent Psychiatry, 36, 5, 637–644.*

Werner, E.E. and Smith, R.S. (1982) *Vulnerable but Invincible: A Longitudinal Study of Resilient Children and Youth.* New York: McGraw Hill.

World Health Organisation (1992) The ICD-10 classification of mental and behavioural disorders: clinical descriptions and diagnostic guidelines. Geneva: WHO.

Wright, J.C., Binney, V. and Smith, P.K. (1995) Security of attachment in 8–12-year-olds: revised version of the separation anxiety test, its psychometric properties and clinical interpretation. *Journal of Child Psychology and Psychiatry, 36, 757–774.*

Zeanah, C. (1996) Beyond insecurity: a reconceptualisation of attachment disorders of infancy. *Journal of Consulting and Clinical Psychology, 64, 1, 42–52.*

26 Some cognitive–behavioural approaches to parenting used in children's in-patient unit settings

Kathleen Morris and Brian Jacobs

Cognitive–behavioural approaches to parenting difficulties are gradually being introduced to the in-patient setting. There is more experience of their use in the USA and a growing body of research literature (Webster-Stratton, 1991; Kazdin, 1997) concerning their application on an out-patient basis. Whilst they approach this important area of difficulties from a very practical approach to change, they should not be seen as in competition with a more psychodynamic understanding of parenting problems and their origins. Indeed, for some parents this approach opens up the possibility of addressing well-defended areas of their personality for sensitive individual psychodynamic work.

At the Bethlem and Maudsley children's in-patient unit, Acorn Lodge, we have used and adapted two different parenting programmes to help parents change their style of child management. The parent–child game (Forehand and McMahon, 1981; Forehand and Long, 1988) has the parent and child on one side of a one-way screen, with the parent using an earbug for active tuition whilst they are playing with their child. The Webster-Stratton programme (Webster-Stratton, 1984; Webster-Stratton, Kolpacoff and Hollingsworth, 1989), originally designed to be used with groups of parents, has been used by us with one or more parents to help them acquire skills through discussion and role play which they then apply at home and on the ward with their child.

The parent–child game (Forehand and McMahon, 1981) provides a practical framework for assessment and treatment during admission. It was originally developed as a training technique for parents of young children with non-compliant behaviours. The model stresses the importance of social learning principles as a means of enhancing treatment outcome and generalisation. Forehand and McMahon also included concepts from normal child development and cognitive behavioural psychotherapy in their model. Work with each parent is carried out where possible.

Clinicians at the Maudsley Hospital have adapted the original model so that it can be used for both assessment and treatment. Initial baseline measures are taken before the treatment begins, and post-treatment assessment measures can later be compared to provide information on progress and potential for the parent–child relationship to change.

On the children's in-patient unit, the technique is used as one approach to assess and help parents develop their parenting skills. It is particularly useful for parents who seem to respond best to learning through doing. Nonetheless, it often leads to greater insight into past patterns of parenting and their origins. The techniques are only one element in helping these parents improve their child management so that the relationship becomes more enjoyable and effective for both parent and child. The parents will also get opportunities to practise this and other work on the ward and at home.

The initial baseline is taken during a ten-minute period of observation as parent and child play together. Both child centred and child directive parenting behaviour are recorded. Examples of child centred behaviour are the uses of praise, smiles, positive touches and verbally giving attention to what the child is doing. Imitation and ignoring minor misbehaviour are also included in this category. Child directive behaviours include commands, questions saying 'No', negative touch and sarcastic comments. Forehand and McMahon have demonstrated (Forehand and McMahon, 1988) that non-clinic samples would typically reveal ratios of child centred behaviour to child directive behaviour at 1 to 1.3–1.75. Distribution in clinic referred parents revealed a higher proportion of child directive behaviour, in the order of 1 child centred to more than 5 child directive behaviours. It is predicted that a successful treatment programme would typically result in ratios of 6:1 child centred to child directive behaviours.

Treatment is carried out in two phases: the child's game and the parent's game. The child's game consists of ten-minute play sessions in a room with a one way mirror and an inductive audio feedback loop, so that the therapist can directly verbally prompt the parent, who wears an earbug, while playing with the child. Direct instruction of child centred behaviours can be given as well as praise and support to the parent, and alternatives to the use of child directive behaviours. The child's game often seems to improve the parent's mood state and sense of self-esteem. The parent may need additional individual therapy, which can be cognitive or brief psychodynamic in style, to help resolve other current overwhelming issues. This combination of approaches can also help parents become more attuned to the developmental stage and needs of their child.

Each ten-minute play session is followed by discussion with the parent. This focuses on discussion of progress, current issues for the parent in their lives and their parenting style. The parents are encouraged to make links to their own childhood experiences with their parents and their own current practice. Often this can be emotionally very powerful for them as they wish not to repeat what they experienced. Sometimes the affect associated with punitive experiences in their own childhood becomes accessible for the first time to the parents through this combination of a behavioural, experiential and reflective approach. As homework the parent and child have a daily play session. Written handouts describing the parent–child game are discussed.

The parent's game is usually initiated once the child's game has proved to be successful. As with other parenting interventions, it is considered very important to improve the nature and quality of the child's experience of their parent as somebody who has a real interest in them and can be attentive to their needs, before introducing non-coercive limit setting techniques. Often it is necessary to break a mutually aversive chain of experience between the child and the parent before each has the psychological space to value the other. The parent's game consists of instruction and discussion with the parent in an educative style on the use of effective commands, ignoring and time out. If necessary, these techniques will have been modelled during the child's game.

It is usual for six sessions to take place before the post-treatment assessment (a repeat of baseline measures) is carried out. Sometimes extended treatment is necessary and valuable.

The H Family

G was referred by her local clinic for further assessment of her aggressive behaviour towards her siblings, and her distractibility and poor concentration at school. She was 6 years old at the time of referral. There were also concerns about the relationship between G and her mother.

G lived with her mother and two younger siblings. Her parents were divorced, and the children had regular monthly visits to their father. G's maternal grandparents lived nearby, and had been supportive, but recently were becoming more upset about her behaviour, so mother had subsequently decreased her contact. At school, G was described as having a short attention span, and she found it hard to settle to a task. She tended to fidget and annoy her classmates, and peer relationships were poor. G was noted to be somewhat over-friendly, and there were concerns that she might be at risk because of this particular behaviour. Admission for the whole family was offered on a day-patient basis. Personal circumstances precluded an in-patient admission.

Assessment of parent

Mother was aged 38, and was unemployed. She had always been close to her mother and used her as a confidante. She had worked as a nursing assistant in a school and met her husband when she was 25 years old. The relationship was never easy because of father's emotional distance; he never wanted children. Mother was keen to start a family, and he reluctantly agreed, but was never much involved in the children's care, or emotionally close to them. After G's birth, mother felt very isolated and had severe post-natal depression. She was treated with antidepressants when G was 22 months old. There were further periods of depression, where mother would tend to apply harsh punishments towards G in particular.

We had no contact with the father and little is known about his background, although he is reported to have come from a close family, and he may have had similar problems to G as a child. He was described as sulky, self-willed, moody and fidgety.

Personality

The mother, Ms H, presented as a pleasant woman, who clearly welcomed the opportunity to talk about her problems. She described herself as isolated and lonely, but in need of some space for herself.

Mental state

Mother described having continuing periods of low mood and said she found it difficult at times to cope with the demands of her three lively children. When she felt depressed, her concentration was poor, and she found it difficult at these times to follow advice about parenting.

Social support

Mother's social worker had organised a regular family aide to visit the home twice weekly. Ms H was unemployed and money was tight.

Her attachment representations were not formally assessed, but she was able to describe how her post-natal depression had a significant effect on her ability to form a stable attachment to G. She found it hard to give warmth or praise and also found it difficult to be physically close to G.

Assessment of G

G did not show distress on leaving her mother. She was initially appropriately shy, but was able to establish good rapport. She said that she sometimes felt blamed for what her siblings did. There was no evidence of formal thought disorder, or delusions, obsessions, compulsions or phobias. Physical examination was essentially normal. Psychological assessment showed that G was of normal intelligence, but with a tendency to answer quickly and impulsively. She was observed by the team to take a parental role towards her siblings, even when her mother was present.

Mother–child interaction

Initial baseline observation showed that Ms H was strict and directive towards G, who in turn was giggly, restless and forced in her speech. There was little praise or positive comment. Mother was then offered a series of sessions following the 'parent–child game' model, where she received direct prompting and instruction from a therapist via an earbug, during play sessions with her daughter. She readily adapted to this, although she found it difficult to ignore minor undesirable behaviours. G's behaviour continued to have a forced quality, and she was ingratiating in a way that her mother found irritating. It was also clear that mother had difficulty in touching G, even when directly invited to do so.

Nursing staff worked directly alongside the therapist, to ensure that mother was encouraged to generalise what she had learned. She was also helped to generate solutions to particular problems, and to practise with the younger children, who could be difficult and demanding at times. Occupational therapists also supervised structured activity sessions with the whole family in order to facilitate further generalisation.

At the post-treatment baseline session, mother was observed to be warmer towards G, praising her frequently and describing positive behaviour. She showed that she could benefit from advice and learn new techniques when offered a high level of input. During this period she reported a lifting of her mood, and clearly valued the individual attention. However, she reported continuing difficulties at home, especially around mealtimes and bedtime.

Summary of assessment and subsequent treatment

G continued to be provocative and impulsive, and tended to bring distress from home into the school setting. It was recommended that she be assessed for a Statement of Special Educational Needs. There was evidence of both disinhibited attachment disorder and oppositional defiant disorder. There was a lack of warmth in the parent–child relationship, with hostility and scapegoating of G, which was further maintained by mother's depression and isolation.

It was clear that despite progress being made during the admission, and mother having more insight, G continued to have difficulties at home and at school. It was felt that intensive support would need to be available locally in order to prevent further breakdown of the relationship. A package of care was therefore negotiated with local services, which included the following elements:

- respite care on a regular basis
- referral of mother to a local adult psychiatrist
- social worker and family aide to continue for home-based support
- anger management and social skills training for G provided by school support service
- individual sessions at clinic for G
- planning meeting in view of the isolation of the family and inappropriate use of sanctions.

Conclusion

The assessment provided evidence of disinhibited attachment disorder in a 6-year-old girl. There was also a history of maternal depression and social isolation. Improvements made during assessment and treatment were being maintained one year later with an intensive package of locally based support being provided and monitored at regular reviews.

USING THE PARENTS AND CHILDREN VIDEOTAPE SERIES

Another approach that we use is that of the Webster-Stratton videotape series (Webster-Stratton, 1984). It consists of commentary, prompts for discussion and role-play, and videotaped vignettes. Summary notes and recording forms are provided for distribution at the end of each session. Topics include Parental Attention, Effective Praise, and Tangible Rewards. Later programmes cover the use of clear commands, ignoring, time out, and the use of logical consequences. Problem solving for both parents and children is discussed. It has been found very important to begin such programmes with parental attention to the child and for the parent to learn to play with the child in a manner that follows their cues with interest, rather than leading the child and trying to teach them. The programme is designed for use with groups of parents with sessions lasting one and a half hours. We have adapted it for use in our setting with individual parents when each topic can typically be covered in one hour. This provides an opportunity for treatment to be paced to suit the individual and for problems directly relevant to the case to be the particular focus as therapy progresses. For example, parents with a poor knowledge of normal child development may benefit from this approach, and it has been successfully used with parents who are receiving modelling and instruction from nursing staff as difficult situations present themselves on the ward. Opportunities for intervention may occur around mealtimes or at times when the child is required to comply with instruction.

The advantage of this approach is that it feels less intrusive to anxious and guilty parents as you are jointly watching other parents' handling of their child rather than commenting directly on their own child management in the room. For some parents this approach will not work – they know the language but do not carry out the actions. For those the parent–child game may be more directly applicable. For other parents, the best approach is to begin with the Webster-Stratton work and move on to the parent–child game later when the parents have gained trust.

Case study

D, aged 7, was a boy who was referred to the unit with a number of complex difficulties. He was an only child who lived with his mother and maternal grandmother, both widows who were bereaved suddenly. Presenting complaints included social isolation, clumsiness, overactivity, poor eating habits, rigid routine, and specific learning difficulties. D was reported by his carers to have a number of phobias and anxieties, which had not responded to intensive treatment. He was born after a difficult pregnancy at thirty-two weeks gestation. He was described as a lazy baby. Motor milestones were not delayed, and D was clean and dry by the age of 3. However, he was bottle fed until the age of six and a half. His carers were noted to be extremely overprotective towards him. They behaved as if any challenge to his wishes would lead to catastrophic results. He attended a mainstream school with individual support in class. Further assessment, including an Autism Diagnostic Interview, and Autism Diagnostic Observation Schedule, confirmed the presence of a pervasive developmental disorder.

The family was offered an admission of two days each week with overnight stays. D's mother and grandmother shared parenting, and it was noted by the team on admission that mother was particularly reticent, while grandmother took a dominant role. During D's admission, a number of treatment approaches were offered. They included individual therapy for mother and grandmother, who both presented as being depressed and in a state of unresolved grief. Nursing staff worked closely with D and his mother, modelling management and coping strategies in a number of situations. Although his carers predicted that D would be extremely anxious, this was not found to be the case on the ward.

D's mother responded positively to individual brief psychotherapy and was observed to be gradually taking a more assertive role with regard to parenting. Grandmother's attendance became infrequent; she gave the reason that she found staying too difficult but we thought it represented mother's increasing assertiveness in the care of her child. D's mother specifically requested help with learning parenting skills and management techniques. Mother was aware that her knowledge of age appropriate behaviour was poor, as they had tended to live on a day to day basis, finding the idea of his eventual maturity too difficult to contemplate.

Mother was offered weekly sessions where the Parents and Children Series (Webster-Stratton, 1984) was used. She kept a folder of the handouts, which she regularly discussed with D's teachers. Handouts consisted of summaries of the week's topic, checklists for evaluating the use of the ideas presented, and homework tasks, such as monitoring the use of praise and positive attention at home.

As D's play was limited in nature, his mother was given advice about age appropriate toys and activities. She was encouraged to use simple reward schemes, for example around bedtime routines, when D was often resistant. She began to use ignoring more effectively, and identified a place in the house where D could sit during time-out. Nursing staff noticed that mother was firmer and more consistent in her management of D on the ward, and was visibly more calm and confident. She demonstrated on several occasions that she was able to generalise what she had learned to the home, particularly when D had tantrums. Their frequency and severity gradually decreased. Mother also related well to problem solving ideas. For example, she noticed one evening that D was agitated, and was able to discuss this with him calmly. He had been upset by a video shown at school on the dangers of electricity. Mother went with D to see his teacher in the morning; he was reassured that the video would not be shown again, and he accepted this. In the past, it was likely that D would have been kept home from school for such a reason. Mother also witnessed teaching staff managing a tantrum and was able to walk away without becoming involved and taking D home. She was very proud of these achievements.

In summary, D's mother, although initially depressed and withdrawn, was able to benefit from a package of treatment, and follow the programme with enthusiasm. She took on a number of new ideas with regard to parenting, generalising them to home and school. She was able to see D's behaviour in the context of his pervasive developmental disorder, and actively plan for his future.

CONCLUSION

Cognitive behavioural techniques for addressing parenting skills can be a very useful adjunct to many in-patient and day-patient admissions. They can deepen the trust between parents and the staff of the unit. There is ample opportunity for parents to practise the skills they learn both on the unit and at home. They can frequently lead to greater exploration by the parents of their learnt automatic responses to their children and the origins of these. These are often powerful motivators for change.

REFERENCES

Forehand, R. L. and Long, N. (1988). Out-patient treatment for the acting out child: procedures, long term follow-up data and clinical problems. *Advances in Behavioural Research and Therapy, 10,* 129–177.

Forehand, R. L. and McMahon, R. J. (1981). *Helping the Non-Compliant Child: a clinician's guide to parent training.* New York: Guilford.

Kazdin, A. E. (1997). Practitioner review: psychosocial treatments for conduct disorder in children. *Journal of Child Psychology and Psychiatry and Allied Disciplines, 38,* 161–178.

Webster-Stratton, C. (1984). A randomized trial of two parent training programs for families with conduct disordered children. *Journal of Consulting and Clinical Psychology, 52,* 666–678.

Webster-Stratton, C. (1991). Strategies for helping families with conduct disordered children. *Journal of Child Psychology and Psychiatry, 32,* 1047–1062.

Webster-Stratton, C., Kolpacoff, M. and Hollingsworth, T. (1989). The long-term effectiveness and clinical significance of three cost-effective training programmes for families with conduct problem children. *Journal of Consulting and Clinical Psychology, 57,* 550–553.

Part VI
Research

27 Research into efficacy and process of treatment

David Imrie and Jonathan Green

STUDIES OF EFFICACY

Efficacy research has a number of different rationales: 1) to justify the existence of in-patient units by showing them to be effective; 2) to make a case for additional resources for in-patient units to enable them to better meet clinical demands; 3) to highlight, through increased understanding of the in-patient care process, strengths and weaknesses in existing practice so that services can be made more effective. This chapter reviews the existing information on the efficacy of in-patient psychiatric care for children, and points up some of the methodological issues raised in this research.

Literature searches were undertaken on 'Psychlit' and 'Medline' and through the reference lists of related papers. These yielded a large number of papers calling for research in the area and proposing various psychometric instruments for use. There were a fair number of small-scale studies, often retrospective and using non-standardised measures, but only a handful of serious attempts to study efficacy of child in-patient units scientifically.

The most authoritative and useful paper to emerge is a review and meta-analysis of research in this field by Pfeiffer and Strzelecki (1990). The authors found a total of thirty-four in-patient unit efficacy studies published since 1975, with the latest publication date 1987; although various areas of study were excluded (e.g. studies of autistic children) to allow a focus on 'severely emotionally disturbed children'. Each of these thirty-four studies provided, in varying degrees, a set of objective data concerning treatment outcomes after in-patient hospitalisation, as well as data on patients and treatment process. The papers varied considerably in methodology and a number of assumptions and simplifications were made in order to integrate their data. The combined data were analysed to assess the predictive power of ten significant patient and process variables with regard to outcome, each variable being supported by data from at least four independent studies. Because of the small number of studies in the meta-analysis, outcome measurements were analysed together regardless of time following discharge, even though the timescales varied from measurements taken at discharge to measurements taken fifteen years after discharge.

Results on these ten study variables were as follows (N = number of studies providing data on each variable):

Intelligence (N = 7): IQ positively predicted good outcome in three studies and predicted poor outcome in one study. IQ showed an overall moderate positive relationship with good outcome.

Organicity (N = 4): All four studies in this area showed 'organicity' (a composite including a number of constitutional variables) to predict poorer outcome and the overall figures show a strong negative relationship between organic involvement and good outcome.

Symptom pattern (N = 13): 'Bizarre, anti-social, and primitive symptoms' were generally predictive of a poorer outcome. Some individual papers found additional predictive symptom patterns, but these symptoms were of negligible predictive value after data integration.

Diagnosis (N = 10): seven of the ten papers showed a relationship between diagnosis and outcome. Diagnoses of psychotic disorders or under-socialised aggressive conduct disorders gave a strong prediction of poor outcome.

Age at admission (N = 12): seven papers found no relationship between admission age and outcome. Overall there was a very weak relationship between younger age and poorer outcome.

Sex (N = 6): Only one study showed any indication of sex having an effect on outcome. The overall predictive value was nearly negligible, weighted towards girls showing better adjustment.

Family functioning (N = 9): six studies showed a positive relationship between family functioning and good outcome, the other three studies found no relationship. Overall better family functioning was a strong predictor of good outcome.

Treatment (N = 4): 'Treatment' is a rather wide variable covering therapeutic alliance, planned discharge, treatment programme completion, and, in one case, 'the efficacy of a cognitive-based problem-solving skills training package'. One study investigated each of these variables, and in each case a good score on the variable was predictive of better outcome.

Length of stay (N = 7): The three largest studies of this variable found a positive relationship between length of stay and outcome; the other four found no relationship. Overall there is a moderate positive relationship between outcome and length of stay.

Aftercare (N = 4): All four studies in this area found that good aftercare was positively related to good long-term outcome.

The diversity of methodologies in the source papers do compromise the meta-analysis somewhat. Pfeiffer and Strzelecki are frank about these problems. They state in summary that whilst their paper provides clear indication concerning predictors of mental health outcome after psychiatric hospitalisation, there is a pressing need for more and better planned research in the future to provide any real clarity of understanding in this area. They make a number of useful methodological recommendations for further studies (see below).

Since 1988, there have been a number of other relevant studies, but many suffer from the same methodological problems outlined by Pfieffer and Strzelecki, the most common being the use of invalidated, non-standardised psychometric instruments. Several (Ney et al., 1988; Dalton, Daruna and Bolding, 1991; Bradley and Clark, 1993) confirm the general finding that in-patient treatment helps the majority of children who receive it in terms of observable functioning rated by clinicians, parents or teachers. In a longitudinal study influenced by Pfeiffer and Strzelecki's findings, Kolko (1992) studied children two, four, or six months after discharge from in-patient treatment and found that poor improvement was predicted by: attention deficit hyperactivity symptoms with depressive symptoms; older age; neurological dysfunction; and a history of abuse. Length of stay and length of follow-up interval (two to six months) showed no effects on outcome. Again the outcome measures were non-standardised instruments composed of two or three point scales. Gerardot (1992) by contrast studied pre- and post-admission scores using the parent-rated child behaviour checklist (CBCL). Mean total, internalising and externalising scores on this instrument fell highly significantly during admission. Although this study largely replicates the finding that in-patient care helps children who receive it, the use of standardised measures allows its easy integration with other studies for future meta-analysis.

A further review paper published since Pfeiffer and Strzelecki (Curry, 1991) draws mainly on the results of a different set of studies. Although mainly focusing on methodological issues, Curry reviewed both child and adolescent in-patient unit efficacy studies, concluding that more favourable outcome functioning is related to: less severe psychopathology; average or above IQ; reactive pattern of symptom onset; participation during hospitalisation; completing the goals of hospitalisation; and continuing therapy after discharge. These findings are in good agreement with those of Pfeiffer and Strzelecki. Curry also finds that studies generally show that a good proportion of children and adolescents treated in residential units show improvements in functioning, but notes strong indications that functioning is variable during the immediate post-discharge period; improvement during hospitalisation (admission to discharge) does not necessarily predict adjustment at follow-up. Like Pfeiffer and Strzelecki, Curry also stresses the need for better planned research in the future and raises a number of methodological issues which will have a bearing on future research strategies.

INVESTIGATION OF THERAPEUTIC PROCESS

The focus of efficacy research is, rightly, on changes which occur in the patients' functioning and symptomatology over the course of a hospitalisation. This has, however, led to a tendency to overlook two other variables, namely: 1) the functioning of the unit and its staff; and 2) the relationship between the patient and the unit. These variables address the therapeutic mode of action of the milieu and are of potential importance in terms of their effect on patient outcome.

Hence it is important that an attempt be made to measure them in efficacy studies to allow these variables to be controlled for.

Ward atmosphere

If the residential component of care characteristic of in-patient treatment is effective, then which are the effective components? If the effect is more than just the removal of the child from their family for a period, then research needs to begin to look at the quality of the environment and the milieu functioning which acts upon the child during admission. Process measures, although sparsely researched in child psychiatry to date, are important not only because of their potential effects on outcome. The relationships between process measurements and outcome allow unit staff to see how their efforts affect their patients, and could provide a real indicator of directions which in-patient treatment should take.

This kind of work in adult psychiatry has been most developed by Moos, with the Ward Atmosphere Scale (Moos, 1974). There have been adaptations of the scale for use in child in-patient units by Steiner (Steiner, Marx and Walton, 1991) and Green and Imrie. The studies of Moos et al. in adult psychiatry (see pages 93–94) emphasise the general characterisation of enduring aspects of the ward culture. Steiner has used his adaptation of the WAS similarly to delineate the characteristics of one unit's milieu and to show that it is relatively stable over a number of years despite considerable turnover of staff.

In contrast, Green and Imrie have aimed to capture more transient fluctuations of a milieu functioning over periods of weeks. These are fluctuations with which ward staff are very familiar and which are very likely to relate to fluctuations in milieu efficacy. Staff will typically talk of times when the milieu undergoes a rapid state change from 'treatment' to 'containment' (see chapter 28). In developing and piloting an instrument which makes a consensus rating of these fluctuations Green and Imrie have tried to investigate some of the influences on such fluctuations (such as staff numbers, skill mix, patient characteristics, ward events) and their consequences (on morale and patient attitudes and behaviour). At present this kind of approach, investigating staff and patient perceptions of the unit milieu along a number of different dimensions, looks a practicable option to pursue.

Therapeutic alliance

Another process variable relates to the therapeutic alliance between family and unit. Although there is a large body of therapeutic alliance literature pertaining to adult psychiatry, summarised in a scholarly review by Hougaard (1994), there has been relatively little exploration of the therapeutic alliance in child psychiatry (Green, 1996). One study addressing the therapeutic alliance in outpatient child psychiatry treatment has been published (Green, 1996) but the obstacles to developing a theory of alliance between a family and the clinical team in in-patient treatment are considerable (Kroll and Green, 1997). To date there appears to have been only one attempt to look at therapeutic alliance in this very different environment of child in-patient psychiatry. Shirk and Saiz (1992), basing their work on a conceptual model by Bordin (1979), looked at therapeutic alliance with children but did not relate their alliance measures to outcome, looking only at the relationships between questionnaire items. Kroll and Green (1997) have developed an instrument to measure staff perceptions of family engagement to the ward and Imrie and Green (unpublished) have developed a measure of child relationship to the ward. Both these measures are currently being used prospectively in a study of treatment outcome. This is a conceptually important area, and should be studied in future efficacy research from the perspectives of the patient, the parents and the staff.

CONCLUSION

The field of research into in-patient efficacy and process is in the early stages of maturity; a stage where there are a relatively small number of disconnected studies in the literature, of uneven quality, using heterogeneous samples and non-shared or non-standardised assessments. There are no randomised controlled studies and no completed studies of treatment process in addition to outcome. The best we can hope for now in this area is a progression to a more mature research enterprise with the emergence of a critical mass of research centres, the development of shared conceptual approaches and instruments, the gradual accumulation of partial but interlocking studies, and an unfolding consensus of knowledge. No doubt the slow development of this field is related to the considerable methodological problems in pursuing the area, as well as the small number of researchers committed to it. The chapter that follows will address these methodological difficulties and attempt to chart a way forward for in-patient research.

REFERENCES

Bordin, E.S. (1979) The generalisability of the psychoanalytic of the working alliance. *Psychotherapy: Theory, Research and Practice*, 16, 252–260.

Bradley, E.J. and Clark, B.S. (1993) Patients' characteristics and consumer satisfaction on an in-patient child psychiatric unit. *Canadian Journal of Psychiatry*, 38, 175–180.

Curry, J.E. (1991) Outcome research on residential treatment: implications and suggested directions. *American Journal of Orthopsychiatry*, 61, 348–357.

Dalton, R., Daruna, J.H. and Bolding, D. (1991) Parents' perceptions of their children's adjustment following short-term psychiatric hospitalisation. *Residential Treatment for Children and Youth*, 8, 3, 71–83.

Gerardot, R.J., Thyer, B.A., Mabe, P.A. and Paston, P.M. (1992) The effects of psychiatric hospitalisation on behaviourally disordered children: a preliminary evaluation. *The Psychiatric Hospital*, 23, 2, 65–68.

Green, J.M. (1996) Engagement and empathy: a pilot study of the therapeutic alliance in outpatient child psychiatry. *Association of Child Psychology and Psychiatry Review*, 1, 4, 130–138.

Hougaard, E. (1994) The therapeutic alliance: a conceptual analysis. *Scandanavian Journal of Psychology*, 35, 67–85.

Kolko, D.J. (1992) Short-term follow-up of child psychiatric hospitalization: clinical description, predictors, and correlates. (University of Pittsburgh School of Medicine, Western Psychiatric Institute and Clinic, PA 15213.) *Journal of the American Academy of Child and Adolescent Psychiatry*, 31, 4, 719–727.

Kroll, L. and Green, J.M. (1997) The therapeutic alliance in inpatient child psychiatry: development and initial validation of a family engagement questionnaire. *Clinical Child Psychology and Psychiatry*, 2, 3, 431–447.

Moore, L.M. and O'Connor T.W. (1991) A psychiatric residential centre for children and adolescents: a pilot study of its patients' characteristics and improvement while resident. *Child Care Health Development*, 17, 4, 235–42.

Moos, R.H. (1974) *Evaluating Treatment Environments: A Social Ecological Approach*. New York: Wiley and Sons.

Ney, P.G., Adam, R.R., Hanton, B.R. and Brindad, E.S. (1988) The effectiveness of a child psychiatric unit: a follow-up study. *Canadian Journal of Psychiatry*, 33, 793–799.

Pfeiffer, S.I. and Strzelecki, S.C. (1990) Inpatient psychiatric treatment of children and adolescents: a review of outcome studies. *Journal of the American Academy of Child and Adolescent Psychiatry*, 29, 6, 847–853.

Shirk, S.R. and Saiz, C.C. (1992) Clinical, empirical, and developmental perspectives on the therapeutic relationship in child psychology. *Development and Psychopathology*, 4, 713–728.

Steiner, H., Marx, L. and Walton, C. (1991) The ward atmosphere of a child's psychosomatic unit: a ten year follow-up. *General Hospital Psychiatry*, 13, 246–252.

28 Methodological issues and future directions for in-patient research

Jonathan Green and Brian Jacobs

INTRODUCTION

The problems in trying to carry out research in child psychiatry in-patient units are significant. Because there is a very low incidence of major psychiatric disorder within this age range the strategies used for the most part in adult services do not apply. This is compounded by the length of stay of children in in-patient units, again rather longer than adult services, leading to a low throughput and the slow accumulation of any series of patients.

Further, the nature of the cases is heterogeneous. Most cases show multiple comorbidity, so that the development of clear populations with few variables is improbable. Inevitably this leads to the need for larger populations to compare and analyse. To complicate matters further, the culture on in-patient units is not stable. It fluctuates, as discussed elsewhere in this volume (chapters 29, 2). This should not produce a difficulty for research provided that the culture fluctuates about a mean. However, it is at least possible that there are features of the culture and practice on the unit that change progressively over time. Methods for recording these matters so that they may be factored into research efforts are still in development.

As an example of the issues, consider one attempt to mount a comparison of in-patient and outpatient treatment for 6–9-year-old boys with severe mixed disorders of conduct and emotion. This used a parent management training approach and was carried out as a pilot study at the Bethlem and Guys Hospitals (Spender et al., 1994). The original concept was to carry out a controlled treatment trial across four London children's in-patient units. One unit had to withdraw because they did not have sufficient staff to deliver the treatment programme in addition to their usual programme. A second unit was, surprisingly, unable to recruit suitable patients during the trial period. The treatment required a weekly two-hour parents' group running concurrently with a social skills and problem solving group for the boys known as 'Dinosaur School' (Webster-Stratton and Hammond, 1997). Assessment of the families was thorough, including screening questionnaires, semi-structured interviews of the parents and the boys, and video recorded tasks of interactions between the boys and each parent. In addition to the programme delivery the therapists for the parents' groups and for the children's groups met separately for weekly supervision. Each group required two therapists and the time spent each week on the trial amounted to five to six hours of clinician's time for each therapist.

In each of the centres it was possible to recruit five families who met entry criteria and were willing to accept randomised assignment to treatment programme together with in-patient admission or treatment programme alone over a four-month period. Each child was regarded as sufficiently severely affected to warrant referral to an in-patient service on clinical grounds. Each family was seen on several occasions for data collection. Data collection was required at entry, during treatment, at discharge and then at one year follow-up.

The research team consisted of four senior trainees, each of whom gave eight to sixteen hours each week to the trial. As the therapy phase of the trial came to an end, one of the two units providing the treatment was suddenly, and inappropriately, closed!

Much useful information was gathered both about the patient group and about the design of appropriate therapeutic interventions for them. One aspect that became very apparent is the expense to families of participating in such research unless their child care and travel costs can be refunded, as they were. What became clear was that such a trial cannot be mounted in earnest without substantial research funding both for the gathering of systematic data and for the payment of the additional clinical time necessary for such structured delivery of treatment. It could not easily replace work currently carried out on an in-patient unit.

Further, the maintenance of uniform treatment across different sites is possible, though difficult. It was clear to all participants that there were differences in in-patient treatment between the two units. There were logistic difficulties in arranging the admissions for those children on the in-patient treatment arm of the trial at the right time to fit with the rest of the research treatment programme because of other constraints of difficult youngsters already admitted. These were overcome but with some considerable cost in stress on nursing staff and others.

The difficulties of this trial are not unique. However, they illustrate the complexity, the high level of staff time involved and the slow pace of any research effort involving group comparison treatment studies in an in-patient setting. The remainder of this chapter addresses specific research issues and potential solutions for the future.

THE WARD AS A CONTEXT FOR RESEARCH

The in-patient unit is a dynamic structure orientated around its own maintenance and the clinical care of a very difficult caseload. To add a research dimension into this can lead to a conflict of priorities and perceived extra burden on staff. Generating a research culture within the unit is at best a gradual task. These issues have been well discussed by Riddle (1989). He emphasises the crucial importance of involving nursing staff from the earliest stages in developing an ownership of the research task. At an administrative level he emphasises the 'Herculean effort' required to combine in one person leadership in the research and clinical fields and recommends a splitting of roles between a clinical director and a research director on the unit. In practice, of course, this is often not possible. It can also be true that that clinical staff perceive research (especially efficacy research) as potentially threatening to their self-confidence and unit culture in an area where therapeutic change can seem to be slow and uncertain. Since efficacy research should implicitly carry in its wake the possibility of change in clinical practice, some unit cultures, biased to preserve sameness, may resist this.

A number of ways of overcoming these difficulties of context have been suggested. Firstly, Gerardot et al. (1992), after studying changes in child behaviour checklist (CBCL) scores over an in-patient admission, and Moore and O'Connor (1991), after attempting retrospective efficacy research using clinical notes, both recommend that a standardised component of evaluative research be built into normal clinical practice. Many units routinely use standardised assessment as part of their workup and it seems reasonable that this can be done without creating too much additional workload. Unit staff will generally know much of the information needed to rate such measures as part of normal, existing procedure; and it seems wasteful that this knowledge is not tapped for research purposes. The very use of these instruments over time can gradually introduce a more self-aware and research orientated attitude into a clinical setting.

The second solution for specific projects is to conduct as much formal data collection as possible using non-clinical staff. In this way the research and clinical tasks are separated, problems of clinical biasing are reduced, and fewer research skills are needed in the clinical staff.

A third suggestion is made by Fiske (1983), Pfeiffer and Strzelecki (1990) and Curry (1991) and echoed widely in the literature in addressing the complexity of the research task in in-patient units. This is that individual research projects are planned on a smaller scale around specific questions and using compatible instruments, with a view to their being integrated with the results of other studies in other centres. This would require a more integrated research culture among people working in the field, such as has occurred in other areas such as mood disorders or autism.

NATURE OF THE CASE MATERIAL

There is a tension between the complexity of variables generated in the kind of research described above and the small number of patients who are treated on in-patient units. This problem is compounded because the multi-variate statistical designs necessary to analyse such data also need large numbers. Pfeiffer and Strzelecki (1990) recommend involving statistical analyses causal modelling. These use discriminant function and multi-dimensional scaling in order to test hypotheses about which of a number of variables may be crucially mediating change, to investigate the interaction between causative factors and the relative strength and variety of predictor variables. The challenge of numbers can be addressed by combining data from different units but this introduces more difficulty in matching between-unit variables. The problem of low numbers needs to be minimised by careful selection of the focus of studies, robust designs that capture important change, and well chosen measures.

ISSUES OF MEASUREMENT

Many of these are generic issues for all child psychiatry research. Measures of change that depend on one perspective or on only limited aspects of functioning such as behavioural symptoms are now generally considered to be inadequate. Pfeiffer and Strzelecki (1990) advocate the use of the tripartite model of Strupp and Hadley (1977) which looks at outcome from three major vantage points: the patient; society; and the clinician. Using more complex measures of psychopathology adds a burden to both practical and theoretical aspects of the research design, but it can help control for a number of aspects of rating bias.

Measures need to be sensitive to change during treatment. Behavioural checklists of the kind developed for epidemiological research are of limited value here and investigator rated interview methods are more suitable.

There needs to be a mix of general and specific, categorical and dimensional measures. Because of the low number and diagnostic variability of admitted patients, as well as high levels of comorbidity, it is impracticable solely to measure change in caseness or diagnostic category. There will however be common elements of psychopathology within most patients that can be measured across patient variability – and these will indeed often be the focus of treatment intervention. These include factors such as overall functional impairment or family dysfunction. Additional to these more general measures, there can be measures around more syndrome-specific symptoms (such as obsessionality or psychoticism) depending on the focus of the study.

A recent outcome study (Green and Kroll, in preparation) has attempted to incorporate these principles into the design of measures. The majority of the clinical assessments were undertaken by an independent research assistant to avoid clinician bias. The study team developed an investigator rated semi-structured interview to rate the UK Health of the Nation Outcome Scales in Child and Adolescent Psychiatry (HoNOSCA) which measures functional impairment in a number of areas. A parallel rating was also made on the CGAS scale; a global rating scale of dysfunction (Phelan, Wykes, and Goldman, 1994; Rey et al., 1995; Jones et al., 1995). Specific symptomatology was assessed using the child behaviour checklist (CBCL, see chapter 6). The possible limitations of the CBCL in relation to change sensitivity are offset by the advantages of the integration of youth self-report, parent, clinician and teacher scales in a coherent assessment, the ability to derive useful categorical symptom clusters from the ratings and the wealth of normative and treatment study data using the instrument. Clinicians made their own ratings of clinical progress and ICD-10 diagnosis and referring clinicians made pre- and post-evaluations using the HoNOSCA and CGAS scales.

Family dysfunction was measured using the Family Assessment Device, which allows ratings from different family members and is in widespread use. New instruments were designed to measure family engagement (Kroll and Green, 1997) and child and parental expectations, attitudes to treatment, and therapeutic alliance. Post-discharge evaluation included patient satisfaction measures.

STUDY DESIGNS

No randomised controlled studies of in-patient treatment have been completed. Clearly this should be the ultimate goal of efficacy research and will depend on the development of methodologies to overcome the difficulties of establishing control settings, and the establishment of robust measures of change and process. A number of models could be proposed.

- *Randomisation with an untreated control group.* Children who are referred for in-patient care are always in acute need, and to not treat a random group of these is not an ethical option.
- *Randomisation between in-patient care and intensive day care/outreach intervention.* There should be little problem in principle with randomising cases of moderate severity to an in-patient or intensive outpatient option. There are certainly some cases where the need for in-patient care is so acute that such a policy would be unethical – but these are arguably the minority. This design would also have the value of testing an assertion that clinicians in in-patient units have long made – that earlier referral of cases before the 'end of the line' would have useful preventative value.
- *Randomisation to a waiting list condition followed by admission.* This is a less demanding design, where referred cases could be allocated to immediate admission or a six-week waiting list before admission. Although attractive in theory, this design would probably represent a weak test of the efficacy of units because of the relatively short length of the control period in relation to admissions that commonly last for three months or more.

A less demanding form of study would be a case control design, utilising a control group that controlled for important treatment variables.

- *Untreated high risk sample control.* Recent reports indicate that there may be many children with severe mental health problems in institutional care settings who are in need of in-patient care but who are never referred for it (Kurtz, personal communication). If a group of such children were identified they could be studied to form a control group. It could reasonably be argued that as the normal care of these children would not involve an in-patient stay, the formation of a control group from these children could be seen as justified.

- *Waiting list control.* Owing to the differing lengths of admission required for different in-patient cases and the demand for in-patient care, long waiting lists are becoming the norm. As waiting times are often a number of months, a control group could be formed from children on the waiting list for in-patient beds. This group could show the untreated progression of mental health problems over a number of months, and could later be matched with studied in-patient cases. This design has the same weakness as the randomisation to waiting list design above.

- *Retrospective case matched design.* It would be possible to match new referrals with discharged patients from whom data had already been collected over a particular timescale and interview parents and teachers of the patients and the children themselves over the same timescale retrospectively. This would be possible because the referral process is lengthy and the child's problems will often have been going on for some time before being brought to the attention of any mental health agency. Obviously retrospective measures are less reliable, but they are likely to be of some use and this is at least an entirely ethical method of obtaining some control data.

WAYS FORWARD FOR CHILD IN-PATIENT RESEARCH

Looking to an ideal future, one could envisage a number of interlocking studies to begin to answer questions about residential in-patient care. Firstly, there is a need for studies into the inputs to in-patient treatment. There are probably considerable variations in input across units (see chapter 27) but multi-centre standardised descriptions of caseload and casemix would be a good basis for further case control studies. Secondly there need to be more studies of the process of treatment as they vary across units. The study reported on in chapter 27 is a beginning in this direction.

In addition to general studies of efficacy on non-selected patient samples described in detail above, there is a place for studies comparing the outpatient versus in-patient delivery of certain treatment techniques for specified groups of patients. Case control or randomised control designs as above could be used. Such studies have been done, for instance, with anorexia nervosa (Gowers et al., 1994) and the IPOPS pilot study (Spender et al., 1994), the former suggesting in that instance (in adolescents) that the residential component of treatment was of questionable value.

The second group of studies could control for the residential component of treatment from a different angle: here groups of patients could be randomly allocated to non-psychiatry residential treatments, as against psychiatry residential treatments. The most viable design here would be to identify a group of children with complex mental health difficulties who are attending Social Services residential units.

A third approach would be to study the variables at admission that might predict outcome of in-patient care. Here one would be looking at the effect of certain characteristics of patients on the process and outcome of in-patient treatment. One example of this is a current study in which the predictor variable of therapeutic alliance with the unit, of both parents and child, is being used in conjunction with a comprehensive evaluation of outcome.

One of the great opportunities in in-patient treatment is the unusual nature and inherent interest of its cases. Single-case designs can capitalise on this. They are particularly useful for investigation of a novel treatment. A variation that increases the power of the conclusions that can be drawn is the use of the multiple single-case study design in which each case acts as its own control. The establishment of a database between several in-patient units would allow unusual constellations of difficulties to become apparent in cases seen across centres. This would allow syndrome description and further investigation of such cases in a way that has been seen throughout the history of medicine. Such a database is currently under discussion. Individual case studies can use multiple baseline observations which, followed by stepped interventions with continued observations on other non-target criteria, can provide some reassurance that the treatment is addressing its specific target, rather than other aspects of the child's difficulties. Similarly, drug treatment trials can be initiated with placebo phases to the treatment. Where medication is of proven efficacy this may not be acceptable ethically but there are still many situations where the information available is insufficient.

The next phase of research should certainly include economic analysis of the various aspects of cost effectiveness of the treatment. The issues here are discussed in chapter 30.

The main solution to the methodological problems hampering efficacy and process research would seem to be a greater emphasis on standardised, change sensitive measurements being made as a part of normal clinical practice in in-patient units. This information will allow efficacy evaluation, and meta-analysis of a much larger data set, particularly if instruments used are compatible. There is a pressing need for this field of research to become less fragmented, for studies to be planned with a view to their future integration with the results of other studies by using standardised measures which cover as many of the relevant variables as possible. Most of all there is a need for routine well planned, evaluative research to become an accepted part of the day-to-day running of in-patient units, as evaluative research will provide a platform for progress in child psychiatric in-patient care. Confidence gained from this could then allow centres to undertake the demanding tasks of randomised trials addressing particular aspects of treatment.

REFERENCES

Curry, J.E. (1991) Outcome research on residential treatment: implications and suggested directions. *American Journal of Orthopsychiatry*, 61, 348–357.

Fiske, D.W. (1983) The meta-analytic revolution in outcome research. *Journal of Consulting and Clinical Psychology*, 51, 1, 65–70.

Gerardot, R.J., Thyer, B.A., Mabe, P.A. and Poston, P.M. (1992) The effects of psychiatric hospitalisation on behaviourally disordered children: a preliminary evaluation. *The Psychiatric Hospital*, 23, 2, 65–68.

Gowers, S. et al. (1994) Outcome of outpatient psychotherapy in a random allocation treatment study of anorexia nervosa. *International Journal of Eating Disorders*, 15, 2, 165–177.

Jones, S.H. Thornicroft, G., Coffey, M. and Dunn, G. (1995) A brief mental health outcome scale: reliability and validity of the global assessment of functioning (GAF). *British Journal of Psychiatry*, 166, 654–659.

Kroll, L. and Green, J.M. (1997) The therapeutic alliance in child inpatient treatment: development and initial validation of a family engagement questionnaire. *Journal of Clinical Psychology and Psychiatry*, 2, 3, 431–447.

Moore, L.M. and O'Connor, T.W. (1991) A psychiatric residential centre for children and adolescents: a pilot study of its patients' characteristics and improvement while resident. *Child Care Health Development*, 17, 4, 235–42.

Pfeiffer, S.I. and Strzelecki, S.C. (1990) Inpatient psychiatric treatment of children and adolescents: a review of outcome studies. *Journal of the American Academy of Child and Adolescent Psychiatry*, 29, 6, 847–853.

Phelan, M., Wykes, T. and Goldman, H. (1994) Global function scales. *Social Psychiatry and Psychiatric Epidemiology*, 29, 205–211.

Rey, J.M., Starling, J., Wever, C., Dossetor, D.R. and Plapp, J.M. (1995) Inter-rater reliability of global assessment of functioning in a clinical setting. *Journal of Child Psychology and Psychiatry*, 36, 5, 787–792.

Riddle, M.A. (1989) Research on a children's psychiatric in-patient service. *Journal of the American Academy of Child and Adolescent Psychiatry*.

Spender, Q., Hill-Smith, A., Phillips, J., Cameron, M. and Jacobs, B.W. (1994) Interviewing boys with conduct disorder: validity issues. Paper presented at the Royal College of Psychiatrists Section of Child and Adolescent Psychiatry, Isle of Wight, September.

Strupp, H.H. and Hadley, S.W. (1977) A tripartite model of mental health and therapeutic outcomes. *American Psychologist*, 32, 187–196.

Webster-Stratton, C. and Hammond, M. (1997) Treating children with early onset conduct problems: a comparison of child and parent training interventions. *Journal on Consulting and Clinical Psychology*, 65, 93–109.

Part VII

Management and finance

29 Childhood, mental health and the law

Michael Shaw

INTRODUCTION

The Children Act (1989) has very significant implications for child mental health services; several aspects are of special interest to in-patient units. First, the Act gives extra weight to the child's wishes in regard to consent to treatment. Second, the Act extends the statutory controls on the restriction of children's liberty to include children accommodated by health services. Third, the Act places particular emphasis on providing services in partnership with parents. Finally, there is encouragement for health, social and education services to co-operate in the best interests of the child.

The government has published guidance on the implications of the Act for the provision of residential care by Social Services but had little to say about the Health Service. Children's competence and consent is currently an area of considerable confusion and debate. We have some guidance on the restriction of children's liberty in health care facilities, but it is fragmentary and expressed in confusing terminology. The remaining issues all relate to the Act's intention to set new standards for the quality of services to children and families. This aspect of the legislation is reflected in the principles which underlie and recur throughout the Act.

The absence of agreed guidelines for good practice has led to much confusion and anxiety (Wolkind 1993). This chapter offers an interpretation of how the law applies to in-patient child mental health services. It cannot be definitive but aims to provide a starting point for further debate and clarification.

CONSENT

The Law

The legal framework for children's consent to treatment derives from the Children Act (DoH 1989), Mental Health Act 1983 (DoH 1993), Family Reform Act (1969) and case law.

The Department of Health's Mental Health Act 1983: Code of Practice (1993) gives the following definition of consent (15.2)

> 'Consent' is the voluntary and continuing permission of the patient to receive a particular treatment, based on an adequate knowledge of the purpose, nature, likely effects and risks of that treatment including the likelihood of its success and any alternatives to it. Permission given under any unfair undue pressure is not 'consent'.

A competent adult can only be treated if he gives his consent (see 'Competence' below). The patient's best interests can never be grounds for imposing treatment on a competent adult. He is entitled to refuse treatment without giving a reason or for reasons which are irrational (Sidaway 1985).

The Family Reform Act (1969) lowered the age of majority to 18 years and gave 16 and 17-year-olds the same right of consent as adults; s8(1) says:

> the consent of a minor who has attained the age of sixteen . . . shall be as effective as it would be if he were of full age; and where a minor has . . . given an effective consent to any treatment it shall not be necessary to obtain any consent for it from his parent or guardian.

The Children Act's approach to consent was influenced by the House of Lords ruling in Gillick (1986). The case considered whether it was lawful to prescribe contraception to a girl under the age of 16 years without her parent's consent. In his judgement Lord Scarman said:

> the parental right to determine whether or not their minor child below the age of sixteen will have medical treatment terminates if and when the child achieves a sufficient understanding and intelligence to enable him or her to understand fully what is proposed.

The ruling has been widely interpreted as giving under-16-year-olds with sufficient understanding an independent right to consent to or refuse treatment (however see Re R and Re W below).

The Children Act explicitly gives competent under-16-year-olds the right to refuse assessment and treatment in specific circumstances. There are five provisions in the Act where 'if the child is of sufficient understanding to make an informed decision he may refuse to submit to a medical or psychiatric examination or other assessment' (s38 (6), s43 (8), s44 (7), and paragraphs 4 (4) (a) and 5 (5) (a) of Schedule 3) and one provision where the child can refuse medical or psychiatric treatment (5 (5) (a) of Schedule 3). However, the Children Act does not address children's competence and consent to treatment outside of the very limited circumstances of care proceedings.

By contrast, Scottish law gives statutory expression to the Gillick ruling; in the Age of Legal Capacity (Scotland) Act 1991, Section 2(40) states:

> A person under the age of 16 years shall have legal capacity to consent on his own behalf to any surgical, medical or dental procedure or treatment where,

in the opinion of a qualified medical practitioner attending him, he is capable of understanding the nature and possible consequences of the procedure or treatment.

The Children Act and accompanying Guidance and Regulations place considerable emphasis on taking account of the child's views. For example 'the ascertainable wishes of the child concerned (considered in the light of his age and understanding)' is one of the factors the court is required to consider in the so called 'checklist' (s1 (3) in regard to s8 and Part IV orders). But the central premise of the Children Act is 'the child's welfare shall be the court's paramount consideration' (s1 (1)). Unlike the competent adult, the competent child's views may be overruled in pursuit of his welfare.

The Act has no provision to protect children whose refusal of treatment has been overruled (compared to the Children Act on Restriction of Liberty, or the Mental Health Act 1983).

Two recent rulings by the Court of Appeal (Re R and Re W) have reinterpreted the Gillick ruling, significantly curtailing a young person's ability to refuse treatment. R was a 15-year-old-girl refusing anti-psychotic medication; Lord Donaldson argued that in the Gillick ruling:

> Lord Scarman was discussing the parent's right to determine whether or not their minor child below the age of 16 will have medical treatment . . . a right of determination is wider than a right of consent . . . I do not understand Lord Scarman to be saying that, if a child was 'Gillick competent' . . . the parents ceased to have a right of consent as contrasted with ceasing to have a right of determination, i.e. a veto. In a case in which the 'Gillick competent' child refuses treatment, but the parents consent, that consent enables treatment to be undertaken lawfully.

Lord Donaldson took a similar view in the case of W, a 16-year-old anorexic refusing transfer to another treatment centre.

Lord Donaldson's rulings are seen by some as idiosyncratic interpretations of both the Family Reform Act 1969 and the Gillick decision (Devereux, Jones and Dickenson 1993; Freeman 1993; and Rylance 1996). But as the law stands, a doctor needs the consent of either the competent child or the child's parents, and a parent's consent will override the refusal of a competent child.

There are other situations where the competent child can be overruled. When a child is in care, the local authority has parental responsibility and can give consent (parents retain responsibility and it is good practice to consult them). Children who are wards can only receive treatment with the leave of the court (Re G-U), and the court can use its inherent jurisdiction to overrule a competent child (Re W) or parent (Re C).

Competence

The concept of competence is central to the law's approach to consent. The Gillick decision defines competence as the ability to understand information about the proposed treatment (Kennedy and Grubb 1994). This includes the treatment's purpose, nature, likely effects and risks, chances of success and any alternatives. The patient may weigh the information differently from the doctor; unwise choices are permitted. The ability to understand is not the same as actual understanding. Nor does understanding imply that a decision is made on a rational basis (we don't choose who we fall in love with on a rational basis).

But, understanding can only be inferred and not observed directly. It is influenced by the quality of information given, and it is difficult to define a level of understanding which is adequate.

In practice, the nature of the proposed treatment affects the level of understanding required (Nicholls 1993). When treatment is simple, effective and free of risk, a high level criterion will be selected and a patient who refuses is more likely to be deemed incompetent. When it is dangerous and the benefits speculative, a lower criterion is selected to protect the patient's autonomy.

Pearce (1994) argues:

> The consequences of withholding consent to treatment are usually much more significant and potentially dangerous than simply giving consent. . . . A more stringent test should therefore be applied when assessing a child's ability to refuse consent than when assessing competence to consent. [He goes on to talk about a striking a delicate balance] . . . there is a danger of using 'in the best interests of the child' as an excuse for poor communication and for failing to take the necessary time to explain the proposed treatment properly. At the same time there is also a risk of placing an unacceptably high level of responsibility on the child which can release parents from their own duty of care.

Competence is an attractive concept but very difficult to apply in ordinary clinical practice. Roth, Meisel and Lidz (1977) are slightly cynical:

> The search for a single test of competency is a search for a Holy Grail. . . . In practice, judgements of competency go beyond semantics or straightforward applications of legal rules; such judgements reflect social considerations and societal biases as much as they reflect matters of law and medicine.

Alderson (1993) is almost alone in having actually talked to children, parents and clinicians about young people's ability to contribute to treatment decisions. She interviewed 120 young people (8–15 years old) undergoing elective orthopaedic surgery, their parents, and 70 health professionals. Surgery was being undertaken for relief of chronic pain, disability or deformity; on average the young people had already had five operations. The young people were asked 'How old do you think you were or will be when you're old enough to decide?' (about surgery). Their parents were asked 'At what age do you think your child can make a wise choice?' The two groups gave a very similar mean age, (14.0 years for the young people and 13.9 for the parents). Girls and their parents thought they would be ready to decide two years earlier than boys and their parents (girls 13.1, their parents 12.8; boys 15.0, their parents 14.9).

In response to a different question: 'Children vary greatly, but what is around the youngest age you think some of your patients could be trusted to make sensible, wise, mature decisions about proposed surgery?' health professionals gave a mean age of 10.3 years.

Alderson asked (questionnaire) 983 school pupils (8–15 years) 'At what age do you think someone is old enough to decide with their doctor about surgery, without their parents being involved?' They gave a mean age (15–17 years) which was higher than the orthopaedic group.

Few children in the orthopaedic group wanted to be 'the main decider' (21 out of 120), and the parents had more confidence in the children's competence than the children had. Asked what they might do if they disagreed with their parents over the decision on surgery, boys were twice as likely as girls to try to get their own way (22 per cent *v.* 11 per cent).

Practice

Young people are not involved in decisions about their treatment as often they should be. Rylance, Bowen and Rylance (1995) looked at consent in a recent immunisation campaign for school-aged children. A questionnaire was distributed to 851 school pupils (11–15 years old) within 21 days of the campaign. 513 (60 per cent) were completed and returned. While 85 per cent of children felt they had sufficient understanding to make a decision, less than 1 per cent considered the information leaflet to be directed at children, and only 7 per cent were asked if they consented. Most did not believe that attending the immunisation session implied consent (65 per cent), or that health professionals should assume that they consented (58 per cent).

There are many reasons for informing children and gaining their co-operation over and above obtaining valid consent. Alderson (1993) cites: out of respect for the child; to answer questions and help the child know what to expect; reduce anxiety; help the child make sense of their experience; warn about risks; prevent misunderstanding or resentment; promote confidence and courage; and increase compliance.

Gaining the trust, co-operation and consent of young people with severe emotional and behavioural problems poses particular challenges. Some will have been subject to extreme forms of coercion and abuse. Sometimes they will (be unconsciously driven to) re-enact their abuse within the therapeutic relationship. Great sensitivity and skill is required to avoid the treatment becoming coercive. For example:

A 12-year-old girl with a history of sexual abuse was dragged to treatment sessions kicking and screaming until staff realised they were abusing her.

> Recognising the mistake gave staff a deeper understanding of the girl's trauma and helped her take more responsibility for her treatment.

Similarly Conduct Disorder can be understood as a coercive cycle between parent and child (Patterson 1982). Such children may try to pick a fight and become triumphant if they believe staff have been thwarted or provoked.

Some disorders are linked to very powerful internal conflicts: for instance in patients with anorexia nervosa the desire to eat becomes linked with a terrible fear of excess. Working with such children, this internal conflict easily becomes externalised with the parents (and therapist) wanting the child to eat and the child resisting. If this polarisation is allowed to go too far there is a danger of the child completely disowning their desire to eat (and live). For example:

> An 11-year-old girl was encouraged to put on weight by earning various privileges. Instead she retreated into her room and gave up the activities she normally enjoyed without protest. Eventually she talked about her own death without any sense of fear or doubt.

In each of these examples, gaining the child's consent is a therapeutic break-through in itself. Failing to gain it makes treatment less effective and may even cause harm. It is often a case of giving children realistic choices: for example, if they don't want to attend their therapy session the child will not be forced, but they are not free to play on the computer. Instead staff talk to them about why they are reluctant to attend their session.

In any long term treatment the patient's motivation is critical to success. Alderson (1993) gives the example of a surgeon advising a 14-year-old girl who was borderline for surgery to consider the options and write to him. Asked about this the surgeon said:

> Unless they're very keen they're unlikely to carry through to completion. ... There are absolute indications, or almost, but there are grey areas, and then it is an awful lot what the patient wants. The treatment sometimes produces problems of its own. There's a lot of choice and weighing up the pros and cons. Yes, children are allowed to refuse.

The child will sometimes refuse treatment despite the most sensitive and skilled approach of staff and parents. Pearce (1994) suggests:

> Every effort should be made to reach a consensus, however protracted this process may be – so long as this does not involve taking unacceptable risks with the child's future health. ... It is usually better to delay treatment until attitudes and relationships have changed – which could just as easily be the professional's attitude as the patient's.

The British Medical Association (1993) have suggested that another health professional be asked to act as an independent arbiter and attempt to negotiate an agreement.

I believe no child (competent or otherwise) should be treated against their will unless they are more likely than not to suffer significant harm without treatment. Even when overruling a child's refusal it is possible to give limited choices. For example:

> A girl suffering from anorexia nervosa has not eaten for days and is now refusing to drink. She is told she will be dead in a few days if this continues and that we will not stand by and let this happen. A minimum daily fluid and electrolyte intake is explained and she is told that her autonomy will be respected while she ensures that she is at no immediate risk of dying. We also stress our belief that her refusal to eat is linked to worries which we are ready to help her with. Her fluid balance and electrolyte are monitored. She will be held and rehydrated by nasogastric tube if her renal function starts to deteriorate.

The Mental Health Act 1983 may be used to treat people of any age. With its requirement for a second opinion, time limited application and opportunity for independent review, it goes further than the Children Act to protect the rights of children treated against their wishes. However there is still a very strong stigma attached to being detained under the Mental Health Act (see Williams and White (1996) for a discussion of options).

GUIDELINES FOR GOOD PRACTICE ON CONSENT

1. Parents and children (whether or not they are competent) should be informed and involved as much as possible in treatment decisions.
2. Treatment can proceed with the parent's consent and the incompetent child's agreement, or the competent child's consent.
3. If either the parent or child refuses, treatment should be delayed for more discussion, modification of the treatment plan or the help of an independent arbiter.
4. It will sometimes be appropriate to proceed with the consent of one parent in the face of opposition from another (see partnership with parents below).
5. On very rare occasions the court might be asked to overrule a parent's refusal (for example if there are grounds for a Care Order).
6. Overruling the refusal of any child (competent or not) should only be considered if:
   (a) discussion and modification of the treatment has been exhausted
   (b) (and) the parents are in favour
   (c) (and) the child is more likely than not to suffer significant harm without treatment.
7. Before treating a child against their will:
   (a) the decision should be confirmed by a second opinion
   (b) (and) a time limit set for reviewing the decision
   (c) (and) the reasons for the decision should be recorded in the notes.

8. Parents or children can withdraw consent at any time.
9. Staff must be aware of the unit's policy on consent.
10. Staff will need training and ongoing support to achieve an appropriate balance between autonomy and protection.

See Alderson and Montgomery (1996) for an alternative approach to good practice.

RESTRICTION OF LIBERTY

The interpretation of the term 'restriction of liberty' is ultimately a matter to be determined by the court. However, the Department of Health guidelines (DoH 1991), para 8.10, view restriction of liberty as: 'any practice or measure which prevents a child from leaving a room or building of his own free will'.

This definition clearly includes physical restraint or locking a child in a room. It could also include standing in the doorway to stop a child who is trying to leave. The term does not apply if for example a child is asked to go to their room and remains there willingly.

Restricting a child's liberty (even for the briefest period) is only permissible if the criteria for 'secure accommodation' are satisfied (s25 (1)). These are:

(a) that:
   (i) he has a history of absconding and is likely to abscond from any other description of accommodation; and
   (ii) if he absconds he is likely to suffer significant harm; or

(b) that if he is kept in any other description of accommodation he is likely to injure himself or others.

While the Act makes no mention of damage to property, the Guidance on Permissible Forms of Control in Children's Residential Care (1993) cites 'immediate action is necessary to prevent injury to any person, or damage to property'.

The use of the term 'secure accommodation' is rather confusing because it refers to any situation where a child's liberty is restricted. In the language of the Act a child could be seen as being in secure accommodation when she is held in one's arms to prevent her from hurting herself. (See Williams and White (1996) for a discussion of secure accommodation for young offenders.)

The definition allows one to act pre-emptively to prevent a child from becoming violent or running away.

A child's liberty can be restricted for no more than seventy-two hours (consecutive or otherwise) in any consecutive twenty-eight days without the authority of the Court (Regulation 10(1)). The consultant (or manager) can ask the court to authorise more prolonged restriction of liberty (DoH 1991, para 8.16). The child is entitled to legal representation and a Guardian Ad Litem (S25 (6)).

In the case of children detained under the Mental Health Act 1983 or section 53 of the Children and Young Persons Act 1933, lawful authority for the restriction of liberty already exists and the criteria described above (s25 (1)) do not apply.

It is the intention of the Act to restrict children's liberty only when there is no other way to prevent injury or other 'significant harm' (s31). If restriction must be used, it should be for the minimum time and employ the least force necessary.

While we may be inclined to see keeping children safe as an integral part of the therapeutic process, the Act forces us to make a clear distinction. Restriction of liberty cannot be used as a treatment and must be clearly distinguished from behavioural therapies such as 'time-out from positive reinforcement'. Like all treatments 'time-out' requires the consent of the child or an appropriate parental authority.

The Mental Health Act 1983 Code of Practice (1993) helps to make a similar distinction, recommending that 'time-out' should:

- last no more than 15 minutes
- never include the use of a locked room
- not use the same room as is used for seclusion.

The government's guidance on the restriction of liberty in hospitals is fragmented, incomplete and the language difficult to follow (DoH (1991), chapters 1 and 8, and DoH (1993)). The following is a suggested way forward based on the detail that is available and interpretation of the spirit of the Act.

GUIDELINES FOR GOOD PRACTICE ON RESTRICTION OF LIBERTY

1. Managers should ensure that all staff understand the definition of restriction of liberty, the circumstances in which it can be used, and the distinction from 'time-out'.
2. Staff should be trained and present in adequate numbers to ensure that children's liberty is restricted with the minimum force and risk of injury.
3. If a locked room is to be used it should be designed to minimise the risk of injury and the child must be continually monitored.
4. Recourse to a locked room is normally a last resort, although some children with a history of abuse become very disturbed if forcibly held, and may calm down more quickly in a room on their own.
5. Restriction should be brought to an end as soon as it is safely possible. There should be a policy of informing (and ultimately requiring the presence of) senior members of the clinical team if restrictions need to continue for more than a relatively short period.
6. All restrictions of liberty must be recorded in the notes; the indications for

its use, the type of restriction, its duration and who authorised it should be included. The running total of hours restriction must be monitored and appropriate action taken well before the 72 hours in 28 days threshold.

7. Children and parents should be informed at the time of admission of the implications of the Children Act for the restriction of liberty and the in-patient unit's own policy for implementing the Act.

8. Parents should be informed as soon as possible when their child's liberty has been restricted.

The locking of external doors and windows at night in line with normal domestic security does not constitute a restriction of liberty (DoH 1991 (1.91 vi)). However, an in-patient unit located, for example, near a busy road or an operating theatre may wish to keep the doors locked at other times for security. As things stand at the moment this is not permitted. This is unsatisfactory and ought to be changed.

The Act prohibits local authorities from using certain punishments in Children's Homes (DoH 1991 (1.91)). In-patient units are not governed by these restrictions but it seems sensible to follow them anyway.

The guidelines recognise that some form of sanction may be necessary in response to behaviours 'which would in any family or group environment reasonably be regarded as unacceptable' (DoH 1991 (1.90)). Sanctions should be contemporaneous, relevant and just and could include reparation, restitution, curtailment of leisure extras or domestic chores.

PARTNERSHIP WITH PARENTS

Acknowledging the crucial role that parents play is established good practice. By the time children are referred to an in-patient unit parents often feel let down, beyond help or ashamed. Building a working partnership may be crucial to parents recovering their sense of purpose and self-respect.

The Act stresses the importance of involving parents in planning and the decision-making process. There is an emphasis on identifying clear goals, having written agreements and regular reviews. When children are accommodated away from home (including in hospital), the Act presumes there will be regular contact with parents. Arrangements for contact should be agreed with the parents and child but there are no specific rules about the frequency of the contact.

While everyone with parental responsibility should be involved in decision-making, disagreement between parents will not prevent decisions being made. The Act says that 'where more than one person has parental responsibility for a child, each of them may act alone' (s2 (7)). Where those sharing responsibility disagree on an issue, the legislation places the onus on the person objecting to a course of action to seek a court order preventing it (Bainham 1990).

The Act calls for a system for handling complaints about the quality of service that includes an 'independent person'. This person should be from outside the organisation under consideration and able to give an impartial view.

GUIDELINES FOR GOOD PRACTICE ON PARTNERSHIP WITH PARENTS

1. Parents need a clear explanation of what admission can offer and what will be expected of the child and family. A written description of the service will be helpful and it will usually be necessary to meet the family more than once prior to admission.
2. It is essential that parents help set the goals of admission.
3. The goals of admission should be as explicit as possible and recorded in the notes with a copy for the child and family.
4. There should be a clear understanding between the parents and the unit about the frequency of parent–child contact.
5. During the course of admission the parents should meet regularly with senior members of the team to review progress with the goals of admission and treatment programme.
6. Where possible reports on the case should be made available to the parents and written in a comprehensible style. Parents should only be denied access with good reason.
7. The parents should be actively involved in decisions about the length of stay and arrangements after discharge.
8. Parents can benefit from meeting regularly with other parents with children at the unit. Such meetings can identify concerns of importance to all families attending the unit as well as providing mutual support.
9. Consideration might be given to involving parents in some aspects of the unit's policy making.
10. The partnership with the parents must be balanced with protecting the confidential aspect of the work with the child.
11. The Act affirms parents' continuing parental responsibility (and their involvement in decision making) even when they are no longer living with the child.
12. When parents disagree with each other the onus is on the parent wishing to block a course of action to take legal steps.
13. The service must be sensitive to the cultural and religious background of the family and aware of racism.
14. Complaint procedures should include an 'independent person'.
15. Working in partnership with parents who are angry, mistrustful of authority, or persecuted by guilt, requires considerable skill and determination.
16. However, this must be balanced by an ability to recognise when partnership with parents has reached an impasse and social services and the court should be involved.

WORKING WITH OTHER AGENCIES

The Children Act (1989, s85 (1)) states that when children are accommodated in hospital 'for a consecutive period of at least three months' the local authority in which the child normally lives should be informed. That local authority is then required to take steps to safeguard and promote the child's welfare during the admission. Most children admitted to in-patient units go home at the weekends (or to some alternative accommodation), so the letter of the law will seldom apply. However, there is no doubt that close co-operation between health, social services and all other agencies is emphasised throughout the Act (see s27 and Schedule 2).

Social services are specifically required to promote contact between a child living away from their home and their parents (Schedule 2 (10)). This includes some provision for local authorities to pay for transport to enable visits (s17 (6)).

GUIDELINES FOR GOOD PRACTICE ON WORKING WITH OTHER AGENCIES

1. Prior to admission, the unit should meet jointly with all the other agencies involved in the case.
2. The professional network and family should agree the role that each agency will play during the admission.
3. It is often necessary for the in-patient unit to co-operate with another agency on a particular task, for example assessment for a statement of special educational need where an agreed timetable is very important.
4. The unit should look for opportunities to collaborate with other agencies who are already working with the family. For example, another agency's therapeutic work with the family prior to admission might continue in collaboration with one or more members of the in-patient team. This approach provides continuity for the family and extends the resources available to the in-patient unit. Continuing collaborative work for a while after discharge helps to ensure gains during admission are maintained.
5. Involved agencies should attend meetings where major management decisions are taken and have access to some reports.
6. The need to work in partnership with the professional network should be tempered by the rules of confidentiality and the family's sensitivities about contact with particular agencies.
7. Social services have an obligation to help if there are financial barriers to maintaining contact between a child in hospital and their parents.
8. Partnership with other agencies needs to be focused around specific issues and not for its own sake. All agencies are far too stretched to attend meetings where they have no particular role to play.

REFERENCES

Age of Legal Capacity (Scotland Act (1991). London: HMSO.

Alderson, P. (1993) *Children's Consent to Surgery.* Buckingham: Open University Press.

Alderson, P. and Montgomery, J. (1996) *Health Care Choices: Making Decisions with Children.* London: Institute of Public Policy Research.

Bainham, A. (1990) *Children – The New Law.* Bristol: Family Law.

British Medical Association (1993) *Medical Ethics Today: Its Practice and Philosophy.* London: BMA.

Children and Young Persons Act (1933). London: HMSO.

The Children Act (1989). London: HMSO.

Department of Health (1991) *The Children Act 1989 Guidance and Regulations,* Volume 4, *Residential Care.* London: HMSO.

Department of Health (1993) *Guidance on Permissible Forms of Control in Children's Residential Care.* London: HMSO.

Department of Health and Welsh Office (1993) *Code of Practice Mental Health Act 1983.* London: HMSO.

Devereux, J.A., Jones, D.P.H. and Dickenson, D.L. (1993) Can children withhold consent to treatment? *British Medical Journal,* 306, 1459–1461.

Family Reform Act (1969) London: HMSO.

Freeman, M. (1993) Removing rights from adolescents. *Adoption and Fostering,* 17, 14–21.

Gillick *v.* West Norfolk and Wisbech Area Health Authority (1986) AC 112.

Kennedy, I. and Grubb, A. (1994) *Medical Law,* 2nd edition. London: Butterworths.

Nicholls, M. (1993) Consent to medical treatment. *Family Law,* 23, 30–33.

Patterson, G. (1982) *Coercive Family Process.* Eugene, OR: Castalia Publishing Co.

Pearce, J. (1994) Consent to treatment during childhood: the assessment of competence and avoidance of conflict. *British Journal of Psychiatry,* 165, 713–716.

Re C (A Minor) (Wardship: Medical Treatment) [1990] Fam 26, [1989] 2 All ER 782, CA.

Re G-U (A Minor) (Wardship) [1984] FLR 811.

Re R (A Minor) (Wardship: Medical Treatment) [1992] Fam 11, [1991] 4 All ER 177, CA.

Re W (A Minor) (Wardship: Medical Treatment) [1993] Fam 64, [1992] 4 All ER 627, CA.

Roth, L.H., Meisel, A. and Lidz, C.W. (1977). Tests of competence to consent to treatment. *American Journal of Psychiatry,* 134, 279–284.

Rylance, G., Bowen, C. and Rylance, J. (1995) Measles and rubella immunisation: information and consent in children. *British Medical Journal,* 311, 923–924.

Rylance, G. (1996) Making decisions with children: a child's right to share in decisions can no longer be ignored. *British Medical Journal,* 312, 794.

Sidaway *v.* Board of Governors of the Bethlem Royal Hospital and the Maudsley Hospital (1985) AC 871.

White, R. (1995) Young people, mental health and the law. In R. Williams and G. Richardson (eds) *Child and Adolescent Health Services: Together We Stand.* London: HMSO.

Williams, R. and White, R. (eds) (1996) *Safeguards for Young Minds.* London: Gaskell.

Wolkind, S. (1993) 'The 1989 Children Act: a cynical view from an ivory tower' (letter). *Association of Child Phychology and Psychiatry Review and Newsletter*, 15 (1), 40–41.

30 Economic evaluation and child psychiatric in-patient services

Jennifer Beecham

BACKGROUND

Central to the development of services for children with mental health problems must be an understanding of the effects of service interventions and their associated resource implications. This is particularly important when considering apparently high cost services such as in-patient psychiatric care (see chapter 31). Purchasers and providers alike need to know not only what a service or intervention can achieve for users, but at what cost. The demand for such information is not solely driven by recent UK governments' commitment to public expenditure constraints and the expansion of market forces. Health care resources are insufficient to meet all wants and needs so the limited (scarce) resources must be used in the way that produces the greatest 'health gain'.

Research results can inform this process. Clinical evaluations are commonly directed at discovering whether one treatment or intervention works better than another. When an economic evaluation is built onto an existing clinical evaluation, it adds a resource or cost dimension, but economic evaluation is not confined to costs. The aim is to discover how limited resources can be used to their best effect by comparing options in terms of both their costs and effectiveness. To facilitate a better understanding of what an economic evaluation might involve, the next section considers the estimation of costs and is followed by a description of the ways these data can be combined with outcomes information.

COSTS ...

The cost of using a particular service or mode of care is not the money spent but should be measured as the value of the benefit forgone (or opportunity lost) by not employing the resources in their best alternative use. Because the current markets in health care are not fully competitive (Donaldson and Gerard, 1993), it is unusual for estimations of the 'best alternative use' and the price to the purchaser to arrive at the same figure. Consequently, for the purposes of an economic evaluation, costs must often be calculated from first principles. The aim is to base the cost measures on the *marginal opportunity cost* of resources, where marginal costs reflect the total cost of including one more client. However, since there are insufficient services for children and young people with mental health problems (Light and Bailey, 1993; Kurtz, Thornes and Wolkind, 1995), *short-run* marginal costs are inappropriate; the costs of setting up new services to expand the overall level of service provision should be included. The convention is to use short-run average (revenue) costs plus the costs of capital (buildings and equipment) and overheads (Knapp, 1993).

Costing in-patient care

In-patient hospital care is expensive and therefore not only commands particular attention from purchasers but should also receive detailed attention from researchers. The most easily available information is the average cost per in-patient day in any given hospital. This *top-down* approach, however, may miss cost variations within the hospital and thus provide a less accurate indication of the resources used in the unit under study. For example, the costs of a long-stay hospital ward for adults are 80 per cent of those of an acute ward and only a third of the costs of a psychiatric intensive care unit (Netten and Dennett, 1996).

Most hospitals in the UK devolve their budget, or certain elements of it, to clinical directorates, so financial responsibility lies closer to the point of expenditure (Woodgates, 1995). This financial process makes the more accurate *bottom-up* costing approach easier – although commercial confidentiality may make access to the data difficult to negotiate. Commonly, wards are considered cost-centres for nursing staff and other direct treatment services (pharmacy, pathology, radiology, for example). Cost centre expenditure statements provide a useful starting point for costing in-patient care but require adjustment in the light of other staff and patient activity data. First, the cost implications of staff attached to that ward who provide support to other parts of the hospital service must be removed and additions made for time inputs from staff (such as clinicians or therapists) not included on the cost centre budget. Second, non-treatment costs must be added. Cost components such as catering, laundry, domestic staff and porters, power and the finance department are often allocated to each cost centre as tariffs or internal recharges, but may require verification of their accuracy. Third, an addition should also be made for the capital cost implications of using the service. This should be calculated as a stream of payments stemming over time from the value of the equipment, buildings and site used by the unit under study (Beecham, 1995).

The final adjustment to the cost centre accounts is to include the costs accruing to other agencies. In the care and treatment of children the main item will be the provision of hospital-based education. The school is likely to provide teaching for pupils resident on a number of wards so costs should be allocated carefully.

The summation of these costs data will provide an estimate of the long-run marginal opportunity cost of providing hospital in-patient care. The unit cost of the service – say per in-patient day – should then be adjusted in the light of the duration of each child's residence: Jaffa (1995) suggests the length of stay for adolescents is commonly one to six months, but can be up to two years. For some studies, more detail will be required on the *intensity* with which the in-patient service is used. Differences might be apparent between children in their medication, the number of tests or investigations undertaken, or in the level of contact with staff and therapists. This disaggregation of ward-level activities to individual patients is complex but will pick up variations in the costs of care *within* the ward.

Comprehensive costs

There are two reasons why the cost calculations should be broader than just those accruing to the hospital. First, in a study that compares in-patient care with another treatment delivery mode, it is important that the scope of the costs measures are similar in each model. For in-patient care, the costs will be all inclusive; therapy, shelter, care, food, heat, etc. are all provided within the hospital. To avoid complex exercises to isolate only, say, the treatment costs (which anyway will distort the costs picture) a similarly comprehensive approach should be adopted for the comparison services. This will ensure that the many 'hidden' cost dimensions are included for those children who are not treated as in-patients. In any randomised control trial of in-patient treatment compared to intensive out-patient treatment such a strict comparison of costs would be necessary (see chapter 28). Hidden costs are likely to accrue through the use of education, social care and other health care services over the treatment period, and to future budgets if childhood problems are untreated.

For an out-patient or day patient service, a method similar to that described above can be applied to estimate the costs of the treatment model, but incorporating data on the intensity of service use will be particularly important. For example, family or group therapy is often undertaken in out-patient sessions, so recording who provides the therapy and how many people attend allows appropriate allocation of costs. In a day treatment unit, many different activities occur within the same centre and the attenders will use component parts of the service in a way that reflects their individual treatment plan (Grizenko, Papineau and Sayegh, 1993). Careful disaggregation of staff activities and the centre's budget will allow a unit cost for each service component to be calculated and allocated to each child according to the duration and intensity with which they use each component.

Green (1994) notes that in-patient treatment allows the child access to specific and individual therapy while simultaneously allowing the rest of the family 'to be seen and heard' (p. 745). Is it not sensible, then, that the financial costs to the family members should be included when exploring the cost and other implications of treatment options?

Costs borne by the family will include the time taken in receiving treatment as well as out-of-pocket expenses (perhaps for travel to the treatment unit or because of changes in work patterns). Moreover, considerable time may be absorbed in providing support (incurring costs) for children and, as with spouse-carers, it is not easy to separate the costs that are the result of usual caring activities and those which are a consequence of the child's mental health problem. The level of input from family members is likely to be different under the various treatment models (for example, children receiving in-patient treatment will not live at home full-time) and, as Seigert and Yates (1980) show, can have a considerable impact when comparing the costs of interventions. Valuing the costs to the family is not easy. In estimating an adequate recompense for informal care from foster carers, Kind (1992) looks at payments to residential social workers and childminders. Other methodological approaches are discussed in Netten (1993) and Smith and Wright (1994). These costs can mount very quickly for families and are often not brought to the attention of clinicians.

There will also be costs to other service providers. The belief that 'day treatment programmes cost less than hospitalisation' (Sayegh and Grizenko, 1991, p. 246) is almost certain to be substantiated if only the costs to the psychiatric hospital are included. However, the criminal justice service, health and education sectors, and social services departments all have statutory duties and powers with respect to young people, with the result that children may use a range of other support services, often with differing intensities. On the one hand, an intensive day programme, plus foster care, plus attendance at a special education establishment may raise the public sector costs above the cost of in-patient care. Indeed, costs to the wider society may also increase owing to the impact of not containing the child, such as vandalism to other people's property (Mirrlees-Black and Ross, 1995). On the other hand, Finney, Riley and Cataldo (1991) found providing psychological therapy within the primary care sector for children with common behaviour, toileting, school and psychosomatic problems reduced the use of other medical care services.

Case-notes are often service-specific. Rarely is sufficiently detailed information recorded on frequency and duration of services received from outside the one directly responsible for the current treatment. For such a data collection exercise, a modified version of the *Client Service Receipt Inventory* can be used to record descriptive data on study members' full support packages in such a way that allows comprehensive costs to be calculated (Beecham and Knapp, 1990). The schedule can be used at each time point for which outcomes data are collected, including discharge plans or receipt of services post-discharge. In a review of in-patient treatment, Hersov notes that 'the goal of reuniting the child with his or her family without the need for further treatment is reached in only a few cases. . . . The majority still require further special help in other hospital units or residential or day-schools for maladjusted children' (1994, p. 992; and see also Grizenko and Papineau, 1992).

There is a second reason for taking a comprehensive approach to costs. Many childhood mental health problems not only impact on current service provision, but will also affect the future service configuration. As the children grow older their symptoms may persist or deteriorate and they may require greater levels of support. For example, psychiatric problems in childhood can lead to behaviour which may become too difficult for parents to contain, resulting in the children being looked after by the local authority. Police or probation workers might intervene as the young people become involved in crime. Greater health and social care service use is likely to be found for the young people themselves, their parents and their future children. There is also the impact of missed school and unemployment on the young people themselves and on wider society (in terms of lost production, increased dependence on social security benefits) or the costs of violence to other people or property. Modelling the costs of the natural course of childhood psychiatric illnesses, therefore, will aid any evaluation of the short- or longer-term economic impact of interventions.

Thus, unless this comprehensive approach to costing is taken, any cost differences found in an evaluation may be due to (unmeasured) shifts in costs burden rather than a reduction in cost. These costs shifts may occur contemporaneously, as the full scope of costs goes unmeasured, or in the future, as the effects of children's mental health problems continue into adulthood or subsequent generations.

Cost variations

As the methodology outlined above illustrates, costs will vary in relation to differences in service provision; higher staff ratios or employing more qualified staff, for example, will mean higher unit costs. A simple comparison of the costs of treatment options will show which is the less expensive service. However, unless it can be shown that the outcome produced by each service is similar, such studies only serve to tell us how much money is spent, not which option is the most cost-effective way of using the resources.

Costs are also likely to be sensitive to a number of factors which are not directly related to the resource inputs. Exploration of these relationships is central to economic evaluation. Costs are, for example, sensitive to a number of service *outputs*. One study of child and adolescent psychiatry provider units showed that higher provider costs (other things being equal) were associated with the presence of in-patient beds, location in London, making inputs to the drug and alcohol service, the number of children referred for self-harm, and the size of the case load (Beecham, Knapp and Asbury, 1996). These are *health care* indicators (Jenkins, 1990) or *intermediate outcomes* (Knapp, 1995) and some can be used as proxy measures of client needs. It is likely, for example, that an in-patient service treats children who, for a number of reasons, require a higher level of support. However, closer examination of service costs and the needs and characteristics of the children served is required to tell us whether this assumption is justified. Detailed information on the frequency and duration of each child's service receipt allows the differences in individual 'care package' costs to be recognised – just as individual measures of symptoms or behaviour allow the differences in health of the children to be retained in the analysis. The examination of associations between these disaggregated cost and need measures can help more accurate predictions of the likely service and cost implications of childhood mental health problems. Indications of the importance of these types of analyses can be found in previous research. Length of stay in an in-patient unit, for example, has been found to be associated with diagnosis (a summary measure of symptoms and behaviour), medication, severity of psychopathology, stressors, and severe tantrums (Borchardt and Garfinkel, 1991; Gold, Shera and Clarkson, 1993).

... AND OUTCOMES

Bringing together cost and outcome data should be central to any economic evaluation in order to explore the level of outcome produced for a given level of expenditure. A number of outcome dimensions can be identified; 'childhood disorders can affect progress in school, social relationships, family relationships, self-help skills, and ability to live independently' (Beitchman, Inglis and Schacter, 1992, p. 231). Treatment is provided with the intention of ameliorating the symptoms of the disorder or the related functional impairments. It is this *change* in the health and welfare of the child which provides measures of final outcome; such changes may prompt discharge from treatment, may continue after discharge, or may not occur until some months or years after the intervention. Outcome and its measurement is considered in more detail in chapter 27.

Economics has developed three main forms of analysis to combine costs and outcome data: cost–benefit analysis, cost–utility analysis and cost–effectiveness analysis (although these terms are not always used consistently by researchers from other disciplines). While the methodology for costs measurement is relatively consistent, the difference between these analytic modes lies in the way they tackle outcome measurement.

A cost–benefit study addresses the extent to which a particular treatment option is socially worthwhile and attempts to value costs and outcomes in the same unit, commonly money, so that a direct comparison of costs and benefits can be made. A direct comparison of costs incurred (say, a new treatment mode) with costs saved is actually a cost–offset analysis. A true cost–benefit analysis must face the problems of outcome valuation, attempting to estimate a monetary value for, say, an improvement in academic performance or social skills. New techniques, such as exploring people's willingness to pay for health care benefits, may aid the use of this form of economic evaluation in the future.

Cost–utility analysis has attracted considerable interest in recent years and has the potential to inform macro-level resource allocation. A cost–utility analysis aims to measure and compare the effectiveness of interventions by assessing and ranking patients' preferences for different health states. Quality Adjusted Life Years (QALYs) are the best known of these measures. The scores can be set against the cost of consuming health care resources to achieve a particular health state. Although cost–utility analysis is still subject to technical difficulties, it is becoming more common in the evaluation of acute health care. There are a few studies of adult mental health care services that use a cost–utility approach

(Wimo et al., 1994; Wilkinson et al., 1992) but none, as yet, which address issues in children's mental health care.

Cost–effectiveness analysis is the most commonly used form of economic evaluation in health and social care studies and is particularly useful where outcomes and costs cannot be valued in the same unit. By retaining outcome data in their 'natural' units of measurement, the findings are more comprehensible to a range of professionals, and a number of perspectives (clinicians, carers, the children themselves) can be incorporated.

In its traditional mode, a cost–effectiveness study uses a single outcome and compares the cost 'per unit' of outcome in each treatment option. If the outcome produced is identical under both interventions, then the intervention that costs least per 'unit' is the more cost-effective. Conversely, if the cost of the interventions is the same, then the more cost-effective option is that from which greater levels of outcome are produced. Yates (1982) described two ways of presenting these data. The first was from an evaluation of different delivery systems of a child management programme. A mean reduction in the behaviours targeted for improvement was identified as the main outcome measurement, and the resulting scores were plotted on a graph against the cost of achieving that level of improvement (p. 283). In the same paper, a matrix is reproduced in which each cell contains information on the number of study members whose functioning score changed from one category to another over the period of treatment (for example, from serious impairment to mild impairment) and the mean cost of resources employed to achieve that level of improvement (p. 285).

Using a single measure of outcome has the advantage of making clear the cost of achieving health gain under certain programmes, but may mean a number of other important outcome measures are ignored or collapsed, as discussed elsewhere in this volume. This may obscure changes that have occurred in other areas of study members' lives and thus provide a less accurate indication of relative effectiveness. For example, Richardson (1992) described the results of an examination of the costs and effectiveness of the residence and counselling programmes in one rural Children's Mental Health Centre. Outcomes were positive in both programmes but the residential option cost over eight times as much as counselling. Using the decision rule discussed above, the residence programme should have been closed in favour of the counselling programmes. However, the Board decided to keep the residence programme open, otherwise fifteen to twenty-five children each year would have been separated from their families by a considerable distance.

A second problem with using a uni-dimensional outcome measure in a cost–effectiveness analysis appears when outcome measures do not move in the same direction. For example, Klein and Slomkowski (1993) reported that medication can allow better regulation of behaviour in children with autism, but will not reverse the lack of social awareness and communication which are key features of autism (p. 531). Kiser et al. (1996) found significant improvements on a number of outcome measures following partial hospitalisation for psychiatric treatment. The study design did not allow comparison of partial hospitalisation with other treatment modes or no treatment but, between admission and one year after discharge, significant improvements were found on all subscales of the child behaviour checklist, except sex problems. Their examination of daily functioning showed the young people had improved in terms of school performance and peer relationships and more of them had found jobs. However, the data on legal status showed negative outcomes. One year after discharge, more adolescents were on probation, more had been incarcerated and more had been in trouble with the police than had been recorded at admission.

Such findings also point to the need to move beyond a simple comparison of group averages of costs and outcomes to obtain information on the relative cost-effectiveness of treatment options. It is between individuals that most variation can be found; quantifying the relationships between costs, treatment procedures, processes and outcomes may determine how to maximise treatment outcomes for a given set of resources (Yates, 1994). Cost functions are one such method of exploring these relationships. They can supplement the other modes of analysis by using a statistical method, such as multiple regression, to 'explain' cost variations by reference to observed measures of need, outcome and other characteristics (Knapp, 1984). Cost function estimations can provide a means of statistical matching when randomisation is not possible, such as in the exploration of child psychiatry provider costs (see above). The approach is also useful when the differences between individuals and/or the services are sufficiently great to warrant further examination. There are few such analyses in the field of child psychiatry research; for a summary of such work undertaken in adult psychiatric care see Knapp, 1995.

CONCLUSION

> The lack of studies of treatment outcomes [but see Part VI of this book] and routine evaluation of intervention programmes have made the services increasingly vulnerable to pressure for containing costs. This situation, if not remedied, has serious implications for therapeutic innovation, and for the development, and even the survival of services.
>
> (Parry-Jones, 1995, p. 299; see also chapter 3 of this book).

This statement has particular relevance for in-patient psychiatric treatment for children and young people as it is an expensive resource and few studies explore for whom this might be an effective – or cost-effective – treatment option (Hersov, 1994; Health Advisory Service, 1995, para 161). Such information should be seen as a highly desirable component of discussions about mental health care, yet in the current world of health and social care markets, this quotation reveals the information deficit in which purchasers must make their decisions.

Although there is a growing demand for economic and cost insights, the supply of cost information is limited. However, there are two lights on the horizon. First, there already exists a small body of research relevant to child psychiatry which incorporates a costs dimension or which considers the issues of a wider health economics agenda (Knapp, 1997). Second, and as this chapter describes, there are already in place economic frameworks, methodologies and techniques which can structure the work so that robust information to inform purchasing strategies can be produced (see also Knapp, 1984; Drummond, 1994; Kavanagh and Stewart, 1995). Given the policy context of developing evidenced-based health care, there is a wealth of work yet to do.

REFERENCES

Beecham, J. (1995) Collecting and estimating costs. In M. Knapp (ed.), *The Economic Evaluation of Mental Health Care*. Arena: Aldershot.

Beecham, J. and Knapp, M. (1990) Costing psychiatric interventions. In G. Thornicroft, C. Brewin and J. Wing (eds), *Measuring Mental Health Needs*. Gaskell: London.

Beecham, J., Knapp, M. and Asbury, M. (1996) Costs and children's mental health services. In A. Netten and J. Dennett (eds), *Unit Costs of Health and Social Care Services 1996*. Personal Social Services Research Unit: University of Kent at Canterbury.

Beitchman, J., Inglis, A. and Schachter, D. (1992) Child psychiatry and early intervention I: the aggregate burden of suffering. *Canadian Journal of Psychiatry, 37*, 230–233.

Borchardt, C. and Garfinkel, B. (1991) Predictors of length of stay of psychiatric adolescent in-patients. *Journal of the American Academy of Child and Adolescent Psychiatry, 30*, 6, 994–998.

Donaldson, C. and Gerard, K. (1993) *Economics of Health Care Financing: The Visible Hand*. Macmillan: London.

Drummond, M. (1994) *Economic Analysis Alongside Controlled Trials*. Department of Health: London.

Finney, J., Riley, A. and Cataldo, M. (1991) Psychology in primary health care: effects of brief targeted therapy on children's medical care utilisation. *Journal of Pediatric Psychology, 16, 4*, 447–461.

Gold, J., Shera, D. and Clarkson, B. (1993) Private psychiatric hospitalisation of children: predictors of length of stay. *Journal of the American Academy of Child and Adolescent Psychiatry, 32, 1*, 135–143.

Green, J. (1994) Child in-patient treatment and family relationships. *Psychiatric Bulletin, 18, 12*, 744–747.

Grizenko, N. and Papineau, D. (1992) A comparison of the cost-effectiveness of day treatment and residential treatment for children with severe behaviour problems. *Canadian Journal of Psychiatry, 37*, 393–400.

Grizenko, N., Papineau, D. and Sayegh, L. (1993) Effectiveness of a multimodal day treatment program for children with disruptive behaviour problems. *Journal of the American Academy of Child and Adolescent Psychiatry, 32, 1*, 127–134.

Health Advisory Service (1995) *Child and Adolescent Mental Health Services*. HMSO: London.

Hersov, L. (1994) In-patient and day-hospital units. In M. Rutter, E. Taylor and L. Hersov (eds), *Child and Adolescent Psychiatry: Modern Approaches*. Blackwell Scientific Publications: London.

Jaffa, T. (1995) Adolescent psychiatry services. *British Journal of Psychiatry*, *166*, 306–310.

Jenkins, R. (1990) Towards a system of outcome indicators for mental health care. *British Journal of Psychiatry*, *157*, 500–514.

Kavanagh, S. and Stewart, A. (1995) Economic evaluation in mental health care: modes and methods. In M. Knapp (ed.), *The Economic Evaluation of Mental Health Care*. Arena: Aldershot.

Kind, P. (1992) *Caring for Children: Counting the Cost*. Discussion Paper 97. Centre for Health Economics: University of York.

Kiser, L., Millsap, P., Hickerson, S., Heston, J., Nunn, W., Pruitt, D. and Rohr, M. (1996) Results of treatment one year later: child and adolescent partial hospitalisation. *Journal of the American Academy of Child and Adolescent Psychiatry*, *35*, *1*, 81–90.

Klein, R. and Slomkowski, C. (1993) Treatment of psychiatric disorders in children and adolescents. *Psychopharmacology Bulletin*, *29*, 525–535.

Knapp, M. (1984) *Economics of Social Care*. Macmillan: London.

Knapp, M. (1993) Background theory. In A. Netten and J. Beecham (eds), *Costing Community Care: Theory and Practice*. Ashgate: Aldershot.

Knapp, M. (ed.) (1995) *The Economic Evaluation of Mental Health Care*, Arena: Aldershot.

Knapp, M. (1997) Economic evaluation and interventions for children and adolescents with mental health problems. *Journal of Child Psychology and Psychiatry*, *38*, *1*, 3–25.

Kurtz, Z., Thornes, R. and Wolkind, S. (1995) *Services for the Mental Health of Children and Young People in England: An Assessment of Needs and Unmet Need*. Report to the Department of Health: London.

Light, D. and Bailey, V. (1993) Pound foolish. *Health Service Journal*, 11 February, 16–18.

Mirrlees-Black, C. and Ross, A. (1995) *Crime against Retail and Manufacturing Premises: Findings from the 1994 Commercial Victimisation Survey*. Home Office: London.

Netten, A. (1993) Costing informal care. In A. Netten and J. Beecham (eds), *Costing Community Care: Theory and Practice*. Ashgate: Aldershot.

Netten, A. and Dennett, J. (1996) *Unit Costs of Health and Social Care Services 1996*. Personal Social Services Research Unit: University of Kent at Canterbury.

Parry-Jones, W. (1995) The future of adolescent psychiatry. *British Journal of Psychiatry*, *166*, 299–305.

Richardson, W. (1992) The use of program-evaluation data in the decision-making process of a children's mental health centre: a case study. *Journal of Child and Youth Care*, *7*, *1*, 61–70.

Sayegh, L. and Grizenko, N. (1991) Studies of the effectiveness of day treatment programs for children. *Canadian Journal of Psychiatry*, *36*, 246–253.

Seigert, F. and Yates, B. (1980) Behavioural child-management cost-effectiveness: a comparison of individual in-office, individual in-home, and group delivery systems. *Evaluation and the Health Professions*, *3*, *2*, 123–152.

Smith, K. and Wright, K. (1994) Informal care and economic appraisal: a discussion of possible methodological approaches. *Health Economics*, *3*, *3*, 137–148.

Wilkinson, G., Williams, B., Krekorian, H., McLees, S. and Falloon, I. (1992) QALYs in mental health: a case study. *Psychological Medicine*, *2*, 52–59.

Wimo, A., Mattsson, B., Krakau, I., Eriksson, T. and Nelvig, A. (1994) Cost-effectiveness analysis of day care for patients with dementia disorders. *Health Economics*, *3*, 395–404.

Woodgates, P. (1995) Multiple division. *Health Service Journal*, 25 May, 28–30.

Yates, B. (1982) Therapy for human service systems: five basic steps for measuring and improving cost-effectiveness. In A. McSweeny, W. Fremouw and R. Hawkins (eds), *Practical Program Evaluation In Youth Treatment.* Charles C. Thomas: Springfield, IL.

Yates, B. (1994) Toward the incorporation of costs, cost-effectiveness analysis and cost-benefit analysis into clinical research. *Journal of Consulting and Clinical Psychology, 62,* 4, 729–736.

31 Commissioning and contracting: implications of the National Health Service reorganisation

Michael Shaw

OVERVIEW

Throughout the world, health care systems are under enormous pressure to change. In developed countries like Britain these pressures include (Smith 1997): 'reaching the limits of the welfare state, exhausting traditional methods and tools for containing costs, and experiencing increased consumer sophistication and demands'.

Over the past ten years the British National Health Service has been radically reorganised by a Conservative government. The changes aimed to improve efficiency, cost-effectiveness and accountability, and to link services more closely with the needs of the communities they serve (see Table 31.1).

Table 31.1 The Conservative government's reorganisation of the National Health Service in the early 1990s

---

The reorganisation attempted to make health care:

- more closely linked to the needs of the communities served, through:
  decentralisation of decision making
  commissioning.

- more effective, by:
  spelling out priorities
  evidence based medicine
  continually monitoring performance
  an increased role for managers

- more cost-efficient, by:
  budget holding
  costing and pricing
  monitoring activity
  tightening the link between money and activity through contracts
  introducing competition

- more accountable, by:
  the separation of purchaser and provider
  a combination of all the processes listed above

The reorganisation has offered the health service some new opportunities, but also created a great deal of anxiety and uncertainty. In their survey of all the children's psychiatric in-patients units in the United Kingdom, Green and Jacobs (see chapter 2) found that most clinicians saw the reorganisation as a 'problem rather than an opportunity'.

The newly elected Labour government seems likely to refine, rather than reverse, their predecessor's approach (Klein 1997). Their white paper (The New NHS 1997) highlights more equitable access to care, switching the emphasis from competition to co-operation, ending the internal market, and reducing bureaucracy

This chapter considers the implications of the health service reorganisation for in-patient child psychiatry. It serves as an introduction to commissioning, contracting, pricing, budget holding and managing change. It highlights where commissioning and contracting fall short of the available guidance on good practice. Finally it examines some options for the future.

COMMISSIONING

Commissioning is a strategy for developing and improving health services. It attempts to ensure that the provision accurately reflects the health care needs of the community it serves. Decisions about priorities are taken locally and based on careful research and consultation. An optimal use of resources is promoted by setting clear objectives and continually monitoring performance.

The starting point in the commissioning process is assessing a community's health care needs. The NHS Health Advisory Service (1995) suggested this should have three elements. First, epidemiological predictions (based on the characteristics of the population) of the type and extent of problems to be expected. Second, research evidence and expert opinion on the efficacy and cost-effectiveness of available treatments. Third, the views of the local community including health care providers, patients and their families.

The next step is to set priorities for developing and improving the service which reflect the community's needs, for example: 'A new fast-track assessment and treatment clinic for hyperkinetic disorder, in a community with large numbers of young children, where non-emergency referrals wait up to a year to be seen by a psychiatrist'.

The performance of the service will then be evaluated in terms of its own priorities. Finally, the priorities themselves need to be updated in response for example to demographic changes or the emergence of new treatments. This creates a circular process where performance is continually monitored and improved and priorities reviewed (see Figure 31.1).

Commissioning is the responsibility of the health purchasers but requires close co-operation between purchasers and providers, for example:

> Changes in priority alter the specifications of the service the health authority wish to purchase. Ideally, a children's in-patient unit will be

included in planning the new service. The final agreement will be reflected in their contract.

Commissioning child mental health services may require additional collaboration from social services and the education authority, for example:

Managing young sexual abusers will be the joint responsibility of social services and health, but have implications for the education authority.

Implementing the commissioning model requires considerable time and sophistication and in practice has proved difficult to achieve. Despite two excellent advisory documents, *With Health in Mind* (Kurtz 1992) and *Together We Stand* (NHS Health Advisory Service 1995), commissioning of child mental health services has been slow to get started. For example, Vanstraelen and Cottrell (1994) questioned all the district health authorities in the North East Thames Region and found purchasers had very limited knowledge of the child mental health services, and made little attempt to establish or monitor quality standards.

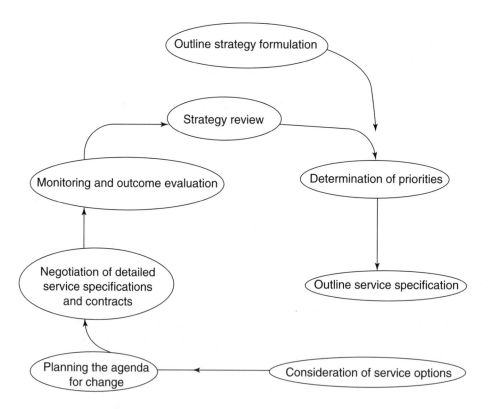

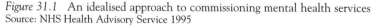

Figure 31.1 An idealised approach to commissioning mental health services
Source: NHS Health Advisory Service 1995

Similarly, Kurtz, Thornes and Wolkind (1994) sent questionnaires to every purchasing authority in England, and received replies from 69 out of 122 (57 per cent). Of these, 52 per cent had begun developing a child mental health strategy but only 28 per cent had a strategy in use. Most purchasing was based on historical patterns and this was the sole basis in 38 per cent of authorities. The Health Advisory Service (HAS), in collaboration with the Centre for Research and Information into Mental Disability at Birmingham University, examined the strategies, purchasing plans and contracts of all the health authorities in England and Wales for 1993–4 and 1994–5. They found that 35 per cent had at least a draft mental health strategy (strategies for child mental health were less well developed). The HAS team also visited 12 providers from a broad spectrum of child mental health services. A positive working relationship between purchaser and provider was rare and there were no examples of co-operation between all three statutory agencies (health, education and social services). The HAS report (1995) concluded 'that commissioning had, in 1993–94, yet to make a significant impact on child and adolescent mental health services'.

Commissioning in-patient child mental health services provides some additional challenges. A significant obstacle is the lack of satisfactory tools to measure key variables in the commissioning process, for example:

> Children requiring in-patient care have complex combinations of problems, and techniques for predicting the prevalence of such combinations are still at a very preliminary stage [NHS Advisory Service, 1995]. Similarly, little is known about appropriate outcome measures for this group.

Table 31.2 Concerns about the provision of very specialised services

---

- Difficulties in relationships with local Child and Adolescent Mental Health Services (CAMHS):
    difficulties of liaison with referrers
    difficulties of discharge planning
    disinclination to share specialist skills with secondary services

- The vulnerability of very specialised services in the internal market:
    lack of contracts for services created difficulties of financial and service planning
    financial insecurity hampered development of new services and restricted their capacity to disseminate specialist skills

- Inappropriate use of very specialised services in providing a source of less specialised interventions in districts with under-developed secondary level services.

- Inappropriate use of local specialist services to provide more specialised care:
    e.g. non-use of very specialised services, on grounds of their cost or insufficient capacity, led to disruption of local CAMHS through disproportionate time and effort being diverted to difficult or extremely challenging cases.

- Poor systems of quality control and performance monitoring:
    the absence of commissioning mechanisms often result in very specialised services not being subject to questions on monitoring of their activity, effectiveness, and efficiency.

The commissioning model requires further refinement when several purchasers commission services from a single provider. Kurtz, Thornes and Wolkind (1994) found 68 per cent of NHS children's and adolescents' psychiatric in-patient units contract with two or more (46 per cent with three or more) health authorities. Green and Jacobs (see chapter 2) report that children's in-patient units in the United Kingdom typically serve a population of 1–2 million, which translates into 3–6 purchasers per unit (on the basis of an average health authority of 320,000 (NHS Management Executive 1994)). In an effort to produce a co-ordinated approach to commissioning by multiple purchasers the HAS report (1995) recommends 'purchasing consortia' and 'lead commissioning authorities', but these have been slow to get started (see below).

Further practical problems with commissioning in-patient services identified by the HAS report (1995) are presented in Table 31.2.

THE CONTRACT

There are broadly three different types of contract. First, a *block* contract, where purchasers pay on the basis of expected activity with no correction for actual activity. Second, a *sophisticated block* contract, which is a variation of the *block* that allows a partial cost correction if activity is above or below a predicted range. Finally, *a cost per case basis* is a pay-as-you-use model typified by the extra contractual referral (ECR.). *Block* contracts give purchaser and provider more financial security, but money does not necessarily follow activity. *Cost per case* provides a direct link between money and activity but makes the market extremely volatile. A *sophisticated block* contract is a compromise between security and money following activity. For example:

> In a year when there are more admissions than predicted, block contracts mean income remains fixed despite extra demands on resources. With sophisticated block contracts there will be a small adjustment in income to reflect extra cases. Under a cost per case arrangement additional cases translate into additional income.

In a questionnaire survey (carried out in 1995) of all children's in-patient units in the United Kingdom, Green and Jacobs (see chapter 2), found that *block* contracts represented a median of 90 per cent of all contracts held (while 8 units out of 29 were completely dependent on block contracting). Most units had less than a quarter of their activity in ECRs, but there were 3 units with 25–50 per cent of activity purchased on an ECR basis. A higher proportion of ECRs means a drop in income if referrals fall and reduced participation in commissioning. On the other hand, it gives the provider much greater control over their prices and priorities.

Child psychiatric in-patient units and other very specialised services share particular problems with contracting (see Table 31.3).

Table 31.3 Problems in contracting for very specialised services

---

- Multiple purchasers
- High cost and low volume:
    individual purchasers may only need to purchase one or two cases a year
- Unpredictable demand:
    demand can vary significantly from year to year
    with tiny volumes a few cases more or less represent huge proportional
    fluctuations
- Purchasers lack expertise

Many of these problems could be reduced if groups of health authorities got together to commission (see section on Commissioning above) and purchased in-patient services. Both the NHS Management Executive (1994) and HAS (1995) have suggested *purchasing consortia* or *lead purchasers*. *Purchasing consortia* are groups of purchasers commissioning and contracting for certain services collectively. Alternatively the service is commissioned by one *lead purchaser* who advises other purchasers on contracting. The HAS (1995) report also recommends a system for under-writing and monitoring services in financial difficulty. The implementation of these recommendations has to date been 'patchy' (The New NHS 1997). The NHS Executive's Commissioning Specialised Services Consultation (1998) recommends the formation of Regional Specialised Commissioning Groups and that Health Authorities commission specialised services like in-patient child psychiatry collectively in the future. It is anticipated that this will largely replace other contracts and extra-contractual referrals (ECRS).

Both HAS (1995) and NHS Management Executive (1994) recommend rolling or long-term contracts for very specialised services. Yet Green and Jacobs (chapter 2) found only two units (out of 29) with rolling contracts applying to more than one year. 'The New NHS' white paper (1997) signals the current Government's intention to replace contracts by three to five year 'funding agreements'.

PRICING

The rules of contracting oblige providers to base prices very closely around costs. There are two types of cost in providing children with in-patient mental health care. First the cost of direct clinical work (such as staff and medicines), second the cost of the organisation needed to support the clinical work (such as management, and building maintenance). Kurtz, Thornes and Wolkind (1994) obtained adequate data to carry out a limited cost analysis on nine (out of 62) children's and adolescent in-patient services. They found 88.3 per cent of total expenditure was on wages, of which 91 per cent went to care staff and 9 per cent to support staff.

The support costs tend to be apportioned according to formulae (such as floor space). However, such formulae throw up bizarre figures, for example 'Services being charged tens of thousands of pounds to have the post delivered'.

There are so few in-patient units that direct competition on the basis of price is unlikely; however health authorities are bound to make comparisons. Variations in the price would be expected to reflect differences in location costs, staff ratios or range of treatment approaches. It is helpful to put in-patient admission in context with other types of residential care for troubled children. The daily rate at children's homes, therapeutic communities, and even specialist foster placements is often similar to that of in-patient units, while secure units cost considerably more.

Charging tends to be either by finished consultant episode (FCE) or by the day. The FCE is administratively easy but a daily charge provides a more accurate reflection of the resources used. It may be appropriate to set an additional charge if a child requires intensive nursing care or is too ill to go home at the weekend (see also chapter 9). Separate charges can also be made for services such as consultation, assessment, and crisis intervention which avert the need for admission.

BUDGET HOLDING

Budgets are increasingly being devolved to clinical teams. Budget holders are given considerable freedom over how they spend their funds but expected to meet all their expenses. For example: 'Budget holding makes it easier to alter the composition of the team in response to change in the nature of the service. But any new investment must be paid for out of savings made elsewhere'. Not everything included in the cost of the service will be held in that service's budget, for example: 'The money to maintain a building is likely to be held in the budget of the department which carries out the building maintenance rather than the service which occupies the building'. In this situation it is possible to have a written agreement between departments specifying the services covered.

Every year the NHS is expected to find cost improvements of around 2 per cent, and depending on the financial state of the trust further savings may have to be found. Because clinical staff pay is such a high proportion of the total cost (see section on pricing above), simply reducing expenditure means cutting clinical posts. An alternative is to generate more income through additional activity such as finding new contracts or setting a higher ECR target.

Occasionally services find themselves with unspent funds which have to be used before the end of the financial year. This can lead to a mad rush, because the extent of any extra money will not be known till the final weeks. It helps to have a list of capital items to be purchased if funds allow, prepared in advance. Alternatively the service may wish to expand its staff on the basis that the extra resources will continue to be available (through extra income or efficiencies).

ADVICE FOR COPING WITH THREATS TO INCOME

Children's psychiatric in-patient units are high-cost, low-volume services where need and outcome are very difficult to measure. As such, they are a vulnerable target for purchasers anxious to find savings. The district health authorities currently contract annually and declare their purchasing intentions six months in advance of the financial year. This provides very little time to mount a fight or prepare for the worst.

The purchasing authorities are currently obliged to pay for any referral initiated by a consultant. The current policy for tertiary referrals is 'notification only' and guidance is contained in a letter to consultants from the Chief Medical Officer Kenneth Calman (21 January 97):

> Consultants in England will no longer be required to obtain prior authorisation from the appropriate purchasing authority before initiating or accepting for treatment a tertiary referral patient who has not been referred within an existing contract. Instead, consultants will need only to notify purchasers of such referrals, with purchasers expected to meet the cost of treatment in much the same way as is already the case for emergency extra-contractual referrals.

This makes the continuing support of referrers extremely important. Rather than make an unsatisfactory contract an in-patient unit may choose to rely on ECRs (see section on the contract above).

There may be an argument for increasing prices. The effect on costs of changes in activity tends to be stepwise rather than linear. There are many costs that will be unaffected by even quite large reductions in activity, for example: 'Ensuring that during the night there are two nurses on the ward, and senior nurses and medical staff on call'. In order to maintain the quality of service at a reduced activity it may be necessary for the prices to go up, for example: 'The cost of providing a comparable service may be very similar whether there are eight children on the ward or ten. Significant savings may only be possible when the numbers fall below six.' The remaining alternatives are for activity to go up or expenditure to come down (see section on budget holding above). The best solution may be a combination of several of these approaches.

Senior managers within the NHS Trust can be important allies. Regional health authorities have very limited powers to intervene. Similarly the Royal College of Psychiatrists or Department of Health are unlikely to get involved, but passing on information about problems may inform wider discussions.

GROWTH AND DEVELOPMENT

It may be possible for a service to grow and develop, where commissioning uncovers unmet needs and additional funds can be found. The alternative is to attract new purchasers.

The HAS (1995) report puts forward the *resource centre*, as a vision of how in-patient services might develop in future (see Figure 31.2.). It is a flexible approach, with interventions tailored to the needs of the individual child and chosen from a *menu* of treatments. There would be a range of treatment packages (instead of the gap we tend to have now between once a week out-patient visits and full admission). The child could move between home, day-patient or residential settings within an integrated programme. Such centres would serve a wide geographical area, collaborate with and support community child mental health services, and provide a focus for innovation, research and teaching.

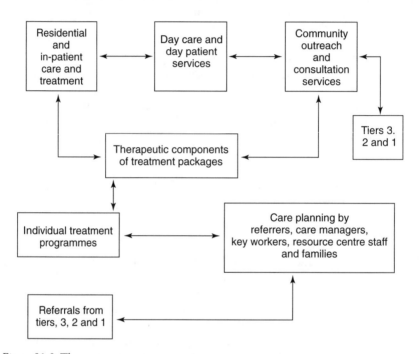

Figure 31.2 The resource centre concept
Note: In-patient units are Tier 4, 'very specialised interventions and care', in the HAS model.

REFERENCES

Department of Health (1997) The New NHS, Modern Dependable. London: HMSO.

Klein, R. (1997) Hastening slowly: Mr Dobson plays a waiting game. *British Medical Journal*, 315, 966.

Kurtz, Z. (ed.) (1992) *With Health in Mind*. London: Action for Sick Children.

Kurtz, Z., Thornes, R. and Wolkind, S. (1994) Services for the mental health of children and young people in England: a national review. London: South Thames Regional Health Authority.

NHS Executive (1998) *The New NHS Commissioning Specialised Services Consultation*. London: HMSO.

NHS Health Advisory Service (1995) *Child and Adolescent Mental Health Services: Together We Stand.* London: HMSO.

NHS Management Executive (1994) *Contracting for Specialist Services.* London: HMSO.

Smith, R. (1997) The future of healthcare systems. *British Medical Journal*, 314, 1495–1496.

Vanstraelen, M. and Cottrell, D. (1994) Child and adolescent mental health services: purchasers' knowledge and plans. *British Medical Journal*, 309, 259–61.

.

Part VIII

Other residential options

Introduction

This section provides two descriptions of provisions that are sometimes used as alternatives to referring to child psychiatric in-patient units. Child psychiatric in-patient units sometimes use therapeutic children's homes or therapeutic schools as longer-term placements following specific pieces of work they have carried out.

Madge Booth writes about a therapeutic children's home where a creative blend of therapies is used. Against a background of behavioural work and containing boundaries, a wide range of active psychotherapeutic games is used to help the children come to terms with their histories. Through this they are often able to move on to a future that is family-based.

Without this work, which can take anything from six to eighteen months, placing these children in families would lead frequently to rapid breakdown of the placement. On other occasions the child might elicit behaviour from decent fosterparents that begins to resemble the original abuse. The reader will notice that this work is longer-term than that which can be undertaken on a child psychiatric in-patient unit.

Longer-term still is a placement for a child at a therapeutic school. Such a placement represents a decision that the child, for whatever reason, is unsuitable to be placed with an alternative family. This may be because their links to their family of origin are too strong to disrupt even though the child may be beyond the family's ability to manage positively. Unfortunately, some children placed in such facilities have very weak links with their families of origin. Richard Rollinson's description is a testament to the potential for these children to change over time. Again the emphasis is non-medical and change takes place over several years.

Each of these authors provides a picture of an eclectic milieu, which is interesting and different from that in in-patient units. How they arrange to support staff, arrange the milieu and how they combine different elements of their approaches, all provide interesting comparisons with child psychiatric in-patient units.

32 Therapeutic children's homes

Madge Booth

INTRODUCTION

Therapeutic communities and therapeutic children's homes work to give the child an enhanced experience. This derives from a theoretical base, maximising all available opportunities to enable the child both to understand and to acquire acceptable standards of behaviour.

Therapeutic communities are sometimes defined as integrated residential and educational environments, which provide psychotherapeutic treatment for exceptionally emotionally damaged children. They are not all of the same model, but they aim to have some, if not all, of the following characteristics:

- A good quality physical environment emphasising care and self-worth.
- Staff and children 'share' the experience of living together to forge a therapeutic alliance and thereby assist the children to achieve change and help them with their problems.
- Staff share and strongly identify with the ethos of the community, some being specifically trained in group work and personal therapies.
- High levels of staff support and of psychiatric and other outside consultancy, focused on particular treatments and therapies offered, are available to all staff.
- A commitment for children to experience alternative care and specialised social life, which allows them to recover from a traumatic external environment.

The role of therapeutic care staff includes fostering and developing in the children self-management, the ability to set their own boundaries, make sensible decisions and generally behave appropriately.

Therapeutic units are sometimes used as an alternative to hospitalisation, or as the second stage of a treatment strategy, prior to the permanent placement of a child within a family. They are able to undertake a psychological assessment of the child's needs (emotional, physical and developmental), responding with an appropriate therapeutic milieu/care plan. Their programmes are 'time limited', constantly reviewed and monitored, requiring full professional reports on the nature and progress of the child's difficulties. As will be seen, their approach to assessment differs from the medical/psychiatric framework discussed in chapter 6 but they often have arrangements to consult child psychiatrists when staff think this is necessary.

Therapeutic units provide a highly specialised, long term, therapeutic environment for the child, but also work with the family preparing them from the outset for the child's return, giving teaching and management strategies.

THE CHILD

Matching the child and the placement is important. Some children will respond better to a behavioural environment whilst others also require intense nurturing play therapy. For some, the priority is a specialised educational environment.

Almost without exception, children referred to the therapeutic unit arrive with the belief of being bad, mad and stupid. In addition to this they often exhibit severe attachment disorders, and/or have the notion of being 'ill'. The small child who has been subjected to poor parenting, along with gross deprivation and neglect, will benefit from an intensive nurturing environment, where good parenting and stimulating play underpin the entire therapeutic process. The child who in addition to the above, has existed in an arena where there are few, if any consistent, boundaries, along with severe physical and emotional abuse, may well require considerably more input than intensive 'good parenting'.

In such cases the child requires much behavioural modification alongside the heavily nurturing, 'good parenting' process.

Where sexual abuse is an added factor, one should then look to those resources which have proven professional and specialised skills, along with qualified personnel, in working with the sexually abused child. This information is available through the Carebase computer centres, which operate across the country. Carebase gives a detailed account of the philosophy, ethos, functioning and staffing levels along with relevant qualifications of all staff and often, inspectors' reports.

Those involved in referring must familiarise themselves with what each resource provides. The younger the child, the greater is the inclination to place in a smaller familial type resource. As a child reaches the age of ten and over, successful outcomes through substitute family placements decrease.

For these older children, small community/group living environments are often far more acceptable to the child, particularly if regular contact with the family is to be maintained. Disharmony between a foster-carer and natural parent can have major disruptive impact on the child.

WINDOWS FOR CHILDREN: A THERAPEUTIC CHILDREN'S HOME

The unit

Windows for children is a small therapeutic community in a large modern family style home. Set in an acre of ground, surrounded by woods, the building has been specifically designed to enable maximum use, yet retain the very important personalised feel of a family home. Each child has their own room, which is light, bright and furnished with appropriate pictures along with the child's own personal possessions. Great attention has been paid to detail, in terms of decor, style of furnishings, and activity areas. There is a large kitchen, which is designed to permit children to cook and be part of its activities. Windows is very much a nurturing unit which works towards enabling damaged and troubled children to move their lives forward.

Windows has a purpose built sound and movement monitor, comprising infra-red sensors, monitoring each child's movements throughout the night, ensuring total safety of every child, yet maintaining their right to privacy. Each room has a very acute sound system, which allows waking night staff to monitor and record, if necessary, the child's sleeping pattern.

All children are aware of its presence, and without exception, check each night to ensure they are 'switched on'. In this way we are able to ensure the total protection of each child, from the potential of abusing children. It allows the early detection of children 'targeting' other children, thereby enabling us to work with the child before an incident occurs.

Each child is encouraged to realise their full potential mainly through highly structured, good, meaningful play. Great emphasis is placed on building a positive environment where children are able to have fun, succeed, and learn. In so doing they address developmental, cognitive and emotional impairments. At the same time they gain an understanding of their life experiences, and develop healthier coping mechanisms.

Entirely through various play techniques we are able to identify areas of concern, and achieve disclosures in severely abused 'silenced' children, without causing further distress and trauma. These also help to alleviate the child's inner pain, anger, guilt, and/or confusion.

The therapeutic process

There are three stages:

Phase 1: Addressing sensory delays

Many children have been so traumatised by their experiences that they have become both physically and emotionally 'frozen'. They are no longer able to laugh or cry appropriately. Many have become inured to pain or discomfort, unable to recognise when they are unwell, or even whether they are too hot or cold (see also chapter 33).

We cannot possibly expect a child to verbalise, or come to terms with, such complex feelings as sadness, anger or frustration, when they are deprived of basic sensory integration of taste, touch, sound, sight and smell. Through 'fun' play these delays are addressed, for example in 'The Smelly-Taste' game.

> The children are divided in small 'teams', and several saucers with varying familiar tastes and smells are laid out at the end of the room or garden. The children then complete an 'obstacle' course, such as carrying a small bucket of water (much fun and laughter is had as children get wet in the romp), over and under obstacles until they reach the saucers with their team members. At this point they assist each other in identifying different tastes and smells, i.e., sweet from sour or bitter, hot from cold, and wherever possible the actual flavour and texture, along with smell. Points or rewards are given, whilst staff ensure each child succeeds at something. The 'winners' earn choosing objects or items for the 'feeling' part of this game. Large bags, full of familiar objects, are placed in the middle of the room, or at the end of a rearranged obstacle course. Again a 'race' is set up where children place just their hands inside the bag, describing to the other children whether the object is hard, soft, smooth or rough, its shape, the material it is made of and if possible its use. The child describing gains points or a reward if the other children are able to guess the object from their description. (Clearly less able or confident children will initially require subtle help from adults.)

In the case of some children it may be necessary to allow them to play individually until they become more trusting and confident.

This type of 'game' not only plays an enormous part in addressing 'sensory delays', but also benefits the child greatly in terms of improving co-ordination and cognitive development. Auditory processing is greatly improved with sound games. Tapes with various sounds such as animal noises, traffic, a swimming pool etc. (any sound which will be of interest or amusing to the child) are played during a quiz or during part of the above game. Children soon learn to enjoy listening to and identifying the sound, in order to be a part of the game and gain reward in some small way. These activities greatly improve attention span.

Remembering items on a tray provides competition between the children and the adults. Walks in the woods, along beaches, at dawn or dusk, in all seasons, along with visits to market places and shopping centres, are all used to get the children to observe, feel, taste and listen to all around them. This has the added advantage of being an additional arena where children can comfortably learn appropriate behaviour.

Implicit is the need for constant praise, encouragement and recognition of gains made by the child. Often the child's behaviour will, for a brief period, appear to regress even further, as they become more in touch with feelings they have long since learned to repress, or have never experienced.

In this early stage we begin the process of eliminating the child's notion of being 'born bad' or of being 'bad, mad and stupid'. We use numerous esteem charts, games and activities in which the child is well able to achieve, and so gain a sense of satisfaction and self-worth. Then and only then will the child entrust the carer with their deepest fears and 'secrets' .

Unless children like themselves, and are aware and proud of their achievements, they will never internalise the vital elements of therapy. They will therefore never make any real progress, other than that which is superficial and very tenuous. Neither will they learn to like others and so develop trust, a key factor in every child's growth and development.

Phase 2: Addressing specific therapeutic issues

During this part of the process, more attention is paid to individual work. Specific games and exercises have been devised to facilitate the talking about and understanding of the particular difficulties encountered by the child. Every piece of work is designed to be experiential and/or highly visual. These must be positive experiences for the child, even when dealing with difficult and painful issues. An example is 'The Button Game'.

> Buttons can be used to demonstrate to a child where they see themselves in any given arena, whether it be within the family, a class, group, or any gathering of people. Buttons are an extremely useful tool in facilitating talking, for children of all ages. We use a very large box of different buttons. The child is encouraged to talk about himself, to choose a button which he feels most represents him and, with help, to explain why. He is then asked to place this button on a large sheet of paper. The child is asked to think about all the people within his family (or the particular area you are attempting to address), and to take time choosing buttons for these people. The child is encouraged to think and talk about all the aspects, good and bad, of the 'button/person' he has chosen. Once this is done the child can then place the button on the sheet of paper. The worker will ask the child to also think about how close or far away they feel this button should be, and why. This continues until the child has selected all the buttons he wishes, placing each on the sheet around themselves, discussing each one and where he feels they should be placed. Many children will feel safer not naming some of the buttons; this is not important, as once they feel they have completed their button picture, the worker can invite the child to glue them down, checking with the child if they are sure the button is where they want it. The child is then asked if they wish the worker to write the names of the buttons beneath them, in case they forget. Having talked about so much, throughout the session, most children find naming the buttons at the end quite easy, and sometimes are visibly relieved. Unnamed buttons can always be named at a later stage, as the child grows more confident. The most important part of this exercise is how easily the buttons facilitate talking. The final picture can

be used to demonstrate to the child whom they see as being close, those people they are uncertain of, and those where there are clearly difficulties. The worker must always ensure and assist the child in seeing there are positive and 'safe' buttons in their world.

It is amazing how well children are able to utilise this medium, often putting aside fantasy, as the buttons do not represent a threat to them. This exercise is extremely beneficial in assisting children to talk safely about those matters they would otherwise find difficult. Many children request to undertake this exercise several times. On each occasion one will observe positive changes in the child's understanding, and their acceptance of particular issues.

Drawing houses with their shapes and people in various colours is used to facilitate talking to resolve confusion around what happened where and with whom. Children find it so much easier to talk when engaged in a structured, meaningful and relevant activity. This is undertaken at the child's pace. No child should be pressurised into facing difficult issues until they feel safe enough to do so.

It is very important to give the child a notion of the positive and good aspects of their past. This is achieved by the use of our 'Good Remembers' candles.

> The child is encouraged to bring forward good memories. Talking of pleasant times and people they have liked and why. With each 'I remember' the child lights a candle and places it strategically on a large tray near their own. Once the exercise is complete and the child has exhausted their memories for that day, the curtains are drawn and the child is shown how (symbolically) their memories can light up the room. They are encouraged to feel the warmth given off by the 'memories', and told how these can never be taken away from them. A photograph is then taken and placed in the child's life book with a list of these memories.

Making up and filming 'plays' (role-play) gives children permission to dress up and be 'someone else'. This allows the children to dress up and 'act out' safely and in a controlled manner, those matters where previously they could only become angry and violent, or totally compliant. Interwoven with these numerous exercises are many light-hearted quizzes, deliberately designed in such a way that every child is able to answer questions. There are also water 'battles' and 'silly' games, during which the child safely learns acceptable touch, all of which increase awareness and understanding, improve co-ordination and so building confidence and self-esteem/worth/image. Impulse control is greatly aided by a simple well-loved party game, 'The Chocolate Game'.

> The children take it in turns to roll a large dice. Each time a six is thrown the child puts on large gloves, a hat and waistcoat; using a knife and fork they attempt to cut a piece of chocolate from a large bar that has been placed in the refrigerator previously. If another child throws a six, they must

immediately pass the clothes to this child and return to their place, even if a piece has been cut. If the child becomes angry or frustrated, a member of staff stands with them, encouraging them to be calm, while the game continues. They are not allowed to participate until they are calm. As the chocolate bar becomes smaller, the child struggles to control themselves (usually breathing deeply and assuring the staff member, 'I am calm now'), in order to rejoin the game before the chocolate bar has been eaten – simple, but very effective in giving the child a notion of self-control.

It is important to ensure that too high an expectation is not placed on the child's behaviour. No child is ever impeccably good. For this reason we allow children to experiment with being 'naughty', giving arenas where it is safe to 'act out', without risk to themselves or others, in privacy with the worker. 'Soft rooms' are excellent for this purpose. In conjunction with the many games and activities, children are encourage to join local groups and clubs, in order to promote the development and improvement of social skills.

Phase 3: Preparation for permanence

In this final stage of the programme much of the work/play centres on preparing the child for life within a family. It is the aim of Windows to achieve permanency within twelve to eighteen months. It is therefore necessary to plan the child's therapeutic schedule to the finest detail, maximising every single opportunity. Numerous games, 'posters' and work sheets are specifically designed for individual children, enabling them to gain a notion of what can realistically be expected from a family, what sort of family they need and their role within the family. For example:

> Large cut out houses are placed around the child's wall. Over a period of weeks much discussion centres around what goes on in the house, and using old magazines and catalogues the child cuts out the various items/people/pets that they feel should be in their prospective home.

In this way the worker can encourage realistic expectations, whilst assessing the child's readiness for the move. Large moving-on calendars are made, where the child and worker plan the weeks and months ahead, preparing the child for each event leading to their departure. Models are made with the child, or cut out people are used, whilst discussion and role play centres around the role of individual family members within the home, and what the expectations would be of the child.

Practical activities allow the child to help with washing up, shopping, helping with meal preparation and being given occasional responsibility for simple chores.

Throughout the child's stay Life Book work to prepare a record of the child's life that they can value and take with them is undertaken. In so doing vital clues are given as to the nature and direction of play required. No effort is too great when making attempts to gain every possible piece of information, inclusive of taking the child on several 'Life Journeys' to facilitate talking and the taking of photographs. To rush or avoid issues when undertaking this vital piece of work could well result in 'missing' the very key which would unlock the child's inner turmoil and distress.

Trying to achieve total consistency from all the adults charged with each child's care is vital. It is a major factor in creating security and stability. Any promise or sanction must be carried through, as would any reward or outing. It is simply not acceptable to say 'I didn't know', when a child is acting out in the most unacceptable manner, because they perceive that they have 'been lied to'. Equally important to the child's well being is the need to impart the very practical skills necessary to develop a child's 'total self'. These basic skills include personal hygiene, dressing appropriately, table manners, consideration for others and cultural awareness, along with the art of conversation.

Case example

Adam was a somewhat overweight nine-year-old boy, exhibiting severe behavioural disorders. He was referred for assessment following several placement breakdowns and many extremely violent episodes, including the stabbing of his father. He had totally wrecked two offices whilst attempts were made to interview his mother. School had always been a tremendous problem, owing to his violent behaviour and total inability to conform to any rules.

Adam refused to participate in any group activity, describing himself as fat, useless and no good. He was extremely violent to any adult who dared to challenge his behaviour in any way. Conversely he was very protective of the younger children, particularly if he perceived there to be an injustice, either by an older child or by an adult, such a situation often resulting in the need to 'hold' Adam until he had calmed sufficiently not to be a risk to others.

He ate constantly, totally unaware of any sense of being full; he would injure himself quite severely without any recognition of pain. On one occasion he was oblivious to the fact that he had clearly sprained his ankle, it being very swollen and bruised after he had kicked a hole in a door.

Individual sensory delay work was undertaken, under the guise of 'helping the little ones' because he was 'so good at making sure things were right for them'. Initially Adam was totally unable to differentiate between iced and tepid water, soft and hard feels, or indeed between sweet and sour foods.

Sensory games exposed a very depressed, confused and angry child who hated everything about himself, trusted no-one and clearly had no sense of 'belonging' anywhere. There was a measure of attachment to his mother, albeit of an extremely anxious nature. Life Book journeys were undertaken with Adam, during which he would become agitated and distressed when in certain areas or meeting previous acquaintances. Subsequent work revealed that he had witnessed, and been party to, considerable violence towards his mother by a previous partner. The button exercise undertaken on more than one occasion with both him and his mother allowed them both to see (and hear from each other) from where many of the difficulties emanated.

Mother came to understand how unsafe and uncared for Adam had felt for many years. Adam realised that his anger and violence stemmed from his mother's own fear of both her former partner and Adam. Using cut out houses and people we were able to show mother and child the need for consistent boundaries. Role-play helped mother to gain the confidence to use her new-found parenting skills. Both took part in many sessions around building a positive environment, learning that this does not just happen, but has to be constantly worked upon by the entire family.

Much time was spent building Adam's confidence so that he could join in group activities. This was achieved by establishing that he enjoyed cooking, and encouraging him to cook various dishes, for which he received much praise.

Posters were drawn up for him, identifying all the things that made him special, i.e. his sense of caring for the little ones, his lovely blue eyes, sense of humour, ability to cook, etc. It was necessary to replace the posters many times, before he finally left them on his bedroom wall. (It is important to replace such visual 'props' immediately a child destroys them, no matter how many times.)

Adam began to participate in group games and also to enjoy initiating the games he was comfortable with. It was explained to him that every one at Windows had to be 'safe'. If he became unsafe he would have to 'miss out' on the games, as it would not be fair to allow him to break the safety rule. Pictures using 'no entry' signs were place around his room, displaying all the aspects of his behaviour that he felt he wanted, or needed to change. One of these pictures would be discussed with him each day. It would be included in a story, role-play and/or a mealtime discussion. (This happens for each child.)

Gradually Adam involved himself in more activities, music times, painting, various group games and clubs. He expressed a love of horses and was enrolled in a local riding stables, which he attended when he was able to display consistent safe behaviour. Adam developed a keen sense of humour, which made him very popular with adults and children alike.

During a game where the entire household are involved in writing positive things on the silhouettes of children (drawn round them on large sheets of paper), Adam announced 'I quite like me, I am good at a lot of things here aren't I?'

Adam had also stopped eating endlessly. He could actually refuse food, recognising when he had eaten sufficient. He was also beginning to take a pride in his appearance and personal hygiene. He began to depend less on adults to put external controls on his behaviour, internalising his own boundaries for acceptable behaviour

Mother maintained contact fortnightly. Prior to her seeing Adam we would meet to discuss various aspects of his behaviour and her parenting of him. It became clear that Adam had virtually 'ruled' by fear. Mother experienced considerable guilt around several major family 'secrets'; not least was the fact that the person Adam believed to be the father of himself and his younger brother was not actually his father. As a result of her guilt, mother had set few if any boundaries or limits on Adam's behaviour; the child had learned that the more he behaved badly, the more mother would 'give in'. She was in fact petrified that her son would discover 'the secret', and had maintained an enormous web of intrigue and subterfuge, in all of which Adam had become almost inextricably enmeshed.

Work commenced with mother that enabled her to be truthful with her son. Adam initially was very angry, but eventually he realised that his youngest brother's extended family treated him differently, because he was not part of their family (they were not his grandparents; hence the lack of presents and interest), rather than because he was a nasty, unlovable little boy.

Adam was able to verbalise his anger and express to his mother how cross and unsafe he had felt within the home, along with the frustration he had experienced at being treated differently by the person he believed to be his father; hence his numerous attacks on him. Adam had clearly been subconsciously aware of the 'divide' between himself and his family. Joint work commenced with Adam and his mother around establishing consistent boundaries, and management strategies for both. Adam commenced mainstream schooling. For the first time, to his pleasure, he found he was 'good', if not better than the rest of the children in his class, going on to win the 'Achiever of the Year' award.

After several months of spending weekends and increasingly longer periods at home, with support from Windows, Adam requested to spend his summer holiday with his mother rather than stay with the group. On his return, grandmother, an aunt and his birth father along with his mother came, all overjoyed at how well the holiday had gone. The entire family was requesting Adam's return. Grandmother required a few sessions to learn how important it was to remain consistent with Adam, and to come to terms with the fact there were no more family 'secrets'. (These sessions were helped by Adam!)

Adam returned home very successfully and remains there happily.

Staffing

I think where Windows differs from many of our counterparts is in how we view the definition of carer. For us it is a central tenet that this definition includes everybody, from the most senior child care practitioner, through the care assistants, domestic staff, administrators, maintenance staff and garden personnel. All are a vital part of the team and all are required to attend training. In this way a high degree of consistency is ensured. Every adult in the building has the understanding to deal with a child in crisis. Windows is based on 'the family'. Every member of staff can and does influence a child's development, which is why *all* are trained in understanding the vital role they play in the 'healing' process.

For any form of residential unit to work, and in particular a therapeutic resource, it is absolutely essential for there to be good inter-staff communication on all levels. To this end, staff are required to maintain full daily logs and file notes on each child, in addition to the communications and message book. Added to this is the full staff and Care Plan meeting each week, which is included in the staff rota, and therefore an integral part of their contracted hours. Short of illness or annual leave, every one has a duty to attend – it is not a matter of choice.

The Windows model requires an extremely high degree of commitment, from highly motivated staff. The selection procedure is long, arduous and specifically designed to sift out those who clearly would not be able to withstand the stresses that such a demanding task would place on them.

Following the informal and formal interviews, potential staff are required to spend a day in the home meeting the children. Their interaction with the group is observed by senior staff on duty, in order to assess their ability to relate meaningfully with the children, along with their ability to take constructive criticism from the feedback. Last, but by no means least, is the need to assess whether they have a child-centred approach.

All applicants who are thus far successful are then requested to attend a 'workshop' day, during which they will undertake several of the exercises and games played with the children, as well as a written assignment on 'Why Play?' or a similar topic.

They will be asked to recall their own childhood experiences and 'share' their thoughts and feelings with their group. This enables us to ascertain those adults who clearly carry their own 'baggage' to a degree which would not be conducive to success in the post for which they are applying. This is also remarkably beneficial in assisting in the protection of the children, team and 'programme'.

All new staff then commence an induction programme, during which they 'shadow' experienced staff. The induction programme includes a reading list and completing several work books:

- *Induction* (this covers the philosophy, policies, principles and procedures in the home)
- *Introduction to Therapeutic Care*
- *The Legal Framework*
- *Child Development*
- *Managing Difficult Behaviour*
- *Building a Positive Environment*

Each work book comes with its own test paper, and requires the participant to display a full understanding, before moving on to the next stage. Weekly tutorials and supervision are an essential requirement. It is expected that all test papers have been undertaken to an acceptable standard, before the probationary period is complete (normally six months). However there are occasions when an extension of the probationary period may be considered.

Knowledge and a full understanding of all the many games and direct work techniques are also absolutely essential. By necessity this requires *all* staff to under-take the very same 'games' and exercises that are carried out with the children; for example, staff do their own eco map, self-esteem charts, buttons, brick wall, candles, trust games, co-ordination games, along with all the 'addressing sensory delay' work. This can be quite a difficult and painful process, hence the need for continuing and regular supervision, meaningful support, regular team building experiences and consultancy.

In this way staff have a full measure of how powerful the work can be, when undertaken appropriately and sensitively. The workers' own experience enables empathy, without collusion, and more importantly lessens the risk of an unhealthy transference.

Six-monthly appraisals are held in order to assess progress, areas which need developing, training needs and those staff who will benefit from further courses, with a view to increasing staff group skills, and enabling staff to gain qualifications, which increase career prospects. Thus job satisfaction and motivation are ensured.

Training is on-going (every member of staff is required to attend their respective training schedules). All staff have fortnightly supervision, six-monthly appraisals, and monthly team building sessions, with the house Consultant Psychotherapist. All staff are required to maintain a positive, child-centred nurturing environment, at all times ensuring that the child's best interests are paramount.

33 A therapeutic school

Richard Rollinson

The ability to form a social relationship depends upon emotional stability; young children under emotional stress do not interact easily with other children or adults. . . . Children cannot learn effectively unless they maintain their emotional and social equilibrium. If children cannot make relationships they will be handicapped in their learning; the ability to learn must at times depend on the ability to relate to a teacher.

(Manning and Sharp, 1977)

Professionals cannot ignore the public concerns about children and young people who are out of control and posing serious challenges to families, communities and schools. Even primary schools now face ever growing problems of managing children who are reported to accept no limits and quickly hit out and hurt anyone whom they regard as in their way. The significant reported rise in exclusions from school bears testimony to this phenomenon as well as to the lack of sufficient resources in schools to deal with such degrees of disruption and risk (Hayden, Sheppard and Ward, 1996).

Even if day schools received a major boost in resources there would still be children who could not be contained, let alone taught, in such circumstances. Their difficulties are not simply restricted to education, but extend to the arena of living in a family and in the local community. The problems which these children present are so long-standing and of such complexity, severity and risk to themselves and others that they interfere profoundly with their social, educational and emotional development (Health Advisory Services, 1995). They require a highly specialised combined treatment intervention of care and education. The need is not in the first instance to learn in the more familiar academic sense; rather it is to learn to live with themselves and others. This capacity occurs naturally amongst most children before the start of their mainstream education; it is often overlooked as the essential foundation both of an individual's 'internal organisation', to manage the educational task, and of a school's organisation of itself, to provide it. These children lack a solid foundation of personality or possess only a badly fractured one. Their educational and emotional difficulties become hopelessly entangled as a consequence. They are unlikely to achieve anything other than the disruption of their own or other children's learning and the efforts of those to teach them, even with at times enormous amounts of individual attention within mainstream settings.

For those very troubled children who are not showing psychiatric disorder of a severity requiring in-patient treatment, one approach is offered within a therapeutic school. Other children might well have gone to a child psychiatric in-patient unit, had a few circumstances at early intervention and referral stage been different, such as a health service provider having become involved first (Kahan, 1994). At the same time a young person presenting with schizophrenia, severe depression with associated suicidal intent, or any acute condition in which the child is an immediate danger to self or others is not likely to be helped in a therapeutic school, at least at such a stage. They are best treated in an in-patient unit. If, following in-patient treatment, concerns remain about the child's underlying emotional and psychological condition a decision will need to be made as to whether community-based help will suffice or whether a referral is appropriate to the residential setting such as a therapeutic school.

The Department for Education and Employment does not separately recognise therapeutic schools. Most such schools are residential and offer care and education together for the purpose of treatment. The approaches, structure, and hence the treatment, in these settings vary widely. Despite this diversity, many of these settings can be grouped, even if loosely and with recognition of some important areas of overlap, into three approaches. (Davie, 1989; Kahan, 1994) These are the psychodynamic, the behavioural and the life/work skills approaches.

The first, psychodynamic, arises out of psychoanalysis and offers many valuable insights about the person derived originally from the analytic perspective. This approach emphasises the psychological forces which motivate behaviours and highlights the importance of feelings. Concern is largely focused on certain key relationships – 'those between self and significant others, past and present experiences and inner and outer reality' (Brearley, 1991).

The behavioural approach is based on the belief from learning theory that all behaviour is learnt. With this approach, if problems find their greatest expression in problem behaviour, then change the behaviour. What has been learnt can be unlearnt; new, acceptable behaviours can replace former undesirable ones. Behaviour modification focuses on the promotion of desirable behaviours and the extinction of inappropriate or anti-social behaviours by recognition and reward (chapter 10). Related to this, token economy systems introduce a behaviour modification programme with the offer of rewards for specified behaviours. Tangible tokens of approval in the short term aim to help the child in the longer term to understand that approval and acceptance for good behaviour and progress is reward enough in its own right.

A third approach, life/work skills, tends to reject what it regards as the too generalised psychological statements about humans and their behaviours in the psychodynamic approach and the too narrow mechanistic explanation of human activity in the behaviourist. Instead, the emphasis is upon the whole person, and learning through self-discovery, from experience and by experiment. This interesting combination of a humanistic perspective and cognitive psychology seeks to influence/adjust the ways children and young people think about or process their perceptions. These include opportunities for constructive work through role-play and rehearsals about issues/situations in which young people have had difficulties.

Treatment and learning in therapeutic schools increasingly recognises the child's right to access to the National Curriculum; but modifications are still necessary to fill gaps in learning and to take account of the emotional and behavioural vulnerability of the children. Thus the aim of each style of therapeutic school, whatever its particular treatment approach or orientation, is to provide education that will enable each child to fulfil his or her full potential. Good organisation and practice is similar to that in mainstream schools. Key features common to all are:

- clear leadership and effective management
- a broad and balanced curriculum
- adequate and appropriate teaching methods and resources
- education plans for children that set targets which can be measured for achievements and outcomes (Greenhalgh, 1994; Grimshaw and Berridge, 1994).

This 'commonality' extends beyond the specifically educational sphere. A number of common features are detectable in the overall practices; most prominent among these are:

1) A physical environment emphasising care and self-worth, actively maintained to a good level.
2) Staff are strongly identified with the ethos of the school and at least some are specially trained in the key features of the declared approach.
3) The importance of a relationship in the treatment. Some argue that the two way relationship between child and adult (whether working or deeply dependent in nature) in all approaches may be of more significance to outcome than any actual treatment or activity itself. Certainly, all approaches require from the adults consistency, reliability and commitment to relationship building as fundamental.
4) For change, a child needs to accept that he has some part in creating and sustaining a problem and be prepared to accept help and work towards resolving it.
5) The approaches require adults to observe behaviour closely and use assessment skills to decide on the nature of any intervention.
6) All approaches acknowledge the existence of thoughts and feelings as well as observable behaviours, even if each approach confers a different meaning and order of importance to these features.
7) There are high levels of support and specialist consultancy available to staff.

Professionals tend to lean towards a therapeutic school with a particular approach because of a combination of their own beliefs, prior experiences and the ways in which a child presents. Children presenting difficulties that appear entirely emotional or behavioural, with a very distinctive and substantial emotional source/component, are often referred to a psychodynamic therapeutic school. Those whose behavioural difficulties seem largely unrelated to long-standing emotional problems are often seen as benefiting from the perceived clearer structures and focused treatment programmes of a behaviourally orien-tated school. Finally, work and life skills are often regarded as beneficial to young people whose alienation from more academic related education is well advanced and who seem intent on/interested in developing more vocational skills within highly structured and activity based programmes.

Since its foundation in 1948 by Barbara Dockar-Drysdale, the Mulberry Bush School has established a wide reputation for helping severely emotionally troubled children of both sexes, aged five to twelve, who have been presenting marked problems in their care and management. Throughout its existence, the school's education and treatment provision has been based on psychodynamic principles developed largely by Donald Winnicott and Mrs Dockar-Drysdale. Within a carefully integrated environment of living and learning, staff seek to help children understand their behaviour and their inner world of feelings in order to provide the emotional containment they need and to support both their emotional recovery and growth and their educational rehabilitation and progress. Children arrive at the Mulberry Bush after a life marked by inconsistent, inter-mittent or absent patterns of caring and nurturing often from infancy. Active abuse is common. Each of the children has had to endure terrible combinations of: disrupted parenting; a poor quality of care leading to chronic discomfort, low expectations, fear and anger; disturbed schooling; physical or sexual abuse and intimidation.

By the time of referral and placement children at the Mulberry Bush School are distressed and deprived to an extent that has severely impaired their functioning in key areas. They are impulsive and unpredictable. They tolerate frustration poorly and discharge their confusions, fears and fantasies directly into actions. Placed with foster families, they relate superficially and often cannot be contained emotionally or safely. They demand more and more of people, seek total control, deny responsibility for their actions and express their vulnerability by their lack of a rudimentary sense of danger and self-preservation. Sometimes they will speak of harming themselves in unplanned, half-formed ways, often it seems to ascertain the effects of such comments upon their carers. In social interactions they are almost completely unable either to be part of a group or to let that group function without their active disruption. Their peer relationships are very poor; friendships are absent or continually fraught. In school they rarely learn from experience, have a poor attention span, cannot generalise from the particular, and can be 'over-concrete' in their thinking. Above all their disruption exhausts their teachers, leaving them on tenterhooks even when the child is quiet. Of course, one child rarely exhibits all these features, and even the child presenting with many, does not do so to a high degree continuously. Invariably there are very positive features about these children who cause such great concern. At times they can be touchingly and genuinely open about their own difficulties and fears, and concerned about others, certainly attitudes and behaviours worth supporting and extending.

'I AM . . . DOESN'T MEAN ANYTHING TO ME'

Following Winnicott and Dockar-Drysdale, the Mulberry Bush School regards these children and their egos as unintegrated – they lack a good enough, continuous and complete sense of self which would aid their healthy growth or be available to fall back upon at times of adversity (Dockar-Drysdale, 1990). Not having achieved this fundamental emotional development, they have no organising centre from which to control their feelings and thoughts. At critical times a strong feeling becomes too unthinkable, any thought too unspeakable; only action, sudden and powerful, remains for the 'expression' of their intolerable predicament borne of emotional fragmentation, confusion and preoccupation with difficulties (Reeves, 1979).

Ultimately, the treatment goal is to offer to children who missed out originally, an experience of ordinary development and learning supplied through the extra-ordinary efforts, knowledge and skills of a group of concerned teachers and carers working together. This should be achieved in presenting the world in manageable doses allowing 'gradual environmental seeping . . . in which the child can best come to terms with the wider world of external reality' (Winnicott, 1965). An essential ingredient in this particular task and environment is a commitment to and emphasis upon relationships. Building and sustaining healthy relationships is the cornerstone. The child needs to experience that whatever behaviour is brought to a worker, sense can be made of it with and for them; a tentative and gradually more secure resolution can be found. With this they may begin to develop that hitherto absent sense of basic trust in people who, as Bettelheim said, have remained 'fundamentally on the side of the child' (Bettelheim, 1987).

As elsewhere, the child's feelings find expression in thoughtless and hurtful words and actions. Yet they are not, as some might fear, permitted to exist in the Mulberry Bush simply to excuse unacceptable behaviour. Such acts are unacceptable anywhere and staff intervene regularly to interrupt them. Yet they do so as part of a larger process of understanding, for example, what is the source of such actions and feelings and what sustains them in the here and now. With active attempts to understand the child, the adults also helping him begin to understand what has been inexplicable in his feelings and behaviour.

So much of the work of helping individuals and groups to learn to live one with another occurs of necessity through adults and children 'living alongside' one another. This is what is most distinctive about a therapeutic school, even for the very young. Each child knows, sometimes quite painfully, that there is work to be done and that each person's responsibilities extend gradually over time and in meaningful ways towards accepting responsibility for others as well as for oneself. Children new to the school cannot hold this awareness consciously. The grown ups can and do so by providing structures and modelling ways of living and learning that allow this to happen. When children are feeling overwhelmed, they can still make progress so long as they know that grown ups recognise and can contain their feelings; that the educational demands on them match their function and are sensitive to their need.

A concentrated and untransformed diet of mainstream input which failed them before will also be indigestible at first in a therapeutic school, until, that is, children are sufficiently settled and trusting to be able to risk what they have failed in before. Even then, small groups and patient individual attention will be necessary. A programme of early years experiences, which through play and other expressive activities helps children to gain the basic skills and confidence on which they missed out before, can become a most effective gateway into more formal educational work. Once on that track, education will draw the child forward in development even if progress is slow; self-esteem grows.

Alongside what Franklin has termed 'the specific and special attitude toward children' (Franklin, 1968) adults in a therapeutic school must adopt a particular 'psychological location' or orientation. They are intermediaries between a child and the events, routines and tasks of the day. In this way children do not feel they are left to fend for themselves. Nor can they easily rush to re-establish their former survival technique of maintaining great emotional distance and defiant 'independence' from adults concerned to offer appropriate care and attention. This psychological location is demonstrated by guiding the child through or towards an experience (bath, food, play, activities, education). 'Being and doing with children' gradually becomes a more complete psychological presence as the child comes to trust in adults, often by a severe testing out of their reliability. The child learns to face important events or transitions with the adult in a marginal physical position or even some distance away. The adult begins to exist in the child's inner world as a continuing safe, containing emotional presence.

The adult has moved steadily from largely 'ego supplying and containing' early on to 'ego supporting and encouraging'. The child's own ego has achieved integration and then gradually been strengthened towards full emotional autonomy. This progression from unintegration to integration is not straightforward and readily managed, even in our setting. Recognising internal and external reality as well as primitive psychological defence mechanisms does not of itself produce change (Reeves, 1993; Brearley, 1991). Within a framework of theory, there must always be the daily adult thinking and talking about the troubled child. We must consider what each is doing or appears to be doing, what they understand or are trying to; where the children are in their journeys towards integration and what are the appropriate adult responses.

'I AM . . . BUT IN BITS'

Some children do appear to have brief periods of an emerging sense of separate self from the outset, at least in the sense of being situated in a body and functionally different from other people. But they quickly become frightened that this differentiation means catastrophe, being overwhelmed by strong feelings or annihilated physically and psychologically. Their efforts to control everything and everyone often end in fraught and tearful breakdowns as they wreak havoc on people and things; the more precious to them, the more vulnerable to destruction at their hands.

For a time, before the tears, many such children seem to 'come alive' as they create chaos with their physical attacks and panic inducing behaviours. It is as if for this group of children the Cartesian declaration of self and awareness 'I think therefore I am' is more accurately expressed as 'by my mess/impact you will know me and I will feel alive, especially when you react'.

At times this powerful disruption is achieved by less chaotic, more controlling means. Some children focus attacks on their teachers, intent upon proving that they cannot learn because their teacher is trying to kill them, often whilst they continue their unprovoked assault on the teacher. They have to protect themselves because nobody else will. A few will even insist further that 'anyway the work was always boring and too easy and that above all it wasn't worth trying to learn anything in such a mess' (of their own making!).

At the Mulberry Bush staff try to anticipate such breakdown and disruption by ensuring that routine is known to the children and adult expectations are clear. When children are aggressive and violent, staff interrupt them, even if it means restraining them. They tell the child in simple words and calm tones at the same time that this must be done for everyone's safety. That, unlike the child, staff can know what the child has done and accept it as a fact and not use it as the reason for the attack that the child fears. This becomes the reliable reference point supporting awareness of healthy separateness within a growing relationship with those whom the child comes slowly to trust.

'BELONGING WON'T LAST'

Some children have an awareness of self in relation to important others. However, accompanying this awareness there can be a terrible anxiety that this 'belonging', being part of something, won't last – that it will be lost. For a time their lives seem a perpetual struggle, one moment desperately seeking proximity/ belonging, the next suddenly beating away the person and the closeness achieved. Sometimes they blame themselves, sometimes others, for the real or feared breakdown of being apart from them. Most difficult is their fear which if expressed in words would say, 'I don't belong; they can't control me; so how can I, alone and apart, do so'. This is expressed behaviourally through rapid swings between competing for exclusive contact and then totally rejecting it. In the face of such bewildering and ferocious swings, people simply could try to keep a lid on them or join the swing by supporting and rejecting the child in equally rapid shifts. Knowing this, we place great emphasis upon providing a special relationship with a particular grown up as a crucial reference for a child's stability. While remaining in contact and pointing out with concerned awareness the effect of their actions on others, the adult in the relationship can praise the individual child and any non-competitive achievements, thus gradually strengthening a sense of steady identity of 'my own self' and worth.

'I AM ONLY A MIRROR OF ME'

Another group of children find very individual ways of showing adults that the pictures they hold and 'live' of themselves, reflect how they feel other people perceive them – their selves more as objects than subjects with other people holding and determining their definition of self. They may wish desperately to be likable and liked, but cannot seem to sustain the behaviour that would make it reasonable to like them. They can be scornful, dismissive and at times quite wild. When interrupted, they will say, often with anger, some variation on the theme of, 'I am shit; my Mum hates me. Who would want anything to do with me'. It is as if deep down each feels that Mum/the carer sees only damaged goods. The child in effect can feel whole enough in relation to a significant other but not yet 'wholesome' in his own right, still somebody else's object, a me 'as in a mirror' (Reeves, 1993).

In response, adults try to challenge the negative behavioural expressions while supporting at every opportunity the positive elements of a child's image. By reinforcing such children's experiences of success and acceptability to others, staff help them improve personal attainments in a context of social responsibility and acceptable standards.

In effect, adults are involved in a physical, psychological and emotional programme of 'emotional holding' (Winnicott, 1965), providing for children a sense of security, consistency and continuity which gives meaning and structure to their living. It is invariably long-term work in residence, dealing as it does with a child's long-term prior experiences and their internal working models; the outcomes in mind from the start are also inevitably long-term.

A specific case example, as regarded by a worker some years ago, although but one child's 'story', may serve usefully to highlight these general points and provide a window through to the therapy through living and learning: see the case study on pp. 407–411.

OUTCOME

As yet the school has done no formal outcomes/follow up studies, although there are proposals to do so. Already however, from a significant number of former pupils with whom the school remains in touch, it is clear that the school has had some transcendent successes, expressed through impressive personal and professional achievements. There are also some very notable and sad failures, where adult efforts appear to have done little to avert continuing individual distress and chaos. For the majority of others known to the school the gains are modest and highly individual. Nevertheless, given the accumulation of adversity in their poor starts and lost opportunities the gains stand as very important to the former pupils themselves, their families and the school (Beedell, 1993). Over the average three years of a child's stay, very often a vicious cycle of damage is interrupted.

Stability in relationships is introduced, based upon an increased capacity in the children to form and maintain these. Finally, the most severe effects of early experiences of deprivation are limited. Where there was largely mindless action, there is now a much greater ability to think and talk. Where there was educational failure, there is now an ability to learn at levels far less removed from their peers; and where there were enforced separations from family life there can be living at home and in the community without resort to substantial levels of support.

By its continuing efforts to achieve its aims of supporting emotional growth and learning, the school remains true to its core belief in the healthy and wholesome potential which exists in children even when they have suffered serious trauma or neglect in their early lives.

MATTHEW – IN FROM THE COLD

Matthew is an attractive, slightly built but wiry child of mixed Nigerian, West Indian and white descent. He was seven years old when he arrived. His mother had been a prostitute who had neglected him. She had died suddenly eighteen months earlier. He had spent nine months with his half-sister Mary and her own two children, both younger than Matt. She was seventeen years older than him and was herself sorely deprived in childhood. The reasons for his reception into care and initial referral to us were his sudden aggressive outbursts which Mary felt unable to control and the emotional flatness that characterised him for much of the rest of the time.

For nearly the first two months of his stay, he presented as so normal that we discussed whether we had made a mistake and taken in a wholly integrated child. He made quite an impression on one staff member when he asked with genuine confusion why children at the school swore so often! Although we were concerned not to expose a normally integrated child to a setting that contained so much potentially disabling underfunctioning, on balance it was agreed not to act too hastily. Despite remaining this way for four months, Matt had presented us with an exaggerated but recognisable pattern of a new child not manifesting his disturbance through disruptive behaviour or breakdowns. Only when he had assured himself that in doing so he did not call down harsh, ruthless punishment upon himself did he 'let go'.

Matt finally gained sufficient confidence to be able to 'expose' his disturbance. Gradually breakdowns in his 'normal' functioning began to appear. Staff noted how single-minded he became, determined persistently to disrupt an activity that had been flowing smoothly, even with him as an eager original participant. Suddenly he would dissolve into a chaotic, raging state when confronted over minor transgressions (a panic aroused by what he felt as someone cutting across his own caretaking survival techniques). Matt had also begun to seek out chaotic individuals and to create unbounded situations in which he could lose/merge himself. Both during and after such occasions of merger or confrontation, grown ups, especially women, felt no real contact with this child. He was cold and distant with no age-appropriate dependency. For a long time he was incapable of shedding a tear in sadness or sorrow. The children themselves found out on a number of occasions just how much of an explosive handful Matt had become – a tiny new boy sitting astride one of their reputedly tough peers, screaming as Matt pummelled him and ripped his hair out.

From the beginning of his placement at the school I had a great deal to do with Matthew. I often saw him and his group to bed at nights and awoke them the next morning. He loved water, relaxing in the baths which I gave him, both the daily ones he had like all the children and the extra ones he would ask to have (something children learn that they can request or have offered to them). Through this close contact in basic child-care I came to recognise an accompanying physical 'numbness' to the emotional flatness he often displayed. At nights Matt would be racked with a rough bronchial cough. I covered him several times each night after he had thrown off all the bedclothes. On the coldest or wettest days I would come across Matt outside, barefoot with only a light T-shirt on his back. This was no conscious attention-seeking behaviour. He was completely out of touch with his bodily sensations.

For almost a year, very little discernible movement was noticed in Matt. There were times when he clearly enjoyed himself; equally the breakdowns and confrontations continued with all adults. The important factor was that the adult who was involved in such breakdowns ensured that he/she saw it through. Often newer staff and women needed the aid of experienced male staff to contain Matt.

During this year in which we 'grasped the bull by the horns' placing Matt with a woman teacher, Jo, he gradually softened. The periods between breakdowns into raging chaos seemed to be lengthening. Jo had put tremendous effort into getting Matt to accept her as the leader of the class group (and hence having the right to direct him within it) and into gaining his acceptance of her as a person. This was not achieved without many battles.

Now Matt's clothing began to go missing under mysterious circumstances in fields or on the roof. He convincingly denied any knowledge of how his clothes came to be hurled away. Our therapeutic adviser suggested that Matt might be doing these things himself in a 'fugue' or dissociated state split off from his conscious awareness, re-enacting much earlier incidents of abandonment or rejection.

If the urge was unconscious, it was not wholly pathological. It might be seen as, 'Look after me through my clothing'. It was in this respect that I acted in the hope of getting closer to Matt himself. I told him that whether he or somebody else was throwing his clothing away was less important than the fact that his clothes seemed to need some, probably temporary, special attention from me. Therefore I had put a chest of drawers in the foyer of the staff flat and was going to look after his clothes there. He would have the same rights (of access) to his clothes as any child; there was simply an extra bit of protection. Matt seemed quietly pleased at this suggested arrangement. He stayed with me as I transferred his clothes. He made no further mention of this directly to me, though he told other children what I was doing and why. Early on he would occasionally ask to come in and just look at his clothes. On such occasions he appeared both reassured and pleased that they were there and intact. There was no further episode of discarded clothes and they remained in the chest of drawers quite some time because Matt clearly preferred them to be there long after it was necessary to protect them in this way.

This special provision by myself to meet a need of Matt's, albeit indirectly expressed, was the first major step in the development of a deep, dependent relationship with me. As such it was a watershed of sorts. From this point onwards movement, though not rapid, was noticeable. The general facilitating environment provided by all the grown-ups in the school – for example the limits set by adults in response to his boundless chaotic behaviour; our refusal to allow him to remain lost behind his own caretaking mechanisms; the investment of each of us in ensuring his being clothed appropriately at all times – had brought Matt to a point where he felt ready to focus upon a particular grown up, me, as a prelude to dependence.

The second major step followed closely upon my caring for his clothing. On a Saturday morning I came across Matt on his bed shouting and cursing at a student. Given what had gone on many times before between Matt and myself and because temporary people like students shouldn't have to bear the brunt of such abuse and manipulation by any child, I took over. The student was taken aback by Matt's venomous verbal assault and could not really describe what had prompted this eruption. Nor did it matter, for, by then, Matt was in a total panic rage, writhing one way and another on his bed for what turned out to be in the end one full hour. It took all my strength to hold him despite his rather small size. He was inaccessible to verbal contact and met my occasional lessening of hold upon him with renewed raging attacks. I felt that about halfway through this episode he picked up my sense of not knowing when or if this battle would ever end. Only later did I realise that I was surely reflecting back to him something of the despair he was needing to give over to me in a very concrete way to contain. However, rather than this realisation driving him to an even greater degree of frenzy, it seemed to have the effect of calming him somewhat. From that point, it was as if this encounter was something that we were sharing. I myself felt able to survive and thus reliably contain his distress. Matt's less frantic actions indicated that a crisis had been passed and he could believe in and accept my ability to contain and care for him. Soon after, he went out as planned with a group to the cinema. I saw him and them off. Matt didn't wave goodbye; I felt drained. However, immediately upon returning he sought me out, stood several feet away from me and smiled. I believe that the chief content to that smile lay in the fact that we had been through something together and I had proved my reliability in an important respect. Saying nothing about what had passed several hours previously, I asked him if he was feeling all right. He said yes, and told me briefly about the film.

This encounter, coupled with my special care for his clothing, provided a strong basis for our relationship to grow. Matt now began seeking aid for small injuries, whereas previously he had been oblivious to physical pain even when a toe-nail had been torn off completely. Now too he could accept comfort from a grown up when he had been angered or hurt. Finally, after nearly two full years in the school he requested a 'special thing' with me. This is the children's shorthand term for a localised adaptation, some regular special time, often weekly, with the grown up upon whom they are focusing. During this time something (or things) is provided by the adult for the child in the present context which enables the child, on the symbolic level, to fill in the gaps in his emotional experience. The adaptation stands as a symbol for the original adaptation. Not untypically Matt asked for some food and a story. He originally wanted peanuts, but I pointed out that this was what his class group had in their weekly story time. Was there not anything he himself especially liked and felt he once or still now didn't get enough of? He was startled at the idea that he might actually have a choice, but he quickly warmed to the notion. He told me that he really 'loved' egg and chips. As for the story, he was much more certain of what he wanted. He specified that the choice could be mine, but it had to be long. The image he was giving me was one of substance. The story had to have a lot behind it – big and long.

Every Monday night in term for the next seven months I prepared a large plate of fried eggs and chips and gave them to Matt. While he was engrossed in the food I read the story. On several separate occasions he told me that an important feature of the book was that it was just for him. I felt that this comment was intended to refer by extension to the whole of the provision, buttressed by the consistency, continuity, and reliability which I myself ensured. Two other points about the importance of the book also became clearer to me over time. First, the tale seemed to awaken in Matt an imaginative capacity which had been absent previously. Second, the book was in part a last protective barrier between Matt and myself, an external focus, not insurmountable but something that permitted him to determine the timing of the growth of his dependence upon me. During these seven months, which felt very long at the time but in retrospect seem much less so, very little beyond what I have described occurred on the surface. Since we feel that there is an element of risk in being in the dark about the direction of intrapsychic processes, the support of the school's therapeutic adviser at this stage was essential. It is possible that a child could use such provision as a pocket to avoid genuine movement. Yet through my consultation with the advisor and based upon my 'feel' of the situation and Matt's verbal and non-verbal hints, there seemed sufficient evidence that Matt was using the experience for being 'filled in' symbolically in those areas where he had missed out as an infant and young child. Further proof that all was going well was discernible in the fact that at the same time outside of the adaptation people continued to have to deal with Matt, but all agreed that there was a softness to him now, and it was growing.

Then on one Monday night at the end of seven months we had started as usual, but just as I began to read Matt interrupted me. He had noticed a Ladybird 'How it Works' book about cameras lying on my floor. It had a picture of an old Brownie camera on the cover. Matt said, 'My mother had one of those cameras'. This signalled the start of a torrent of communication from him on topics he had never discussed previously in the school. The next three 'special times' each lasted over an hour, as compared with the usual half an hour, and almost all of Matt's talk was about earlier experiences with and memories of his mother, his brother and his sister. Much of it was descriptive, but it was so much more too. Most memorable for me was his description of an incident that occurred while he was with his Mum. They had been out walking together and had both seen a vicious street-fight. He cringed several times as he related the details to me. In fact, violence was a theme that ran strongly through many of his recollections, seeing his sister hit his nephew with a carving knife in anger being another memory mentioned. On one occasion he spent over half an hour painstakingly drawing out (and constructing with chips) the ground plan of the holiday chalet and camp (complete with rides and things you could do) where he had gone the previous summer. The animation which he brought to the task was a marvel to behold in this child who had been so accurately described as 'emotionally flat' when he first came to us. At one point he burst out happily, 'I really wish you could have been there'. Near the end of this phase he also looked directly at me and said, 'I have a really good memory, you know'. Though I immediately thought it, I did not mention that until these recent weeks he had not seemed able to afford a memory. Yet clearly now he had reached a point where he could verbalise what previously for him had been unutterable.

In the following months a great deal more movement was realised, both within and without our special relationship. While never reaching the level that it did over the several weeks I have just described, his communication about important aspects of his past life and present feelings never dried up. With other grown ups he was able to accept admonitions with appropriate signs of guilt and often a readiness to make genuine reparation. His low self-image underwent a transformation too. He now informed me when pieces of clothing were too small or worn and he requested a special brush and comb set appropriate for his type of hair. In the very vital areas for Matt of relationships with women, movement was still measured in small steps. Yet despite being an area in which his ability to function was fragile, Matt himself sought out help insofar as he did not avoid women.

Matt remained with us for a further two years after the critical period of ego integration described. I do not suggest that he left us with the trauma of his past experiences wholly exorcised. Nevertheless there was a warmth and depth to the departing child that contrasted sharply with the tiny, vague yet volatile figure who had entered the school.

REFERENCES

Beedell, C. (1993) *Poor Starts, Lost Opportunities and Hopeful Outcomes*, London: Charterhouse Group.

Bettelheim, B. (1987) *The Good Enough Parent*, London: Thames and Hudson.

Brearley, J. (1991) 'A Psychodynamic Approach to Social Work', in J. Lishman (ed.) *Handbook of Theory for Practice Teachers in Social Work*, London: Jessica Kingsley

Davie, R. (1989) 'Behavioural Problems and the Teacher', in T. Charlton and K. David (eds) *Managing Misbehaviours*, London: Longmans

Davis, M. and Wallbridge, D. (1981) *Boundary and Space*, London: Karnac Books.

Dockar-Drysdale, B. (1990) *The Provision of Primary Experience*, London: Free Association Books

Franklin, M. (1968) 'Human Relations in the Institutional Treatment of Children', in R.J.N. Todd, (ed.) *Disturbed Children*, London: Longman.

Greenhalgh, P. (1994) *Emotional Growth and Learning*, London: Routledge.

Grimshaw, R. and Berridge, D. (1994) *Educating Disruptive Children*, London: National Children's Bureau.

Hayden, C., Sheppard, C. and Ward, D. (1996) *Primary Age Children Excluded from School*, Portsmouth: Portsmouth University Social Services Research and Information Unit.

Health Advisory Services (1995) *Together We Stand: The Commissioning, Role and Management of Children and Adolescent Mental Health Service*, London: HMSO.

Kahan, B. (1994). *Growing up in Groups*, London: HMSO.

Manning, K. and Sharp, A. (1977) *Structuring Play in the Early Years at School*, London: Ward Lock Educational.

Reeves, C. (1979) 'Transference in the Residential Treatment of Children', *Journal of Child Psychotherapy*, 5, 23–37.

Reeves, C. (1993) 'Unintegrated States and the Process of Integration', *British Journal of Psychotherapy*, 9, 4, 414–427.

Winnicott, D.W. (1965) 'Integrative and Disruptive Factors in Family Life', in *The Family and Individual Development*, London: Tavistock.

Part IX

Conclusions

34 Summary and conclusions: implications for the future

Brian Jacobs and Jonathan Green

This book began by outlining a number of the challenges currently faced by in-patient child psychiatry. How does the content of the intervening text indicate that these challenges are being addressed?

THE MOVE FROM RELATIVELY CLOSED TO RELATIVELY OPEN SYSTEMS

The text reflects a general systemic change in the structure and orientation of in-patient child psychiatry: from units that are relatively closed systems to ones that are relatively open. A sign of this is the time now devoted to communication with external structures and the emphasis on collaborative therapeutic work with family and referring agencies. Such developments are essential although they put extra demands on staff organisation (there has rarely been any increase in staff provision to accommodate such increased roles). But taken to the extreme, the move towards open boundaries can end up threatening a basic raison d'être of in-patient units: the provision of a boundaried residential treatment milieu. In the USA for instance, some units have become no more than holding environments pending triage or crisis resolution. Such developments raise urgent questions; firstly about the nature and effectiveness of the internal treatment environment that units should be providing – and for whom? Secondly there is the question of the relationship of this treatment environment to the external world – whether family, referrer or purchaser. These two broad areas will be addressed in turn.

FUTURE DIRECTIONS FOR THE IN-PATIENT THERAPEUTIC ENVIRONMENT

Range and specificity of treatment

In-patient units offer intensive care to the whole family and not just to the resident child (chapter 8). This is part of the 'open system' approach that modern in-patient units have adopted in keeping with the systemic understanding of multiple origins and effects of child mental illness. The residential milieu can best be seen as providing an environment of specialised adapted psychological care responding to extreme situations and children's complex needs. Much of this book describes various approaches to creating such an environment of adapted care and also emphasises the specificity with which the milieu must adapt to the variety of needs in its child patients. Part V of the book is devoted to specific adaptations of in-patient care to specific clinical problems and disorders. The pattern of care necessary to treat children, for instance with autism (chapter 25) is different from that needed for children with conduct disorder (chapter 19). The modern unit needs both sensitivity and specificity in adapting, within a single setting, to a range of children and of disorders.

Such specificity creates challenges for admissions policy. While on the one hand units need to strive to meet the needs of all the referring constituencies outlined in chapter 1, it is clear that there are advantages in specialisation, in terms of clarity of treatment organisation and staff morale. Do specialist units (for eating disorders for instance) provide a better treatment environment than generic units? There certainly do appear to be advantages with the concentration of specialist skills and gains in staff efficiency in some cases. Cotton (1993), quoted in chapter 9, argues that increased staffing ratios are needed in units taking a wide mix of psychopathology. In most areas the issue will be academic, as there will be insufficient young people requiring admission to justify a unit specialising in one area of psychopathology. Even where there are sufficient cases, there may be reservations about, say, the range of age often covered in specialist units.

Our review of current practice in UK units (chapter 2) makes clear that clinicians in this country are very aware of such dilemmas. While up to half of children admitted to in-patient units have some form of generic conduct or behaviour disorder, there is great variation in the overall profile of other disorders admitted. Dilemmas regarding specificity will remain a major issue for clinical management. It would be useful to have empirical evidence to work on.

Evolving treatments

This book describes ways in which treatments used elsewhere in child and adult mental health services are adapted for in-patient use. One of our themes has been to suggest ways in which such adaptations can be carried through; for instance in the contexts of family therapy, behaviour or cognitive therapies, psychodynamic therapies and parenting assessment and training (Part V). The in-patient unit needs to continue to adapt new and different generic mental health treatments for its own purposes. Some, when adapted to the developmental stage of the child, are promising (such as cognitive behavioural approaches to behavioural difficulties). Others, such as ECT, are only rarely appropriate. As elsewhere we need to work towards increasing specificity in matching treatment to need and refining treatment protocols.

New styles in the delivery of treatment need to be, and are being, developed and researched (chapter 27). A number of possibilities can be contemplated:

- partial admissions
- family admissions
- intensive outreach work
- a 'hospital at home' approach
- emergency admissions.

Partial admission

Here a child is admitted for part of the week only, spending much of their time at home. On the face of it this is an attractive option, reducing treatment impact on the family and increasing unit efficiency. However, a word of caution is needed. Cases worked in this way can require at least as much professional work as full admissions. For the child there is the repeated requirement to adapt to changes of environment and many of our patients are poor at just this. This can outweigh any advantage gained by having them at home for more of the time. The pattern of service and treatments described in this book points out the need for *both* in-patient and day-patient services.

Family admission

This can counter the problems relating to family fragmentation during admission, allowing an intensive period of family orientated work at a crucial time. The 'Mothers Unit' at Oxford (chapter 24) offers one of the few UK child psychiatry orientated services of this kind at present but there are more commonly facilities for family admission in other countries such as Holland. An attractive model is that of 'pulses' of brief family admission during a child's treatment. This has been tried in some units. It may allow an intervention to take root in the family's style of managing certain situations and thus shorten overall admission time. It would be useful to have further studies on this.

Intensive outreach

Intensive outreach can extend the degree of liaison with local services. Some work could be carried out at the unit using its full resources whilst other parts of the work might be provided in the child's own school and local clinics. This could be combined with work in the family home. Could such programmes substitute for admission on occasion? Quite possibly, with well-organised teams – however there are staffing implications.

The hospital at home

This approach aims to recreate the intensity of in-patient admission in the child's own home and has been tried in some paediatric work. Small teams of nursing and other staff would work for many weeks in the child's home, staying through the night on occasion. The advantage of such a model would be the intensity it could create. This would also be its disadvantage. Many families might find the pressure too great. It would not allow social skills work to be carried out in the same way, though there would be a more normal peer group to interact with in the child's home school. The model would be very demanding on staff. Such developments might possibly improve efficacy but they are likely to be more expensive because of the high level of personal contact necessary in psychiatric care. A base in-patient or day-patient team would be necessary as a source for the high level of skills necessary to work in this style and to maintain skills. Again, comparative trials of such interventions against in-patient care (including economic evaluation) would be useful.

Emergency admission

Emergency admissions are de rigueur in medical settings and referrers often find it frustrating and counterintuitive if child and adolescent psychiatry wards resist them. The reasons need to be fully explained. Emergency admission, while attractive in reducing immediate crisis, may be therapeutically inappropriate for the child. Pressure to admit may be great because local services have difficulty finding a more appropriate placement, but once admitted, pressure for them to act is reduced and the child can languish, inappropriately placed.

Nevertheless, many units do have a commitment to the concept of emergency admission. Our practice is to offer an initial brief (about one week) admission during which time a normal preadmission assessment is carried out before any commitment to keep the patient longer is made. Referring districts can guarantee access to emergency beds but only if they are prepared to reserve an empty bed at their expense for much of the year: this may be impracticable. A degree of risk management has to be accepted on both sides.

Researching the evidence base for treatment

In-patient care, like other aspects of medical treatment, aims to become more evidence based. This is a major challenge since so much of milieu treatment is intrinsically difficult to study. In chapter 9, Green and Burke discuss theoretical approaches to an evidence base for milieu treatment, and in Part VI, Imrie, Green and Jacobs discuss the research base that has so far been established and potential paths forward for in-patient research. This project remains a major and exciting challenge that will have to be tackled piecemeal. We have indicated that there is useful existing data about the general efficacy of children's in-patient psychiatric services (chapter 27), but that there are not yet good controlled studies comparing in-patient treatments to intensive out-patient programmes. Evidence is accumulating for the efficacy of in-patient care for specific disorders, for instance in obsessive compulsive disorder (chapter 21) and the treatment of severe early parenting failure (chapter 24). Comparative trials of out-patient or day-patient with in-patient care could now be carried out for specific conditions controlling for case complexity and for severity of symptoms and psychosocial impairment. With the shortening of in-patient admissions, some opportunities for teasing these matters apart have disappeared and current methods of funding in-patient admissions in the NHS can militate against randomised controlled trials. However, as other short-term treatments have been developed, the comparative effect of these can be investigated.

Single case design studies for psychological or drug treatments are well suited to in-patient units because of the opportunity for detailed observation of the child. Such trials can include obtaining observations from parents in the home setting as well. Research into treatment process such as the nature of the engagement between families and in-patient services is important. Is this a predictor of outcome of the intervention? How can it be improved?

As research on in-patient care gradually matures, we suggest (chapter 28) that a series of interlinked studies using reasonably common methodologies should be established. As in other areas of child mental health services, there is a need for measures of outcome that can be routinely applied. With the development of measures that appropriately reflect case complexity and change, both clinicians and service commissioners will become more sophisticated in shaping future services. The disciplines of research, such as the training of staff to deliver treatments consistently to written manual standards, have clinical benefit as well as research use. We do not underestimate the difficulties involved in developing a research culture in clinical teams, however (chapter 28).

Quality standards

The development of appropriate quality standards for children's in-patient units is underway (Bryce, 1996). There are issues concerning care, treatment, responsiveness and liaison, including quality and timeliness of information to referrers and others. Units should be working with their commissioners and with other units to develop appropriate measures both to maintain and to further raise standards of service. Such standards will codify the best practice already seen in many in-patient units.

Sustaining the therapeutic culture

Children's in-patient units are complex organisations. They bring together large multidisciplinary teams, many of whom have other professional commitments. Management in this context is extremely demanding. There is a delicate balance to be struck to enable a lively, healthy setting for a number of children with differing problems. Staff themselves need nurturing in order to provide a nurturing culture on the unit. Similarly both children and the staff need a sense of structure which has some flexibility but is safe (chapters 14 and 15).

We have highlighted the rudimentary knowledge and guidance concerning appropriate nursing levels and skill mix to work with different types of youngsters. This is a matter for concern. All clinicians will have had the experience of being unable to admit a child because the nursing staff have become overstretched by the children already on the ward. We have to develop better measures of dependency and better preadmission predictors of likely dependency levels (chapter 8). These should help in avoiding the mix of patients becoming too dependent, often accompanied by major behavioural difficulties in children. The maintenance of morale and skills development in the nursing group is vital to a healthy ward milieu (chapter 28)

Evaluation and prevention of unwanted effects

Modern in-patient units are particularly sensitive to a variety of unwanted effects resulting from their treatment. This theme is addressed throughout the book, but two chapters pursue detailed arguments. Green and Jones (chapter 18) offer a systematic review of potential unwanted effects of milieu treatment and their anticipation or minimisation, whilst Newbold and Jones (chapter 17) address various aspects of 'institutional abuse'. As Newbold and Jones state, it would be foolish and irresponsible to assume that in-patient treatment is not potentially harmful. They propose new forms of team organisation to counter such difficulties.

Much discussed is the potential damage of separating young children from their parents. Concern about this has led to relaxing of visiting policies, reluctance to admit young children without their parents and a shift to become more family oriented in approach. But there are still occasions when the separation from parents can be therapeutically beneficial. Sometimes family relationships have temporarily broken down. On other occasions the child may have been abused at home and this can only become apparent when the child feels protected in a safe setting. Parents may themselves have become unwell. Whilst neither of the first two reasons is sufficient in itself to precipitate a hospital admission in preference to accommodation by the local authority, admission can provide important asylum in all three circumstances. As Newbold and Jones state, the child's right to appropriate admission and care needs to outweigh understandable scruples about family disruption; this often requires consideration with fellow professionals as well as purchasers.

Clarification of the law regarding in-patient care

The Children Act (1989) has major implications for residential units, but the particular case of psychiatry in-patient units is not tackled explicitly in the Act's provisions and will need to be the subject of developing case law. A cogent view of our responsibilities in relation to this legislation is outlined in chapter 29. The applicability of the legislation is uncertain in places; many of the guidelines from the Department of Health have not been tested in the courts. It is wise to try to observe the spirit of the Children Act but we take the view that there may be occasions when one should be prepared to go to court to justify a particular course of action if it is thought to be in the child's best interests.

Liaison and communication outside the unit

This book shows many examples of units striving not only to provide an environment of adapted care in their own functioning, but also communicating constantly with the wider environment. Part II emphasises modern theories of admission practice (chapter 4) and discharge planning (chapter 7), approaches that embody active collaboration with external agencies. French and Tait emphasise how the educational management within in-patient units needs to articulate closely with the wider national curriculum and school provision (chapter 12). Similarly, the open system aspect of in-patient care is emphasised in areas of commissioning, management and finance in Part VII. Commissioners, referrers and health economists ask challenging questions of the effectiveness and appropriateness of the residential option. As in so many other areas of public life, 'marketing' and communicating about the institution to others are critical aspects of its effective functioning. In-patient treatment will survive by being both useful and by being seen to be useful. Clinical managers will have to put increasing energy and resource into meeting this need and not rely solely on the spare time efforts of hard pressed clinicians – this means specific managerial time set aside for external liaison or 'marketing'.

Communication with referrers about appropriate admission

Children with mental health disorders continue to be admitted to inappropriate settings. Some are inappropriately placed on adolescent or (particularly worry-ingly) on adult psychiatric wards; more frequently, they are nursed in paediatric settings. Sometimes the latter is appropriate but if staff are busy with children suffering physical illness or anxious about having psychiatric patients, they can resent their admission and convey their feelings to children and parents. It is hardly surprising that this can be suboptimal. If in physical medicine it is accepted that the best results are obtained in specialist units, psychiatric dis-order should be no different. At various points this book aims to clarify the criteria for problems that need in-patient psychiatry care and what can properly be managed in other ways.

Liaison with local teams

Much of the book reflects increased liaison between in-patient services and local mental health teams from the originating district and with professionals from other services such as education and social services. There is nevertheless some way to go. Distance from the service can limit liaison work as can the busy timetable of colleagues in both local services and the in-patient unit itself. Further, once families have engaged with in-patient unit staff and come to trust them, they can be very reluctant to re-engage with local services (see chapter 7).

Units can work with their local child mental health service to provide backup to enable them to hold more worrying cases in the community provided they are able to admit urgently. For example, colleagues may be able to work with youngsters who are depressed or who have anorexia nervosa for longer, if they know that they have the support of an in-patient unit if the child becomes too ill. Units can provide training and consultation for cases that may not need the full resource of the in-patient service. Specialist knowledge of other appropriate placements can prevent admission. Alternatively, a consultation with referring professionals and a family can clarify new directions for work between them without the need for admission. All these ways of working meet the role suggested by the NHS Health Advisory Service report (1995).

Equity of access

Children's in-patient units continually need to improve ways to make their services equitably available. It is often more effective and efficient for members of the team to visit local services at a distance for meetings than requesting that they attend the unit on all occasions. For some families, attending units that are at some distance can be more than they are able to manage. Should we be providing transport? Is it economic *not* to do so? If units supply effective treatment the answer must be that we should provide transport. Stressed parents with responsibility for several young children may only be able to engage in regular treatment and to visit their child regularly if we support them practically.

Similarly, we have to ask ourselves whether we are making ourselves sufficiently available and welcoming to all racial and cultural groups. For some, there are huge hurdles of cultural shame to overcome to access our services. This emphasises the importance of developing an appropriate cultural and ethnic mix among the staff of the unit at all levels of seniority.

We have not specifically addressed the needs of children with moderate or severe learning disabilities in this book and this reflects a clinical reality. Children's in-patient units are able to help some of these young people but there are difficulties if they need a great deal of help with their self-care. Current mental health services do not well meet the needs of the significantly learning disabled child (this is also true of most outpatient services). This matter needs urgent attention but will require substantial funding.

Hearing the users' voice

It is most helpful to have feedback from users. Obtaining honest feedback can be helped by periodic surveys. Involving parents in development of ward policy can be enlightening and lead to helpful suggestions. It can also improve their sense of self-esteem. Hearing the children's voices is important. They may have different views from their parents. Enlisting the help of the Trust audit services can aid this work.

Children's in-patient units as a training and resource centre

In-patient units should be seen as a part of a resource centre providing the intensive care element of child psychiatry (NHS Health Advisory Service,

1995). They can used in a coherent manner to provide education in therapeutic skills for those who will later work in community settings such as child psychiatry, nursing, social work, clinical psychology, occupational therapy, family therapy and experiential therapies such as art and movement therapies. Training experience in the management of the complex cases seen in in-patient units is invaluable to all these groups. In outreach, specialist skills in the management of disturbed and difficult children can be taught to professionals elsewhere such as other mental health settings and special schools.

The need within the milieu to provide specialist adapted psychological care for children in extreme situations leads to further opportunities for treatment innovation. In-patient staff undertake difficult parenting/therapeutic tasks around everyday basic care in a parallel relationship to that of parents at home. This gives in-patient teams unique opportunities both to understand the pressures on parents resulting from a particular disorder, and to generate solutions to difficult parenting and care problems (chapter 14). The consequences of this for service development and research are only beginning to be exploited by in-patient units. If they are to fulfil their role as core components of 'resource centres' then this is an area that should be addressed. Innovations must be subject to controlled comparison with existing models of treatment.

Inter-unit collaboration

Because they each constitute a small critical mass, in-patient units will need to collaborate more with each other, within areas of clinical practice, training and research. This should be reflected in joint audit, in research, in shared training events and in secondment of staff where particular skills are to be developed. Each of these initiatives is now beginning to occur in the UK.

Audit of in-patient work can occur in at least two forums. Firstly, it can be linked to other community and hospital-based child and adolescent mental health services. This provides such units with a healthy context in which the benefits of their service can be measured against other priorities. Secondly there can be audit with other in-patient units because the of the specialist nature of the tasks undertaken.

Health economics and commissioning

The current distribution of in-patient services across the country does seem to reflect major population areas (chapter 28) but some central planning may be needed so that access to these scarce resources can be optimised. Like other expensive, low volume, highly specialist services, in-patient units are vulnerable to cuts being made by single purchasers in isolation from others who would wish the service to continue and develop. The resulting dissipation of skills does not produce an equal benefit elsewhere and once the critical mass of the core team has been lost it is very difficult to reassemble it in a new form.

Within health needs assessment we must ensure that those children who most need and are most likely to benefit from the service are referred. We must also consider the implications for provision for these needy children after discharge. New methods of approaching health needs assessment suggest that there is a finite core group of complex disorders in the community who are usually known as a problem to some agency. Unfortunately they are often not matched to the specific service that would be appropriate to their needs (Kurtz, Thornes and Wolkind, 1994). Research-led needs assessment of this kind will be crucial to future development of in-patient service provision.

Too many children are not being referred until their difficulties have grown to a point where intervention is unlikely to succeed. Too often, following admission and treatment, in-patient teams have difficulty in accessing the right follow-on provision for a child because it is expensive and has to be funded by other services. Wrangling over money and consequent delay so often leaves the child and family without the right provision and the unravelling of health gains made during admission – this is a scandalous waste of resource and too often reflects a basic lack of common understanding and joint planning between agencies. We need new models of partnership between local commissioning services (health, education and social services) so that they accept joint ownership of the needs of these multiply disadvantaged children. One sign of such a partnership will be an increasing willingness to combine their resources to fund subsequent longer-term placements when necessary.

Equally, in-patient psychiatric units cannot and should not provide a service to fill the gaps in outpatient services or gaps in other agency services. Such a misuse of the resource is expensive and leads to inefficiency in their core task.

Economics

The NHS reforms have brought these matters into clearer focus (chapter 31). What has become very evident is that decisions about the cost of mental health matters in childhood have to take into account the full costs of treatment, including those to the family and to other agencies. This must be set against the current costs of failing to treat where effective intervention is available and also the longer-term costs both to the National Health Service and to other services. The closure of adult mental hospital beds saves money only for those patients where provision in the community is less expensive. This is obvious but often forgotten. The more dependent patients cost more to sustain in community settings (Leff, 1992). The same may also be found for some child psychiatry patients, but information is not available yet.

Funding hospital schools

The mechanism for funding hospital schooling continues to pose a threat in the UK system of provision. Such schools are essential to in-patient child psychiatry provision. Equally, children's in-patient units provide very helpful advice to Education Authorities. Children have a right to education whilst in hospital but sometimes the Education Authority feels disaffected because it was not the referring agent and the child did not appear to be causing a problem in their local school. Nonetheless, the authority in the child's home district has to pay for the intensively staffed education provided in the hospital special school. At present, the Local Authority that hosts the hospital unit has to fund the hospital school and recharge the child's sending Local Education Authority. There is an argument that such schools should be centrally funded, to enable an appropriate national funding formula to be applied across these unusual, but important schools. This is unlikely to happen.

DO WE NEED IN-PATIENT UNITS?

Finally we can address this question – by asking what the effect would be on children and services if in-patient units no longer existed. Certainly, lack of intensive care and treatment for some very disturbed children would lead to unrelieved distress; and there would be other consequences. It is likely that a proportion of complex cases, failing to improve in outpatient settings, would disappear from the sight of child psychiatrists only to reappear as difficult problems for the education authorities and social services and a worry to other professionals. The difficulties in this group would be likely to escalate rather than resolve over time. Long term morbidity and burden on services into adulthood is likely to result: alcohol or drug abuse and self-harm; personality difficulties, problems with parenting their own children and continuing behavioural difficulties. All this is a heavy price for society to pay for the failure of earlier provision. Of course, this is still the outcome for some patients that *do* enter child psychiatry in-patient units but there is evidence (Part VI) beginning to accrue suggesting that for significant numbers of children a path of inappropriate provision and deterioration can be diverted following an in-patient admission.

END WORD

One of our major objectives has been the demonstration of the necessity for the integration of biopsychosocial perspectives in children's in-patient work. It is a holistic approach that draws on the medical model and psychological theories from the behavioural to the psychodynamic; and that integrates these with careful assessment of educational strengths and social realities. It practises in a complex systemic framework of understanding the meaning and effects of behaviours and attitudes in the family and in the wider community. Our work is energised by the very richness and complexity of this undertaking with complicated cases and the knowledge that in-patient treatment can produce a unique benefit to the lives of many referred children.

Our final word is to make an acknowledgement of the difficult and often personally painful work done by the children and their families during in-patient treatment. Their commitment to change, despite the difficulties, is often moving and humbling. They must, at times, feel challenged by the therapeutic demands placed on them but they so often show a powerful persistence to work for change. Far too often they have been offered over-simple or partial solutions for complex difficulties. The ongoing impact of successful in-patient care can be rewardingly shown by youngsters returning to the ward years later 'just to say hello' and to update staff on the development of their lives.

REFERENCES

Bryce, G. (1995) *Commissioning Inpatient Psychiatric Services for Children and Young People in Scotland*. A report for the Scottish Health Boards General Managers Group. (Can be obtained through the Greater Glasgow Health Board.)

Cotton, N.S. (1993) *Lessons from the Lion's Den: Therapeutic Management of Children in Psychiatric Hospitals and Treatment Centres*. San Francisco, CA: Jossey-Bass.

Leff, J. (1992) Problems of transformation. (Special Issue on changing mental health care in the cities of Europe.) *International Journal of Social Psychiatry*, 38, 16–23.

Kurtz, Z., Thornes, R. and Wolkind, S. (1994) *Services for the Mental Health of Children and Young People in England: A National Review*. London: South Thames Regional Health Authority.

NHS Health Advisory Service (1995) *Child and Adolescent Mental Health Services: Together We Stand*. London: HMSO.

Subject index

Name index